Communicating
Effectively

EIGHTH EDITION

Saundra Hybels • Richard L. Weaver II

Learning Solutions

Boston   Burr Ridge, IL   Dubuque, IA   New York   San Francisco   St. Louis
Bangkok   Bogotá   Caracas   Lisbon   London   Madrid   Mexico City
Milan   New Delhi   Seoul   Singapore   Sydney   Taipei   Toronto

Communicating Effectively, Eighth Edition

Copyright © 2007 by The McGraw-Hill Companies, Inc. All rights reserved. Printed in the United States of America.
Except as permitted under the United States Copyright Act of 1976, no part of this publication may be reproduced or
distributed in any form or by any means, or stored in a data base retrieval system, without prior written permission of the
publisher.

This book is a McGraw-Hill Custom Publishing textbook and contains select material from *Communicating Effectively*,
Eighth Edition by Saundra Hybels and Richard L. Weaver II. Copyright © 2007, 2004, 2001, 1998, 1995, 1992, 1989,
1986 by The McGraw-Hill Companies, Inc. Reprinted with permission of the publisher. Many custom published texts
are modified versions or adaptations of our best-selling textbooks. Custom versions contain only material selected by the
professor. Depending on what material is included/excluded, gaps in pagination may occur. Some adaptations are printed in
black and white to keep prices at a minimum, while others are in color.

67890 QGT QGT 11

ISBN-13: 978-0-07-340040-2
ISBN-10: 0-07-340040-8
part of
ISBN-13: 978-0-07-332724-2
ISBN-10: 0-07-332724-7

Learning Solutions Specialist: Judith Wetherington
Production Editor: Carrie Braun
Printer/Binder: Quad/Graphics

Brief Contents

Contents

Part Two
Interpersonal Communication

7 Interpersonal Relationships 154

1

The Communication Process

OBJECTIVES

After reading this chapter, you should be able to:

- Explain communication needs and relate them to your life.
- Define *strategic flexibility (SF)* and explain where its power lies.
- Define *communication* and explain it as a process.
- Describe the types of communication.
- Define and explain the importance of *intercultural communication*.
- Discuss the principles of ethical communication and the foundation out of which ethical conduct is most likely to grow.
- Discuss the ways you can improve your own communication skills.
- Explain how Internet communication relates to the model of communication and the four characteristics that make it unique from normal face-to-face communication.

THE FOLLOWING ARE THREE EXAMPLES THAT REVEAL THE POSITIVE ROLE speech communication courses can play in the lives of students. For Ashley, Andrew, and Wanda, they served as pivotal points for changing their lives.

When Ashley visited her guidance counselor in high school, Mr. Vernon, she was really on a personal quest to find out more about herself and to get an expert's advice about her college potential. Ashley had goofed around in high school—far more interested in the social whirl than anything academic. After telling Mr. Vernon what she was doing in high school, and after examining her grades, he uttered the excruciating words: "I'm afraid you're not college material." Those six words were the very wake-up call she needed. In a required speech communication course at a small liberal arts college where she was accepted because of her parents' pleading, she discovered what she needed: an instructor who saw her potential, a course that offered specific information and activities that motivated her and reinforced her talents, and a result—a solid A—that proved she definitely had college potential. It was her speech communication instructor who discovered this bright, fun, articulate young woman who could do anything she put her mind to.

My name is Andrew, and I want to tell you this in the first person: I have never acted before, but my friends said I was a natural-born actor. When I came to college, I was sitting in the cafeteria among a horde of talking, milling students. They all seemed so confident, directed, and older. I was hoping no one noticed me sitting there alone. In walking across campus, I saw the "call" posted on a kiosk. The drama department was looking for actors for an upcoming play. Auditions were the following week. I went to the library, checked out a copy of the play, and read it in one sitting. Although terrified, I tried out. My name did not appear on the call-back sheets, but I knew I could do better, and I knew it could happen. I realized at that moment that any knowledge I could gain about effective communication, and any experience I could get, would help me build the confidence and poise I needed. The course in speech communication was essential for me to face myself and the future I wanted.

Don't ever think that majoring in subjects such as philosophy, literature, or speech has little value in our society because they won't help you get a good job. This crass materialism infects too many students, parents, and employers. I (Wanda Jean DuCharme) studied speech communication at a midsized midwestern university because I wanted to polish my communication skills. I went on to get a master's degree in both speech and English, and now I earn a substantial income as a business consultant, and I run my own business. How did my background prepare me for the work I do now? I learned to think and organize ideas. I could discern patterns and form valid conclusions. I could communicate with senior management, workers, and the public alike. I learned to question, listen, and put ideas into words. My philosophy is, "Do what you love, and the money will follow."

EVERYONE NEEDS COMMUNICATION SKILLS

Your success in this world depends on effective communication skills. The problem isn't a lack of ability to communicate; the problem is simply that you have never mastered the skill. Even the very top students from highly competitive schools frequently are unable to write clearly or make persuasive presentations.[1] This is true for two reasons: (1) We take communication for granted. After all, we've been communicating since we were born, with that much practice, why wouldn't we be good at it? (2) We often think we are better at it than we really are.

If you were told that there were skills that are *more important* to your success than a knowledge of computers, more important than any job-specific skills, and more important than your knowledge of any content area or major, would you want to pursue those skills and improve your ability to perform them? Those skills—basic oral and written communication skills—are the most frequently cited factors in aiding graduating college students to both obtain and sustain employment. The list of studies that support this conclusion goes on and on.[2]

What are the benefits? Why should you take a speech communication course seriously? As a result of a speech communication course you will feel more confident about yourself, you will feel more comfortable with others' perceptions of you, you will experience greater ease in reasoning with people, you will use language more appropriately, and you will have improved critical thinking skills.[3]

This author (Richard) decided on a career in medicine in junior high school. All the courses I took targeted me in that direction. In high school I focused primarily on math and science courses—taking all the school offered. During my first two years at the University of Michigan, as a premedicine major, I did the same. Then came the university's required speech course. Not only did I do well in the course, I decided to use my last free elective slot to schedule a second speech course, and I was hooked. I found out what I could do with a speech major, how it both complemented and supplemented any other major, and I pursued it for the rest of my college career—both at the undergraduate and graduate levels.

Here is what I discovered that made me switch from a premed major to speech. First, I discovered that speech communication is the ultimate people-oriented discipline. I had pursued premed because I wanted to be in a people-oriented business. I loved the idea that here was a discipline that would develop my thinking and speaking skills. In speech I could apply my imagination, solve practical problems, and articulate my ideas. I was truly free to be human.

The second factor that made me switch majors was that I wanted to be a leader. I knew what skills were important to this goal. Ask yourself, what skills should leaders possess? They are the very same skills every college graduate should have, and they are the same as those that more than 1,000 faculty members from a cross section of academic disciplines selected: skills in writing, speaking, reading, and listening; interpersonal skills, working in and leading groups; an appreciation of cultural diversity; and the ability to adapt to innovation and change.[4] These are all skills that are developed, discussed, emphasized, and refined in a basic speech communication course. They are the central focus of this textbook.

The third and final ingredient that made me switch majors resulted from my study and experience. I recognized the importance of communication skills to my success. Whether it was oral presentations, time spent in meetings, interpersonal skills, interactions with other employees, or use of multimedia technologies, developing effective communication skills was going to be vital in all areas of my life.

Patrick Combs, author of the book *Major in Success*, includes a chapter titled "Classes Worth Their Weight in Gold." In this chapter he admonishes his readers to "Take a course that includes discussions and practice on delivering persuasive speeches, body language, assertive communications, and audiovisual aids. . . . In our society, shyness is not considered an asset." Combs writes, "A speech course can help you feel confident speaking to one or 1,000. And you can apply this confidence to situations that occur more often than in public speaking: speaking well over the phone; speaking up in class;

making a good impression in an interview; and expressing your ideas in a meeting."[5] Combs then adds this sentence in capital letters: "THE ABILITY TO COMMUNI-CATE EFFECTIVELY HAS BEEN CONSISTENTLY RANKED THE NUMBER ONE PERFORMANCE FACTOR FOR PROFESSIONAL SUCCESS."

STRATEGIC FLEXIBILITY (SF)

Strategic flexibility (SF) means expanding your communication repertoire (your collection or stock of communication behaviors that can readily be brought into use) to enable you to use the best skill or behavior available for a particular situation. Let's say you're caught in an unfamiliar situation, but you realize that if you can communicate your position effectively, you will free yourself from this uncomfortable position. You suddenly need all of the best skills and behaviors you can call upon. SF is a primary characteristic of successful people, a vital component of excellent relationships at work and at home, a trait of effective group leaders and participants, and the attribute of public speakers who can adapt to changing circumstances or unexpected occurrences.

People who possess SF are happier and more fulfilled because they are not only aware of their own communication skills and deficits, but also they can bring to bear on any situation they encounter a broad range of potentially valuable behaviors. Going into a new situation, they don't always know exactly what will be required, but they realize that their own background, experience, and repertoire will be sufficient to not just meet the new circumstances but to succeed in them as well. The knowledge that SF provides yields confidence and security, and helps reduce any unnecessary and unwanted fear.

Those without SF are those who approach every situation with their own limited resources. Often, this results in knee-jerk responses that depend on nothing more than the same set of behaviors used to approach any and every situation that confronts them. The problem with this approach is that there is no single way to behave in the world. The world is too complex; problems are too complicated; circumstances are too intricate and involved. It's a little like the leader who applies exactly the same set of solutions to every problem saying "You may not like my solutions, but at least you know exactly where I stand." This is discomforting information simply because it shows no recognition of SF. All problems require different sets of solutions that result from study, thought, and the serious application of a wide variety of potential behaviors.

The power of the SF concept is in its application. The six steps of SF make this possible. These steps will allow you to take SF into the world and apply it to the real-life circumstances you encounter daily:

1. **Anticipate** = Think about potential situations and the needs and requirements likely to arise because of them. The key to anticipation is forecasting. Remember Louis Pasteur's famous dictum: "Chance favors only the prepared mind."

2. **Assess** = Take stock of the factors, elements, and conditions of the situations in which you find yourself. The key to assessment is alertness.

3. **Evaluate** = Determine the value and worth of the factors, elements, and conditions to all those involved and how they bear on your own skills and abilities. The key to evaluation is accuracy.

4. **Select** = Carefully select from your repertoire of available skills and behaviors those likely to have the greatest impact on the current (and future) situations.

Here, one must also predict and forecast the potential effects of the skills and behaviors that will be used. The key to the selection process is appropriateness.

5. **Apply** = Now, with care, concern, and attention to all the factors that are likely to be affected—including any ethical considerations that may be appropriate—apply the skills and behaviors you have selected. The key to application is relevance.

6. **Reassess and reevaluate** = For every action taken, there is likely to be feedback as well as actions taken by others as a direct result of those taken by you. There will be other effects as well—some immediate that can be observed, some long-range that can only be surmised and anticipated. Reassessment and reevaluation may result in the application of further skills and behaviors needed to clarify, extend, continue, or even terminate the situation. The key to reassessment and reevaluation is accurate, careful observation.

Creativity

Another factor that must be mentioned within the umbrella of SF is the notion of **creativity**—the capacity to synthesize vast amounts of information and wrestle with complex problems. Creativity is not a rare or special power, and it relates directly to communication because every time you open your mouth, the unique combination of words emitted is a creative extension of who you are. Creativity requires this synthetic ability—this capacity to draw together and make sense of vast amounts of information. The more information you have (from whatever sources you can draw upon, including this instructor, this course, and this textbook), the more you have to bring to or bear upon your noticing, remembering, seeing, speaking, hearing, and understanding language and nonverbal communication. Not only are these processes important—a definite understatement—but they also allow you to search and transform the spaces on this earth you occupy. Your creativity frees you to generate possibilities, which of course is the very foundation of SF.

So, what you have is a complementary set of processes that are interwoven and mutually contributing: Creativity offers some of the creative force that drives successful SF, and SF provides the opportunities when you can apply your best creative thinking to a task.

To live, then, is to communicate. To communicate effectively is to enjoy life more fully. Consider this textbook, then, a *guide* for empowering effective communicators—for encouraging both SF and creativity. On the premise that increased knowledge helps you do things better, let's begin with a discussion of how communication works.

COMMUNICATION IS A PROCESS

A Definition of Communication

Communication is any process in which people share information, ideas, and feelings. It involves not only the spoken and written word but also body language, personal mannerisms, and style—anything that adds meaning to a message.

Each of the three opening stories illustrates communication as a process. When we say communication is a process, we mean that it is always changing.[6] When Ashley visited her guidance counselor, she looked for any sign from Mr. Vernon that would encourage her. Instead, she received a negative verbal message of six words: "I'm afraid you're not college material." This message stimulated a number of internal messages of motivation: "I'll show him. I *am* college material. I'll prove it."

The messages Andrew received also show how communication is always changing. Think, first, of the internal messages of lack of confidence, indecision, and immaturity he experienced while sitting in the cafeteria. Think, second, of the cognitive dissonance (mixed internal messages) he experienced trying to reconcile those messages with those from his friend about becoming a great actor. Think, third, of the messages he gave himself when he tried out for the play, saw that he was not on the call-back sheets, knew that he could do better, then pursued a course of action that would build his confidence and poise.

Finally, Wanda Jean DuCharme began her academic career with both direction and focus. Think about how her communication changed as she learned to think, organize ideas, question, listen, and put ideas into words. It changed, too, as her self-confidence and personal strength grew when she discovered she could communicate using her body language, personal allure, and engaging style in communicating with senior management, workers, and the public.

Knowing that communication is a process contributes positively to SF and creativity because it provides a foundation for growth, development, and change. Basically, it supports the kind of changes likely to occur as you read, experience, criticize, and put into practice the ideas, theories, and knowledge gained from a textbook and course in speech communication.

The Elements of Communication

The communication process is made up of various elements; sender-receivers, messages, channels, noise, feedback, and setting. Figure 1-1 shows how all these elements work together. The amoebalike shape of the sender-receiver indicates how this person changes—depending on what he or she is hearing or reacting to.

Sender-Receivers

People get involved in communication because they have information, ideas, and feelings they want to share. This sharing, however, is not a one-way process where one person sends ideas and the other receives them, and then the process is reversed. First, in most communication situations, people are **sender-receivers**—both sending and receiving at the same time. When you are discussing a problem with a close friend, your friend may be talking, but by listening closely, you are acting as a receiver. By paying careful attention, putting your hand on his or her arm, and showing genuine concern you are sending as many messages as you get, even though you may not say a word.

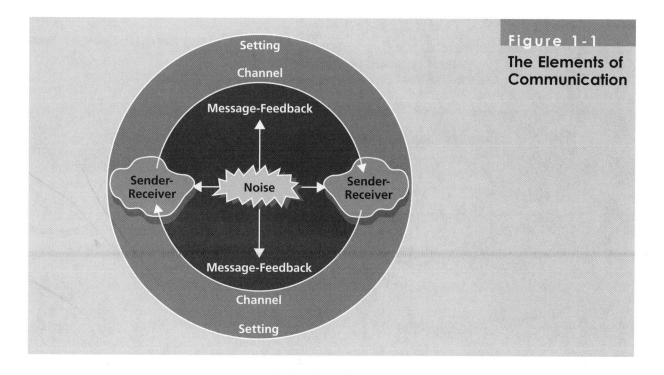

Figure 1-1

The Elements of Communication

Second, in all situations, sender-receivers share meaning. In your discussion with a close friend, both of you share the language and also share understanding of the situation.

Messages

The **message** is made up of the ideas and feelings that sender-receivers want to share. In the situation above, your close friend's message dealt with what had happened to him or her and how he or she was dealing with it, while your message was one of comfort and support. Meaning, however, is *jointly created* between sender and receiver. That is, it isn't just a sender sending a message to a receiver. There is no message at all if there aren't common symbols, like an understanding of each other's language. There is no message—or, perhaps, a very weak one—if there are no common referents, like understanding what the other person is talking about. How often, for example, do you "tune out" teachers if you have no idea where they are coming from?

Notice in Figure 1-1 that the message-feedback circle is exposed behind the amoeba-like sender-receiver shapes. This reveals that your "presence" within a message-feedback situation influences you. More than common symbols and common referents, presence can have powerful emotional, intellectual, physical, and, perhaps, spiritual effects. Think of being in the presence of a message-feedback occurrence between you and the president of the United States; an actor you admire; a priest, rabbi, or minister; or your professor. In these cases, it may not be the setting (to be discussed in a later section), or any other aspect of the message that influences you. It is simply being present within that message-feedback situation.

Ideas and feelings can be communicated only if they are represented by symbols. A **symbol** is something that stands for something else. Our daily lives are full of symbols. We all know that the eagle stands for the United States, the Statue of Liberty equals freedom, and roses express love. Two people walking close and holding hands reflects romance, books represent knowledge, and teachers stand for instruction.

Feedback and nonverbal communication are important when we communicate with others.

All our communication messages are made up of two kinds of symbols: verbal and nonverbal. The words in a language are **verbal symbols** that stand for particular things or ideas. Verbal symbols are limited and complicated. For example, when we use the word *chair*, we agree we are talking about something we sit on. Thus, *chair* is a **concrete symbol,** a symbol that represents an object. However, when we hear the word *chair*, we all might have a different impression: A chair could be a recliner, an easy chair, a beanbag, a lawn chair—the variety is great.

Even more complicated are **abstract symbols,** which stand for ideas. Consider the vast differences in our understanding of words such as *home, hungry,* or *hurt*. How we understand these words will be determined by our experience. Since people's experiences differ to some degree, individuals will assign different meanings to these abstract words.

Nonverbal symbols are ways we communicate without using words; they include facial expressions, gestures, posture, vocal tones, appearance, and so on. As with verbal symbols, we all attach certain meanings to nonverbal symbols. A yawn means we are bored or tired; a furrowed brow indicates confusion; not looking someone in the eye may mean we have something to hide. Like verbal symbols, nonverbal symbols can be misleading. We cannot control most of our nonverbal behavior, and we often send out information of which we are not even aware.

Many nonverbal messages differ from one culture to another just as symbols differ from culture to culture. Black is the color for funerals in Western cultures; in Eastern cultures, that color is white. The crescent moon of male-oriented Islam used to be the symbol for female-oriented worship of the moon mother in ancient Arabia.[7] In one culture, showing the sole of your foot when you cross your legs is an insult. In another culture, respectful behavior is shown with a bow; while in still another, deep respect is shown by touching the other person's feet. Whether or not you are aware of nonverbal messages, they are extremely important in all cultures. Albert Mehrabian, a scholar of nonverbal communication, believes that over 90 percent of the messages sent and received by Americans are nonverbal.[8]

Channels

The **channel** is the route traveled by a message; it is the means a message uses to reach the sender-receivers. In face-to-face communication, the primary channels are sound and sight: We listen to and look at each other. We are familiar with the channels of radio, television, CDs, newspapers, and magazines in the mass media. Other channels communicate nonverbal messages. For example, when DeVon goes to apply for a job, she uses several nonverbal signals to send out a positive message: a firm handshake (touch), appropriate clothing (sight), and respectful voice (sound). The senses are the channels through which she is sending a message.

Feedback

Feedback is the response of the receiver-senders to each other. You tell me a joke and I smile. That's feedback. You make a comment about the weather and I make another one. More feedback.

Strategic flexibility is an important aspect of jointly created messages. The ability to change messages in ways that will increase your chances of obtaining your desired result is exactly what SF is all about, and the need to change underscores the importance of SF in communication. People are infinitely varied in their individual traits, and even though you think you have created a message with common symbols and referents, it may not be true. Using SF, you can adapt, change, adjust, correct, or do whatever is needed to get the result you wish.

Feedback is vital to communication because it lets the participants see whether ideas and feelings have been shared in the way they were intended. For example, when Dele-tha and Jordan decide to meet on the corner of 45th and Broadway in New York City, it would be good feedback for one of them to ask, "Which corner?" since the four corners at that particular intersection are among the busiest and most crowded in the city.

Sender-receivers who meet face-to-face have the greatest opportunity for feedback, especially if there are no distractions—or little noise. But, often in these situations a limited amount of feedback occurs because rather than being sensitive to the feedback, communicators are busy planning what they are going to say next. **Sensory acuity** means paying attention to all elements in the communication environment. Are you paying attention to what others are saying? Are you aware of how they are saying it? Do their nonverbal messages support or contradict their verbal messages? Are you gaining or losing rapport with the other person? Is your communication bringing you closer to achieving your objective? Are you aware of distractions or noise that can derail your communication? You begin to notice at once the contribution that sensory acuity can play in all six steps of SF.

Noise

Noise is interference that keeps a message from being understood or accurately interpreted. Noise occurs between the sender-receivers, and it comes in three forms: external, internal, and semantic.

External noise comes from the environment and keeps the message from being heard or understood. Your heart-to-heart talk with your roommate can be interrupted by a group of people yelling in the hall, a helicopter passing overhead, or a weed wacker outside the window. External noise does not always come from sound. You could be standing and talking to someone in the hot sun and become so uncomfortable that you can't concentrate. Conversation might also falter at a picnic when you discover you are sitting on an anthill and ants are crawling all over your blanket.

Internal noise occurs in the minds of the sender-receivers when their thoughts or feelings are focused on something other than the communication at hand. A student doesn't hear the lecture because he is thinking about lunch; a wife can't pay attention to her husband because she is upset by a problem at the office. Internal noise may also stem from beliefs or prejudices. Doug, for example, doesn't believe that women should be managers, so when his female boss asks him to do something, he often misses part of her message.

Semantic noise is caused by people's emotional reactions to words. Many people tune out a speaker who uses profanity because the words are offensive to them. Others have negative reactions to people who make ethnic or sexist remarks. Semantic noise, like external noise and internal noise, can interfere with all or part of the message.

Setting

The **setting** is the environment in which the communication occurs. Settings can have a significant influence on communication. Formal settings lend themselves to formal presentations. An auditorium, for example, is good for giving speeches and presentations but not very good for conversation. If people want to converse on a more intimate basis, they will be better off in a smaller, more comfortable room where they can sit facing each other.

In many situations the communication will change when the setting changes. For example, in the town where one of your authors lives there was an ice cream stand just outside the city limits. People parked in front, got out of their cars, and walked up to a window to order their ice cream. On warm evenings, the place attracted many of the area's teenagers. After years of great success, the owner retired and sold the stand. The new owners decided to enclose it and make it more restaurantlike. You still had to order at the window, but because of the new addition at the front of the building, no one could see you anymore. Once you had your ice cream, you could take it to your car or eat it in the restaurant at one of the tables.

The new restaurant was certainly comfortable. You no longer had to stand in the rain, the place was open year-round, and you could sit down at a table and have dinner. However, comfort wasn't the issue: Every teenager deserted the place and headed for the Dairy Queen down the road. Why? So that they could be seen. For them, eating ice cream was secondary to participating in the social ritual of interacting with or being seen by their peers. In other words, the setting was an important part of their communication.

Setting often shows who has power in a relationship. The question "Your place or mine?" implies an equal relationship. However, when the dean asks a faculty member to come to her office, the dean has more power than the faculty member. When a couple meet to work out a divorce agreement, they meet in a lawyer's office, a place that provides a somewhat neutral setting.

Settings can have a significant influence on communication.

In his book written specifically for college students, Patrick Combs writes in the opening two paragraphs of Chapter 1, "On the Road to Greatness":

Think of the students around you. What personal characteristic do you think will make the difference between those who become great at something and those who never rise above mediocrity? Intelligence? Family background? Confidence?

The answer is surprising. Benjamin Bloom, a professor at the University of Chicago, recently studied 120 outstanding athletes, artists, and scholars. He was looking for the common denominators of greatness and mastery. The study concluded that intelligence and family background were NOT important characteristics for achieving mastery of a desired skill. The only characteristic that the 120 outstanding people had in common was extraordinary drive.

Source: *Major in Success: Make College Easier, Fire Up Your Dreams, and Get a Very Cool Job* (p. 3), by Patrick Combs, 2003, Berkeley, CA:Ten Speed Press.

The arrangement of furniture in a setting can also affect the communication that takes place. For example, at one college, the library was one of the noisiest places on campus. Changing the furniture solved the problem. Instead of having sofas and chairs arranged so that students could sit and talk, the library used study desks—thus creating a quiet place to concentrate.

All communication is made up of sender-receivers, messages, channels, feedback, noise, and setting. Every time people communicate, these elements are somewhat different. They are not the only factors that influence communication, however. Communication is also influenced by what you bring to it. That is the subject of our next section.

COMMUNICATION IS A TRANSACTION

A communication transaction involves not only the physical act of communicating but also a psychological act: Impressions are being formed in the minds of the people who are communicating.[9] What people think and know about one another directly affects their communication.

The Three Principles of Transactional Communication

Communication as a transaction—**transactional communication**—involves three important principles. First, people engaged in communication are sending messages continuously and simultaneously. Second, communication events have a past, present, and future. Third, participants in communication play certain roles. Let's consider each of these principles in turn.

Participation Is Continuous and Simultaneous

Whether or not you are actually talking in a communication situation, you are actively involved in sending and receiving messages. Let's say you are lost, walking in a big city that is not familiar to you. You show others you are confused when you hesitate, look around you, or pull out a map. When you realize you have to ask for directions, you look for someone who might help you. You dismiss two people because they look like they're in a hurry; you don't ask another one because she looks as though she might be lost too. Finally you see a person who looks helpful and you ask for information. As you listen, you give feedback, through both words and body language, as to whether you understand.

As this person talks, you think about how long it will take to walk to your destination, you make note of what landmarks to look for, and you may even create a visual image of what you will see when you get there. You are participating continuously and simultaneously in a communication that is quite complicated.

All Communications Have a Past, a Present, and a Future

You respond to every situation from your own experiences, your own moods, and your own expectations. Such factors complicate the communication situation. When you know someone well, you can make predictions about what to do in the future on the basis of what you know about the past. For example, without having to ask him, Lee knows that his friend Jason will not be willing to try the new Indian restaurant in town. Lee has been out to eat with Jason many times, and Jason always eats the same kind of food, burgers and fries. Lee also knows that Jason doesn't like changes of any kind, so he knows better than to suggest that they go out of town for a concert because he knows that Jason will respond that they should wait until the group comes to their town.

Even when you are meeting someone for the first time, you respond to that person on the basis of your experience. You might respond to physical traits (short, tall, bearded, bald), to occupation (accountant, gym teacher), or even to a name (remember how a boy named Eugene always tormented you and you've mistrusted all Eugenes ever since?). Any of these things you call up from your past might influence how you respond to someone—at least at the beginning.

The future also influences communication. If you want a relationship to continue, you will say and do things in the present to make sure it does ("Thanks for dinner. I always enjoy your cooking"). If you think you will never see a person again, or if you want to limit the nature of your interactions, this also might affect your communication. You might be more businesslike and thus leave the personal aspects of your life out of the communication.

All Communicators Play Roles

Roles are parts you play or ways you behave with others. Defined by society and affected by individual relationships, roles control everything from word choice to body language. For example, one of the roles you play is that of student. Your teachers may consider you to be bright and serious; your peers, who see you in the same role, may think you are too serious. Outside the classroom you play other roles. Your parents might see you as a considerate daughter or son; your best friend might see the fun-loving side of you; and your boss might see you as hardworking and dependable.

Roles do not always stay the same in a relationship. They vary with others' moods or with one's own, with the setting and the noise factor. Communication changes to meet the needs of each of your relationships and situations. For example, even though Eduardo and Heidi have been married for 10 years and have three children, they still try to reserve Saturday night for a romantic date. While they are out, they try not to talk about children and family issues. Instead, they focus on each other and what the other is thinking and feeling. On Sunday morning, their roles change. Eduardo fixes breakfast while Heidi gets the children ready to go to church. Now their roles are children and family centered.

The roles you play—whether established by individual relationships or by society—may be perceived differently by different people. These perceptions affect the communication that results. For example, Tom, in his role of youth director, is well organized and maintains tight control over the activities he directs. The kids who play the games he coaches know they have to behave or they'll be in big trouble. Therefore they speak to him in a respectful voice and stay quiet when they're supposed to. To

Working with classmates as a group, create a model of communication as a transaction. Drawing on everything that each person has read and all the information received in class, the group is to develop a complete model of communication as a transaction by following each of these steps:

Step 1: Talk through the process of communication as a transaction, making certain each group member contributes his or her thinking.

Step 2: Create a list of all the elements that need to be included in a model of communication as a transaction. Remember to include, as well, any important subpoints to the major principles.

Step 3: Have each member of the group create the same visual representation of the model in his or her own notebook. Each aspect of the model should be entered simultaneously, only when it is agreed upon by all members.

Step 4: One member of the group should explain the group's model to the entire class.

If there is time before this group exercise is complete, discuss as a group the question, "Why are visual representations effective tools for explaining a theory, idea, or process?"

---

some kids, however, Tom's discipline seems rigid and inflexible. These kids avoid the youth center; they choose not to communicate with him at all.

TYPES OF COMMUNICATION

As you can see in Figure 1-2, there are different kinds of communication. The figure shows four of the kinds most often used: intrapersonal, interpersonal, small-group, and public communication. In this section we will also discuss intercultural and computer-mediated communication.

Intrapersonal Communication

Intrapersonal communication is communication that occurs within you. It involves thoughts, feelings, and the way you look at yourself. Figure 1-3 shows some of the things that make up the self, hence, intrapersonal communication.

Because intrapersonal communication is centered in the self, you are the only sender-receiver. The message is made up of your thoughts and feelings. The channel is your brain, which processes what you are thinking and feeling. There is feedback in the sense that as you talk to yourself, you discard certain ideas and replace them with others.

Even though you are not directly communicating with others in intrapersonal communication, the experiences you have had determine how you "talk" to yourself. For example, think about the intrapersonal communication—all the internal messages—that Andrew (in the second opening example in this chapter) may have been creating while sitting in the cafeteria among a horde of talking, milling students who all seemed so confident, directed, and older: "What am I doing here? I am not like all these people. I don't have their confidence and security. I don't know what I want. I am so young and immature when I compare myself with them."

Interpersonal Communication

Interpersonal communication occurs when you communicate on a one-to-one basis—usually in an informal, unstructured setting. This kind of communication occurs mostly between two people, though it may include more than two.

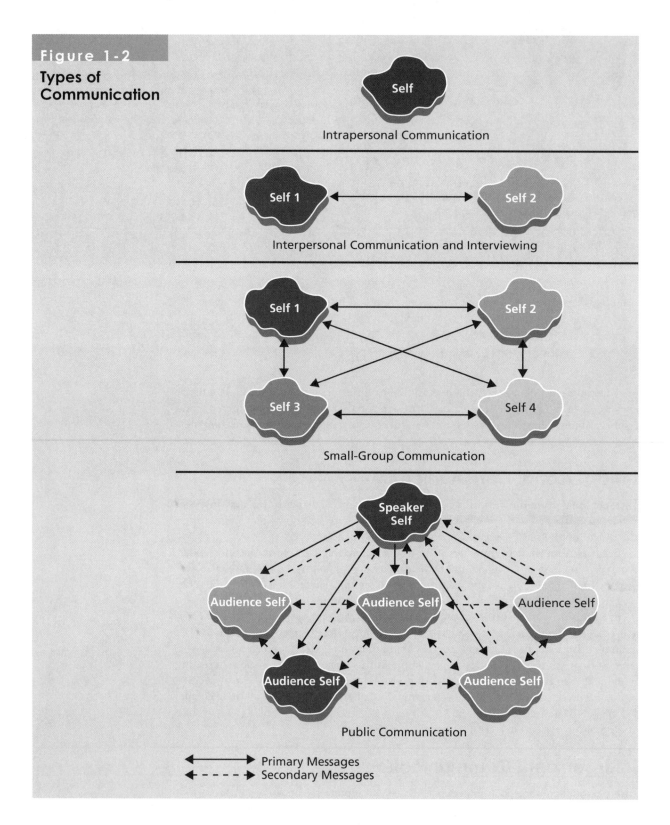

Figure 1-2

Types of Communication

Intrapersonal Communication

Interpersonal Communication and Interviewing

Small-Group Communication

Public Communication

Primary Messages
Secondary Messages

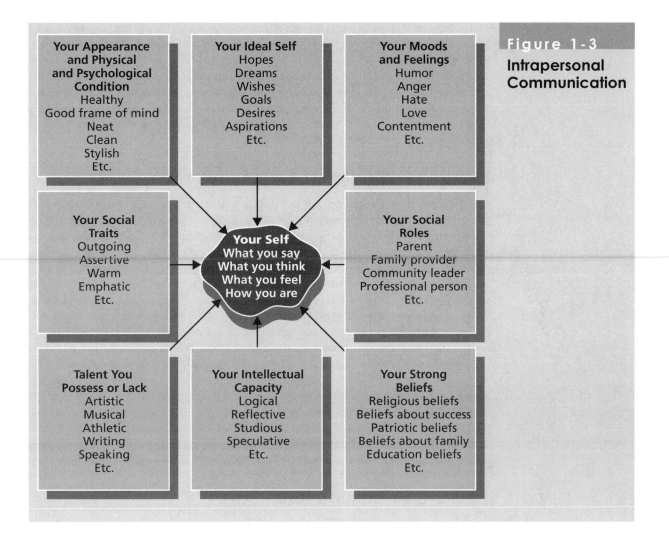

Figure 1-3

Intrapersonal Communication

Interpersonal communication uses all the elements of the communication process. In a conversation between friends, for example, each brings his or her background and experience to the conversation. During the conversation each functions as a sender-receiver: Their messages consist of both verbal and nonverbal symbols. The channels they use the most are sight and sound. Because interpersonal communication is between two (or a few) people, it offers the greatest opportunity for feedback. Internal noise is likely to be minimal because each person can see whether the other is distracted. The persons involved in the conversation have many chances to check that the message is being perceived correctly. People who want to engage in interpersonal communication usually look for informal and comfortable settings.

Small-Group Communication

Small-group communication occurs when a small number of people meet to solve a problem. The group must be small enough so that each member has a chance to interact with all the other members.

Because small groups are made up of several sender-receivers, the communication process is more complicated than in interpersonal communication. With so many more people sending messages, there are more chances for confusion. Messages are also more structured in small groups because the group is meeting for a specific purpose. Small groups use the same channels as are used in interpersonal communication, however, and there is also a good deal of opportunity for feedback. In keeping with their problem-solving nature, small groups usually meet in a more formal setting than people involved in interpersonal communication.

Computer-Mediated Communication

Computer-mediated communication (CMC) is defined as "a wide range of technologies that facilitate both human communication and the interactive sharing of information through computer networks, including e-mail, discussion group, newsgroups, chat, instant messages, and Web pages."[10] Using this definition alone, CMC is strictly about the variety of channels that serve as conduits for conveying messages and feedback between senders and receivers. However, when CMC is conjoined with digital literacy—"the ability to understand and use information in multiple formats from a wide range of sources when it is presented via computer"—then the combination of CMC and digital literacy fits neatly into the communication model presented earlier in this chapter with few changes except for the type of CMC technology used.[11]

The most important aspects of CMC over face-to-face communication (FtFC) include the fact that CMC occurs over a single channel, it is asynchronous (the time and place for communication is at the discretion of the individual), and the mode of communication can support thought-out prose. CMC also exhibits social leveling (it brings all people, of whatever status they hold in society, to a near-equal footing or level) as the cues to social status are removed. There are a wide variety of reasons—personal, interpersonal, and experimental—why you would choose CMC over FtFC.

Public Communication

In **public communication** the sender-receiver (the speaker) sends a message (the speech) to an audience. The speaker usually delivers a highly structured message, using the same channels as in interpersonal and small-group communication. In public communication, however, the channels are more exaggerated than in interpersonal communication. The voice is louder and the gestures are more expansive because the audience is bigger. The speaker might use additional visual channels, such as slides or the computer program PowerPoint. Generally, the opportunity for verbal feedback in public communication is limited. The audience members may have a chance to ask questions at the end of the speech, but usually they are not free to address the speaker during the speech. However, they can send nonverbal feedback. If they like what the speaker is saying, they may interrupt the speech with applause. If they dislike it, they may fidget a lot or simply stop paying attention. In most public communication, the setting is formal.

Intercultural Communication

There are cultural and technological forces that are now reshaping the world. It is the communication skills—whether of senders or receivers—that determine how well individuals, organizations, industries, and even nations do in acquiring and applying knowledge, thus broadening their chances for success in this information-driven world. The better you are at negotiating the cultural issues in communication, the greater the competitive edge you gain in a global society.

When we talk about **culture,** we mean "the ever-changing values, traditions, social and political relationships, and worldview created and shared by a group of people bound together by a combination of factors (which can include a common history, geographic location, language, social class, and/or religion)."[12] Cultures could include the Amish or Pennsylvania Dutch, groups with a common history. Cultures could include the Japanese or Taiwanese, groups with a common geographic location. Cultures also could include those who speak the French or Islamic languages.

By **co-culture,** we mean people who are part of a larger culture but also belong to a smaller group that has some different values, attitudes, or beliefs. For example, co-cultures could include the socially elite, those in the top 1 percent income bracket, the Baptists, Catholics, Unitarian-Universalists, or Jews—all part of the larger U.S. culture, yet smaller groups possessing some different values, attitudes, and beliefs. African Americans, Native Americans, Hispanic Americans, and Asian Americans make up large co-cultures within the U.S. culture. Within the U.S. culture are co-cultures made up of gay and lesbian people, older people, and people with physical disabilities.

To help people understand each other better, scholars, teachers, and worldwide business leaders have developed the field of **intercultural communication**—the communication that occurs whenever two or more people from different cultures interact. This field studies how differences between people affect their perceptions of the world and, thus, their communication. Of course, there is no way to understand all cultures and co-cultures. There are, however, certain characteristics that occur again and again, and the study of intercultural communication rests on these characteristics.

Why should you be concerned about intercultural communication? What if your job involved coordinating international student services and exchange programs at your university or college campus? What if you were the manager of a biotech com-

Every year the United States becomes more culturally diverse.

pany responsible for leading a diverse team of scientists doing innovative research? What if you were a member of a campus group interested in gathering the support of diverse groups on campus to extend an invitation to a controversial speaker? In each case, to overlook the different cultural backgrounds of those receivers might mean your communication would be less constructive and may result in misunderstandings and breakdowns as well. There are inherent cultural issues associated with any form of communication.

Although people throughout the world have many characteristics in common, there are also many differences. Thus, if people from different cultural or co-cultural groups want to communicate, they must be aware that they may have different systems of knowledge, values, beliefs, customs, and behaviors. For example, crossing your legs in the United States reveals a relaxed attitude, but in Korea it is a social faux pas. In West Africa, the comment "You've put on weight" means you look healthy and prosperous and is a great compliment; in America it is an insult. In Japan, they put business cards in safe places and handle them with great care, because they view them as an extension of the person, in America they are viewed as a business formality and convenience, and Americans are quick to put them away, a behavior insulting to the Japanese.[13] Understanding differences and then utilizing them in the preparation, development, and presentation of your ideas can only help you become a more effective communicator.

ETHICAL COMMUNICATION

Ethical communication, a component of each of the six types of communication, is communication that is honest, fair, and considerate of others' rights. Communication is honest when communicators tell the truth; it is fair and considerate when they consider listeners' feelings. Most people reading this believe that truthfulness, accuracy, honesty, and reason are essential to the integrity of communication, just as it is written in the National Communication Association's (NCA's) Credo for Ethical Communication.[14]

The problem, of course, is neither with what you know to be true nor with what you want to have happen. The problem occurs as you are faced with complex demands (too much being asked of you), limited resources (like time), or the easy access to alternatives to ethical behavior (being handed an exam, paper, or speech)—or what is often likely, the combination of some or all of these. There is always the very human temptation to try to make life easier by nullifying some of your fundamental ethical responsibilities. That, of course, is when your true ethics are revealed.

You have undoubtedly heard numerous excuses for unethical conduct. The most often may be "I didn't know that was considered unethical." Others include "Everyone does it," or "I'm sorry, I just didn't have the time [to be ethical]," "What harm is there in it?" "I've been sick," "I've never done it before," "You know, I'm very busy." It is not surprising that those who engage in unethical behavior have quick and easy excuses for what they do. No excuse, of course, is good enough to justify truly unethical conduct.

Why should you be concerned about ethical communication? It is clearly stated in the NCA's Credo: "Unethical communication threatens the quality of all communication and consequently the well-being of individuals and the society in which we live."[15] As the Credo states in its opening paragraph, ethical communication is "fundamental to responsible thinking, decision making, and the development of relationships and communities within and across contexts, cultures, channels, and media. Ethical communication enhances human worth and respect for self and others."[16] Because of the worldwide publicity given to the unethical practices of large corporations such as Enron, Tyco, WorldCom, and in the mutual funds industry, there is an increasing trend for organizations to integrate a code of ethics into their daily activities.

"Questions of right and wrong arise whenever people communicate," the Credo states, thus, it is important to establish a basic code of ethics as you begin a course in speech communication. As you read the following principles of ethical communication, notice the two ethical communication themes of caring and responsibility. These seven principles have been paraphrased from the Credo:

- Protect freedom of expression, diversity of perspective, and tolerance for dissent.

- Strive to understand and respect others' communications before evaluating and responding to their messages.

- Help promote communication climates of caring and mutual understanding that protect the unique needs and characteristics of individual communicators.

- Condemn communication that degrades individuals and humanity through distortions, intolerance, intimidation, coercion, hatred, or violence.

- Commit yourself to the courageous expression of your personal convictions in pursuit of fairness and justice.

- Accept responsibility for the short- and long-term consequences of your own communication, and expect the same of others.

- Avoid plagiarism—presentation of the work of another person in such a way as to give the impression that the other's work is your own, whether it be:

  - the verbatim use of part of a book or article without using quotation marks and without citing the original source.

  - paraphrasing another's words without noting this is a paraphrase essentially taken from another source.

  - using another person's illustrative material without citing the source and, thus, giving credit where credit is due.

  The basic idea in avoiding plagiarism is simply to give credit when using someone else's ideas. If you have any doubts, give the credit—using a footnote or a reference *during* (as part of) the communication.[17]

Sometimes it is easy to look at what goes on in this world and develop a hardened, insensitive, and unfeeling attitude toward ethics: proper conduct. But if you conduct yourself as an ethical person in your dealings with family, friends, and others, refraining from activities that may be construed as unethical—whether they are governed by written or unwritten codes of personal conduct, rules, or regulations—and if you continue your wholehearted commitment to being a credible, quality person who demonstrates care, consideration, and dedication to values and morals, you will promote ethical thinking and living and be an example to others.

COMMUNICATING EFFECTIVELY

Once you understand the process of communication, you can begin to understand why communication does or doesn't work. In an ideal communication situation the message is perceived in the way it was intended. But when messages don't work, it is useful to ask these questions: Was there a problem with the message? Was the best channel used? Did noise occur? Knowing the right questions to ask is essential to building skills in communication.

Most of us already have considerable communication skills. You have been sending and receiving verbal and nonverbal signals all your life. Nevertheless, you have probably had times when you have not communicated as effectively as you should. If you got a lower grade on a paper than you expected, you unintentionally hurt somebody's feelings, or if the instructor did not understand a question you asked in class, you are not communicating as effectively as you could.

Where to Begin

The information about communication is so vast that most of us could spend a lifetime studying the subject and not learn even a fraction of what there is to know. However, as you begin your study of communication, the following five questions are a good starting point.

Which Communication Skills Am I Most Likely to Need?

Find out what communication skills are important to you. What do you intend to do in your life? What kind of work do you expect to do? What communication skills are required in this work? Which of these skills do you already have? Which ones need improvement? Which ones do you need to acquire?

For example, a career in business requires almost every communication skill. You need interpersonal skills to get along with the people you work with, intercultural communication skills if you are going to work with people from other countries, and public-speaking skills for making presentations. Although you may use some communication skills more than others, at one time or another you are going to need every one we have discussed in this chapter.

Which Communication Skills Am I Most Lacking?

Which kinds of communication are most difficult for you? Intrapersonal? Interpersonal? Intercultural? Small group? Public speaking? What are the symptoms of difficulties in these areas? What problems do you have to overcome before you can perform effectively?

Many people would prefer to avoid, rather than work in, the area that gives them the most trouble. For example, if you are anxious about public speaking, you might feel inclined to avoid any circumstance where you have to give a speech. A better approach, however, would be to get over this fear: You'll be able to offer a wedding toast, give a presentation at a meeting, consider many more job possibilities, and so forth. If you can conquer fear by plunging in and practicing the thing that gives you the most trouble, you will expand the possibilities in your life.

How Can I Get Communication Practice?

Are there situations, other than class, where you can practice communication skills that will be useful to you? Are there groups and organizations you can join that will help you develop these skills? It's always a good idea to take what you have learned in class and try it out on the world. Using new skills helps to develop and refine them.

Where Can I Get Help?

What people do you know who will help you develop communication skills and give you feedback on how you are doing? Are there people you can ask who will give you support when you are trying something new and threatening? Are you willing to ask them to support you? You can usually count on this kind of support from your friends. Don't you have a friend who would be willing to listen to one of your speeches and tell you whether it works and how you might improve it? Also, don't forget your instructors. Many of them sit in their offices during office hours hoping that students will drop by.

What Timetable Should I Set?

Have you set a realistic timetable for improvement? Knowing that it is difficult to learn new skills or break bad habits, are you willing to give yourself enough time? Your speech communication class is going to last for a semester or a quarter, and although you will be making steady progress in your interpersonal communication and public-speaking skills, change will not happen overnight. The act of communicating—whether with a single person or a classroom audience—takes time and effort. The most realistic timetable is one in which you say, "I'm going to keep working at this until I succeed."

THE INTERNET AND THE COMMUNICATION PROCESS

The landscape of the Internet along with all aspects of technology and communication continues to change quickly. The problem with relating the Internet to the communication process is that the Internet contains many different configurations of communication. **Synchronous communication** means talk that occurs at the same time—with no time delay. With respect to senders and receivers, it could be one-to-one, one-to-a few, one-to-many, or even many-to-one. The best examples of synchronous communication are instant messaging (IM) and chat rooms. **Asynchronous communication** does not occur at the same time, such as e-mail messages or when you seek information from Web sites. For those familiar with the Internet, Usenet, electronic bulletin boards, and Listservers are asynchronous. The words *synchronous* and *asynchronous* help categorize Internet communication, but also reveal some of the problems in trying to categorize it.

The point here is not to confuse but to show the role of the Internet in the sender-message-receiver elements of communication pictured in Figure 1-1. Sometimes the elements are configured similar to the model; sometimes they are put into entirely new configurations.

An Internet model of communication must have an active receiver who emits information, interacts with—or has the potential of interacting with—the sender or Web site and selects his or her own information and decodes it according to personal interests. Because of the influence of the Internet and the active character of the public (a mass of active receivers), the Internet has become one of the most important elements of public opinion formation.

Messages can be as simple as conversations between two people, but they can also be traditional journalistic news stories created by a reporter or editor, stories placed on Web logs (blogs) by people with unknown or uncertain credentials, stories created over a long period by many people, or outdated stories that have been stored on a Web site and never updated since their creation years ago—the latter is called Web rot.

Although the channel for the communication may be one computer—or a network of computers—with another, settings can vary from one's home or office to anyplace where one can carry a laptop or gain computer access. You have seen people with laptops in airport terminals, waiting for a bus, or in hospital waiting rooms. Cell phones provide yet another means of access.

If how we communicate is affected by the tools we use to communicate, then it should be clear that the communication we have with others via the computer is significantly different from communication we might have via the telephone, a written letter, or a face-to-face meeting. We will explore some of these differences in the Internet communications sections in every chapter.

Perhaps the major difference the Internet introduces into communication is the removal of face-to-face communication. Face-to-face interactions will increase with direct video links between computers. The Internet's effect on communication has four characteristics that make it unique from normal face-to-face communication. The first is **globalization**—there are no limitations because of borders. The second is **temporality**—there are no limitations because of time. The third is **access to roles.** Whoever has the technical capacity to receive messages with a computer can also send them. Senders and receivers do this without restrictions on their roles, whether it involves being a student, commentator, reporter, businessperson, citizen, politician, or some fabricated identity. The fourth characteristic is **content openness.** There are no limitations on content. Within the obvious boundaries of a computer's capabilities, content can take on any form desired by senders and receivers. Just as a message may be typed, videotaped, audiotaped, or simply visualized, news too can be communicated via text, games, or letters.

These characteristics make audiences more independent of traditional media sources, but they involve a loss of control over source reliability, selection of information, and control over verification. It increases risks because of the loss of traditional journalistic controls—or any controls—over the information market, and, as a result, it raises the responsibility for Internet users to be wise consumers.

The Internet will continue to lead to changes in how people communicate, solve problems, and create knowledge. It will continue to evolve. What we can do is examine, assess, and evaluate the changes and how they affect senders, receivers, messages, feedback, channels, and settings—interpersonally, at work, in groups, and in public-communication settings.

Do You Have Strategic Flexibility?

For each question circle the numerical score that best represents your performance, skill, or ability using the following scale; 7 = Outstanding; 6 = Excellent; 5 = Very good; 4 = Average (good); 3 = Fair; 2 = Poor; 1 = Minimal ability; 0 = No ability demonstrated.

1. Do you try to anticipate situations—think about them *before* they occur—to prepare yourself mentally (and physically) for what is likely to happen?   7 6 5 4 3 2 1 0

2. Do you generally look at new situations with an eye toward determining if communication will be needed or required by you?   7 6 5 4 3 2 1 0

3. From your assessment of a situation, is it easy for you to determine *when* communication is necessary?   7 6 5 4 3 2 1 0

4. Do you find it easy to know—once engaged in communication— what the purpose of the communication is? What people hope to accomplish?   7 6 5 4 3 2 1 0

5. When you are with a group of people, can you—from simple, preliminary observations—determine what their needs and assumptions are?   7 6 5 4 3 2 1 0

6. When you are with a group of people, do you automatically know what their relationship is to you?   7 6 5 4 3 2 1 0

7. Do you also know what your relationship to this group of people is?   7 6 5 4 3 2 1 0

8. Are you able to anticipate how an audience would use any communication you shared with them?   7 6 5 4 3 2 1 0

9. When you are talking with another person, or other people, are you able to determine—in advance—what effect your communication *should* have on them?   7 6 5 4 3 2 1 0

10. Can you tell from preliminary assessments what kind of communication might be appropriate in particular situations?   7 6 5 4 3 2 1 0

11. Do you feel you have the breadth of knowledge, experience, and skills to more than effectively meet most of the communication-related situations you encounter?   7 6 5 4 3 2 1 0

12. Do you feel comfortable when you encounter a situation where you know you will have to communicate?   7 6 5 4 3 2 1 0

13. Do you feel confident, secure, and free of nervousness when facing communication situations?   7 6 5 4 3 2 1 0

14. When you have to communicate with others, do you feel as if the behaviors and skills you put into use are the same ones you always use?   7 6 5 4 3 2 1 0

15. When you communicate, do you feel like you use some of the techniques, styles, or behaviors of the other gender?   7 6 5 4 3 2 1 0

16. Do you believe there is a possibility of and value for expanding your range of communication skills and behaviors?   7 6 5 4 3 2 1 0

Go to the *Communicating Effectively* CD-ROM and the Online Learning Center at **www.mhhe. com/hybels8** to see your results and learn how to evaluate your attitudes and feelings.

CHAPTER REVIEW

SUMMARY

Everyone needs good communication skills. Effective communication will help you feel more confident about yourself, more comfortable with others' perceptions of you, greater ease in reasoning with others, better at using language, and improvement in your critical thinking skills. It is the ultimate people-oriented discipline, fundamental to effective leadership, and a key to professional success.

Strategic flexibility (SF) means expanding your communication repertoire to enable you to use the best skill or behavior available for a particular situation. People who possess SF are happier and more fulfilled because they can bring to bear on any situation a broad range of potentially valuable behaviors. The six steps of SF are anticipate, assess, evaluate, select, apply, and reassess and reevaluate.

Creativity is the capacity to synthesize vast amounts of information and wrestle with complex problems. Your creativity frees you to generate possibilities, which of course is the very foundation of SF.

Communication is an ongoing process in which people share ideas and feelings. The elements of communication include sender-receivers, messages, channels, feedback, noise, and setting. The essence of communication is meaning making, and meaning is jointly created between sender and receiver.

Every communication is a transaction. Viewing communication as a transaction focuses on the people who are communicating and the changes that take place in them as they are communicating. It also implies that all participants are involved continuously and simultaneously; that communication events have a past, present, and future; and that the roles the participants play will affect the communication.

Six types of communication are discussed in this book. Intrapersonal communication is communication within oneself. Interpersonal communication is informal communication with one or more other persons. Small-group communication occurs when a small group of people get together to solve a problem. Computer-mediated communication refers to a wide range of technologies that facilitate both human communication and the interactive sharing of information through computer networks. It is discussed in the in-text appendix. Public communication is giving a speech to an audience. Intercultural communication occurs whenever two or more people from different cultures interact.

Ethical communication, a component of each of the six types of communication above, is communication that is honest, fair, and considerate of others' rights. Underlying the seven principles of ethical conduct paraphrased from the National Communication Association's Credo are the themes of caring and responsibility. Proper ethical conduct often grows out of an individual's personal commitment to live an ethical life.

Communication can be improved if you concentrate on several important areas. Find out what communication skills are important to you. Discover the kinds of communication that are most difficult for you and work to improve them. Seek out people who will help you develop these skills and give you support and feedback, and set a realistic timetable for improvement.

The Internet plays with the sender-message-receiver features of the elements of communication. There are four characteristics that make it unique from normal face-to-face communication: globalization, temporality, access to roles, and content openness. The Internet will continue to lead to changes in how people communicate, solve problems, and create knowledge.

KEY TERMS AND CONCEPTS

Use the *Communicating Effectively* CD-ROM and the Online Learning Center at **www.mhhe.com/hybels8** to further your understanding of the following terms.

mhhe.com/hybels8

Abstract symbol 10
Access to roles 24
Anticipate 6
Apply 7
Assess 6
Asynchronous communication 23
Channel 10
Co-culture 19
Communication 8
Computer-mediated communication (CMC) 18
Concrete symbol 10
Content openness 24
Creativity 7

Culture 19
Ethical communication 20
Evaluate 6
External noise 11
Feedback 11
Globalization 24
Intercultural communication 19
Internal noise 11
Interpersonal communication 15
Intrapersonal communication 15
Message 9
Noise 11
Nonverbal symbol 10
Public communication 18

Reassess and reevaluate 7
Roles 14
Select 7
Semantic noise 12
Sensory acuity 11
Sender-receivers 8
Setting 12
Small-group communication 17
Strategic flexibility (SF) 6
Symbol 9
Synchronous communication 23
Temporality 24
Transactional communication 13
Verbal symbol 10

QUESTIONS TO REVIEW

1. What are the most frequently cited factors important to aiding graduating college students both to obtain and sustain employment?

2. What is the meaning of strategic flexibility (SF)?

3. What are the six steps of SF, and what is the key to each step?

4. What is the role of creativity in communication?

5. Why is communication called a process?

6. What is the significance in knowing that meaning is jointly created between sender and receiver?

7. What are the differences between the symbols that make up communication messages?

8. Why is communication called a transaction? What are the three principles of transactional communication?

9. How do intrapersonal and interpersonal communication differ from each other?

10. What is the difference between culture and co-culture?

11. Why should you be concerned about intercultural communication?

12. What are the principles of ethical communication, and what is likely to be the foundation for ethical conduct?

13. What are the four characteristics that make Internet communication distinctive from face-to-face communication?

14. What are the risks involved regarding Internet communication?

mhhe.com/hybels8

Go to the self-quizzes on the *Communicating Effectively* CD-ROM and the Online Learning Center at **www.mhhe.com/hybels8** to test your knowledge of the chapter concepts.

Self, Perception, and Communication

After reading this chapter, you should be able to:

- Explain the role of self and perception in communication.
- Describe self-concept and how it is formed.
- Describe the ways you have to improve a weak or poor self-concept.
- Point out the understandings that Alford Korzybski's theory ("The map is not the territory") clarifies.
- Explain how the Internet relates to the self and communication.
- Explain each of the perceptual steps of selecting, organizing, and interpreting.
- Explain perceptual filters and the ways that they may influence your perceptions.
- Explain the difference between objective reality and a subjective point of view.
- Describe the different ways you have of adjusting to perceptual influences.

R AANI BENAZIR WAS A SHY 17-YEAR-OLD LIVING IN BANGLADESH (FORMERLY known as East Pakistan). Raani lived in a large house with her parents and one younger sister and brother. Although Raani attended private school because her father worked for the government, she knew her chances of attending an American university were slim because very few from her country ever did so and because she was not number one in her graduating class. Having heard of Raani's desire, a friend of her father's gave him a scholarship form for Raani to complete. Raani's computer skills and English fluency came to her aid, and she was accepted. In her first-year student orientation class, she met Cheryl Davis, another new student, who helped her understand U.S. customs, interpret others' behaviors, and clarify perceptions and observations.

Raani, experiencing her first time in the United States, was overwhelmed. Her shyness, being a female from a country where women generally occupy a secondary position (to males), and her newness to the university and to this country all created an environment that, in most cases, would produce a weakened self-concept, distorted perceptions, and hesitating (or ineffectual) communication. For Raani, however, it both challenged and motivated her. It was, after all, her dream, and she was determined to be the best she could be—to fulfill her dream and then some.

THE ROLE OF SELF AND PERCEPTION IN COMMUNICATING EFFECTIVELY AND STRATEGIC FLEXIBILITY

An obvious question when beginning a chapter titled "Self, Perception, and Communication" is "What does this have to do with communication?" Or, perhaps, "Why do I need to know this?" Both self and perception are foundations for effective communication. Your **self-concept** is how you think and feel about yourself. Self-concept and perception are so closely related that they are often difficult to separate. **Perception** is how you look at others and the world around you. Now, here's the connection: How you look at the world depends on what you think of yourself, and what you think of yourself will influence how you look at the world. Thus, your communication—the words and nonverbal cues you use when you talk with others—will be a direct and obvious result of both your self-concept and perceptions. As noted in Chapter 1, your communication is always changing because, in part, your self-concept and perceptions are always changing.

Realize that your self-concept can set limits on your behavioral possibilities. Because of your self-concept, you may consider yourself unlovable, irrational, inadequate, incompetent, worthless, or inferior. If you think of yourself as unlovable, this may cause you to believe you are ineligible for the love of another person. If you think of yourself as irrational, this may cause you to believe that you are ineligible to render logical, well-grounded judgments and decisions.

Another limitation imposed by your self-concept has to do with risk taking. Being who you take yourself to be, some action or experience becomes unthinkable. To take *that* action or have *that* experience would so violate who you are that, should you do it, you could no longer take yourself to be the same person. You would be forced to see yourself as someone different. Think of what it might take, for example, to leave a destructive relationship, defend your rights in an assertive and forceful manner, or take the initiative to lead a group in a dramatic new direction.

A third limitation imposed by your self-concept relates directly to perception, but because of its importance, needs to be restated. You will perceive the world in ways that are in keeping with your self-concept. For you, that will be "just the way the world is." If you, for example, think of yourself as "world's greatest failure," then you might read anyone else's positive comments about you as cases of misunderstanding or praise as ill-motivated, deceitful flattery. To have a self-concept, then, is not just to have a certain appraisal of yourself, it is to live in a certain world.

Imagine, for a moment, Raani's situation. Undoubtedly, how she thinks and feels about herself is determined in part by the role and perception of women in Bangladesh, by the way she was raised by her parents, and by the perceptions and reactions of her friends and teachers. It will take her a while to understand the place that women hold in the United States and how she fits into those roles, the function of students at a university and how active they must be to impact their own education, and the perceptions and reactions of her new friends and instructors.

Because Raani has defined the differences as challenges, and has used her situation to motivate personal growth, development, and change, you can see how readily both her self-concept and perceptions will change and how her communication will change as well. Improvements are likely to be observed in her readiness to ask and answer questions, speak out on her observations and perceptions, and take a more active, assertive role in her relationships with others. If you could stand back and observe Raani's changes, you would likely see a much stronger, more certain, and—definitely—more effective communicator emerge.

How do self-concept and perception fit into the six steps of strategic flexibility? First, with stronger self-confidence, you will have a sturdy base of operations—more strength and confidence in your ability to anticipate, assess, and evaluate communication situations. Second, with more accurate perceptions you will increase your repertoire of available skills and behaviors, thus you will have more from which to select and, likely, more accuracy and precision in their application. Reassessment and reevaluation become more effective as well because the context for all your actions will be broader, more immediate, and relevant.

What is important to know is that it doesn't take much change in your self-concept or in your perceptions to influence your communication. The starting point can be just as soon as you want it to be. Nothing is likely to change if you are closed-minded, reluctant, and hesitant or full of fear, doubt, and concern. Nothing is likely to change either if you think you know everything you need to know, or if you think there is no need or room for improvement. You must be open to change, since change is going to happen. You must be open to new findings and understandings. And you must be open to options, alternatives, and possible new choices. It can be a great journey, but without a commitment from you, there's likely to be no journey at all—just words on a page or ideas that travel in one ear and out the other—if, indeed, they get that far.

SELF-CONCEPT

The case of Raani Benazir reveals that the self is mobile, personal, self-reflexive (causing one to think and reflect), and subject to change. Although she was born into a rigid social structure in her native country of Bangladesh, in the United States she became freer to create her own identity. (The words *self* and *identity* are being used synonymously.) How she thinks and feels about herself is socially constructed as she assumes different roles throughout her lifetime. Her identity is established as a result of mutual recognition from others combined with self-validation. For example, those who had contact with Raani discovered a soft-spoken, intelligent, witty, and incredibly perceptive individual who was more than willing to share her background, history, and insights—mutual recognition. Because of what they discovered and the respect and admiration they revealed, Raani became more outspoken, charming, and humorous—self-validation. Her thoughts of being a second-class citizen (how many women are often viewed in Bangladesh) changed, and she emerged from a self- and culture-imposed shell to become more self-confident, self-assured, and self-reliant.

Just as in Raani's case, your self-concept is based on the values of the culture and the community you come from. Your culture tells you what is competent and moral by defining attitudes and beliefs; the community you belong to tells you what is expected of you. The extent to which you reflect the attitudes and beliefs of your culture and live up to the expectations of your community will determine how you see yourself. If Raani were to spend her life in the town where she grew up, her self-concept would be formed by a very limited group of people. When she moved from Bangladesh to the United States, there were many more influences. If she moved between two or more cultures—which she might do because of her interest in international relations—the influences would be even greater.

Self-concept is made up of three distinct elements: reflected appraisals, social comparisons, and self-perception. Let's look at each of them.

Reflected Appraisals

Remember the story of Tarzan? Although Tarzan was a human, he believed he was an ape because he was brought up by apes and had no human experience. Tarzan's story reminds you that you are not born with an identity—others give it to you. Your parents, your friends, and your teachers all tell you who you are through **reflected appraisals:** messages you get about yourself from others. Most reflected appraisals come from things people say about you. Your college speech communication instructor may say you are a good speaker, your peers may say you are a good friend, and your coach may tell you that you must work harder. All such messages from others help create your self-concept.

Besides being given messages about yourself, you are also given lines to speak.[1] These lines are often so specific that some people refer to them as **scripts.** Some scripts are given to you by your parents, and they contain directions that are just as explicit as any script intended for the stage. You are given your lines ("Say thank you to the nice woman"), your gestures ("Point to the horsie"), and your characterizations ("You're a good girl/boy"). The scripts tell you how to play future scenes ("Everyone in your family has gone to college") and what is expected of you ("I will be so happy when you make us grandparents"). People outside your family also contribute to your scripts. Teachers, coaches, religious leaders, friends, the media, and the Internet all tell you what they expect from you, how you should look, how you should behave, and how you should say your lines. Sometimes you receive the messages directly, and sometimes you get them by observing and then imitating others' behavior.

Writer and radio personality Garrison Keillor gives a list of scripts we get as we are growing up. Have you heard any of them or used them on your own children?

I. I don't know what's wrong with you.
  A. I never saw a person like you.
    1. I wasn't like that.
    2. Your cousins don't pull stuff like that.

B. *It doesn't make sense.*
   1. *You have no sense of responsibility at all.*
   2. *We've given you everything we possibly could.*
     a. Food on the table and a roof over your head.
     b. Things we never had when we were your age.
   3. *And you treat us like dirt under your feet.*
C. *You act as if*
   1. *The world owes you a living.*
   2. *You've got a chip on your shoulder.*
   3. *The rules don't apply to you.*

II. *Something has got to change and change fast.*
   A. *You're driving your mother to a nervous breakdown.*
   B. *I'm not going to put up with this for another minute.*
     1. *You're crazy if you think I am.*
     2. *If you think I am, just try me.*
   C. *You're setting a terrible example for your younger brothers and sisters.*

III. *I'm your father and as long as you live in this house, you'll—*
   A. *Do as you're told, and when I say "now" I mean "now."*
   B. *Pull your own weight.*
     1. *Don't expect other people to pick up after you.*
     2. *Don't expect breakfast when you get up at noon.*
     3. *Don't come around asking your mother for spending money.*
   C. *Do something about your disposition.*

IV. *If you don't change your tune pretty quick, then you're out of here.*
   A. *I mean it.*
   B. *Is that understood?*
     1. *I can't hear you. Don't mumble.*
     2. *Look at me.*
   C. *I'm not going to tell you this again.*[2]

If you were given positive reflected appraisals when you were young, you probably have a good self-concept; if the appraisals were largely negative, your self-concept may suffer. The messages you receive about yourself can become **self-fulfilling prophecies**—events or actions that occur because you (and other people) have expected them. For example, at the beginning of the semester Professor Farley said to Kevin, "You're going to be a very good student." Because of this expectation, Kevin wanted to be a good student and worked hard to live up to Professor Farley's prophecy. Similarly, negative prophecies can have a negative impact. If someone tells a child that he or she will "never amount to much," there is a good chance the child will not.

Social Comparisons

When you compare yourself with others to see how you measure up, you are making a **social comparison.** Social comparisons are not just important, they are necessary in helping develop an accurate self-perception. An accurate self-perception is crucial for navigating and responding to the social world through effective communication.

If you think about it, you can't evaluate yourself without some form of comparison. You may, for example, compare yourself with your peers. You might ask, "Do I look as good as she does?" or "What grade did you get on your midterm?" or "What kind of car do you drive?" If you are a parent, you might compare your child to your friend's child. "Can he talk yet?" "Did she get a position on the softball team?" In your job, you are likely to ask yourself if you are doing as well as your co-workers. Did you get as big a raise as your colleague got? Does the boss ever notice you and praise your work? The answers to these social comparison questions all contribute to your self-concept.

Social comparisons are pivotal to self-evaluations. They depend less on objective circumstances than on how you judge yourself in relation to others on particular attributes. You prefer to compare yourself to others who are similar for the attribute of concern. For example, the first question in the paragraph above, "Do I look as good as she does?" may refer to body image. Social comparisons also can be employed to gather information about highly valued attributes (personality, money, or success), social expectations (appropriate attire and expected behavior), and norms (rules, laws, and acceptable practices). That is why comparisons are likely to be made to a variety of targets—there is such a broad range of information needed.

Let's focus on a single attribute of concern: body image evaluation. The repeated media images of thin females and muscular males make these forms seemingly the standard of attractiveness. The gender differences in the attributes associated with body image are those that would be expected. Weight is the primary feature predicting body dissatisfaction among women. Height and shoulders—or muscular shape—is the attractiveness concern of males. From where do the standards come? Pressures for the proper body image come from parents, peers, dating partners, as well as the media. They can be direct, such as a parent encouraging a daughter to diet or a son to lift weights, or indirect, such as a peer voicing admiration of a particular model who reveals the attributes. Constant exposure is likely to make both men and women self-conscious about their bodies and make them obsess over and consider their physical appearance a measure of their worth. Of course, this is both a narrow and limited measure.

In a single day, you see many images of how people should look and behave. In a lifetime, you may receive 40 to 50 million commercial messages. Magazines, movies, and videos all contribute to what the "ideal you" should be. Even if you can discount

The way we see ourselves is often a reflection of how we compare ourselves with others.

As a group, work together to list as many items as you can think of over which you have direct control. Each should be an item that will help people like those in your group to *appreciate themselves more*. After listing items, arrange them in hierarchical order with the most important items listed first. With the list complete, answer the questions that follow.

In her book *In the Dressing Room with Brenda*, Brenda Kinsel suggests some of the following items:

- the color or curl of your hair
- the shape or form of your body
- how your eyes open every morning and allow you to see life
- how your legs take you to your car or to your classes every day
- how your fingers can soothe a sore muscle

Which of the following plays the most important role in determining which items get listed and why: reflected appraisals, social comparisons, or self-perception? Which of these three is likely to have the most impact on each of the members of your group?

What is the point of this group exercise? Kinsel suggests two points:

1. When you begin practicing appreciation, it gets easier.

2. Self-appreciation has its most direct effect on your self-concept.

Source: *In the Dressing Room with Brenda: A Fun and Practical Guide to Buying Smart and Looking Great*, by Brenda Kinsel, 2001, Berkeley, CA: Wildcat Canyon Press (a division of Circulus Publishing Group, Inc.).

these images as being unrealistic, many of the people around you believe them and judge you and others by what they see and hear.

Self-Perception

You think, feel, speak, and act in accordance with your self-image. The way you see yourself is called **self-perception.** The process of accumulating views of your self is both complex and ongoing. Consciously and subconsciously you weigh whether others' thoughts, attitudes, actions, and reactions will work for you. It is a little like putting pieces of a puzzle together; however, not only does the puzzle picture constantly change, but seldom does anyone have all the pieces that make up the picture. Even when you may have a puzzle piece in your hand, the piece may not fit where you think it goes, or it may not fit the picture you thought it would. Why is this process so confusing?

First, self-perception is made up of so many variables. They include physical, social, intellectual, and spiritual elements such as convictions about principles; basic personal wants and desires; moral, religious, and political feelings; as well as responses to personal freedom, social controls, and oppression of one kind or another. They include, too, how you respond to failings and difficulties (or achievements and successes) as well as mental stress and self-deception.

Second, self-perception depends on the phase of your development, which is constantly changing as well. Often, as one ages, one becomes more open to the ideas of others, okay with being wrong, less attached to particular outcomes, and better listeners.[3] When all is said and done, self-perception is a little like what a state trooper told a woman when he stopped her for speeding: "My measure of your speed is but a momentary picture of what occurs in a fraction of a second. That's all it can be."

Numbers of variables and constant change, however, don't deny the importance or application of self-perception. Accept your self-perception as a momentary picture. What can you do to make it positive? First, make certain you have a positive attitude,

In his article "Lacking in Self-Esteem? Good for You!," Andrew Sullivan writes that self-esteem isn't all that it's cracked up to be. Drawing on the research performed by Brad Bushman of Iowa State University and Roy Baumeister of Case Western Reserve University, Sullivan writes:

Self-esteem can also be an educational boomerang. Friends of mine who teach today's college students are constantly complaining about the high self-esteem of their students. When the kids have been told from Day One that they can do no wrong, when every grade in high school is assessed so as to make the kid feel good rather than to give an accurate measure of his work, the student can develop self-worth dangerously unrelated to the objective truth. He can then get deeply offended when he's told he is getting a C grade in college and become demoralized or extremely angry. Weak professors give in to the pressure—hence, grade inflation. Tough professors merely get exhausted trying to bring their students into vague touch with reality.

Questions

1. Have you experienced people who think they are God's gift and who are offended if other people don't treat them that way?
2. Can you see how inflated egos can be substituted for a proper sense of self— that is, how distortion can become reality?
3. What are some ways to enhance the realistic and natural development of self-esteem?

Source: "Lacking in Self-Esteem? Good for You!", by A. Sullivan, *Time*, October 14, 2002, p. 102. © 2002 TIME Inc. Reprinted by permission.

because how you think about what you do will affect your persistence, attitudes, and achievements. Second, keep your focus objective. For example, look specifically at what is required to achieve success—the steps, resources, or abilities—and not at subjective elements such as your feelings, reactions, and interpretations of the events, people, or situations. Third, try to focus on small achievements because your ability to perform successfully will have a direct effect on your actual performance. Your state of mind clearly impacts your ultimate performance.[4]

Gender, Sex, and Self-Concept

Several research studies show that men and women gain their self-concept in different ways.[5] Two researchers found that when forming self-concept, men give the most importance to social comparisons, whereas women attach more importance to reflected appraisals. Men put more value on reflected appraisals from their parents, while women give more importance to reflected appraisals from their friends.

Other studies have shown that female self-confidence comes primarily from connections and attachments, while male self-confidence comes primarily from achievement.[6] This relates to research findings about gender and language. (In Chapter 5 we discuss how women's language is tied to social networks, while men's language is tied to competition and achievement.)

Although your family and peers may influence how you act as a male or female, there is some evidence that your sexual identity is established when you are born. Researchers know this because of a terrible accident that occurred to an infant boy when he was eight months old. A surgeon was trying to repair a fused foreskin and accidentally cut off the boy's penis. Because the doctor thought he could never live as a boy, he recommended to the parents that they rear him as a girl. When the parents agreed, his testicles were removed and a vagina was constructed.

From this point on, the parents treated the child as a girl. They got her feminine clothes, gave her toys that girls liked, and even put her in the care of a female psychiatrist to help her adjust.

The child, however, never accepted her female identity. She tore off the dresses, refused the dolls, and looked for male friends. Instead of using makeup like her mother, she imitated her father by shaving and urinating standing up.

When she was 12, the doctors began estrogen treatments that enabled her to grow breasts. She did not like the feminizing effects of the drug and refused to take it. When she was 14, she refused any more treatment to feminize her. By this time she was so unhappy that her father told her what had happened to her, and her first feeling was that of relief.

At this point she went back to being a man. The youth took male hormone shots and had a mastectomy (an operation to remove breasts), and a surgeon began to reconstruct male genitals. Although the surgery was only partially successful, he married and he and his wife adopted children.

From this and other cases involving ambiguous genitals in newborns, many scientists have concluded that an infant with a Y chromosome will be a boy, regardless of his genitalia, and that nothing will ever change this.

Psychological Safety and Risk

Ask some second-semester seniors what they are afraid of. Chances are they will reply that they are very apprehensive about going out into the world. Will they find jobs? Can they survive outside the structure of university life? What is the world like? What is their place in it?

For most of us, **psychological safety**—the approval and support that we get from familiar people, ideas, and situations—is important. However, as the late psychologist Abraham Maslow, who worked in the area of self-fulfillment, pointed out, the needs for safety and growth pull us in opposite directions. Maslow believed that in order to grow, people have to abandon some of the safe areas of their lives and take some psychological risks.[7]

A **psychological risk** involves taking a chance on something new. It could be getting to know someone different from us, trying to understand a different point of view, or even moving to a new place. Taking a psychological risk helps improve one's self-concept. For example, when students go away to college, they must leave the safety of home, friends, and family. This is such a great risk that some first-year students spend a week or two away from home, decide they can't stand it, and drop out of school. The majority who remain, however, discover that they can cope on their own. This new knowledge helps improve their self-concept.

Going away to school involves psychological risks—taking a chance on something new.

New college students take risks not only in leaving home but also in being exposed to new ideas. For example, a student who has heard pro-choice ideas at home or in church will take a big risk if he or she tries to really understand a person who is pro-life, and vice versa. Similarly, it's risky for an athlete or a sports fan to try to understand the point of view that high schools might improve if they dropped competitive sports. The problem with taking the risk of really understanding a different point of view is that you might be changed. If you do change, you face the possibility that your family and friends probably will not change and you won't completely fit in anymore. Inevitably, whenever you take a risk, your circle of safety grows smaller.

Often, your first response to ideas that conflict with your own is to refuse to even listen to them. If you take this course, you choose psychological safety. When you take a psychological risk, you are ready to test your self-concept by considering ideas from another person's vantage point. For example, when you are in college, your religious beliefs might be threatened by a philosophy course or by late-night talks in the dorm with other students. If your beliefs are challenged, you might respond by no longer going to church or, in the extreme, by no longer believing in your church or even in religion. When this happens, you have taken a risk. When you go home, if you tell your parents what has happened, they probably are going to be upset; if you don't tell them, a gulf will grow between you and them as a consequence of your doing something so risky.

CAN YOU IMPROVE YOUR SELF-CONCEPT?

If you have any doubt that we, as a society, are obsessed with self-concept or self-esteem, look in the self-improvement section of any bookstore or library. You will find literally hundreds of books—each guaranteeing that if you read it, you will feel better about yourself and will change your self-esteem from negative to positive. One thing that many self-help books say is that the use of self-affirmations will assist you in raising your self-esteem. William Swann, PhD, of the University of Texas–Austin, suggests that self-affirmations, even when endlessly repeated, don't work and may even leave you more demoralized than before using them.[8]

According to Annie Paul, in her review article on "Self-Help," "The only way to change the final product—your self-esteem—is to change what goes into making it—feedback from other people." Then, she quotes Swann, who says "If you find yourself in bad relationships where your negative self-view is getting reinforced, then either change the way those people treat you by being more assertive, or change who you interact with."[9] In one of the most succinct, profound, and instructive summaries, she writes, "Stand up for yourself. Surround yourself with people who think you're great, and tell you so. Do your best to live up to their high opinions. And be patient. Self-esteem is the sum of your interactions with others over a lifetime, and it's not going to change overnight."[10]

You should know that a positive self-concept may have nothing to do with success. Researchers have found that criminals and juvenile delinquents often have high self-esteem.[11] Even though self-esteem may not be connected to success, a positive sense of who you are is good because it will make you feel happier.

Where Should Change Begin?

What is important to understand as you begin any kind of improvement program is that a poor self-concept is part of many human problems. For example, it could be part of a lack of purpose, inadequate motivation, lack of confidence, sadness and pessimism, lack of assertiveness, self-put-down games, and even the lack of wisdom and equality in selecting a mate. When it is related to sadness, just one of these human problems, it could relate to self-criticism, anger turned inward, guilt, shame, feeling inferior, low self-concept, and pessimism. That is why a poor self-concept isn't an easy problem to overcome. Wouldn't it be great if you could just erect a mental wall that would block out all your previous problems, and begin anew, with a blank slate—much as Raani Benazir did in our opening example?

Where would you start if you could erect a solid barrier between where you are today and where you were yesterday (see Figure 2-1)? First, silence your internal critic, nip negative thoughts in the bud, and stop bullying yourself. Replace criticism with encouragement and treat yourself kindly. Second, stop depending on others for your self-esteem; do your own self-evaluation. Stop letting others dominate your life. Take responsibility for your feelings. Just as you can't make others feel happy, don't expect others to make you feel happy or good about yourself. Third, accentuate your strengths and assets. Fourth, accept yourself—warts and all. Give yourself permission to decide that you're doing the best you can. Fifth, avoid your perfectionistic tendencies—the tyranny of all the "shoulds" in your life. Accept flaws, mistakes, and imperfections as part of being human. Sixth, avoid your overreactions to criticism. You needn't feel guilty about things beyond your control.

There are other areas, too, where you can begin to change. A seventh way to get to where you want to be is to modify your negative traits. Focus on what you *can* do, not

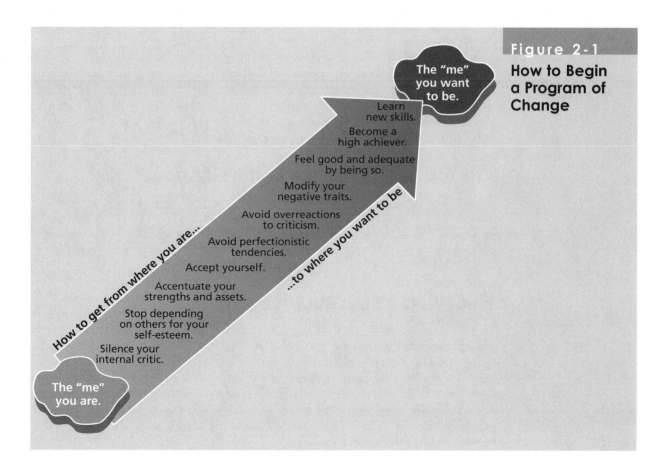

Figure 2-1

How to Begin a Program of Change

on what you can't. Eighth, feel good and adequate by being good and adequate—behave morally. Ninth, become a high achiever. It is more about doing what is expected of you, and then some, than it is about high intelligence or excessive brilliance. Tenth, learn new skills. Open yourself to new possibilities, areas for potential growth, and new ways to develop positive attributes. Eleventh, don't feel responsible for everything. Don't try to be all things (and do all things) for people. Twelfth, forgive and forget. Avoid hanging on to painful memories and bad feelings. Your past can control you if you don't control it. Finally, begin a program of personal change in specific desired areas by working through the following steps.

What Do You Want to Change about Yourself?

Pick one area in which you would like to improve yourself. See if you can figure out why you have had problems in this area. Were you given a script saying you were inadequate in this area? Are you living out a self-fulfilling prophecy?

Are Your Circumstances Keeping You from Changing?

Are you living in circumstances that are holding you back? Do the people around you support you if you want to do something differently, especially if it involves taking a risk? Sometimes the people you live with try to hold you back—even though they might not be conscious of doing so. For example, one spouse says to the other, "Why do you want to go to Europe? We haven't seen all of the United States yet."

Sometimes you are locked into roles that are uncomfortable for you. Many women feel trapped when their children are small; some people hate their jobs; some students hate school. Are you in a role that you have chosen for yourself, or has someone else chosen it for you? Has someone else defined how you should play this role? Can you play this role in a way that will make it more comfortable for you? Can you change the role so that you can be more like the person you want to be?

Are You Willing to Take Some Chances?

Colleges and universities offer great chances to take some risks. Take a course from a professor who is rumored to be hard but fair. Study a subject you know nothing about. Join a club that sounds interesting—even if you don't know any of its members. Many colleges and universities also offer opportunities to study abroad or to take an internship. Going abroad is especially helpful in building self-confidence.

What Would Be a Realistic Goal?

Too often, people decide they are going to change their behavior overnight. Students who habitually get poor grades will often announce that this semester they are going to get all A's. This is an unrealistic goal. If you are going to try to change your behavior, see if you can break down the problem into steps you can handle. Let's say that you are shy but would like to speak up more in class because you often know the answers. Why not set a goal to speak up once a week in one class? That is probably a goal you can manage. Once you feel comfortable with that, you might increase your goal to speaking up two or even three times a week.

Can You Discipline Yourself?

The old saying "Nothing succeeds like success" applies to a positive self-concept: As soon as you experience success, you start feeling better about yourself. Sometimes people think they are unsuccessful because they are not motivated enough. Typical thinking might be, "If only I could motivate myself, I would get better grades." People who think this way confuse motivation with discipline. There's no way to motivate yourself to take out the garbage, do the dishes, or study your class notes. These jobs can be done only through discipline: You say, "I am going to do this job for one hour—whether or not I want to do it is irrelevant." This sort of discipline is what leads to success, which, in turn, helps you feel better about yourself.

Are There People Who Will Support You?

Whenever we try to bring about a change in ourselves, we need to surround ourselves with people who will support us. These are people who understand how difficult it is to change and who understand our desire to do so. Take the example of speaking up in class. If you are very apprehensive about doing this, you might consider discussing the problem with an instructor you like and trust. Tell him or her that you are occasionally going to try to say something, and ask for his or her support. Also tell a couple of friends in your class what you plan to do. Just having other people know what you are trying to accomplish often provides good moral support. Not all people will support you, and some may even consciously try to defeat you. For them, the possibility that you might change is too threatening.

When you have found some people to support you, it's important that you tell them what you want to do and give them some direction as to how they can help you.

Can You Be More You-Centered?

People who lack self-esteem often spend a lot of time looking inward at their miseries, while people who seem happy and content with themselves seem to spend their time interacting with others. If you look inward all the time, you are probably making yourself more miserable. For a few days, experiment with relating more to the people around you. Just asking someone "How was your day?" or "How is your semester (or quarter) going?" shows that you are interested.

If you have an opportunity to bestow some praise, do it. Look for situations around you in which you can praise people, and express your praise with genuine feeling. Tell your mother that her meatloaf tastes great, tell a professor that her class was really helpful on an internship, tell a friend that she looks wonderful in green. When you act positively toward others, they will act positively toward you, and this, in turn, will make you feel better about yourself.

THE MAP IS NOT THE TERRITORY

It was the father of general semantics, Alford Korzybski, who stated, "A map is not the territory it represents, but if correct, it has a similar structure to the territory, which accounts for its usefulness." You have maps inside your head that describe the things outside your head. The maps inside your head represent the territory outside your head.

Figure 2-2

The Map Is Not the Territory

The more accurate your maps are, the better equipped you are to function within society. The accuracy of your maps is a measure of your sanity. But, remember that nobody has completely accurate maps.

What this means for you is simply that your perception of reality is not reality itself, but it is your own version of it—your "maps." In Figure 2-2, the person is bewildered because from the map being held there was no way to know that the mountains on the horizon even existed. Even a road map doesn't accurately depict the territory it is supposed to represent. Your maps, likewise, are distorted because you jump to conclusions with little or no evidence, ignore parts of the territory, see only what you want to see, see things as black and white rather than in shades of gray, and apply labels to people and situations and then refuse to see beyond the labels.

There are some important understandings that Korzybski's theory clarifies for both self-concept and perception. The first has to do with how your maps are created. There is so much information in the world that you can't take it all in, let alone make sense of it all. So what you do is create internal maps of reality that you can refer to as you navigate through life. Your maps contain countless beliefs, values, generalizations, decisions, and numerous other mental aspects about how you see yourself and your relationship to the world around you. Just as a road map, it is a scaled-down version of reality. And just as a road map, maps don't show everything. As you get more information, your maps change.

Now, imagine what people's maps might look like if they grew up with trauma or abuse? Their maps might be useful for navigation within their family unit, but they wouldn't be accurate when they got out into the world on their own. For example, their maps might tell them that other people will hurt them (not realizing that some will and others may not), and their maps may cause them to miss out on many beautiful parts of life. What happens in your life occurs because of your maps of reality—your mind creating experiences based on your maps.

The second understanding is that you react to the maps inside your head, not the territory outside your head. You react to the maps and not to what the maps represent. For example, if your maps tell you that a certain piece of music is pleasant, you will listen to it. If your maps tell you that the same piece of music is unpleasant, you will not listen to it. It is not the music that you are drawn to, it is your maps of the music. The same occurs in elections. You look not to the candidates when you choose how to vote, you look instead to your maps of the candidates.

The third understanding is that no two people can have exactly the same maps. Problems in communication occur when you try to impose your maps upon another person—or other people. Empathizing with others requires learning to recognize the structure of others' maps—seeing the world through their eyes—thus being able to understand and relate to them respectfully and accurately. It helps to know that their maps are likely to be just as jaundiced by their own interpretations as yours are.

No two people have exactly the same maps because people's upbringing, genes, and values differ. But even more, just because two or more things have the same label, they are unlikely to be identical. One American, for example, is not the same as another American, just because they are both Americans. Also, nothing exists in isolation; everything is affected by surrounding conditions. You might appear ignorant when discussing economics with a professor of that subject, but seem like a genius when discussing it with your friends who know little about economics.

The fourth understanding is that to create personal change requires changing maps. There is a natural and understandable desire to protect old maps. That is because they become comfortable. You know how to navigate with these maps, and replacing them with new ones is a little like trying to find your way around a new supermarket. Not only are maps comfortable, they are habit forming. Even when they may not be as useful as they could be, you depend on them because they are what you have. You know where the bread, milk, and cereal are supposed to be in the supermarket. Letting maps go causes temporary chaos, but reconfiguring, reconstituting, or reorganizing maps at a higher level can result in relief from the problems and limitations of the old maps—new abilities to deal with what was previously stressful, perplexing, or overwhelming. You learn where things are located in the new supermarket, and your trips there become efficient, effective, and satisfying.

STRATEGIC FLEXIBILITY
When you permit changes in your maps of reality, you increase your strategic flexibility because new maps are likely to work better than old maps.

The fifth understanding is that your maps of reality are *not* who you are— the map is *not* the territory. Rather, your maps are simply a convenient tool you use to navigate through life. To understand that your maps are not who you are but simply a navigation tool will help you understand that maps need to go through the chaos and reorganization process for personal growth to occur. It will help you understand that map "changes" do not represent you in the process of falling apart. The **map is not the territory.** Trying to hold old maps together creates dysfunctional feelings and behaviors such as fear, depression, anger, anxiety, substance abuse, many physical diseases, and numerous other more serious mental problems.

Knowing that the map is not the territory will help you look forward to map changes. Why? Because new maps are likely to work better. New maps will allow you to be a happier, more peaceful person. New maps are likely to produce positive change. And because of the relationship between self-concept and perception, new maps will allow you to come at the world more accurately, see things with greater clarity, and understand events, others, and ideas with increased precision..

THE INTERNET, SELF, AND COMMUNICATION

The Internet presents an opportunity seldom, if ever, offered to the adventurous. When engaged in conversations in chat rooms, posting messages on bulletin boards, or even in the construction of blogs or Web pages, Internet users have the option of presenting their real and authentic self to their Internet audience, or creating their own identity. It is impossible to determine how many Internet users choose one course over the other; however, in chat rooms, most participants—for the sake of anonymity (and often, safety)—select to use a pseudonym or clever descriptor to identify themselves.

Technology allows users to become invisible—at least, their perception of invisibility. Actually, Internet users leave cyberfootprints wherever they go, but despite this reality, the perception of invisibility persists. The fact that many people may be engaged in similar activities leads to this perception of invisibility because, the rationale is, any single person's actions are a mere "drop in the pond" and, thus, are unlikely to be detected.

How does this bear on the self-concept? When people are in the process of developing their self-concept and, at the same time, are active users of the Internet, they are obviously influenced by the lack of tangible feedback and perceptions of invisibility, and it isn't clear how this will affect their development and internalization processes.

What is interesting about the social identities created on the Internet is that, according to some research, it depends on perceptions we have of the Internet. Because it is through our relationships with others that we discover ourselves, it may be that Internet communication, which enables a higher level of self-disclosure because of its relatively anonymous nature, promotes self-discovery for some, better than communication in real life.[12] Some computer-mediated communication (CMC) partners engage in more intimate questions and deeper disclosures than those in ongoing face-to-face relationships.[13]

When the Internet is perceived as a sociable medium, the disclosures on ICQ (instant messaging) tend to be open, personal, intimate, honest, and in great extent about negative feelings and opinions. When people perceive the Internet as a personalized medium, disclosures will be more about themselves. And when the Internet is perceived as sensitive, warm, and active, the disclosures appear more private and intimate but the contents are more negative and undesirable.[14]

There are two important conclusions regarding the Internet, self, and communication. First, people who have more positive self-evaluations have more positive self-disclosures in both the offline world and the cyberworld. To be more specific, the Internet simply provides another channel for the same kind of communication that occurs in the real world. People who gain satisfaction in communication have a more positive self-image and are more eager to disclose themselves on the Internet or in instant messaging.

Second, how people perceive the Internet determines how they use it. Those who perceive it as a warm medium are more likely to disclose private and intimate information including negative or undesirable things about themselves. Just as when trust is developed in a relationship, a warm and safe environment develops at the same time. Perceived as a sociable medium, disclosures are open, personal, intimate, and honest. Perceived as a personalized medium, disclosures are about themselves.

The point is simply that for those who find effectiveness and success in real-life communication, they are likely to find success and effectiveness in Internet communication in the same way—whether it be self-perception, self-development, or self-expression. Much depends on their perception of the Internet; however, those with a positive self-concept are more likely to perceive it as just another channel of communication—an additional way to share knowledge, ideas, and information.

PERCEPTION

Perception, you will recall, is how you look at others and the world around you. Acts of perception are more than simply capturing incoming stimuli. These acts require a form of expectation, of knowing what is about to confront you and preparing for it. These expectations or predispositions to respond are a type of perceptual filter called **psychological sets,** and they have a profound effect on your perceptions. "Without expectations, or constructs through which you perceive your world," writes John Ratey, associate clinical professor of psychiatry at Harvard Medical School, "your surroundings would be what William James called a 'booming, buzzing confusion,' and each experience truly would be a new one, rapidly overwhelming you. You automatically and unconsciously fit your sensations into categories that you have learned, often distorting them in the process."[15]

For example, how you view a new instructor depends on your views of all the instructors you have had in the past. How you think about forming a new romantic relationship depends on the romantic relationships you have had in the past. Your knowledge, background, and experiences form the psychological sets and, thus, provide the matrix—that which gives shape or form to anything—into which any new idea or event is placed

The Perceptual Process

Your perceptions affect more than your direct interactions with people. They also influence your response to all the information around you. Whenever you encounter new information, whether it's from a television program, a newspaper, the Internet, or another person, you go through a three-step perceptual process: You select the information, you organize it, and you interpret it.

We do not all perceive information in the same way. Even when several people have access to the same information, they are likely to select, organize, and interpret it in different ways. Let's say, for example, that three different people read the same newspaper: Omar is a Syrian who is studying in the United States; Caroline is an American who has been an exchange student in Syria; and Jim is an American who has never traveled.

When Omar reads the paper, he looks for (selects) news about Syria. In his mind he organizes the information on the basis of what he already knows. He may

Whenever you encounter new information you go through a three-step perceptual process: You select the information, you organize it, and you interpret it.

interpret it by asking the meaning of certain government actions or by thinking that the reporter has the wrong slant on the story. Caroline goes through a similar process. She has a high interest in stories about Syria because she has been there. She, too, organizes what she reads according to what she knows about the country. However, she may interpret the news stories differently because she doesn't have as much information as Omar. Also, her interpretation will probably be from an American point of view. When Jim reads the newspaper, he skips all the stories about Omar's country. He has never been there and has no immediate plans to go there. In fact, he skips all the news about the world and goes directly to the sports section. These three people are all exposed to the same information, but they all perceive it differently.

Deletions, Distortions, and Generalizations

Any perceptions you have are less than perfect because of deletions, distortions, and generalizations.[16] **Deletions**—blotting out, erasing, or canceling information—must occur first because your physical senses are limited. Your sight, hearing, touch, taste, and smell are the means you use to get information, but those senses focus only on those aspects of the environment that are most important for your survival. Your senses are not capable of perceiving everything in your external environment. Deletions occur, too, because of your beliefs. If you believe something to be true, you have an almost infinite capacity to delete information that contradicts that belief. In addition, if you believe something to be true, you will go through your life searching for information that supports that belief and ignore information that does not.

In addition to deleting information, you also distort much of the information from your environment. **Distortions** involve twisting or bending information out of shape. You distort information, first because you observe only a small part of your external environment. Since what you observe is such a small part of the whole, you must fill in the blanks—specifically add information—to make your information make sense. The other reason you distort information is so that it will support your existing beliefs and values—fit into your psychological sets.

In addition to deleting and distorting information, you draw generalizations based on little substantial information. **Generalizations** involve drawing principles or conclusions from particular evidence or facts. Once you have observed something a few times, you conclude that what has proven true in the past will prove true in the future as well. Generalizations are important to your survival. Getting burned by putting a hand on a hot stove will give you a conclusion about the consequences of putting your hand on a hot stove in the future. If you had several bad experiences with members of the opposite sex, of a different race, of a different culture, or of a particular organization, you might generalize that *all* members of the opposite sex, a different race, a different culture, or a particular organization are bad. Then, all future experiences are filtered through that belief, information that contradicts the belief is deleted, and you distort other information so it will support the belief.

Keep these three activities in mind as you read the next section on perceptual filters. Realize that even before perceptual filters come into play and certainly while they are operating as well, deletion, distortion, and generalization are also influencing the information.[17]

Perceptual Filters

Deletions, distortions, and generalizations are important and affect your perceptions, but perceptual filters can be even more important. **Perceptual filters** are limitations that result from the narrowed lens through which you view the world. For example, your biologic makeup has a significant influence. If your biologic makeup differs from that of the predominant society—if you are obese, short, or unattractive, for example—you may have difficulty securing and maintaining a positive self-concept because of the distortions your senses cause. You automatically see things differently than members of the predominant society.

Other significant influences on your perceptions include your culture, values, and beliefs. You, like most people, find it easier to communicate with members of your own culture. Many of your customs (e.g., Halloween), values (e.g., everything should be clean), and beliefs (all humans are created equal)—as well as your manners, ceremonies, rituals, laws, language, religious beliefs, myths and legends, knowledge, ideals, accepted ways of behaving, and even your concept of self—are culturally determined.

There are numerous other influences, such as the ways you have for coping with and tolerance for stress as well as your conflict resolution strategies.[18] If through your upbringing you have developed inadequate coping patterns to adapt to stress or resolve conflict you narrow your lens, and your perceptions will be distorted. One major influence would be the familial patterns you observed between your parents and between your parents and you or other siblings. For example, some of the patterns you may have observed could include the excessive use of denial, projection of blame and responsibility, hypersensitivity to criticism, and rationalizing of failures. Destructive behaviors may have included overeating, excessive smoking or drinking, the overuse of over-the-counter medications, or illicit drug use. Even high rates of illness as a result of high blood pressure, ulcers, irritable bowel syndrome, frequent headaches or neck aches may also have been influential.

Other influences on your perceptions could include your previous experiences. Many failures rather than successes may create difficulty. If you attribute your successes to luck, chance, or the influence of powerful others rather than to your own personal behavior, this could be a factor. If you have suffered stressful life events such as financial difficulties, problems on a job, change or loss of a job, relationship concerns, sexuality concerns, divorce, or moving, particularly if they have been cumulative, your perceptions could be affected. Illnesses, traumas, and surgery, too, can create alterations in self-esteem, body image, and personal identity and can influence your perceptions. Even your current physiological state can influence your perceptions. Insufficient nutritional food, lack of sleep, or a serious night of drinking and the consequential hangover can be influential.

Our purpose here has not been to cast a negative light on the role of your perceptions in creating and maintaining your self-concept; rather, it is to show how many factors are likely to filter your perceptions. Any changes from the norm—the perceptions of those who make up your predominant society—will influence your perceptions in some manner. Because there are so many influences, and because these influences are likely to combine in unknown ways and even have some cumulative effect, there is no way to predict or know how much effect the influences on your perceptions have nor how your self-concept is altered. What is interesting is that even self-assessments are likely to be distorted, since the self doing the assessing is also subject to the distortions!

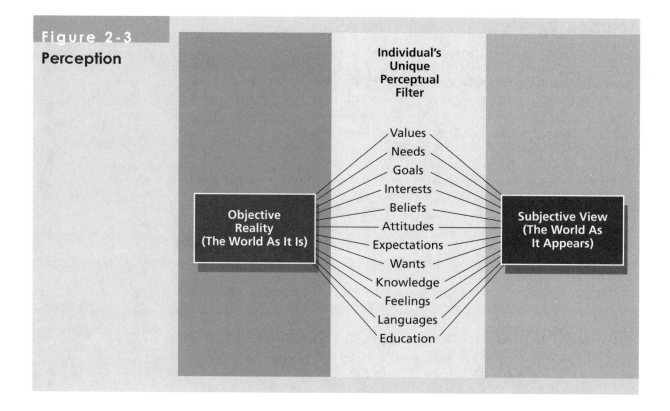

Figure 2-3
Perception

Individual's
Unique
Perceptual
Filter

Values
Needs
Goals
Interests
Beliefs
Attitudes
Expectations
Wants
Knowledge
Feelings
Languages
Education

Objective
Reality
(The World As It Is)

Subjective View
(The World As
It Appears)

Adjusting to Perceptual Influences

George A. Miller, the psychologist, said, "Most of our failures in understanding one another have less to do with what is heard than with what is intended and what is inferred." It would be great to believe that there were no such thing as perceptual filters. It would be great to believe that you come at the world straight on and that objective reality is, indeed, your reality. It would be great to believe, because of the truthfulness and honesty with which you conduct your life, that any observation you make is accurate, precise, and correct—that the conclusions you draw conform exactly to truth or to the standard set by the norm of others in your culture. Unfortunately, this is *never* the case. The fact is, your perceptions and the conclusions you draw from them represent, as noted in Figure 2-3, your reality, your subjective view, or the world as it appears to you.

The difference between **objective reality**—the actual territory or external reality everyone experiences—and a **subjective view**—your personal mental maps of the world—is easy to demonstrate. It is the difference between an examination, or the actual written document that contains the questions (objective reality), and your maps of that examination (subjective reality) which are constructed from your beliefs about the need for examinations, your attitudes toward examinations, your expectations regarding this particular examination, your knowledge about what is likely to be on the examination, and your related thoughts regarding your preparation, as well as your feelings (anxiety or apprehension).

If you think about it, if you were affected by any one of the perceptual influences listed in the section on perceptual filters—lack of sleep, for example—you would experience some distortion from the norm. Whether or not you knew the distortion was occurring might depend on the severity of the influence (three nights without sleep), the circumstances in which you found yourself (taking a final exam), or whether you had other comparisons to make; that is, you had a way to compare your sensory data (observations) with that of others. (Others thought the exam was fair; you thought it unfair.) You have drawn a conclusion that is true based on your perceptions.

Stay healthy, get rest, and exercise. Make every effort to come at the world as healthy, well rested, and sufficiently exercised as possible. Because perception depends on your senses, the better condition that your senses are in, the more likely they will respond in proper ways. It is more likely that you will be aware of and adjust to perceptual influences when you have a proper state of mind and body. For example, can you imagine getting physically and emotionally upset with an instructor because of an exam you felt was unfair after three days of no sleep, living on Mountain Dew, isolated in your room, and trying to study a semester's worth of notes in a day and a half?

Avoid hasty conclusions. If you feel it is necessary to publicly announce a conclusion, then state it tentatively rather than as a conclusion. For example, rather than stating that you know that flying saucers exist because you saw strange lights in the sky last night, why not offer your observations in a tentative way that will allow exploration and discussion: "You know, I saw strange lights in the sky last night. Did anyone else see any strange lights?"

Take more time. The third method for adjusting to perceptual influences follows from the last one. Take more time. When it is said patience is a virtue, nothing could be more succinct or accurate. Time has a number of benefits. It allows you to gather more facts. With more facts, it is likely your conclusions will change. Time also allows you to think about your observations and conclusions. For example, you might overhear another conversation about the strange lights in the sky, or read a newspaper article about a meteor shower last night, or the glow from locally launched weather balloons. How often have you discovered that your first impressions were wrong—that, for example, you could not tell what a book was about by its cover alone?

There is an important caution to be aware of as you search for information. As noted previously, when you believe something to be true, you will find information to support that belief. That statement introduces the caution. Your external environment contains ample evidence to support all beliefs about a subject.[19] If you believe that most people are bad and will lie, cheat, steal, and otherwise injure you, you can find plenty of evidence in the news and in your daily encounters with others to support that belief. If you believe that most people are good and will behave in honest, caring, and courageous ways, you can find plenty of evidence to support this belief as well. The point of gathering information is to seek evidence that might suggest your beliefs are in error or that other explanations exist for the conclusions you have reached.

Be available. A fourth method for adjusting to perceptual influences follows from the previous methods. Be available to see the other person's viewpoint. Availability, here, means both physical and psychological openness. How often in the heat of an argument could you not stop long enough to really listen to another person's side? Rather, you were so upset you were framing your own ideas, choosing your own words, defending yourself from attack, and trying to outdo, outmaneuver, and outwit the other person. The advantage of counting to 10 to allow your emotions to calm, or stepping back and taking more time, or just trying to put yourself in the other person's shoes helps you become more available. The question "Did anyone else see strange lights?" reveals availability and openness.

There are two other ways you have to adjust to perceptual influences.

Be committed. Commit yourself to seeking more information. Commit yourself to having additional information before making any judgment. Commit yourself to being as fully informed as you would expect others to be with you before sharing their conclusions. Buy a local paper, for example, and examine it for possible explanations of strange lights in the sky. Listen to a local newscast for information. Go ask or make a call to a local expert who might have an answer. It is this kind of climate—the kind of climate in which educated and informed conversation and dialogue can take place—that is likely to produce additional perspectives, alternatives, and conclusions.

Be prepared to change. If everything has worked thus far, you are likely to get information, hear viewpoints, or gain perspectives, alternatives, or conclusions that you did not originally have. If this is true, you must be prepared to change accordingly. Whatever adjustments are necessary, you must be ready to make them. This is why it is important to avoid making hasty conclusions at the outset. In that way, changes at this point will be unnecessary. You simply adjust internally. If you expressed a hasty conclusion, now you must admit the error or openly reveal the adjustment necessary to accommodate the new information, viewpoint, perspective, alternative, or conclusion, and you can't save face, or protect yourself from embarrassment. Publicly admitting an error is difficult for anyone. As it turned out, the strange lights in the sky were a number of planes returning to the local airport at the same time, having all been at the same air show in another state. From the ground, at night, depending on your position or location, the planes lit up the night sky.

As you take steps to reduce the effect of perceptual influences on you, you will notice changes simply because the information you will get is likely to be more accurate and dependable. It will be better information for use in building a stronger self-concept.

STRATEGIC FLEXIBILITY
When you anticipate, assess, evaluate, and select, be ready to change instantaneously and adjust accordingly because of new viewpoints, perspectives, alternatives, or conclusions.

What Do You Think of Your Self?

Please mark each statement in the following way:
If the statement describes how you usually feel, put a check in the column *Like Me*.
If the statement does *not* describe how you usually feel, put a check in the column *Unlike Me*. For this inventory, there are no right or wrong answers.

	Like Me	Unlike Me
1. I'm pretty sure of myself.	_____	_____
2. I often wish I were someone else.	_____	_____
3. I'm easy to like.	_____	_____
4. I never worry about anything.	_____	_____
5. I find it very hard to talk in front of a class.	_____	_____
6. There are lots of things about myself I'd change if I could.	_____	_____
7. I can make up my mind without too much trouble.	_____	_____
8. I'm a lot of fun to be with.	_____	_____
9. I always do the right thing.	_____	_____
10. I'm proud of the college work that I do.	_____	_____
11. Someone always has to tell me what to do.	_____	_____
12. It takes me a long time to get used to anything new.	_____	_____
13. I'm often sorry for the things I do.	_____	_____
14. I'm never unhappy.	_____	_____
15. I'm doing the best work that I can.	_____	_____
16. I give in very easily.	_____	_____
17. I'm pretty happy.	_____	_____
18. I like everyone I know.	_____	_____
19. I like to be called on in class.	_____	_____
20. I understand myself.	_____	_____
21. Things are all mixed up in my life.	_____	_____
22. I'm not doing as well in college as I'd like to.	_____	_____
23. I can make up my mind and stick to it.	_____	_____
24. I have a low opinion of myself.	_____	_____
25. I don't like to be with other people.	_____	_____
26. I'm never shy.	_____	_____
27. I often feel upset in college.	_____	_____
28. If I have something to say, I usually say it.	_____	_____
29. I always tell the truth.	_____	_____
30. Most people are better liked than I am.	_____	_____
31. I always know what to say to people.	_____	_____
32. I often get discouraged in college.	_____	_____
33. Things usually don't bother me.	_____	_____

Go to the *Communicating Effectively* CD-ROM and the Online Learning Center at **www.mhhe. com/hybels8** to see your results and learn how to evaluate your attitudes and feelings.

mhhe.com/hybels8

Source: In J.P. Robinson, P. R. Shaver, & L. S. Wrightsman, *Measures of Personality and Social Psychological Attitudes* (San Diego: Academic Press, 1991), pp. 127–31. Adapted from S. Coopersmith, *The Antecedents of Self-Esteem* (San Francisco: W. H. Freeman and Company, 1967,) Used with permission.

CHAPTER REVIEW

SUMMARY

Both self and perception are foundations for effective communication. Self-concept is how you think about and value yourself. Perception is how you look at others and the world around you. How you look at the world depends on what you think of yourself, and what you think of yourself will influence how you look at the world.

Self-concept comes from three sources: reflected appraisals, social comparisons, and self-perception. Scripts and self-fulfilling prophecies also influence your self-concept. If people are willing to give up some of their psychological safety and take some risks, their self-concepts will become more positive.

Although being accepted by others may be more important than it should be, is a fleeting and temporal circumstance, and is based on their viewpoint alone, the fundamental components start with accepting your self. It also means accepting who everyone else is and changing your attitude.

Improving your self-concept is not easy because a poor self-concept is part of many human problems. To start, you must silence your internal critic. Then, stop depending on others for your self-esteem, accentuate your strengths and assets, accept yourself, avoid your perfectionistic tendencies, avoid your overreactions to criticism, modify your negative traits, behave morally, become a high achiever, learn new skills, don't feel responsible for everything, and forgive and forget.

To focus on a single area for improving your self-concept, decide what you want to change, consider your circumstances, take some chances, set reasonable goals, use a program of self-discipline, find people who will support you, and act positively toward others.

Alford Korzybski's theory that the map is not the territory means that your perception of reality is not reality itself but only your version of it—your map. Problems in communication occur when you try to impose your map upon another person. To create personal change requires changing your map. Map changes do not represent you in the process of falling apart; often, they work better, create greater happiness, produce positive change, and increase the accuracy and clarity of perceptions.

Those who find success in real-life communication will find success and effectiveness in Internet communication. For the adventurous, Internet users have the option of presenting their real and authentic selves. Those with a positive self-concept will perceive the Internet as just another channel of communication.

The perceptual process includes the steps of selecting, organizing, and interpreting information. Perceptions are less than perfect because of deletions, distortions, and generalizations. Also, numerous perceptual filters will have an effect on your perceptions. Because there are so many influences, and because these influences are likely to combine in unknown ways and even have some cumulative effect, there is no way to predict or know the effect of the influences on your perceptions nor on how your self-concept is altered.

Adjusting to perceptual influences requires that you stay healthy, avoid hasty conclusions, take more time, be available and committed, and be prepared to change. Strategic flexibility—especially the steps of anticipating, assessing, evaluating, and selecting—requires a readiness to change instantaneously and adjust appropriately not just because of new viewpoints, perspectives, alternatives, and conclusions, but because people often come to wrong conclusions. Your interpretations of reality—your mental maps—need to be checked continually to see how accurately they represent the territory, and being prepared to change is part of that process.

CHAPTER REVIEW

KEY TERMS AND CONCEPTS

Use the *Communicating Effectively* CD-ROM and the Online Learning Center at **www.mhhe.com/hybels8** to further your understanding of the following terms.

mhhe.com/hybels8

Deletions 46
Distortions 46
Generalizations 46
Map is not the territory 43
Objective reality 48
Perception 30

Perceptual filters 47
Psychological risk 37
Psychological safety 37
Psychological sets 45
Reflected appraisals 32
Scripts 32

Self-concept 30
Self-fulfilling prophecies 33
Self-perception 35
Social comparisons 33
Subjective view 48

QUESTIONS TO REVIEW

1. What is the role of self and perception in communication?

2. How is the self-concept formed?

3. What are the differences among reflected appraisals, social comparisons, and self-perception? Which one is likely to have the most influence on self-formation?

4. In what specific ways can you make your self-perception more positive?

5. What are the fundamental components of being accepted?

6. What are the ways you can improve a weak or poor self-concept?

7. What is the value of Alford Korzybski's theory (The map is not the territory), and how does it contribute to strategic flexibility?

8. What are the influences of the Internet on self and communication?

9. What are the three steps of the perceptual process?

10. What role do deletions, distortions, and generalizations play in perception? Can you give an example of each?

11. What are some of the perceptual filters that narrow the lens through which you view the world?

12. What is the difference between objective reality and a subjective view, and why is this important in communication?

13. What are some of the ways you can adjust to perceptual influences, and which aspect of adjustment contributes most to strategic flexibility?

mhhe.com/hybels8

Go to the self-quizzes on the *Communicating Effectively* CD-ROM and the Online Learning Center at **www.mhhe.com/hybels8** to test your knowledge of the chapter concepts.

Intercultural Communication

After reading this chapter, you should be able to:

- Define the role intercultural communication plays in communicating effectively and in strategic flexibility.

- Offer a clear definition of *culture* and *co-culture*.

- Explain what it means to possess a cultural identity.

- Relate intercultural communication to the model of communication.

- List and briefly explain six dimensions or frameworks for studying cultural differences.

- Explain the potential barriers to intercultural communication.

- Distinguish among assimilation, accommodation, and separation strategies, and explain their purpose.

- Explain the influence of the Internet on intercultural communication.

M Y NAME IS STANLEY MARTINEZ, AND I WAS INTRODUCED TO GANGS, drugs, and violence at an early age. My uncle, a burly man covered in tattoos who was just released from the state penitentiary, taught me the rules of our neighborhood, and those rules, along with drugs and alcohol, served as my school of survival. I grew up fast, and the inner strength gained from my uncle's advice, my ability to watch and listen, and my common sense caused the home boys I ran with to make me their gang leader. Their trust in me not only gave me courage and comfort but it also empowered me. They also broadened my perspective.

All through my life it was as if I were outside myself looking in, and when I lost gang members because of useless deaths on the street, addictions to drugs, and unwanted pregnancies, I realized I had a higher purpose. A member of the Chicano Youth Center (CYC) helped me secure a job, and my employer put me in contact with the Educational Opportunity Program (EOP) which helped me enroll in college. In ethnic studies classes I learned of my heritage, and I didn't just begin to appreciate my culture, I began to proudly share it with others.

For my first speech in my speech communication class, I dressed as a gang member and talked about my life story. Halfway through the speech I took off a layer of clothing to reveal a shirt and tie, and I talked about the biases and prejudices of mainstream society that push down members of our ethnic cultures. It was in my speech communication class that I made a commitment to dedicate my life to breaking down the barriers that prevent home boys and home girls from entering college.

In this chapter we first look at the role of intercultural communication in communicating effectively and in strategic flexibility. Then we look at the word *culture* and the importance of understanding your role as a cultural being. In the next section, we discuss the importance of intercultural communication. Then we relate this topic to the model of communication discussed in Chapter 1. We present six dimensions or frameworks for studying cultural differences. There are four barriers to intercultural communication, and we examine how to deal with the barriers—which includes a discussion of dominant and nondominant cultures. We look at ways for improving intercultural communication, and, finally, we discuss the influence of the Internet.

THE ROLE OF INTERCULTURAL COMMUNICATION IN COMMUNICATING EFFECTIVELY AND STRATEGIC FLEXIBILITY

In Communicating Effectively

What does intercultural communication have to do with communicating effectively? First, we must all agree that it is communication skills—both sending and receiving abilities—that determine how well individuals, organizations, industries, and nations do in both acquiring and applying knowledge. The better the communication, the greater likelihood of success. Second, we must all agree that because of globalization and the importance of information, there is a rising new category in the world known as the **knowledge class.** It is a class supported solely by its participation in the new information industries with little, if any, reliance upon traditional manufacturing, production, or agriculture. The ability of members of this knowledge class to effectively negotiate the inherent cultural issues in communication will give them a competitive edge in a global world.

Closer to where you live, perhaps, the relevance of intercultural communication is no less important. What if it were your job to coordinate international student services and exchange programs on your college campus? What if you were the manager in a biotech company, responsible for leading a diverse team of scientists doing innovative research?

The world today is characterized by an ever-growing number of communications between people with different linguistic and cultural backgrounds. It is likely that you will make such contacts because they occur in the areas of business, military cooperation, science, education, mass media, entertainment, and tourism, and because of immigration brought about by labor shortages and political conflicts—as well as informally in Internet chat rooms and on Internet bulletin boards. Just a quick example will make this point. The U.S. Department of Education found that close to 40 percent of public school students were minorities in 2000, up from close to 30 percent in 1986. Also, the number of students who spoke a language other than English at home rose by 46 percent from 1979 to 1999. Many teachers are faced with teaching a diverse student population.[1] The communication throughout all these contacts needs to be as constructive as possible if misunderstandings and breakdowns are to be avoided.

In Strategic Flexibility

Intercultural communication has a direct and noticeable effect on each step of strategic flexibility. In the first step (anticipate), you will have a new slant or angle from which to think about potential communication situations. The needs and requirements will be different than without this new knowledge, and forecasting may require the introduction of new or different skills and abilities.

In the second step (assess), the factors, elements, and conditions of situations in which you find yourself will be different. Becoming alert to the introduction of these new ingredients will become easier as your experience broadens. In the third step (evaluate), you will more accurately be able to determine the value and worth of the factors, elements, and conditions and how they bear on your own skills and abilities. Because you will have developed more skills and abilities, in the fourth step (select) you will find it easier to select those most likely to affect the situation.

In the fifth step (apply), you will take greater care and concern and give greater attention to the factors that are likely to be affected. You will understand how to judge their relevance with greater accuracy, and when you reassess and reevaluate your actions you will have increased sensitivity to the intercultural demands of communication situations and how you can enhance, nourish, and encourage further communication efforts.

WHAT IS CULTURE?

Culture is not a box but a fluid concept that is an ever-changing, living part of you, reflecting your learned, socially acquired traditions and lifestyles. The following is a useful definition. As you read it, recognize that there are no hard edges; rather, there are phenomena that tend to overlap and mingle. **Culture** is:

> *The ever-changing values, traditions, social and political relationships, and worldview created and shared by a group of people bound together by a combination of factors*

The words you choose reflect your culture because that is where you learned them, and that is where they originated.

(which can include a common history, geographic location, language, social class, and/or religion).[2]

The word **worldview** means an all encompassing set of moral, ethical, and philosophical principles and beliefs that govern the way people live their lives and interact with others. Your worldview governs the way you think, feel, and behave whether you realize it or not and affects in a major way how you view every aspect of life—physical, spiritual, emotional, moral, sociological, and mental.

Culture is significant in your life because it is part of you. It includes your patterned, repetitive ways of thinking, feeling, and acting.[3] Thus, it is not only maintained but often expressed through your communication. When Jonathan left a prominent position at a prestigious company, his best friend, Adam, explained his departure this way: "Voicing concern and choked with emotion, Jonathan was no longer able to step up his efforts, as his American dream turned into a nightmare, his emotional roller coaster came to a full stop. Sending shock waves through family and friends, he said his final good-byes, and called it quits." Not only was Adam's communication full of cliches, but each one—eight in two sentences—was uniquely American. Where do the words you choose come from? They reflect your culture because that is where you learned them, that is where they originated, and they are likely to be all you know!

Because it is part of you, culture not only influences your perception of your self and your perception of others (discussed in the last chapter) but your perception of everything in life with which you have contact. Think about what might be considered true American values and freedom: things like democracy, individualism, property, equality, freedom, community, and justice. The degree to which you accept these as your own values is also the degree to which you measure your sense of self on those same values. For example, you would feel better about yourself if you were actively involved in your democracy (being informed of the positions of political candidates and voting), expressing your individualism (being assertive and sticking up for your rights), and owning property (having a nice car).

YOU ARE A CULTURAL BEING

One desired outcome from reading about *culture* is that you will recognize and accept *yourself* as a cultural being. **Cultural identity,** composed of ethnicity, culture, gender, age, life stage, beliefs, values, and assumptions, is the degree to which you identify with your culture, and it is determined by the values you support. If you were born and raised in the United States, your cultural identity involves the degree to which you identify with being American. But, it doesn't stop there. You have a number of cultural identities—being a member of the student body, a particular race, a specific age group, a religion, and so on. The word **co-culture** represents nonwhites, women, people with disabilities, homosexuals, and those in the lower social classes who have specific patterns of behavior that set them off from other groups within a culture.[4] Which cultural identity is prominent depends on the situation, the people you are with, and the conversational topics.

Stanley Martinez in our earlier example was clearly a member of a gang co-culture. Although that co-culture was distinguished by members who followed the rules of the neighborhood and were often characterized by the use of drugs, alcohol, and violence, he was a member of two other cultures as well. First, he was a Latino American, a large co-cultural group where he lived. He grew up speaking Spanish, living in overcrowded conditions, and suffering extreme social discrimination—having been called lazy, shiftless, lawless, and violent, all unfortunate, negative stereotypes that had a direct effect on his self-concept. Second, he identified with being an American. Born and raised in the United States, his cultural identity involved a very clear identification with the beliefs, values, and assumptions of the dominant culture. The co-cultures of Martinez and their relationship to the dominant culture are depicted in Figure 3-1.

There are three things that you need to understand about possessing a cultural identity. First, cultural identities are learned. You learn the ways of thinking, acting, and feeling from your family first, then from your friends and communities. Second, cultural identities vary in strength. Morgan, for example, had all the speech and language patterns, all the actions and reactions of a typical American student. All were so deeply embedded within her that she wasn't even aware of it until she visited Australia with her debate team.

Third, cultural identities vary in their content. For example, not everyone would define what it means to be an American in the same way, just as students have different ways of defining what it means to be a student. The importance of this point becomes evident when you begin to generalize about cultures. To what extent do you value freedom, pleasure, social recognition, and independence. These are values often

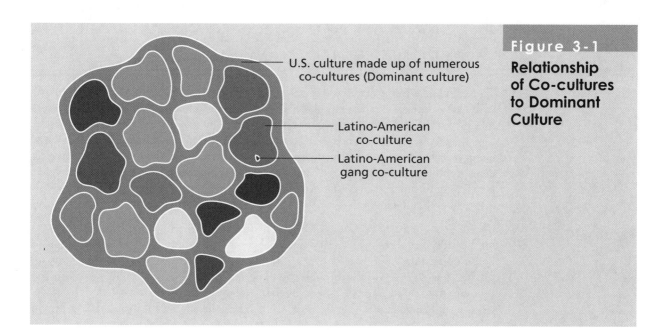

U.S. culture made up of numerous co-cultures (Dominant culture)

Latino-American co-culture

Latino-American gang co-culture

Figure 3-1

Relationship of Co-cultures to Dominant Culture

ascribed to members of the U.S. culture. What if you were a Japanese American and you held cultural identities for both these cultures? The Japanese culture values self-sacrifice, harmony, and accepting traditions—values that, in part, directly contradict those of the U.S. culture.

When you realize all the cultural identities people possess, you also can see the perplexities associated with the *intersection* of issues of race and ethnicity, language, religion, gender and sexual orientation, generation and age, and so forth, as they operate within individuals. These factors interact and come out differently in different people. Understanding cultural identities offers insights into how individuals relate to the many groups to which they belong, but not only that, to understand others, and yourself, you need to realize the variety of groups that create their (and your) cultural identity.[5]

Cultural identity can be a complex issue. For example, a second-generation girl, living in a minority area, whose parents are Korean immigrants, whose friends are Spanish-speaking co-workers, identifies herself as Korean American, a woman, or an American depending on the **context**.

Cultural identity can be a simple issue, too. Some groups create their own co-cultures to isolate themselves from others. In many cities the immigrants still seem to live and work in isolation and resolve to protect their heritage by maintaining all vestiges of their culture and not assimilating. Regarding your perception of others, you might perceive them based on the same set of values—those that you hold dear.

"Culture is a mental set of windows through which all of life is viewed."[6] It is more than an environment or geographical location in which you live, and it is more than any single component of your personality or background, including your race, ethnicity, nationality, language, gender, religion, ability or disability, or socioeconomic status. These components—and certainly the way they combine and interact—affect your social and educational status as well as your family, community, and professional interactions. Culture is the way you make sense of your life.[7]

From this brief discussion of culture it is easier to understand intercultural communication. When a message is created by a member of one culture, and this message needs to be processed by a member of another culture, **intercultural communication** takes place.[8]

THE IMPORTANCE OF STUDYING INTERCULTURAL COMMUNICATION

The chances for contacts with people from other cultures have increased dramatically with changes in the workplace; U.S. businesses expanding into world markets in a process of globalization; people now connected—via answering machines, faxes, e-mail, electronic bulletin boards, and the Internet—to other people whom they have never met face-to-face; the ever-increasing mobility of U.S. families; and the changing demographics within the United States and changing immigration patterns as well.[9] It is precisely this increased contact that makes studying intercultural communication so important. (See Figure 3-2.)

Understanding Your Own Identity.   The first reason for studying intercultural communication is to develop a sensitivity to various cultural heritages and backgrounds to better understand your own identity. In her book *Torn Between Two Cultures*, Maryam Qudrat Aseel says, "It was through the experience of living and being raised in the United States that I came to truly appreciate and understand my own religion, heritage, culture, and language."[10] Your decisions about the values you want to adopt or continue

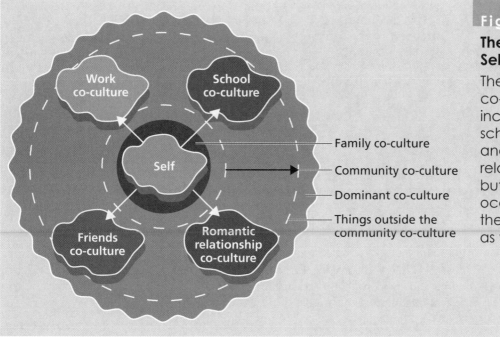

Figure 3-2

The Multicultural Self

The community co-culture may include work, school, friends, and romantic relationship, but these may occur outside the community as well.

Labels in figure:
- Work co-culture
- School co-culture
- Self
- Friends co-culture
- Romantic relationship co-culture
- Family co-culture
- Community co-culture
- Dominant co-culture
- Things outside the community co-culture

holding, the lifestyles or orientations you wish to pursue, and even the friends you want to have—not to mention the major, occupation, or profession you desire—are affected by racial, cultural, gender, and social-class factors that affect your personal identity, who you are and who you want to be.[11]

Enhancing Personal and Social Interactions. The broader your outlook, the more tolerant and accommodating you become. The chances of having close, personal, interactions with those different from you—whether in age, physical ability, gender, ethnicity, class, religion, race, or nationality—are increasing daily. Such relationships help you learn about the world, break stereotypes, and acquire new skills.[12]

Solving Misunderstandings, Miscommunications, and Mistrust. Until recently our nation has not learned, nor has it needed to learn, to be multiculturally competent.[13] The study of intercultural communication will not just unlock doors closed for generations; it will open those doors and, thus, resolve misunderstandings, miscommunications, and mistrust through honest, open, positive, healthy communication. People not only fear, but they also distrust the unknown. Trust is gained through knowledge and understanding.

Enhancing and Enriching the Quality of Civilization. Recognizing and respecting ethnic and cultural diversity are important steps on the road to valuing the ways in which diversity enhances and enriches the quality of our civilization. According to Carlos Cortes, "many multiculturalists today seem unwilling to deal with the growing factor of intermarriage. Too much of multicultural education is frozen into a kind of group purity paradigm, when in fact, intermarriage is one of the enormous changes that is taking place in America. For example, one-third of all Latinos born in the United States now marry someone who is not Latino. . . . What will these cultural blends be like?"[14] In

STRATEGIC FLEXIBILITY
Strategic flexibility requires learning about the world, breaking down stereotypes, and acquiring new skills. Greater tolerance and accommodation will expand your available skills and behaviors as you anticipate, assess, evaluate, and select from your repertoire. In addition, you will reveal greater care, concern, and attention as you apply those skills.

Working Together

The word *multicultural* means different things to different people. The commonly held view suggests that being multicultural means being tolerant of racial and ethnic minorities, mainly of their dress, language, food, religious beliefs, and other cultural manifestations.

For this activity, allow each member of your group to express his or her ideas and feelings on each of the following questions:

1. Multiculturalism seeks to preserve distinctly different ethnic, racial, and cultural communities (co-cultures) without melting them into a common culture. Is this definition of U.S. society an acceptable one?

2. Can diversity be preserved while also establishing a unifying set of cultural symbols—symbols like language? Should teachers in the United States, despite their background or current geographic location, teach students in English alone?

3. Should the word *multicultural* include—in addition to ethnic, racial, and co-cultures—struggles against sexism, heterosexism, classism, linguisism, and ableism?

4. Does multiculturalism encourage racial and ethnic harmony as well as cross-cultural understanding?

2002 there were 1,674,000 interracial marriages, close to a 40 percent increase in 22 years.[15] When you consider the potential for the new perspectives, cultural insights, and unique wisdom that intermarriages can produce, there is no doubt about the corresponding increase in the quality of our civilization.

Becoming Effective Citizens of Our National Communities. **National communities** are co-cultural groupings within the country. National communities were established from the beginning as "our forefathers acquired the lands of Native Americans, 34 percent of the territory of Mexico in 1848, and the island of Puerto Rico in 1898."[16] Prior to the 1960s, most of the immigrants to the United States came from Europe, but of the million or so immigrants who now enter the United States every year, 90 percent are from Latin America and Asia. A study by the Population Reference Bureau suggests that by 2050 the United States will be a global society in which nearly half of all citizens will be from today's racial and ethnic minorities.[17]

INTERCULTURAL COMMUNICATION AND THE COMMUNICATION MODEL

Using our broad definition of *culture*, and with the clear understanding that much of communication is intercultural, you can also see how much influence intercultural communication has had on the model of communication in Chapter 1.

It Influences Senders and Receivers. If my values, traditions, social and political relationships, and worldview are different from yours, given the same subject to respond to and with everything else in the assignment the same, I will compose a significantly different response. As the differences among communicators become greater, the results in thoughts, feelings, and messages become more divergent as well.

It Influences Messages and Feedback. When my parents taught in Pakistan, they were told that raising a question in the classroom is considered an affront to a respected and esteemed authority: the teacher. Instead of interpreting the lack of student response as indifference or lack of understanding, my parents encouraged students to respond among themselves with the teacher as overseer, guide, and outside resource. Jun Liu, in his book *Asian Students' Classroom Communication Patterns in U.S. Universi-*

ties, attributes silence in Asian cultures to politeness, the pace of the discussion in U.S. classrooms, fear of wasting class time, and face saving with other international students or with the professor.[18]

Both verbal and nonverbal messages are affected by intercultural communication. Most Americans pay attention and show respect in the classroom by maintaining eye contact with teachers. But Navajo students in the classroom show respect by avoiding eye contact.

It Influences the Setting. Setting can refer to the way communication fits into history: past, present, and future. It also describes how communication fits into a relational setting, such as the influences of power and distance, individualism versus collectivism, or femininity versus masculinity. It can refer to gender, ethnicity, or nationality.

Setting, too, can relate to your own position within a speech community. If you are the only person with a physical disability in an otherwise abled environment, or the only gay man or lesbian in a heterosexual environment, you may face specific expectations or have people project their motivations on your communication.[19]

STUDYING CULTURAL DIFFERENCES

There are a number of ways to contrast a group of cultures to another group of cultures.[20] Geert Hofstede examined cultural distinctions based on deeply rooted values and derived five dimensions.[21] A sixth dimension, Edward T. Hall's high context versus low context, follows our discussion of Hofstede's five dimensions.[22]

Cultural differences are manifest in the cultural identities of the people, as the examples within each category will reveal. Cultural identity influences behavior including choices of symbols, heroes and heroines, rituals, and even the values one chooses.

The dimensions discussed here are general tendencies only. They are not always true of a culture, nor true of everyone in a culture. Jackie Low is a good example. Raised in Ohio, she has never been to China, never spoken a word of Chinese, and did not know much about China. Anyone who assumed from her looks that Jackie was Chinese would have been incorrect.

Iris Chang, in her book *The Chinese in America,* verifies Jackie Low's experience when she says about the ethnic Chinese in America: "None can truly get past the distinction of race or entirely shake the perception of being seen as foreigners in their own land."[23]

Power Distance

Power distance is a way of contrasting a group of cultures to another group of cultures by measuring social inequality in each. You will notice power differences in family customs, the relationships between students and teachers, the young and the elderly, language systems, and organizational practices. When Lennie observed Tupac—who was from Africa, a high-power-distance country—he noticed he always did as he was told by their boss, who Lennie thought was authoritarian, dictatorial, and unfair, and wasn't afraid to say so. When he talked to Tupac, he realized most people from Africa consider their boss a benevolent dictator and do as they are told.

Continents with high power distance include Africa, Latin America, and Near Eastern countries. Low-power-distance countries include the United States, Germany, China, and Great Britain.

Our way to contrast a group of cultures to another group of cultures is to use the dimension of power distance—social inequality. The picture reveals potential power distances between students and teacher as well as between the younger and the elderly.

View "Culture and Self," clip #9, on the CD to further understand the value of examining cultural differences.

Individualism versus Collectivism

The degree of integration and orientation of individuals within groups is referred to as **individualism versus collectivism.** When Elaine worked with the Peace Corps in Argentina, she learned about collectivist cultures. Working hand in hand with Eduardo Puerta, a native Argentinian, she realized he had never worked side-by-side with a female and needed to be in control and maintain face. In their discussions, she also came to understand his devotion to his family and preference for government control over the economy and press. Knowing about collectivist cultures helped Elaine not just understand Eduardo, but learn from and respect him as well.

You will notice that people in individualistic cultures such as Great Britain, the United States, Canada, France, and Germany value self-expression, view speaking out as a way to solve problems, and use confrontational strategies to deal with interpersonal problems. In collectivist cultures such as many Arab, African, Asian, and Latin American countries, people have unquestioning loyalty to the group, and when in conflict they use avoidance, intermediaries, and other face-saving techniques.

Femininity versus Masculinity

A way of contrasting a group of cultures to another group of cultures that looks at the division of rules between men and women is called **femininity versus masculinity.**

High-feminine cultures believe women should be nurturant, concerned for the quality of life, and reveal sympathy for the unfortunate. In general, feminine cultures allow cross-gender behaviors. High-masculine cultures believe men should be concerned about wealth, achievement, challenge, ambition, promotion, and that they should be assertive, competitive, tough, and recognize achievements. Masculine cultures are more likely to maintain strictly defined gender roles and, thus, have distinct expectations of male and female roles in society. High-feminine cultures include Africa and the Nordic countries of Europe. High-masculine cultures include Latin America, Great Britain, Japan, and the United States.

Uncertainty Avoidance

Uncertainty avoidance compares tolerance for the unknown when contrasting a group of cultures to another group of cultures. When Amelia entered her math classroom on the first day, she was startled to realize her teaching assistant was from Japan. Because Amelia knew Japan was a low-uncertainty-avoidance country, she was able to put into perspective much of what she learned from Junji Akimoto. Junji behaved quietly without showing aggression or strong emotions. Easy-going and relaxed, he ran an open-ended class.

Cultures that feel threatened by ambiguous and uncertain situations and try to avoid them prefer formal rules to control social behaviors. The best example is China. Low-uncertainty-avoidance cultures need few rules and accept and encourage dissenting views and risk taking. Countries with low uncertainty avoidance include Latin America, Africa, and Japan. The United States is considered "medium" on this dimension—neither high nor low.

Long-Term Orientation

Long-term orientation measures the trade-off between long-term and short-term gratification of needs. This dimension was added by Hofstede as a result of his work with Michael Bond.[24] Bond labeled it Confucian dynamism. Elisha's roommate, Mei Li, explained by example that virtuous behavior in China means acquiring skills and education, working hard, and being frugal, patient, and persevering. Knowing what long-term orientation meant helped Elisha bond with Mei Li and appreciate her industriousness.

Those at one extreme on this dimension—having long-term orientation—admire persistence, ordering relationships by status, thriftiness, and having a sense of shame that emphasizes care for others and being loyal and trustworthy. China, Japan, and other Asian countries have an extraordinary long-term orientation toward life. At the other extreme—with short-term orientation—are countries like Finland, France, Germany, and the United States where people value personal steadiness and stability but do not have as much respect for tradition because it prevents innovation, nor for saving face, which can hinder the flow of business. These countries, too, favor reciprocation of greetings, favors, and gifts as related to social rituals.

High Context versus Low Context

High context versus low context contrasts how much information is carried in the **context** (high) and how much in the code or message (low).[25] In high-context communication most of the information is already in the person; very little information is in the coded, explicit, intentionally transmitted part of the message. For example, in the Japanese, African, Mexican, Asian, and Latin American cultures most of the meaning of a message is either implied by the physical setting or is presumed to be part of the individual's beliefs, values, and norms. Often, in long-term relationships communication is high context because the slightest gesture, quickest glance, or briefest comment is interpretable without explicit statements or extended explanations.

Why? Because most of the information has already been experienced. Few explicit statements or extended explanations are necessary unless new areas of experience or discussion occur. Some people who date a lot tire of it simply because of the time it takes to move from low context to high context—often the preferred mode of communication because it is easier and doesn't require as many explanations and clarifications.

Most Western cultures prefer low-context messages in which the majority of the information is in the communication itself—not in the context. Computer instructions are low context because they require that every space, period, letter, and number be precisely in the right location; there are no exceptions. All the information is in the instruction, or the instruction does not work.

These six dimensions are basic frames of reference to help you appreciate differences. No culture is better than another; no culture is strange; no culture is unusual or foreign. Using these tools will help reduce misunderstandings by encouraging empathy, tolerance, respect, and perhaps, a more accurate interpretation of messages from people of another culture group.

BARRIERS TO INTERCULTURAL COMMUNICATION

Some people do not know about other cultures, and some do not want to know. There is no doubt that both ignorance (lack of knowledge) and naivete (lack of sophistication) can be important barriers to intercultural communication.

In this section, we will briefly consider ethnocentrism, stereotyping, prejudice, and discrimination. These are barriers because each is constructed around a judgment made before any communication takes place that then biases the communication that follows. All communication has a past, present, and future; barriers are part of the past that influence the communication that takes place now and affect all that follows in the future.

Ethnocentrism

When I lectured in Australia, I was told never to show arrogance or in any way to reveal condescension or become patronizing. It was wise advice. My hosts had warned me not to be ethnocentric: a common occurrence, they said, when Americans spoke to Australians.

Ethnocentrism is the belief that one's own cultural group's behaviors, norms, ways of thinking, and ways of being are superior to all other cultural groups. Ethnocentrism is not to be confused with *patriotism*, which is devotion to one's country. Ethnocentrism carries devotion to the extreme point where you cannot believe that another culture's behaviors, norms, ways of thinking, and ways of being are as good or as worthy as your own. It becomes a barrier in intercultural communication when it prevents you from even trying to see another's point of view—that is, when it hampers all attempts at empathy.

Stereotyping

Stereotypes are oversimplified or distorted views of another race, another ethnic group, or even another culture. They are simply ways to categorize and generalize from the overwhelming amount of information we receive daily.

The problem with stereotypes is that whether they are positive or negative, once they are established, it is difficult to remove them. Sometimes they exist in our subconscious; these are even more difficult to discard because we are less aware of them. We tend to pick up information from our environment that supports the stereotypes rather than denies them. This simply embeds them more deeply. To remove them, we must first recognize them, then we must obtain individual information that will counteract them.

n her book *The Majesty of the Law*, Supreme Court Justice Sandra Day O'Connor discusses survival in an increasingly multinational environment:

> We live in a world that is constantly shrinking. Cellular phones, fax machines, beepers, e-mail—all of these new forms of communications have made it much easier for us to talk to one another, no matter where we are. We need, however, more than technology to communicate with people from other nations. We need language skills. We need deeper understanding of foreign cultures. We need to know how to survive in an increasingly multinational environment.
>
> Many of our schools recognize this need, and many parents are taking great interest in language training. High schools now offer more than French and Spanish. They are adding Japa-

nese and Russian as well. American businesses have been in the forefront of this move toward what newspapers constantly herald as the "globalization" of trade. There are McDonald's restaurants in Moscow, Kentucky Fried Chicken franchises in Beijing.

Source: *The Majesty of the Law: Reflections of a Supreme Court Justice* (p. 231), by Sandra Day O'Connor, 2003; New York: Random House.

Questions

1. What signs have you noticed that we are now living in an increasingly multinational environment?

2. What implications do these changes hold for you?

3. If you were trying to prepare the next generation for the changes occurring in our culture, what suggestions would you make?

Prejudice

Prejudice is a negative attitude toward a cultural group based on little or no experience.[26] The difference between stereotypes and prejudice should become clear in this example: When Chris was young, his parents told him never to go into the city because Mexican gangs ruled the city streets at night. Chris, of course, then had the preconceived notion that all Mexicans were bad people. From this stereotype Chris formed a prejudice against Mexicans. The stereotype told him what a group (Mexicans) was like; the prejudice told him how to feel about the group. All this changed when Chris worked for the city to help pay his way through college, and almost all his co-workers were Mexicans. Their attitude toward Chris as well as their behavior quickly changed the stereotype and altered his prejudice.

Discrimination

Discrimination is the overt actions one takes to exclude, avoid, or distance oneself from other groups.[27] Discrimination takes stereotypes and prejudice one step further—to action, whether overt or covert. You can discriminate against someone subtly by slightly turning away your body when in a conversation, or by avoiding eye contact with them. You can discriminate against people by hurling verbal insults at them. You can discriminate, too, by using physical violence, systematically eliminating the group from which the individual comes, or even in extreme cases by using genocide, as when autocratic tyrants exterminate racial or national groups. Yet another form of discrimination occurs when you exclude others from jobs or from other economic opportunities.

Obviously, discrimination can be interpersonal when you do it against another person, collective (when a number of individuals or a group perform the discrimination), or institutional (when a business or industry chooses not to serve a particular group of people).

DEALING WITH BARRIERS TO INTERCULTURAL COMMUNICATION

For accurate communication to occur, sender-receivers must be operating from the same perceptual point of view. This is usually not a problem when we are interacting with people from our own race or culture; however, when we communicate with someone from a different race or background, we must realize that this person will be operating from an entirely different point of view.

Communication between Nondominant- and Dominant-Group Members

Much of the literature about communication is written from the point of view of the dominant, or majority, culture. In the United States **dominant culture** includes white people from a European background, while **nondominant culture** includes people of color; women; gays, lesbians, and bisexuals; and those whose socioeconomic background is lower than middle class.

When people are not part of a dominant culture, how do they communicate with people who are? In a tantalizing piece of research, Orbe looked at how people from nondominant groups (people of color; women; gays, lesbians, and bisexuals; and those from lower socioeconomic backgrounds) communicated with people from the dominant group.[28] He found that nondominant members adopted one of three basic strategies when they wanted to confront oppressive dominant structures and achieve success: assimilation, accommodation, and separation.

Assimilation Strategies

When nondominants use **assimilation,** they drop cultural differences and distinctive characteristics that would identify them with the nondominant group. As you can see in Table 3-1, there are three types of **assimilation strategies.**

Nonassertive Assimilation. In this type of assimilation, minority members want to belong to the majority group, but they do not want to use aggression to get there. In order to achieve acceptance, they emphasize what they have in common with the

Table 3-1	**Assimilation**	
Nonassertive	**Assertive**	**Aggressive**
Emphasizing what the dominant and nondominant groups have in common	Carefully preparing for meeting dominant-group members	Disassociating from one's own group
Acting positive	Manipulating stereotypes	Copying dominant-group behavior
Censoring remarks that might offend the dominant group	Bargaining	Avoiding interaction with other co-cultural groups
Avoiding controversy		Ridiculing oneself

dominant group and sometimes censor themselves to fit in. However, it often comes at a terrible cost, as you can see in the following passage:

> I spent the fifties essentially either going to graduate school or beginning my career as a teacher who was very much in the closet—and very much attempting to hide the fact that I was a lesbian. And that meant putting down and holding down a whole part of myself that was really vital to my being. I have these visions of faculty parties or church parties or picnics to which I would oftentimes go with a gay man friend of mine, and we would put on an incredibly good show.[29]

Assertive Assimilation. In assertive assimilation, people are likely to take a stronger approach to fitting in. They will often carefully prepare for an encounter with the dominant group. They may overcompensate by trying to be twice as smart, twice as witty, and so forth.

African American writer Patricia Raybon, in her book *My First White Friend*, describes her assertive assimilation stage, which occurred when she was a child living in a predominantly white culture:

> I was reared to smile, to be polite, to say please and thank you and not to act ugly. I was reared to be the cleanest, nicest, smartest, kindest black child I could possibly be. That would make people like me. White people especially.[30]

Aggressive Assimilation. In this type of assimilation, minority-group members want to fit into the dominant group at any cost. They will imply that there are no differences between the two groups and will be careful to not do or say anything that would indicate their difference, such as speaking in a dialect or making reference to their own group's behavior. They are so eager to be part of the dominant group that they might ridicule the group they belong to.

Accommodation Strategies

The next main category consists of accommodation strategies. **Accommodation** works toward getting the dominant group to reinvent, or at least change, the rules so that they incorporate the life experiences of the nondominant group. The three types of **accommodation strategies** are summarized in Table 3-2.

Nonassertive Accommodation. In nonassertive accommodation, the person does not act in any way that would cause dominant-group members to be defensive or cautious but tries to make people more aware of the group she or he belongs to and tries to change stereotypes they might have. For example, Anna who is Mexican often talks to her co-workers about her friends who are professionals, trying to break the stereotype of Mexicans as manual laborers.

Assertive Accommodation. Those who use this strategy try to achieve a balance between their own group and the dominant group. They try to get their own group's members to know the dominant group by sharing something about their lives; they also attempt to educate others about their group's members. Often they will choose a member of the dominant group as a mentor who can guide, support, and assist them.

They also try to educate the dominant group about their group's culture. Maria, for example, persuades some dominant-group members to go to a Mexican restaurant and guides them through the menu.

Aggressive Accommodation. The strategy in this approach is to get into a dominant group and try to change it, although nondominant-group members may confront

Table 3-2   Accommodation

Nonassertive	Assertive	Aggressive
Increasing visibility	Letting DG members know who they really are	Confronting members of the DG when they violate the rights of others
Avoiding stereotypes	Identifying and working with DG members who have similar goals	Referring to DG oppression of NG
	Identifying members of the DG who can support, guide, and assist	
	Educating others	

Note: DG = dominant group; NG = nondominant group.

dominant-group members to gain an advantage. For example, a woman on a committee that brings international scholars to the university may point out that no women have been chosen. Persons using aggressive accommodation may also warn dominant-group members of their history of oppression.

Separation Strategies

In the third category of strategies, nondominant-group members have given up. In **separation,** nondominants do not want to form a common bond with the dominant culture, so they separate into a group that includes only members like themselves. During the 1960s and 1970s, many African Americans and women, unhappy that power structures were not changing quickly enough, formed separate groups that excluded members of the dominant group as well as nondominant-group members who did not share their views (Black Muslims exclude other blacks as well as whites). Some of these groups still exist today. Table 3-3 outlines the three types of **separation strategies.**

Nonassertive Separation.   In this type of separation, the nondominant person avoids the dominant group whenever possible. Although the nondominant may work

Table 3-3   Separation

Nonassertive	Assertive	Aggressive
Maintaining barriers between themselves and the DG	Asserting their voice regardless of the consequences	Making direct attacks on DG members
Keeping away from places where DG members are found	Making references to DG oppression with the goal of gaining advantage	Undermining the DG by not letting its members take advantage of their privileged position

Note DG = dominant group; NG = nondominant group.

with dominant-group members, he or she won't go out to lunch with them or socialize after work. Through verbal and nonverbal cues, the dominant group senses that this person wants to be left alone. For example, when Tom, who is gay, is asked whether he is going to the office Christmas party, he answers no because he knows that the man he lives with would not be welcome.

Some nondominant groups make no attempt to become part of the dominant group. An example is the Hmong people who immigrated to the United States because they were no longer safe in Laos. Anne Fadiman describes them after they had lived for 17 years in the United States:

> *Seventeen years later, Foua and Nao Kao use American appliances but they still speak only Hmong, celebrate only Hmong holidays, practice only Hmong religion, cook only Hmong dishes, sing only Hmong songs, play only Hmong musical instruments, tell only Hmong stories, and know far more about the current political events in Laos and Thailand than about those in the United States. . . . It would be hard to imagine anything further from the vaunted American ideal of assimilation, in which immigrants are expected to submerge their cultural differences in order to embrace a shared national identity.[31]*

Assertive Separation.   Persons practicing assertive separation work to form organizations where they can be separate from the dominant group. While in these groups, they work against any dominant-group messages that imply the dominant group is superior and they are inferior. One communication strategy they use is reminding the dominant group of their oppression. Patricia Raybon, whose passage we quoted in the assimilation discussion, describes some of the feelings that led to her assertive separation stage:

> *White people—that relentless, heavy presence. Never benign. Never innocent. "White people" as a category embodied in my view a clear and certain evil—an arrogant malevolence—that had done unspeakable things that I couldn't ignore because I knew the facts of these things. Names and dates and numbers. And the facts haunted me and the numbers justified my hate for all of the evil that I believed white people had done.[32]*

Aggressive Separation.   In aggressive separation, people separate from the dominant group and expect their fellow nondominant-group members to do so too. They are very critical of those who practice assimilation or accommodation. It is not uncommon for groups fighting against oppression to separate from the dominant group.

If members of these groups have to have interaction with the dominant group (for example, at work), they will try to undermine the dominants by not letting them take advantage of their privileged positions. For example, an employee would bring legal action against his or her boss for discrimination.

The Consequences of Nondominant- and Dominant-Group Communication

Orbe's research does not lead to a very optimistic picture of American society. If we depict his results on a continuum, as in Figure 3-3, on one end are people who want to belong so much that they are willing to give up or suppress their own cultures, while on the opposite end are people who have decided that they cannot live in the dominant culture of the United States and have gone off on their own. In a country that prides itself on being a place where people from all cultures can live in harmony, nothing on the continuum is acceptable to our vision of what democracy should be.

Figure 3-3

Nondominant Persons' Communication to Dominant Groups

Belongers									Separatists

Nonassertive assimilation
Assertive assimilation
Aggressive assimilation
Nonassertive accommodation
Assertive accommodation
Aggressive accommodation
Nonassertive separation
Assertive separation
Aggressive separation

IMPROVING INTERCULTURAL COMMUNICATION

Sometimes in an intercultural-communication situation with a person different from us, we may interpret the other person as *abnormal, weird,* or simply *different.* It is important to learn to control the human tendency to translate "different from me" into "less than me."[33] Rather, we need to raise questions. Are there effective ways of dealing with different kinds of people? Can I develop a repertoire of five or six approaches that will help me reach others in real and meaningful ways?[34]

Pay attention to your words and actions. It is only through your thoughtful communication with others that you become aware of your own thinking patterns, assumptions, perceptions, prejudices, and biases.[35] When students come to Cruz-Janzen's classes expecting to learn how to communicate with nonwhites, she tells them they are first going to study themselves, their gender, racial, ethnic, cultural, socioeconomic, and physical (ability, disability, and appearance) socialization. Cruz-Janzen has a very clear motive in this: "As long as whites continue expecting others to explain themselves, whites are setting themselves as the norm, the normal ones, against whom all others must be judged and measured."[36]

Control your assumptions. An **assumption** is a taking for granted or supposition that something is a fact. You can learn from generalizations about other cultures, but those generalizations turn sour when you use them to stereotype or oversimplify.[37]

- Don't assume that there is one right way (yours) to communicate. Question your assumptions about the "right way" to communicate.

- Don't assume that breakdowns in communication occur because others are on the wrong track. The point isn't "who is to blame for the breakdown?" it is "who can make the communication work?"[38] Remember, ineffective communication can occur for a variety of reasons:

  - You may not have transmitted your message in a way that can be understood.

  - Others may misinterpret what you say.[39]

- Don't assume that the preferred rules of interpersonal relationships you have learned in your culture apply universally across all cultures. They do not.

STRATEGIC FLEXIBILITY
To apply the steps of strategic flexibility may require that you ask questions that help you more accurately anticipate, assess, evaluate, select, and apply your abilities and skills. Questions can also help you demonstrate the care, concern, and attention that may reveal true sensitivity— opening the doors to effective intercultural communication.

One popular way to educate people who will be entering another culture is to provide them with lists of do's and taboos. The Internet, for example, is good at providing such lists. Here is what Linda Beamer and Iris Varner think of such lists:

The do's and taboos lists are usually accurate, but their helpfulness is limited: One-sentence advice on behavior is like seeing a snapshot from a movie. It is accurate, but without the content of the movie's story line, character development, or even the specific episode, the snapshot's significance may not be understandable. Lists of do's and taboos can't explain why you should or should not behave in a particular way in a particular place. Lists can't possibly be comprehensive. And even if a business traveler were armed with a very long list, who can consult a list for every nuance in every different country? It's no wonder that businesspeople may seem to discard tips on do's and taboos in favor of simply being themselves and acting the same way abroad that they would at home. And yet most businesspeople know that business as usual—doing what they do at home—can be counterproductive when doing business abroad.

Source: *Intercultural Communication in the Global Workplace* (p. 11), by L. Beamer and I. Varner, 2001, New York: McGraw-Hill/Irwin.

Questions

1. Have you ever seen or used a list of do's or taboos? Have you found them helpful?

2. Do you think a list of do's and taboos would serve the purpose when you just don't have time to make a thorough or comprehensive introduction to the new culture?

3. What do you rely on when you have no instructions of any kind and you are in a new culture? How do you behave? How do you know what to do?

- Don't assume that your cultural definitions and successful criteria of conflict management apply universally across all cultures. They do not.[40]

- Don't assume because another's values and beliefs differ from your own that you are being challenged.

- Don't assume that you can learn about intercultural communication by staying in your comfort zone. Even if it is awkward at first, you need to expose yourself to different cultures.[41]

- Don't assume you know what is best for someone else.

Engage in transpection. Instead of assuming—a process most people begin quickly, naturally, and often subconsciously—take a moment to relax and reflect. **Transpection** is the process of empathizing across cultures.[42] "Achieving transpection, trying to see the world exactly as the other person sees it, is a difficult process. It often involves trying to learn foreign beliefs, foreign assumptions, foreign perspectives, and foreign feelings in a foreign context. Transpection, then, can only be achieved by practice and requires structured experience and self-reflection."[43]

Striving *toward* transpection can help you avoid assumptions and move you closer to tolerance, sensitivity, respect, empathic listening, and effective communication responses. Listen carefully to others, understand their feelings, be interested in what they have to say and sensitive to their needs, and try to understand their points of view.[44]

Gain knowledge. The greater your cultural and linguistic knowledge, and the more your beliefs overlap with those from other cultures, the less likelihood for misunderstandings.[45] You need to read, observe, ask questions, and visit places where there are people from different races and ethnic backgrounds.

When Madison found out her new roommate was from Saudi Arabia, she immediately worried because of what she'd heard in the media about Saudi terrorists. She went online to find out more about the country—customs, traditions, religion, and anything else she could discover. The words *Saudi Arabia* produced over 11 million Web sites. Using online resources such as The World Factbook, Saudi Arabia Information

Resource, Saudi newspapers, and the Lonely Planet World Guide, Madison strove toward transpection to help herself avoid assumptions.

Gain experience. You cannot learn how to be a good communicator just by reading, observing, asking questions, or doing research on the Internet. But gaining experience doesn't require making actual visits to foreign countries or foreign cultures. Find an individual of another culture, and ask if the two of you could have a conversation about intercultural communication. With that as your focus, ask some pointed, specific questions designed to help you better understand him or her and others of the same culture. The following 10 questions are designed to get your conversation started:

- How do you, or other members of your culture, cope with and adapt to unfamiliar cultural environments?
- How can members of other cultures begin to communicate with members of your culture?
- What factors can increase our effectiveness in communicating?
- If we had a conflict, what strategies would be successful for managing it?
- What important factors contribute to the development of interpersonal relationships with you or with members of your culture?
- What changes have you noticed in yourself as a consequence of your experiences in a new culture?
- How can I become more *intercultural* as a result of our contact and communication with members of your culture?
- Can we develop community with members of your culture?[46]
- What are some of the worst offenses people outside your culture make in communicating with you or with members of your culture?
- What do you feel are some of the worst offenses you have made as you have become acclimated into this culture?

There are other ways to gain experience in intercultural communication—to obtain a broader worldview. Frequent ethnic restaurants, watch world news in addition to local news, read books written by authors from other countries, learn another language, and when countries with which you are unfamiliar are mentioned, find them on a map. Listen to world music, rent foreign films, and travel—whether in person or through videos. Your local library has dozens of videos on foreign countries. But don't just observe. Converse with people of other cultures. Take part in cultural celebrations that differ from your own. Volunteer to serve on committees, teams, or groups in which members of other cultures will be serving. Listen, engage, and keep asking questions. Take time to understand what people believe about childrearing, educational opportunities, world politics, and life in general.

How you learn about intercultural communication will depend on your willingness to find it out. You will see that the knowledge and understanding you gain is well worth any effort you put forth.

THE INTERNET AND INTERCULTURAL COMMUNICATION

One of the most important influences on intercultural communication is the Internet. We are increasingly linked together across the globe, and we can connect with people on the other side of the world as quickly as we do with friends and family at home.

Assess Yourself

Cultural Awareness Self-Assessment Form

For each statement circle the numerical score that best represents your performance, skill, or ability using the following scale:
7 = Outstanding; 6 = Excellent; 5 = Very good; 4 = Average (good); 3 = Fair; 2 = Poor; 1 = minimal ability; 0 = No ability demonstrated.

1. I listen to people from other cultures when they tell me how my culture affects them. 　　　7 6 5 4 3 2 1 0

2. I realize that people from other cultures have fresh ideas and different points of view to bring to my life and to the workplace. 　　　7 6 5 4 3 2 1 0

3. I give people from other cultures advice on how to succeed in my culture. 　　　7 6 5 4 3 2 1 0

4. I give people my support even when they are rejected by other members of my culture. 　　　7 6 5 4 3 2 1 0

5. I realize that people outside my culture could be offended by my behavior. I've asked people if I have offended them by things I have done or said and have apologized whenever necessary. 　　　7 6 5 4 3 2 1 0

6. I realize that when I am stressed I am likely to make myself and my culture right and another culture wrong. 　　　7 6 5 4 3 2 1 0

7. I respect my superiors (boss, teacher, supervisor, group leader, etc.) regardless of where they are from. I do not go over their heads to talk to someone from my culture to try and get my way. 　　　7 6 5 4 3 2 1 0

8. When I am in mixed company, I mix with everyone. I don't just stay with people from my culture, or only with people from the dominant culture. 　　　7 6 5 4 3 2 1 0

9. I go out of my way to work with, recruit, select, train, and promote people from outside the dominant culture. 　　　7 6 5 4 3 2 1 0

10. When people in my culture make jokes or talk negatively about other cultural groups, I let them know that I don't like it. 　　　7 6 5 4 3 2 1 0

TOTAL POINTS: _____

Go to the *Communicating Effectively* CD-ROM and the Online Learning Center at **www.mhhe.com/hybels8** to see your results and learn how to evaluate your attitudes and feelings.

mhhe●com/hybels8

Source: Adapted from *Cultural Awareness Self-Assessment Form 3*, I CANS (Integrated Curriculum for Achieving Necessary Skills), Washington State Board for Community and Technical Colleges, Washington State Employment Security, Washington Workforce Training and Education Coordinating Board, Adult Basic and Literacy Educators, P.O. Box 42496, 711 Capitol Blvd., Olympia, WA 98504. Retrieved March 14, 2003, from **http://www.literacynet.org/icans/chapter05/cultural3.html**

The Internet serves as a vehicle not only for searching for common values and understanding, but also for hearing and seeing in real-time events that take place thousands of miles away. It can bridge the culture gap among nations of the world. For example, it has helped worldwide organizations function by bringing together people from different physical locations with common interests and goals. More than 45,000 Muslims had joined Naseeb.com by February 2004, after it went online in the fall of 2003. Monis Rahman, who founded Naseeb, said the word means "destiny" in Arabic, Urdu, Persian, Malaysian, Indonesian, Turkish, and Hindi.[47] In fact non-English-language website growth has overtaken English Web site growth, and by 2007 Chinese will be the most common language on the Internet. All those with access to the Internet now have the opportunity to expand their horizons by learning how to communicate, relate, collaborate, and understand their changing world.

CHAPTER REVIEW

SUMMARY

Intercultural understanding increases both sending and receiving abilities, making communication between people with different linguistic and cultural backgrounds as constructive as possible. With broader experience, the care and concern you demonstrate will not just nourish intercultural communication but will encourage further communication efforts as well.

Culture is the ever-changing values, traditions, social and political relationships, and worldview created and shared by a group of people bound together by a combination of factors (which can include a common history, geographic location, language, social class, or religion).

To accept yourself as a cultural being means embracing a cultural identity composed of ethnicity, culture, gender, age, life stage, beliefs, values, and assumptions. A cultural identity is learned, varies in its strength, and varies in its content as well.

Five reasons for studying intercultural communication include (1) better understanding your own identity, (2) enhancing your personal and social interactions, (3) helping solve cultural misunderstandings, miscommunication, and mistrusts, (4) valuing the ways it enriches the quality of our civilization, and (5) becoming effective citizens of our national communities.

Intercultural communication influences the communication model first by its effect on the values, traditions, social and political relationships, and worldview of senders and receivers; second, by its effect on verbal and nonverbal messages; and, third, by the influences it has on the historical setting, relational setting, and a person's position within a speech community.

Power distance relates to social inequality. Individualism versus collectivism relates to the degree of integration and orientation of individuals. Femininity versus masculinity pertains to the division of roles between women and men. Uncertainty avoidance describes the degree of tolerance for the unknown. Long-term orientation relates to trade-offs between long-term and short-term gratification of needs. Finally, high versus low context refers to the amount of information already contained in the person or context versus the amount in the coded, explicit, transmitted part of the message.

The four barriers to intercultural communication include ethnocentrism, stereotyping, prejudice, and discrimination. To deal with barriers, nondominant-group members use one or more of three main strategies to get what they want from dominant-group members: assimilation, accommodation, or separation.

Five ways to improve intercultural communication are: (1) pay attention to your own words and actions; (2) control your assumptions; (3) engage in transpection—the process of empathizing across cultures; (4) gain knowledge; and (5) gain experience.

The Internet offers a vehicle for searching for common values, understandings, and approaches to managing a world of different cultures.

KEY TERMS AND CONCEPTS

Use the *Communicating Effectively* CD-ROM and the Online Learning Center at **www.mhhe.com/hybels8** to further your understanding of the following terms.

mhhe.com/hybels8

Accommodation 69
Accommodation strategies 69
Assimilation 68
Assimilation strategies 68
Assumption 72
Co-culture 59
Context 60
Cultural identity 58
Culture 57
Discrimination 67

Dominant culture 68
Ethnocentrism 66
Femininity versus masculinity 64
High context versus low
  context 65
Individualism versus collectivism 64
Intercultural communication 60
Knowledge class 56
Long-term orientation 65

National communities 62
Nondominant culture 68
Power distance 63
Prejudice 67
Separation 70
Separation strategies 70
Stereotypes 66
Transpection 73
Uncertainty avoidance 65
Worldview 58

CHAPTER REVIEW

QUESTIONS TO REVIEW

1. What is the role intercultural communication plays in communicating effectively and in strategic flexibility?

2. What are the strengths and weaknesses of the definition of *culture* offered in this textbook?

3. What does it mean to possess a cultural identity?

4. Can you make a case for the study of intercultural communication?

5. What are the likely components of a multicultural self?

6. How does intercultural communication relate to the model of communication?

7. What are the six dimensions that can be used as a framework for studying cultural differences?

8. What are four barriers to intercultural communication, and how do they work? Why are they considered barriers?

9. What are the three ways members of a nondominant group work to get what they want from dominant-group members?

10. What are some ways for improving intercultural communication?

11. What is the process of transpection, and why is it important?

12. What is the influence of the Internet on intercultural communication?

mhhe.com/hybels8

Go to the self-quizzes on the *Communicating Effectively* CD-ROM and the Online Learning Center at **www.mhhe.com/hybels8** to test your knowledge of the chapter concepts.

Listening

After reading this chapter, you should be able to:

- Explain the role of listening in strategic flexibility.

- Distinguish among the elements of the Integrative Listening Model (ILM).

- Differentiate and give an example of each of the four listening styles.

- Clarify the effects of culture and gender on listening.

- Differentiate between good listeners and poor listeners.

- Distinguish among and give the key characteristics of active, critical, and empathic listening.

- Explain how you can talk so others will listen.

- Identify the three areas where the Internet is likely to have an effect on listening.

PATRICIA REYES WAS BORN A CHEERLEADER—PRETTY, EXUBERANT, AND communicative. Even before she could talk she would mimic the gestures and sounds of others. As an only child her parents enjoyed the sound of her voice and encouraged and reinforced her, because her voice was music to their ears. Throughout elementary school she was warned by her teachers to "stop talking" and "listen." But Patricia loved talking more than listening. In high school she would often get assignments confused when given orally by teachers because she wouldn't listen closely to the details. She would have to spend more time on assignments because her attention and concentration skills suffered—her mind easily wandered. Patricia had difficulty sustaining relationships with others because she found it difficult to listen to others with attention and care. Seldom did others feel validated or supported by her because of her ineffective listening habits.

It was part of a class in gerontology (the scientific study of the process and phenomena of aging) when Patricia, at last, had to directly confront her "problem." Throughout the class students had to make regular visits to a nursing home, and the instructions were clear: "You are to listen to the patients. Let *them* talk. You may briefly reflect on their comments but only to encourage *them* to talk more." Patricia followed her instructions to the letter, and she discovered a whole new world: that others had valuable ideas, interesting insights, and their own life stories. It was the very wake-up call she needed, and it turned her life around.

The **Integrative Listening Model (ILM)** provides a framework for assessing listening both systematically and developmentally. **Listening** includes the processes of listening preparation, receiving, constructing meaning, responding, and remembering.[1] Each of these processes will be discussed in the next sections, as well as how this framework of listening relates to the framework established in Chapter 1 for strategic flexibility. In addition, the process of remembering is discussed more fully in a separate section.

THE ROLE OF LISTENING IN COMMUNICATING EFFECTIVELY AND STRATEGIC FLEXIBILITY

When you reexamine Figure 1-1, "The Elements of Communication," in Chapter 1, you will notice that there is no element labeled "listening." It is not mentioned there as one of the elements of communication, and yet, you know intuitively that listening is an essential component of effective communication. Now look at Figure 4-1.

When you look closely at the ILM framework for listening previously discussed, you realize that listening—just like strategic flexibility—actually begins *before* the elements contained in the model. **Listening preparation** includes all the physical, mental, and behavioral aspects that create a readiness to listen. These are the same aspects that you bring to any communication situation as you **anticipate** (SF) the various needs and requirements likely to arise.

Second, according to the ILM framework, listening involves the element of receiving. This is where the process of listening begins to relate to the elements in the model of communication. **Receiving** is the process of taking in, acquiring, or accepting. It occurs through the various senses (hearing, seeing, smelling, touching, and tasting) and happens within sender-receivers as they receive all the cues, signals, and impulses. Listening is one part of the whole perceptual process discussed in Chapter 2. It is similar to, but not the same as, the **assessment** stage of strategic flexibility in which all the

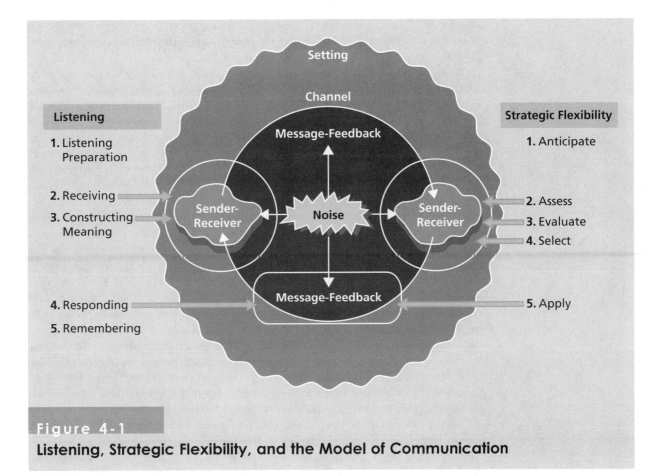

Figure 4-1

Listening, Strategic Flexibility, and the Model of Communication

factors, elements, and conditions of situations are considered. Assessment assumes the receiving process has taken place.

There is an important distinction between hearing and listening that takes place at the receiving portion of the framework. You hear sounds—such as words and the way they are spoken—but when you listen, you respond to much more. Hearing is a physiological process involving the various parts of the ear, whereas listening is a more complicated perceptual process involving your total response to others, including verbal as well as nonverbal communication.

Receiving messages is accomplished with your ears in conjunction with your other four senses, and it involves hearing, *not* listening. It is only when you move to the next part of the framework that listening occurs.

Third, according to the framework, listening involves constructing meaning. **Constructing meaning** is the complicated and unique process of making sense of the cues, signals, and impulses received. It goes on in the brains of sender-receivers. A unique aspect of human beings is the ability to make meaning. Although you often think of listening as connected with hearing alone, it usually requires the full and active use of all the senses. For example, let's say that you are at a crowded party with a potentially romantic partner. Your partner utters the words "I love you," which you hear quite clearly above the sounds of the people and music around you, but you don't fully understand why those words were said in this context, nor what their full meaning might be. You see that your partner may have had too much to drink, you smell the odor of beer, your partner's touch appears to be suggestive, and the kiss revealed the taste of beer. You heard the words, but you can see that only when all the senses come into play can you construct meaning from those words.

One significant part of constructing meaning involves focusing your attention on particular stimuli. In the "I love you" example, notice how the words rang out loud and clear above the sounds of the people and music around you. **Selective attention** is the ability to focus perception. Although you may be able to focus your attention in specific ways, most people's attention spans are very short. Few people, for example, can give full attention to a message for more than 20 seconds.[2] Something in the message reminds you of something else, or you disagree with the message and let your mind wander. Fortunately, you are able to quickly refocus your attention on the message, but every listener and speaker should be aware of just how easily attention can go astray.

As another part of constructing meaning, you must assign meaning to the cues, signals, and impulses—deciding what in the message is relevant and how it relates to what you already know. Assigning meaning is an important process before responding because you must weigh what the speaker has said against the personal beliefs you hold, question the speaker's motives, wonder what has been omitted, or even challenge the validity of the ideas. As in the "I love you" example, you may understand *what* was said, but do you fully understand *how* it was said? When you assign meaning, you give meaning to the speaker's tone of voice, gestures, and facial expressions as much as you do to his or her words.[3]

Constructing meaning involves two steps in the strategic flexibility process as you can see in Figure 4-1. There is no way to make sense of cues, signals, and impulses if **evaluation** (SF)—determining the value and worth of the factors, elements, and conditions—fails to occur at the same time. This is the only way to determine how all those cues, signals, and impulses bear on your own skills and abilities. Constructing meaning also involves **selection** (SF): carefully selecting from your repertoire of available skills and behaviors those likely to have the greatest impact on the current (and future) situations.

Fourth, according to the ILM framework, listening involves responding. **Responding** means using spoken or nonverbal messages to exchange ideas or convey information. In strategic flexibility it is the same as **applying**—with the appropriate care, concern, and attention to all the factors that are likely to be affected, including any ethical considerations that may be appropriate—to apply the skills and behaviors you have selected.

From the "I love you" example think about all the potential nonverbal elements that could affect how you might respond: the clothing or dress of the other person; the gestures made while speaking the words; the body movement, posture, and touch; and, perhaps, most important, the way the words were spoken. An additional element might be the setting in which all of this takes place. What would be the appropriate response? What would you say to the other person who has just said, "I love you"?

The fifth stage of the listening process is **remembering,** as shown in Figure 4-2. A number of strategies that will help ensure that information is being learned well and stored securely in your memory system are discussed in the next section.

In strategic flexibility, the process is complete when the steps of reassessment and reevaluation have taken place. This is just as important in the listening process. You simply need to look back at what has taken place and determine its value, worth, success, effectiveness, or efficiency in light of what you expected.

To review, the listening process has five stages: listening preparation, receiving, constructing meaning, responding, and remembering. Figure 4-2 shows these five stages and offers examples to illustrate how they might occur.

Often, all of these aspects of the framework for listening occur instantaneously, sometimes without conscious effort. Understanding these aspects may help you assess if and where the process breaks down. It may help you slow down the process so that all the information you

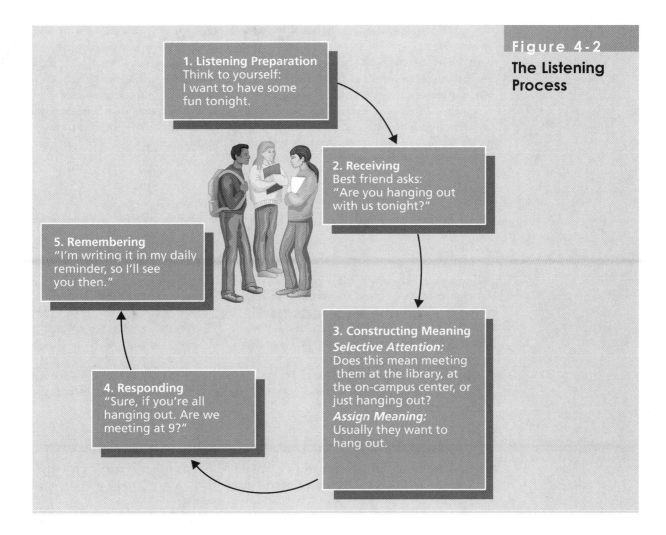

Figure 4-2

The Listening Process

need can be obtained. Sometimes, for example, patience allows time for more observation and the collection of more information. It may also help you better understand why others may not understand what you say. A pause, for example, may allow time to reflect on what and how you said something but, too, on the full meaning of the other's response.

REMEMBERING INFORMATION

There are a number of techniques useful for remembering information, but there is no single right way or best way to improve your memory. All techniques require your motivation and dedication to the task, because when you are motivated, you concentrate harder, and concentration makes information easier to remember. Motivation is a key; using mnemonic devices (used for remembering information that is to be memorized, but not necessarily understood) is unlikely to create any long-term effect. Information that is simple, clear, and vivid is more easily remembered as is anything that is unusual, funny, or personal.

There are four major techniques. The first is organization. Find a pattern, structure, order, plan, format, or framework. The second is association. Make the things you want to remember relate to each other or to categories you already understand. Group them, if possible. The third technique is visualization. Picturing what you want to remember creates a strong, vivid memory of it. The fourth is repetition. When you repeat ideas, you burn them into your memory. Reading them into a tape recorder, for example, and listening to them repeatedly implants them by sheer repetition. Other techniques often associated with assisting memory include creating rhymes, acronyms, and abbreviations.

Much of the effectiveness of remembering information will depend on the notes you take, because notes will reduce the amount of information. Also, with good notes, it will make it easier to use the memory techniques outlined above.

NOTE-TAKING SKILLS

Just as active listening is essential to effective note taking, effective note taking is essential to remembering information. There are those who recommend that you not take notes so you can focus your attention wholly on what the speaker is saying. If you are blessed with a great memory, this method may work for you. There are others who will tape a lecture so they can give it their full attention while it is occurring, then write notes from the tape. The problem with taping lectures is finding the time to listen to the tapes. Taking notes—whenever you do it—has four benefits. First, it will help you remember the information. Second, it will help you organize what the speaker is saying. Third, it may aid in your understanding of the information. Fourth, it is likely to require you to think.

Having been a large-group lecturer for the basic speech communication course for many years, I (Richard) was often asked how to take notes in my lectures. Here is the essence of my advice:

- Sit where you can easily see and hear the lecturer. Also, sit where you can see the board and any slides or overhead projections that might be shown.
- Do not try to write out everything that is said. Think before you write, but don't get behind. If you get behind, leave a blank where you are (to be filled in later, if possible), and move ahead to where your lecturer is right now.
- Feel free to record the lectures using a small, inconspicuous recorder. If you plan to do this, ask lecturers for their permission before making a recording. If you record, make sure you write down everything on the board or slides in your notes.
- Jot down notes of the main and minor points of the lecture. Often, supporting material can be filled in later.
- Listen carefully for verbal or nonverbal cues that indicate key or essential points.
- Write legibly, and use abbreviations wherever possible. If you cannot write clearly enough so that you can understand your writing later, make certain you allow time to decipher your notes before they grow cold. Reviewing notes later that make no sense can be disheartening.
- If you record the lecture, compare your notes of the main and minor points with the information on the tape, as you listen a second time. Taking notes and recording at the same time will help you remember the information better.
- Fill in any details missed the first time through as you listen to the tape, but do not copy down everything.
- Annotate and highlight any key points or essential information.
- If you did not record the lecture, compare and discuss your comprehension and notes with other students.

- Review your notes shortly after the lecture to reinforce both your memory and understanding of the contents.
- Once you have your notes reduced to the essence of the lecture, review them several times just before the examination.

If you find information particularly difficult or challenging, and you must remember it for an examination, once you have reduced your notes to their essence, read them into a tape recorder, as mentioned in the previous section. Then listen to your notes in your car, at home in your room, or whenever a spare moment occurs. Listening to them over and over will help you learn the material thoroughly. If you think this level of commitment—actually following all these recommendations—is too much for you, it might help you to understand that it all depends on what you want out of college. A college education is what you make of it.

LISTENING STYLES

Most of you have discovered, after being in school for so many years, that there are different ways of learning and different ways of listening. Researchers have identified four different kinds of listening styles.[4] In a **people listening style,** you are concerned with the other person's feelings. You seek out common interests with others and respond to emotions. This listening is common among couples, families, and best friends.

In an **action listening style,** you want precise, error-free presentations, and you are likely to be impatient with disorganization. A boss, for example, might ask for a report from one of the division heads on how the company is doing. She would expect this report to be focused and to the point.

In a **content listening style,** you prefer complex and challenging information. Since this information is generally abstract, you can listen without emotional involvement and then evaluate information before you make a judgment. A doctor might, for example, ask for information from his colleagues on how a particular patient should be treated. Because of his training and experience he will not have difficulty understanding a complex medical explanation.

The final style is **time-style listening.** In this style, you prefer brief and hurried interaction with others and often let others know how much time they have to make the point. Newspeople, getting ready for a television newscast, need to get information quickly and efficiently because they are always working against the clock, so they are likely to be time-style listeners.

For the most part, you do not have just one listening style—although you may prefer one over some of the others. You listen in all the ways discussed here depending on the circumstances. To a roommate, for example, you will use a people style, for a group project you may reveal an action listening style, in a lecture it may be a content listening style, and racing out to run errands in a short amount of time, you may adopt a time-style method of listening before you go.

The most skillful listeners are able to adapt their listening styles to the circumstances. If you haven't learned to do this, you will have a problem in some of your interactions with others. For example, when a person is complaining about a co-worker, she would probably prefer a people-style listener. Yet her boss, who is short of time, wants her to state her problem, listen to his suggestions, and then leave his office—a reaction that will leave her feeling unsatisfied.

When you work with people, it's important that you be aware of their listening styles. For example, if you want some critical reaction to a paper

STRATEGIC FLEXIBILITY
Because of your quick ability to anticipate, assess, evaluate, and select from your repertoire of available skills and behaviors, you will be able to adapt your listening style to the circumstances.

you have just written, a content-style listener will be more helpful than a people-style listener because the people listener wouldn't want to hurt your feelings by pointing out your mistakes.

Some research shows that a person's listening style might depend on the culture he or she comes from. One study that compared American, German, and Israeli speakers found that Americans were the most people centered and were likely to pay careful attention to the feelings of the people they were talking to while Israelis concentrated more on the accuracy of the messages. Germans were the most active listeners and often interspersed questions as they listened.[5]

Culture and Listening

More and more, intercultural encounters will become an important part of your every-day life whether it is in casual encounters, business transactions, interviews, or telephone conversations. Much of the misunderstanding in such encounters can be traced to problems in listening, and when experiencing such problems it is essential that you demonstrate both empathy and sensitivity to cultural differences.

As discussed in Chapter 3, intercultural communication often requires that you adjust the ways you approach fundamental aspects of communication—aspects that you may consider normal. For example, you may have to adjust your vocabulary. Both colloquial language and figures of speech often confuse those from other cultures. "The plan was really screwed up," could be restated as "The plan failed completely." Another adjustment might include the elimination of poetic language such as the use of metaphors and literary examples.

There are other adjustments as well. You may need to simplify your grammar. The complex grammar that frequently results from long sentences needs to be altered. Short sentences, for example, and simple grammar can be used instead. Informal communication styles may confuse non-native speakers who learned more formal English in school; thus, choosing a more formal style may help. Referring to culture-specific rituals and activities may be confusing, too.

Intercultural communication interactions are not always marked by misunderstanding, confusion, and hurt feelings. Often, however, varying degrees of misunderstanding, confusion, and hurt feelings do interfere. For example, the British find it rude and manipulative to be asked their full names. Americans, on the other hand, seek others' full names as a way of showing friendship. To be aware of potential misunderstandings is the first step toward adapting and adjusting your communication.

Lack of knowledge, insufficient language, and even lack of sureness about the conventions that underlie the use of language in intercultural situations create difficulty. For example, a convention the Japanese are known for is gracious apologies, even at the slightest mishap, and even when the fault is not theirs. In a New York supermarket, a member of the Japanese culture had her shopping cart bumped by another shopper's cart, and turned immediately to say "Oh, sorry," even though it wasn't her fault.

Willingness to ask questions, seek clarification, admit errors and difficulties, and reveal empathy, will help resolve many intercultural communication problems. Often, you need to understand that using your own cultural rules, even when speaking to someone from a different culture or co-culture, may not just be inappropriate, but it may offend, too. The more you know and the greater your willingness to achieve accurate, effective communication, the better your chance of being both an effective listener and communicator.

"There is no denying that women have an edge in the listening category," says Audrey Nelson in her book *You Don't Say: Navigating Nonverbal Communication Between the Sexes* (p. 264). However, men have a responsibility as well—"sit face to face, make continuous eye contact, touch (if appropriate), and employ nonfluencies like 'uh huh' and 'umm' to indicate they are listening. They should also eliminate any props or barriers to listening, which means putting away the remote, turning off the game, or setting aside the newspaper," she adds.

On the other hand, while women appear to be the champions in the listening department, they still have some homework to do! They must be sensitive to a man's level of discomfort when they are actively listening! He may dislike all the attentiveness (face-to-face position, eye contact, touch); in fact, it can cause him to shut down. Women must be patient—involved, but not too intense. They can self-disclose, but shouldn't tell too much, too soon. It may overwhelm the man. Remember, he is wrestling with his own feelings, and he's listening even though he may not be maintaining eye contact. If he really appears distracted and tuned out, ask him, "Is this a good time for you? You seem distant." Giving attention is generally not a man's forte! (p. 265)

Source: *You Don't Say: Navigating Nonverbal Communication Between the Sexes*, by Audrey Nelson, 2004, New York: Prentice Hall/The Berkley Publishing Group (a member of Penguin Group (USA) Inc.).

Questions

1. Why does most of the burden for effective listening—or communication within relationships—fall on the woman's shoulders and not the man's?

2. Why do men have to engage in all this "touchy-feely stuff"? Shouldn't female relationship partners just know that their male partners care about them and what they are saying?

3. Do you think that men and women truly think differently about feelings?

4. When a woman perceives that a man is not listening, could there be a variety of possible explanations? Could it be, for example, that the man is inattentive, unable to "understand" her, or unwilling to empathize with her? How often does not listening have a variety of explanations?

Gender and Listening

Anyone who has had some experience in the world might suspect that men and women listen differently. For example, how often have you heard the complaint, "My boyfriend/ husband doesn't listen to me" or "You never listen to me"?

Scholars who have studied communication between men and women have discovered that men and women have different listening styles. In the study of cultural listening styles mentioned above, the researchers found that in all three cultures (American, German, and Israeli) women were more likely to be people listeners than were men.[6]

Deborah Tannen, a linguist whose work is discussed in detail in Chapter 5, maintains that men and women come from different communication cultures: Women are interested in relationships and networking, while men are more interested in competitive communication.[7] This theory explains why a husband does not show much interest when his wife tells him about two people who were quarreling at her work. By the same token, the wife pays little attention when her husband talks about the batting averages of some of the players in the major leagues.

Tannen has also found that when men and women talk, women are more likely to be the listeners. Curious about how long this communication behavior has existed, Tannen went back to the literature of earlier times. She found that little has changed over the ages: In Shakespeare's fifteenth-century *Julius Caesar*, Portia begs Brutus to talk to her and not to keep his secrets from her. Tannen says that the culture of boys is based on status and that to maintain their status boys will hold the center of attention by boasting and telling jokes or fascinating stories; the same thing was true of the hero of *Beowulf*, an eighth-century saga.[8]

Notice in the Another Point of View box by Audrey Nelson the interpersonal adjustments necessary by both men and women to try to accommodate the differences in their listening styles. If you consider listening to be important, then you will not be able to continue listening in the same ways you have in the past, and that is precisely the point Nelson is making.

One problem women have to face when they enter the executive or professional world is getting men to listen to them. When Sandra Day O'Connor, the first female Supreme Court justice, was asked what problems she had in her career, she replied that the greatest problem was not being listened to. Finally she found a technique that made people pay attention to her: "I taught myself early on to speak very slowly—enunciating every word—when I wanted someone's undivided attention."[9] Her strategy makes sense: When we find that someone's attention seems to be fading, we are inclined to talk faster.

Another mistake women are likely to make in a business setting is to smile and wait their turn instead of using the male tactic of jumping into the discussion when they have something to say. Men don't follow the female system of taking turns. Patricia O'Brien advises that if women want to be listened to at work they should sit at the middle of the conference table where they can't be ignored, speak with conviction, avoid disclaimers such as "I might not be right but . . . ," and go directly to the main point, omitting the details.[10]

THE DIFFICULTY OF LISTENING

As discussed in an earlier section, listening preparation includes all the physical, mental, and behavioral aspects that create a readiness to listen. There is far more in that statement than what meets the eye. If listening was as natural, easy, and successful as it appears, there would be no need for a whole chapter on the topic. Physically, mentally, and behaviorally, most people are *not* ready to listen well. Figure 4-3 shows some of the factors that have a bearing on senders and receivers.

Because these aspects are likely to affect any listening you will do, but also how effective that listening is likely to be, let's just list some of the factors. They are listed here in no particular order simply because at any given point in time, any one of them might be the cause (or result) of poor listening. Your attitude (tense, worried, anxious, or troubled), knowledge (comprehension, understanding, or expertise), and abilities or skills (adeptness, talent, or training) will be factors. Your state of mind is also important because listening is hard work. Laziness alone can affect your listening. The setting (environment, location, or position) might have an impact as well as how open-minded (unprejudiced, nonpartisan, neutral, nonjudgmental, nondiscriminatory, objective, broad-minded, or tolerant) you are. Your attention to the stimulus (some people have a very short attention span), empathy with the person or subject being discussed, and respect for the other person could have an effect. Also, your physical well-being matters. Being tired, hung over, or ill might have an effect just as much as if you are rushed, stressed, or tense.

There is an additional factor as well. Speakers speak at approximately 125–250 words per minute. Listeners listen at something greater than 600 words per minute. Some researchers have actually suggested that listening may occur at a rate of 1,000–3,000 words per minute. The point is, no matter whom you are listening to, they are speaking slower than you are listening. What do you do with the difference? What does anyone

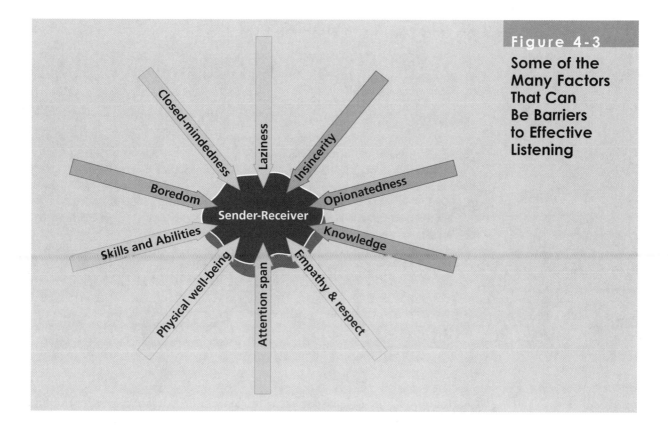

Figure 4-3

Some of the Many Factors That Can Be Barriers to Effective Listening

do with the difference between speech speed and thought speed? What you do with that difference may determine how effective you are as a listener, and suggestions will be provided in this chapter. Any wonder people don't listen well?

Steven Golen did some research on the factors and barriers to effective listening.[11] Out of 23 potentially important factors in listening, the 6 listed in Table 4-1 are the ones that stood out. How these factors turn into barriers are listed as well. When you examine each of the barriers in Table 4-1, are they familiar? How many have you actually experienced?

Four other factors cause difficulty in listening: cognitive dissonance, anxiety, control, and passiveness. **Cognitive dissonance** occurs when you feel conflict because you hold two or more attitudes that are in opposition to each other. For example, when Dr. Roman came into the classroom, you knew you would have difficulty listening because you were fearful, scared, and afraid. You were told he had high standards, a fearless attendance policy, and a tendency to humiliate students not prepared for class. It was Dr. Roman's approach to the class, however, that created the cognitive dissonance. Talking casually with you and your classmates, he defended his grading policy, explained the importance of attending class, and clarified the need to be prepared. His genuine warmth and caring made it difficult for you to listen because it didn't conform to what you had been told.

Anxiety is a disturbance that occurs in your mind regarding some uncertain event, misgiving, or worry. Many college courses create anxiety because so much is uncertain, there are so many misgivings, and the nature and structure of courses and examinations cause worry. It cannot be avoided. Just knowing that you have an exam coming up later in the day can cause you not to listen well in classes or lectures earlier the same day.

Table 4-1   **Factors and Barriers to Effective Listening.**

Factors	Barriers
Laziness	Avoid listening if the subject is complex or difficult.
	Avoid listening because it takes too much time.
Closed-mindedness	Refuse to maintain a relaxing and agreeable environment.
	Refuse to relate to and benefit from the speaker's ideas.
Opinionatedness	Disagree or argue outwardly or inwardly with the speaker.
	Become emotional or excited when the speaker's views differ from yours.
Insincerity	Avoid eye contact while listening.
	Pay attention only to the speaker's word rather than the speaker's feelings.
Boredom	Lack interest in the speaker's subject.
	Become impatient with the speaker.
	Daydream or become preoccupied with something else when listening.
Inattentiveness	Concentrate on the speaker's mannerisms or delivery rather than on the message.
	Become distracted by noise from office equipment, telephone, other conversation, etc.

Source: Adapted from "A Factor Analysis of Barriers to Effective Listening," by S. Golen, *The Journal of Business Communication*, 27 (Winter 1990), p. 32.

Control is the desire to have governing influence over a situation, and **controlling listeners**—like Patricia Reyes, in our opening example—prefer talking to listening. They seek to control their listeners by looking for ways to talk about themselves and their experiences. Often, they do not notice nonverbal signals from others, ignore signs that their listeners are bored, and even overlook overt verbal comments like "I'd better get going" or "I just noticed how late it is."

Passiveness involves the suspension of the rational functions and the reduction of any physical functions to their lowest possible degree. Passive people believe that listening involves no work. If you believe that you don't have to do anything, that you can just sit back and listening will happen, then you are in serious trouble. To learn—especially in situations where the speaker or the subject is not very interesting—requires a serious and concerted effort. So often students put the responsibility on the instructor: "Make it interesting, and I will listen." Education, however, often demands that students actively participate in the learning (acquisition of knowledge) process.

LEARNING TO LISTEN

You have now read about the role of listening in communicating effectively and in strategic flexibility. You have also read about the effect of culture and gender on the process and the difficulty of listening. Are you aware of how much time you are likely to spend listening? Estimates vary, but some listening researchers estimate that the majority of people spend as much as 60 to 70 percent of their waking hours communicating. About 9 percent is time spent writing, 16 percent is in reading, 30 percent is in speaking, and 45 percent is in listening.[12]

Figure 4-4 shows the average percentage of time people devote to the four communication skills: listening, speaking, reading, and writing. If you spend 70 percent of your waking day engaged in some form of communication, and if you are awake for 16 hours, then you are communicating in some way during 11 of those hours. Of that time, you spend 7 hours listening. You listen more than you do any other human activity except breathe. Although you spend the greatest amount of time listening, it is the skill that is taught the least.

Listening is a skill that can be learned, but like any skill, it has to be practiced. Listening well is habitual, and if the habit of good listening isn't deeply entrenched through constant practice, you are likely to fall back on your ineffective, unproductive, and unprofitable listening patterns.

Michael Purdy, writer and researcher on listening, conducted a study of 900 college and military students aged 17 to 70 which showed the traits of good and poor listeners:

A good listener:

1. Uses eye contact appropriately.

2. Is attentive and alert to a speaker's verbal and nonverbal behavior.

3. Is patient and doesn't interrupt (waits for the speaker to finish).

4. Is responsive, using verbal and nonverbal expressions.

5. Asks questions in a nonthreatening tone.

6. Paraphrases, restates, or summarizes what the speaker says.

7. Provides constructive (verbal or nonverbal) feedback.

8. Is empathic (works to understand the speaker).

9. Shows interest in the speaker as a person.

10. Demonstrates a caring attitude and is willing to listen.

11. Doesn't criticize, is nonjudgmental.

12. Is open-minded.

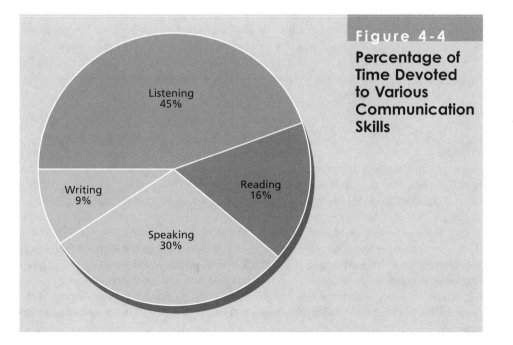

Figure 4-4

Percentage of Time Devoted to Various Communication Skills

A poor listener:

1. Interrupts the speaker (is impatient).
2. Doesn't give eye contact (eyes wander).
3. Is distracted (fidgeting) and does not pay attention to the speaker.
4. Is not interested in the speaker (doesn't care; daydreaming).
5. Gives the speaker little or no (verbal or nonverbal) feedback.
6. Changes the subject.
7. Is judgmental.
8. Is closed-minded.
9. Talks too much.
10. Is self-preoccupied.
11. Gives unwanted advice.
12. Is too busy to listen.[13]

STRATEGIC FLEXIBILITY

Changing your listening habits will give you more insights, ideas, suggestions, and knowledge on which to base all steps in strategic flexibility. Effective listening—like perception—is bedrock (down to fundamentals or the truth of the matter) in strategic flexibility.

If you wanted to change your listening habits, the Purdy study offers 12 guidelines for change: use good eye contact, be attentive and alert, be patient and don't interrupt, use responsive verbal and nonverbal expressions, ask non-threatening questions, paraphrase, restate and summarize, offer constructive feedback, reveal empathy, show interest, demonstrate a caring attitude that shows you are willing to listen, and be nonjudgmental and open-minded. If we were to add one additional guideline, it would be to build your vocabulary. The more words you learn, the better listener you will become.

If you avoid those characteristics of a poor listener, and if you are flexible in your listening style (people-, action-, content-, or time-style listening), you are likely to develop a positive, constructive, and worthwhile listening habit that will, through use, become deeply entrenched. You can speed this entrenchment by challenging your listening ability—seeking out situations many try to avoid rather than experience. You must stretch if you want to grow. Force yourself to listen carefully to sermons, political speeches, lectures, debates, and other material that requires concentration. Given today's movies, television, the Internet, and computer games, seldom is such concentration required. It will, however, be rewarded by your gains in insights, ideas, suggestions, and knowledge in general—let alone your increased ability to listen.

THREE KINDS OF LISTENING

Just as you might choose a different style of listening when you are in different situations, there are three different approaches that can be taken in three different kinds of circumstances. In the classroom, or in a lecture hall, you would engage in **active listening**—making a mental outline of important points, thinking up questions or challenges to the points that have been made, and becoming mentally involved with the person talking. This is sometimes referred to as listening for information. **Critical listening** includes all the ingredients for active listening, but it includes, in addition, evaluating and challenging what is heard. Critical listening often occurs when you are being persuaded to do something or when you are exposed to advertising. **Empathic listening** involves trying to understand what others are feeling from their point of view and reflecting those feelings back. This often occurs with friends and family members. Because each of the three kinds of listening requires a different set of skills, we will briefly discuss each one.

Active Listening

Because this is the most common kind of listening that occurs in college, we will devote most of our time to it. We use it, too, to obtain directions, understand others, solve problems, and share interests. In an earlier section, we discussed the difference between speech speed and thought speed, and we asked the question "What do you do with the difference?" It is a crucial

Our first experiences of learning to listen usually come from our parents.

question in active listening simply because, if you don't know about the difference, or if you don't know what to do with the extra time, it is easy to become bored, distracted, or otherwise mentally disengaged. There is no speaker who can keep up with the speed of your thinking. So, what do you do with the difference? Here are six suggestions. They are specifically designed to keep your mind focused, connected, and centered.

First, *identify the **central idea,*** the essential thought that runs through the speech or communication. Once identified, look for **main heads**—the points that reinforce the central idea. Then, once main heads are located, listen for **supporting points:** the material, ideas, and evidence that back up the main heads. This can be a memory tool as well, because when you remember the central idea, the main heads often follow. Main heads without a central idea may look like a number of unrelated points that make no sense and can easily be forgotten. Central ideas tie fragmented ideas together and give them meaning.

Second, *form a **mental outline***—a preliminary sketch that shows the principal features of the speech or lecture. Often, such an outline gives you clues about the way speakers or lecturers are thinking, what they want you to know, and how they are going to move through their material. When you have a mental outline, it allows you to see the forest, not just the individual trees.

Third, *predict what will come next.* To predict is simply to forecast or to try to make something known beforehand. Why do this? Remember the overall goal: to keep your mind focused. Since attention comes in spurts—as little as 20-second intervals—you must force yourself to concentrate, and prediction is a mind game that can keep you tuned in to what is going on.

Fourth, *relate points to your experience.* Good listeners attempt to relate material to their own experiences. Not only does this add meaning to the information but it also makes the information more memorable. Adults often do well when they go back to school simply because they have more experiences to which to relate the new information they receive.

Fifth, *look for similarities and differences.* How is the information you are receiving similar to or different from what you already know? Sometimes similarities

This is a two-pronged activity. In your group you are to answer two questions. Everyone in the group should have an opportunity to answer the first question, and all the responses should be put into hierarchical order with the most important one (voted on by all group members) placed first and the least impor-tant answer placed last. Then move to question two, and proceed in the same manner—brainstorming with everyone participating, first, then placing the responses into hierarchical order.

Question 1: Why don't college students ask more questions in class?

Question 2: What *specifically* could be done to get college students to ask more questions?

and differences are obvious. For example, you hear that all Chinese people use chopsticks to eat their food. This is an obvious difference from the American or European practice of using forks. A more subtle difference emerges when you examine the natural resources of each of these cultures to see how they might influence the creation of eating utensils. Bamboo, for example, is found throughout China, so it is not surprising to find that many chopsticks are made of bamboo.

Sixth, *ask questions*. When you ask questions of yourself, you challenge, test, stretch, and demand more. This not only is energy producing but is likely to be exciting, stimu-lating, and inspiring as well. When you find questions you can't answer, write them down or try to remember to ask the speaker or lecturer.

Although it seems likely that college students would ask questions, most of them do not. When researchers studied classes in a variety of subjects, they discovered that over a 30-hour period students asked only 108 questions, or 3.6 per class. Of the 108 questions, 29 were about classroom procedures ("Will this be on the test?"); 27 were information seeking ("What date did that happen?"); 23 were for clarification ("Will you repeat that definition again?"); 13 were confirmation ("Am I correct in thinking that . . . ?"); 13 were asking instructors' opinions; and 3 did not fit into any of these categories.[14]

Critical Listening

Ideally, all communication should be listened to critically. When you are receiving new information, however, it is sometimes difficult to evaluate it critically because you do not know much about the subject—or possibly about the speaker either.

When people are persuading you to do something or believe something, critical listening is vitally important. One way to put yourself in the proper frame of mind is to think of yourself as a reporter. As a journalist, get answers to each of the following questions of who, what, when, where, why, and how. Who benefits? Who gets hurt? What happened? What can I do about it? When did it happen? Where did it happen? Why did it happen? Why is this important? How did it happen? Questions beginning with *who, what, when, where, why,* and *how* can be rephrased in any way that will make sense to you; they simply give you a place to begin your questioning.

There are five jobs you have in connection with critical listening. The first is to *determine the speaker's motives*. With a commercial ad—certainly a persuasive communi-cation—the motive is simply to determine: Who wants to sell you a product or services? With political candidates, the motive may be more complex. They want to be elected, so the most important question is why? Are they after money or power? Do they want to bring about social change? Do they want to keep things the way they are?

Your second job is to *challenge and question ideas*. Where did the speaker get his or her information? Did it come from sources generally regarded as credible? Is the speaker quoting the information accurately or taking it out of context? Does the speaker identify his or her sources of information so that the audience can check them later? Is important information omitted? Is contrary information overlooked?

Your third job is to *distinguish fact from fiction*. A **fact** is something that can be verified in a number of ways, which might include experiments, direct observation, or books by authorities. Everyone who applies the same test or uses the same sources should be able to get the same information. An **opinion** is a personal belief. That cinnamon comes from the bark of a tree is a fact that can be found in any number of books and encyclopedias. That cinnamon is tasty in foods, especially cookies, is an opinion because some people will disagree. During the course of a day you hear many more opinions than facts, so it is important that you, the listener, make the distinction.

Although all facts are equally true, some opinions are more reliable than others. You are, for example, more likely to trust the opinions of speakers who have similar beliefs to your own, who have been right before, who have a high degree of authority or credibility, or whose opinions have been (or are) supported by people you respect.

Your fourth job is to *recognize your own biases*. Sometimes there are messages you don't hear because they contradict your attitudes and beliefs. In some cases, you might not even be aware that you are blocking out messages. One study found that although jurors had heard instructions about the rules of circumstantial evidence, only 40 percent correctly followed the instructions. The authors of the study concluded that this misunderstanding of the law was not merely a matter of poor listening. They believed that jurors were likely to misinterpret the law—to listen to and consider circumstantial evidence—because they didn't believe in the law.[15] The tendency to interpret information in light of your beliefs can lead you to distort the information you hear. As a listener you must be aware of your values and attitudes, especially when you hear information you might resist or disagree with.

Your fifth job in critical listening is to *assess the message*. Assessment can take place as part of listening preparation, the receiving process, constructing meaning, responding, remembering information, or—as in strategic flexibility—in reassessment and reevaluation just after or long after the situation has taken place. To **assess** is to determine the value of something. Basically, it is a critical process: chewing over what you have heard before you swallow it. Ideas that may seem acceptable when you first hear them may not be as palatable when you have had time to think about them. This is especially true for important ideas: It is essential to reflect on them before they become part of you and of your thinking.

The important thing in assessment is to learn to delay taking a position until you receive all the facts and other evidence, until you have had a chance to test them in the marketplace of ideas, and until you have had an opportunity to chew over everything before digestion. Figure 4-5 is a critical listening evaluation checklist for a speech or lecture.

Empathic Listening

Empathy is the process of mentally identifying with the character and experiences of another person. Often, it involves the emotional projection of your self into another's life—or their life as revealed by and through their communication. It is all about feelings. Michael P. Nichols, who has written about listening, points out that when you listen with empathy, you have to suspend your ego and immerse yourself in the other person. Only by doing this will you be able to enter into his or her feelings.[16]

Listening to other people's feelings, as noted in the introduction to this section, is not just a way of giving emotional support, but it is a way of creating intimacy with others as well. To do this effectively, you need to recognize what feelings are involved,

Figure 4-5

Critical Listening Evaluation Checklist for a Speech or Lecture

1. Were you able to make any accurate predictions about what the speaker was going to say? What helped you to do so?

2. What was the speaker's central idea? Was it clearly stated?

3. Do you have any ideas of the speaker's motive for giving this speech? If you know the motive, does it make the speech more or less believable?

4. What kinds of supporting points were used to back up the speaker's ideas? Were these points based on evidence you respect?

5. What questions would you like to ask the speaker? Are they questions that clarify what the speaker has said or questions that ask for more information?

6. Think of one or two ways you would like to challenge the speaker.

7. 0ow would you evaluate this speech? What did the speaker do well? Was there anything the speaker could have done to make the speech better?

let speakers tell you what has happened, and then encourage them to find the solution to their problem.

Identify the emotion(s). First, listen to what the other person is *really* saying. If, for example, your roommate comes back to your room and says, "I am going to kill my advisor!" he is obviously not saying that he literally plans to kill her. What is he really saying? In this case, it would be reasonable to assume that your roommate is feeling anger. If you respond with "Boy, you really sound mad," you create the opportunity for your roommate to tell you what has happened.

Listen to the story. Another part of an empathic response is to listen attentively. As the whole story comes out, there is no need to respond with anything very specific. At this point the person just wants to be listened to. You can show your interest and concern if you listen and look sympathetic—not like you are ready to leave for your next class.

Let's go back to your roommate and his problem with his advisor. What happened to make him so angry? He explains that his advisor overlooked one of his requirements, and to fulfill it means he must take an overload, take the course in summer school, or graduate late.

After your roommate has told you the whole story, he is not quite so mad, but he's still pretty upset. As you listen, you discover other feelings in addition to anger. He feels betrayed because he thinks his advisor never really liked him and is doing this on purpose. He feels humiliated because he has told all his friends exactly when he would be graduating and how much coursework he has yet to complete. Usually people do not feel just one emotion—they have a whole assortment of them.

If you can let your roommate talk through the entire problem, without making judgments but by offering support, it is likely that the full range of the problem will be revealed. One way to reach this point is through **paraphrasing:** restating the other person's thoughts or feelings in your own words. If your roommate says "I just feel like giving up," an appropriate paraphrased response might be, "You sound like you are very upset." (You know dropping out of school is not a realistic option, so you don't include it in your paraphrase.) This response not only helps identify the feelings but it also helps find out whether you have been hearing accurately and shows that you are paying attention. A paraphrased response provides a mirror for the other person's remarks.

Finally, *let the person work out the problem*. Sometimes just listening and letting people explain what is upsetting them largely solves the problem. You often hear someone say, "I feel better just because I've talked to you." People frequently want to vent their feelings, and once they have done so, they feel better.

But sometimes merely listening is not enough; your roommate has a problem, and he wants some help in solving it. In such a situation, the best approach is usually to trust the other person and his or her ability to work out the problem. This does not mean, however, that you ignore the problem. Empathic listening includes helping others find a way to solve the problem.

The last step in empathic listening, then, is to give the person a chance to work out the problem. In the case of your roommate, you don't want to say "You should quit!" Let him decide what he wants to do. If the emotion in the situation has died down, it might be appropriate to ask some general questions such as "What are you thinking about doing?" It might also be possible to ask some questions that may lead to a solution the other person has not thought of: "Could you go to the department where the course is offered to see if there is a way to 'place out' of it?" "Do you think your advisor might have made a mistake?" "Would it be possible to get credit for the course because of all the other related courses you have already taken?" "Do you think this course is offered on a campus near your home where you could take it along with your job next summer, and then transfer the credit?"

The important thing to remember at this stage is that you do not have to solve the problem. If you try to solve every problem that people bring you, you will put a heavy burden on yourself. Think of the person with the problem as "owning" that problem. This attitude also will help the other person grow in his or her ability to deal with problems.

When strong emotions are involved, people often need a sounding board. To be there and to utter an occasional "Oh," "Mmmm," or "I see" is often enough. Much comfort and support is derived from just being listened to.

Table 4-2 compares active, critical, and empathic listening. Notice that there are significant differences. A strategically flexible person will be aware of the differences and will respond appropriately.

Table 4-2 Active, Critical, and Empathic Listening Compared

Active Listening	Critical Listening	Empathic Listening
Identify the central idea	Determine motives	Identify the emotion(s)
Form a mental outline	Challenge and question ideas	Listen to the story
Predict what comes next	Distinguish fact from opinion	Let the person work out the problem
Relate points to your own experience	Recognize your biases	
Seek similarities and differences	Assess the message	
Ask questions		

This African American woman shows through her communication that she is an empathic listener.

TALKING SO OTHERS WILL LISTEN

There is a downside to the technology-oriented, information-driven society that you are experiencing, and that is a corresponding reluctance to listen. Whether it is distractions, preoccupations, time limitations, or the difference in the slow rate of others' speaking to you versus the rapid pace of gaining information from the media and from the Internet—how accustomed you've become to having your attention span satisfied by video games, chat room banter, and fast-paced television programs—the fact is, you do not listen well nor does anyone else. Whether this represents a societal change or simply a continuation of a well-documented, ongoing problem is not the point. The point is, what can be done when you realize others are not and will not be listening to you? Is it a hopeless situation?

Although there are numerous techniques for reaching out and grasping the attention of others, the following are some that may work. Often, a combination of techniques works best. We'll briefly discuss assertiveness, getting to the point, being prepared, writing down ideas, being flexible, and changing your vocal style.

First, and perhaps most obvious, you need to be more assertive. In the article "Talking Back to Your Doctor Works," Greider says, "Studies show that doctors remember best the cases of assertive patients. Medical outcomes are also likely to be better."[17] See the Consider This box. These results are likely to apply across communication contexts. It has long been an established research result that assertive behavior tends to be associated with positive outcomes.

The doctor–patient relationship represents one significant example where listening is often a problem:

Next time you visit your doctor keep in mind one crucial if little-known rule: catch 23.

The catch works this way: Doctors typically will listen to a patient's "opening statement" little more than 23 seconds before changing the subject or "redirecting" the talk.

That means you, the patient, must talk not only fast, but compellingly, even knowledgeably, to get his or her attention. That's important for your doctor to fully grasp what's bothering you.

Too often doctors don't. In fact, researchers increasingly are finding that one big reason treatments don't work—or aren't prescribed at all—is because of problems in the way doctors and patients communicate.

Or, more precisely, fail to communicate. And when communication fails, the results can be disastrous.

Late last year the National Academy of Sciences (NAS) reported that some 7,000 patients die every year because of medication errors.

Even more alarming, the NAS found medical errors in hospitals cause between 44,000 and 98,000 deaths every year.

Some mistakes can be avoided, experts believe, if doctors and patients do a better job talking to each other.

Questions

1. Have you ever had this happen to you? How have you handled it?

2. Are there other situations—other than doctor–patient relationships—in which you have discovered that effective listening was a problem? Lawyer–client? Salesperson–buyer? Parent–child? Teacher–student?

3. What are the barriers, hurdles, or restrictions that cause you to be reluctant to deal with the other person in such relationships in an effective manner?

Source: "Talking Back to Your Doctor Works," by L. Greider, *AARP Bulletin*, February 2000.

Second, knowing that the other person is likely to be a weak or indifferent listener, avoid idle chit-chat and friendly conversation and get to the point fast. In advance of the conversation, think about what you want to say, how you plan to say it, and what you want from the other person. Then, try to follow your plan. The point isn't to memorize a speech; rather, it is to move rapidly toward your point.

Third, do your homework—that is, know what you are talking about. If some research is necessary to gather facts and relevant information, go to the library or use the Internet to ferret out the facts that will make your case or back up your position. Well-informed people tend to get the ear of others, as opposed to those who either do not know what they are talking about or are simply willing to hear the ideas of others and make no significant contribution of their own.

Fourth, write down your most important points or questions, and prioritize them. A list of ideas has always been associated with a rational, judicious, well-thought-out approach. Even if you do not use your notes, writing them out will assist you in organizing your ideas and phrasing them in the most effective way. When you put your most important ideas first, it is more likely they will be heard or noticed. Otherwise, they may be hidden in the middle or end of your conversation, or they may come too late for the attention span of your listener.

Fifth, have some options in mind, and be willing to listen. You are more likely to get the attention of others when you appear flexible and willing to listen yourself. The old adage "It takes one to know one" suggests that if you want someone to listen to you, you must also be willing to listen to them. But preparation and forethought does not necessarily mean all the alternatives have been considered. Thus, remember that this is a conversation; it is two-way. You must be willing to prepare your ideas and, in turn, listen to the ideas of others.

STRATEGIC FLEXIBILITY
When you assess, evaluate, and select from your repertoire of available skills and behaviors, you must appear flexible. As we say in this paragraph: "You must be willing to prepare your ideas and, in turn, listen to the ideas of others."

Sixth, try to change your vocal style. For some people—as indicated earlier in this chapter—this may mean slowing down your rate of delivery. If your pace tends to be slow already, or plodding, speeding up may be a useful approach. Often, it may simply be a need for variety. A change in volume, either louder or softer depending on the circumstances, may also help.

There are many ways to talk so others will listen. These suggestions will get you started, but overriding any of them are, of course, the courtesy and respect you need to demonstrate. Being assertive, for example, is not an excuse for being aggressive and thoughtless. Avoiding idle chit-chat and friendly conversation is not an excuse for overlooking necessary or important human concerns and connectiveness. You should make all decisions in the context of good judgment, common sense, thoughtfulness, and **propriety**—the character or quality of being proper, especially in accordance with recognized usage, custom, or principles.

Throughout all of this—your use of techniques to get others to listen to you—you need to recognize that there are some people who will not listen to you no matter what you do. Fortunately, these people are likely to be few and far between. You should not be disappointed if the techniques you use fail to work. The bottom line is: Communication involves a large number of factors or variables. No situation is the same as any other. No one has or ever will have control of all the factors or variables; no one has that kind or level of control. The more experience you have, the more practice that you engage in, and the more you believe in yourself and your abilities, the more likely you will be successful. Success is never guaranteed.

THE INTERNET AND LISTENING

There are three areas where the Internet is likely to have an effect on listening. The first has to do with what speakers are likely to bring to their presentations because of the Internet—and, coordinately, what this means for listeners in an Internet-saturated world. The second has to do with the increased amount of information listeners are likely to possess because of Internet accessibility. The third concerns the listening materials available.

The Internet has provided a benchmark for improved communication. It is the dawning of a new era of communication that is listener focused, listener directed, and listener dominated. Why? Because of the ease and accessibility of an overwhelming amount of information. People have no excuse for being uninformed—unless they choose *not* to take advantage of this resource. Thus, they now can focus and direct their information specifically toward their listeners. It is an enormous challenge and an incredible opportunity for speakers to inform, educate, and persuade.

The second issue has to do with what listeners are likely to possess because of the Internet. This issue is closely related to the first, but it removes listening from strictly a public-speaking context. As noted, wide channels of information are now available because of the Internet. With this supply, listeners can expect full disclosure from others. Professionals, for example, are expected to communicate clearly and sensitively. Doctors must listen carefully, notice the body language of patients, show empathy, and offer patients more information. Because of the Internet patients know more about their own illnesses and the treatments for those illnesses. With careful observation and a sensitive, empathic approach, doctors can focus on what is known and, thus, make their assessments, diagnosis, and treatment more complete and more specifically tailored to individual patient needs and knowledge.[18]

Third, and finally, what listening materials are available on the Internet? The word *listening* written into the Google search engine produced 116,000,000 hits (October 18,

Are You a Good Listener?

For each statement circle the numerical score that best represents your listening ability using the following scale:

7 = Outstanding; 6 = Excellent; 5 = Very good; 4 = Average (good); 3 = Fair; 2 = Poor; 1 = Minimal ability; 0 = No ability demonstrated.

1. I listen for the other person's feelings, not just to the words he or she says.	7 6 5 4 3 2 1 0
2. I paraphrase what other people say to me.	7 6 5 4 3 2 1 0
3. I don't interrupt.	7 6 5 4 3 2 1 0
4. I am open-minded to ideas, some with which I may not agree.	7 6 5 4 3 2 1 0
5. I remember what people say.	7 6 5 4 3 2 1 0
6. I am willing to express my feelings.	7 6 5 4 3 2 1 0
7. I don't complete other people's sentences even when I think I know what they are going to say next.	7 6 5 4 3 2 1 0
8. I make eye contact.	7 6 5 4 3 2 1 0
9. I don't think of what I'm going to say next while the other person is talking.	7 6 5 4 3 2 1 0
10. I ask the person questions to get more information and show that I am interested in what he or she is saying.	7 6 5 4 3 2 1 0
11. I am comfortable with silence.	7 6 5 4 3 2 1 0
12. I am aware of a person's body language and my own body language.	7 6 5 4 3 2 1 0

TOTAL POINTS: _____

Go to the *Communicating Effectively* CD-ROM and the Online Learning Center at **www.mhhe. com/hybels8** to see your results and learn how to evaluate your attitudes and feelings.

mhhe.com/hybels8

Source: Adapted from *Assessing Your Listening Ability*, I CANS (Integrated Curriculum for Achieving Necessary Skills), Washington State Board for Community and Technical Colleges, Washington State Employment Security, Washington Workforce Training and Education Coordinating Board, Adult Basic and Literary Educators, P.O. Box 42496, 711 Capitol Blvd., Olympia, WA 98504. Retrieved October 18, 2005, from **http://www.literacynet.org/icans/chapter05/assessing.html**

2005). The words *Listening on the Internet* produced 38,500,000 hits, and enclosed in quotation marks, the same three words produced 738 hits. The first site (http://ec.hku.hk/vec/listening/listint.htm) explains that listening material on the Internet use two kinds of software: Real Audio and Shockwave. To use material on the Internet, you will need to check that your computer is capable of running the latest versions of the software.

There are numerous sites listed on the Internet related to listening. Some are specifically designed for English as a Second Language (ESL) students. There is the English Listening Lounge; a BBC site by which you learn English by radio; a Voice of America (VOA) Special English site where the speaking rate is reduced and a simplified vocabulary is used for those learning to speak the English language; and other sites.

The point is that the Internet is making a significant difference in the way it is producing a new breed of listeners, in the additional wide variety of general information that it makes available, and in offering those with difficulty in listening or those with weak comprehension skills a place to go to learn, practice, and improve.

CHAPTER REVIEW

SUMMARY

Of all the communication faults people are accused of, not listening probably ranks as number one. Listening is a skill, and like any other skill it must be learned and practiced.

The Integrative Listening Model (ILM) includes the processes of listening preparation, receiving, constructing meaning, responding, and remembering. It begins before the elements of communication in the model in Chapter 1 with listening preparation, and it continues after the elements depicted there with the process of remembering. Listening, because it is one aspect of the process of perception, is essential to all steps in strategic flexibility.

There are numerous strategies that will help you ensure information is being learned well and stored securely in your memory system. All require conscious effort. Just as active listening is essential to effective note taking, effective note taking is essential to remembering information. Effective note taking requires commitment on your part as well.

Culture has an effect on listening simply because of the potential misunderstandings that can occur. Adjustments in vocabulary, grammar, or informality may need to be made. Gender has an effect because men and women listen differently. Understanding the differences will aid in effective communication.

There are as many factors, or combinations of factors, that cause difficulty in listening as there are listeners. One element is the difference between speech speed and listening speed. In addition to the six factors singled out by Steven Golen, there are the factors of cognitive dissonance, anxiety, control, and passiveness as well.

To be a good listener, you must become actively involved in changing your listening habits. In his study of good and poor listeners, Michael Purdy offers 12 guidelines for change. In addition to building your vocabulary, you need to challenge your listening ability by seeking out situations where concentration and careful listening are required.

There are three kinds of listening discussed in this book: active listening (sometimes referred to as listening for information), critical listening, and empathic listening. Active listening involves identifying a central idea, forming a mental outline, predicting what comes next, relating points to your experience, seeking similarities and differences, and asking questions. Critical listening involves determining motives, challenging and questioning ideas, distinguishing fact from opinion, recognizing your biases, and assessing the message. Empathic listening involves identifying the emotion, listening to the story, and letting the person work out the problem.

When you discover that those you want to listen to you are not listening, the techniques of assertiveness, getting to the point, being prepared, writing down ideas, being flexible, and changing your verbal style are ways—or combinations of ways—for reaching out and grasping attention. Whatever techniques you choose, you need to avoid being aggressive and thoughtless and show courtesy and respect. All decisions should be made using good judgment, common sense, thoughtfulness, and propriety.

The three areas where the Internet may have an effect on listening include what speakers are likely to bring to their presentations because of the Internet; the increased amount of information listeners are likely to possess because of Internet accessibility; and the wide variety of listening materials available on the Internet.

KEY TERMS AND CONCEPTS

Use the *Communicating Effectively* CD-ROM and the Online Learning Center at **www.mhhe.com/hybels8** to further your understanding of the following terms.

QUESTIONS TO REVIEW

1. What is the role that listening plays in strategic flexibility?

2. What are the elements of the Integrative Listening Model (ILM), and how do each of the elements relate to the model of communication discussed and illustrated in Chapter 1?

3. What are the four kinds of listening styles, and why is it helpful to know someone's listening style if you are communicating something important?

4. What effects are culture and gender likely to have on listening?

5. What are the factors that make listening difficult?

6. If you wanted to become a better listener, what are some of the ways you have to improve?

7. What are the strategies you can use to remember information?

8. What skills are involved in effective note taking?

9. How do identifying the central idea, main points, and supporting material, and forming a mental outline contribute to better listening?

10. In addition to listening for information and asking questions, what must be added when you are listening critically?

11. What is empathic listening, and what are some of the circumstances in which you might use it?

12. What are some of the techniques you can use to reach out and grasp the attention of others when you must talk so others will listen?

13. In what areas does the Internet affect listening?

mhhe.com/hybels8

Go to the self-quizzes on the *Communicating Effectively* CD-ROM and the Online Learning Center at **www.mhhe.com/hybels8** to test your knowledge of the chapter contents.

5

Verbal Communication

After reading this chapter, you should be able to:

- Briefly describe how you acquired your ability to use words.
- Describe the relationship of the Sapir-Whorf hypothesis to strategic flexibility.
- Explain how language is symbolic.
- Explain Hayakawa's ladder of abstraction and why it is important.
- Explain the function of role in a language environment.
- Define *style*.
- Describe differences between women's language and men's language.
- Define *report-talk* and *rapport-talk*.
- Explain differences between standard American English and dialect.
- Describe the ways in which speaking and writing differ.
- Describe some of the ways to make your verbal style clearer, more vivid, and more ethical.
- Describe the four influences of the Internet on verbal communication.

WESLEY COLEMAN DIDN'T KNOW HOW LUCKY HE WAS. He had two parents who cared deeply about him and who were determined to give him a better life. His parents knew that people who communicate clearly, respond quickly, tell interesting stories, and make compelling arguments have a distinct advantage. Those who can't are put at a distinct disadvantage. Even while Wesley was in the womb, his mother would read him stories of adventure, challenge, and risk. In his early years, Wesley loved to be read to, and whenever he visited his grandparents, he would beg to have them sit with him and read. His parents created a ritual of reading Wesley stories before going to bed, and these stories always stimulated his imagination. Soon he was reading to them, and always he was learning new words—building his vocabulary. Wesley loved to write, and he would keep a journal just to record his thoughts on things in this world. He would write short stories and read them to anyone who would listen. Wesley's was a world of words. His friends admired him because he was so verbal and eloquent. Teachers appreciated his class contributions because he had a way with words. It was his verbal acumen, his success in school, and his desire to help others that led him to law school. Wesley went on to become a successful trial lawyer, but he credits his success to parents who took an active interest in his development of language skills.

The flip side to Wesley Coleman's ability in acquiring and using proper languaging skills, as his parents were well aware, can be devastating. In his book *A User's Guide to the Brain*, John Ratey, a clinical professor of psychiatry at Harvard Medical School, states it succinctly: "When people . . . fail to make proper language connections, or do not stop and consider what they are saying, they wind up not only with speaking, reading, or writing problems—which are bad enough—but with difficulty sustaining social relationships, making moral decisions, controlling anger, and even feeling emotions."[1] The potential repercussions of poor language acquisition and use are enormous, to say the least. There is even evidence that a poor command of language may inhibit your ability to imagine and think up new ideas.[2]

So, when you learned to use language in the elementary grades, you did more than master the basic skills. You learned to express feelings and opinions, and, as you matured, to support your opinions with sound arguments and research. You became aware of the many purposes for which language is used and the diversity of forms it can take to appropriately serve these purposes and a variety of audiences. You learned to use the language and forms appropriate for different formal and informal situations—for example, the formal language of debate, the figurative language of poetry, the technical language and formal structures used in report writing. In sum, through your mastery of lan-

Protests and demonstrations will probably have a lot of connotative language.

guage, you have experienced expressive and communicative powers, and you appreciate language as both a source of pleasure and an important medium for recording and communicating ideas and information.

Language is just as important in your personal life. How you use language will affect your relationships with friends and loved ones. Failures in relationships with friends and family are often attributed to a failure of language. Lack of effective communication is often cited as a leading cause of marital breakups.

THE ROLE OF VERBAL COMMUNICATION IN COMMUNICATING EFFECTIVELY AND STRATEGIC FLEXIBILITY

Communicating Effectively

When you look at the model of communication presented in Chapter 1, it may be too obvious to say that the verbal communication component takes place in the message-feedback element of the model—the words that make up both message and feedback. It may be obvious, but that is far more simplistic than what actually occurs. It overlooks the importance of the senders and receivers. For example, how *you* acquired your ability to use words depended on three factors: (1) native architecture, (2) cognitive development, and (3) environmental influences. See Figure 5-1 for some of the elements involved.

With respect to your native architecture, you can thank the presence of the FOXP2 gene—among others—which enabled the emergence of behaviorally modern humans (those with the ability to use language) somewhere between 120,000 and 200,000 years ago. The fact that the FOXP2 gene makes clear is that as a human being, you have inborn language-transmission and language-acquisition devices—native architecture. This nature architecture transforms the surface structure of language, which appears in

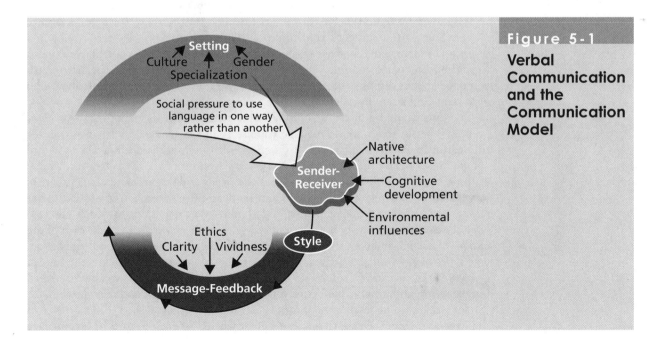

Figure 5-1

Verbal Communication and the Communication Model

the model as message-feedback, into an internal deep structure, which appears in the model as sender-receiver, that you readily understand.

Cognitive development is the development of the thinking and organizing systems of your brain. It involves not only language but also mental imagery, reasoning, problem solving, and memory development. It began well before your birth as your brain took in information and created paths to a storage area for each bit of information.

Much of your brain "wiring" resulted from environmental influences that took place as your parents and siblings played with and had conversations with you, explained what was happening as you went through your days, introduced you to new activities and environments, encouraged you to explore and experiment, gave you choices, read to you, were interested in your interests, let you know it was okay to make mistakes, and loved and were proud of you. This was your language-acquisition support system. You were analyzing language content long before you were discovering and understanding grammatical structures.

Just as your communication with others is directly affected by other senders and receivers, the messages and feedback that take place, and the setting and cultural environment in which they occur, these are also the precise elements that affect its development in you, as noted earlier.

Strategic Flexibility

Verbal communication is a key component in strategic flexibility as well. Edward Sapir (1884–1936)[3] and Benjamin Lee Whorf (1897–1941),[4] Sapir's pupil, proposed a theory, the **Sapir-Whorf hypothesis,** that suggests that the language you use to some extent determines or at least influences the way in which you view and think about the world around you. This simply means that your thoughts are affected by or influenced by your language. When you want to talk about how you feel, you are at the mercy of the language you possess. When you are thinking about something that you have perceived, your linguistic habits predispose certain choices of interpretation. When you see automobiles at an intersection, it is what you know about the red, yellow, and green colored lights that helps you understand what is happening and what the choices are.

It is important to underscore the vital connection that exists between oral language and reading, writing, and critical thinking.[5] An increase in any one area results in a direct and proportional increase in ability and skills in the others. The bottom line is this: The better understanding you have of verbal communication, and the more words you have at your disposal, the more complete will be your ability to think about and view the world around you.

One understanding that the Sapir-Whorf hypothesis instills is that it is a two-way process. That is, the kind of language you use is also influenced by the way you see the world. In the strategic flexibility framework, the more you know about verbal communication, and the more words you have at your disposal, the better you will be at thinking about potential situations and the needs and requirements likely to arise (anticipate)—your view of the world and its possibilities; the better you will be at taking stock of the factors, elements, and conditions of situations in which you find yourself (assessment); the better you will be at determining the value and worth of the factors, elements, and conditions (evaluation); the better you will be at selecting from your repertoire of available skills and behaviors those likely to have the greatest impact (selection); the better you will be at applying the skills and behaviors you have selected (application); and, finally, the better you will be at reassessment and reevaluation.

Here, then, is one fascinating interrelationship, and you can see it in Figure 5-1 in the large arrow from setting to sender-receiver labeled "social pressure." The language of a culture and co-culture together with the unique language of a sender-receiver represent a subtly selective view of the world. This combination of languages and pressures tends to support certain kinds of observations and interpretations and to restrict others. Such transformative power—with the strength of being able to alter your very nature—goes largely unnoticed and, often, even when manifest, retreats to transparency. Thus, the influence of language on strategic flexibility is always present, but is likely to be subtle, difficult to perceive, and often transparent.

HOW WORDS WORK

When you say a word, you are vocally representing something—whether that thing is a physical object, such as your biology textbook, or an abstract concept, such as peace. The word is, as noted in Chapter 1, a symbol: It stands for the object or concept that it names. This is what distinguishes a word from a random sound. The sounds that are represented in our language by the letters *c a t* constitute a word because we have agreed that these sounds will stand for a particular domestic animal. The sounds represented by the letters *z a t* do not make up a word because these sounds do not stand for anything. A word that stands for a concrete and emotionally neutral thing—such as the word *mailbox*—can usually be interpreted with good fidelity because most people respond primarily to its **denotative meaning**—that is, its dictionary definition.

Other words stand for abstract concepts that evoke strong feelings. Words such as *freedom* and *love* are easily misunderstood because they carry a lot of **connotative meaning**—the feelings or associations each individual has about a word. For example, when you hear the word *love*, you don't just think about the word; you probably associate it with a person or an experience you have had. The connotative aspect of words may cause problems in communication because a single word may evoke strong and varied feelings in listeners. Think of the many different reactions people have to the phrases *affirmative action* and *axis of evil*. Figure 5-2 illustrates the difference between connotation and denotation. Notice, too, that your thoughts about the tree are influenced by your language, as discussed in the previous section on strategic flexibility.

Although you need abstract connotative words to express ideas, precise denotative words work best when you want to convey information or get things done—like giving directions or following a recipe. Figure 5-3 shows S. I. Hayakawa's "ladder of abstraction" from his book *Language in Thought and Action*.[6] The **ladder of abstraction** is a diagram of how we abstract through language, classifications, types, categories, and so on. It assists communicators in finding the right rung on the ladder with enough detail (e.g., examples and illustrations) for clarity, yet not so much that the detail gets in the way of the communication. It has been adopted and adapted in hundreds of ways to help people think clearly and express meaning.

At the bottom of the ladder in Figure 5-3 are examples and illustrations. Farmer Jones's Bessie is a single example, and because of language, you can classify, categorize, and label Bessie—due to its similarities and dissimilarities in features to other organisms—as a cow. Such a label raises the level of abstraction from a specific example (Bessie) one rung up on the ladder to a category of animals called cows.

You can observe this particular cow in an environment with other animals such as horses and pigs. One step up on the ladder, in a broader, more abstract, less restrictive classification, you can say this cow is part of Farmer Jones's livestock. His livestock exists within an environment with Farmer Jones's buildings and equipment. Taken together, you move one rung up the ladder of abstraction, and you group his livestock,

Figure 5-2

The Difference between Connotation and Denotation

Your view of the tree

dictionary definition of the tree

Connotation

Denotation

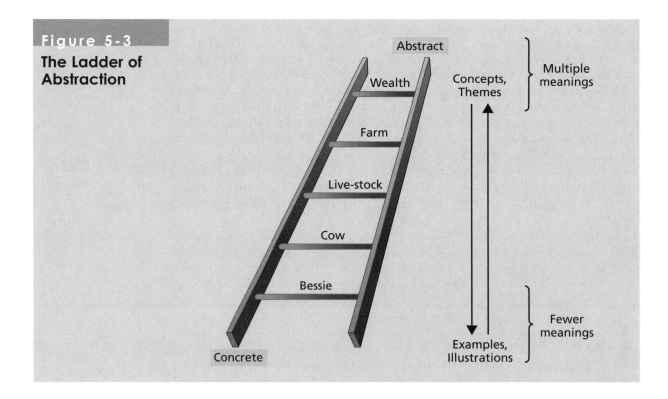

Figure 5-3

The Ladder of Abstraction

Abstract

Wealth

Farm

Live-stock

Cow

Bessie

Concrete

Concepts, Themes

Multiple meanings

Examples, Illustrations

Fewer meanings

buildings, and equipment using a new category or label that is even more abstract—farm. Finally, this farm contributes to an even more abstract classification that you can call Farmer Jones's wealth.

A level 5 abstraction might be people of the world. Level 4 could be U.S. society; level 3 could be people who are dominant in that society; level 2 could be spoiled children; and level 1 could be your brother Tim. The more level 1 abstraction you use in your communication, the more likely you will be understood by your listeners. For example, if you are trying to describe a woman and you mention that she wore Birkenstocks and a jean skirt, you have evoked a specific image in your listener's mind. If, on the other hand, you said the woman was dressed in casual attire—a level 2 abstraction—the listener's impression is not as specific, and he or she is free to interpret your meaning in ways that you may not intend. The woman could be wearing a bathrobe and slippers because that, for some people, is casual attire. Using the levels of abstraction carefully will help convey meaning to your listeners.

Why else is the ladder of abstraction useful? First, it will help you better analyze your communications, understandings, and misunderstandings. If a friend down the hall shouted to you "Hey, your econ book is on the floor at your door," that says something more specific and meaningful to you than if the friend said, "Hey, part of your education is sitting out in the hallway." Notice in this example the words *econ book* were substituted for *Bessie* in Figure 5-3, and *education* was substituted for *wealth.*

Second, it will help you immunize yourself against political propaganda, advertising, and vacant rhetoric (talk that has no substance behind it). If a politician visiting campus said, "And, if elected, I will centralize educational opportunity and expedite a new system of open access," you would quickly notice his or her operation at a high level of abstraction because the politician's words contain no specifics, only generalized, highly abstract references. Recognizing this, you might inquire, "What exactly do you mean? What do you plan to do?" What the candidate might mean is that he or she plans to eliminate the major you are pursuing (centralize educational opportunity) by moving it to another state campus, and lower standards (expedite a new system of open access) by making the state system open to anyone who wishes to attend college—with no prerequisites and no standardized admission tests. This could, you might quickly discover—once the level of abstracted language is reduced—drastically alter the value of your college diploma.

Third, you will make a number of personal adjustments as you become more aware of your own abstracting. You will better differentiate between what happens, what you sense of what happens, what you describe of what your senses sense, and what you infer (a much higher level of abstraction) from what you describe. Think about it this way: What actually happens (e.g., a car accident) to you is concrete and specific—low on the ladder of abstraction. What you sense of what happens (e.g., an interference in your life) depends on your background and experiences and is likely to be high on the ladder of abstraction (abstract) because of all the multiple meanings you use to make meaning of what actually happens (the concrete). Knowing this, to describe what happens, you must make a switch from the interference (abstract) to the accident itself (concrete). What you infer, at an even higher level of abstraction, could include the interference of alcohol, cell phone usage, young, inexperienced drivers, or lousy road signs. Once you realize this, you begin to respond more conditionally to what happens in your life because things are not always what they seem to be. A simple car accident can be road rage, a way to collect on an insurance policy, a mechanical malfunction, or any of a

STRATEGIC **FLEXIBILITY**
Here, then, are a number of adjustments you need to make as you anticipate, assess, evaluate, and select. Delay your responses, leap to fewer conclusions, snap to fewer judgments, and make fewer inappropriate assumptions and the care, concern, and attention required as you apply your skills and behaviors will not just increase, but the entire application step will be more accurate and relevant.

dozen possibilities. You will delay more of your responses, leap to fewer conclusions, snap to fewer judgments, and make fewer inappropriate assumptions.

There are situations when abstract language works best. For example, when you want others to know some general information (like about a dying parent, or a crash that killed a close friend), but details would not be necessary. Here is a story that circulated via the Internet with just the sender's name attached, that reveals the power of abstract over concrete language:

> *The Smiths were proud of their family tradition. Their ancestors had come to America on the Mayflower. They had included senators and Wall Street wizards. They decided to compile a family history, a legacy for their children and grandchildren. They hired a fine author. Only one problem arose—how to handle that great-uncle George, who was executed in the electric chair. The author said he could handle the story tactfully. The book appeared. It said, "Great-uncle George occupied a chair of applied electronics at an important government institution, was attached to his position by the strongest of ties, and his death came as a great shock."[7]*

When you study a language, whether it is your native tongue or a foreign one, you must learn what the words stand for; that is, you have to know both their denotative and their connotative meanings. You must also know how to put the words together to make the phrases and sentences that express relationships between the words. This is the *grammar* of a language.

Because the United States has been a one-language nation, many Americans do not understand how language and perception of the world are connected. Americans sometimes complain that immigrants to the United States do not learn and use English. However, if you accept the theory that language influences your world and your perception of it, you see that learning a language is not just a matter of learning a sign system: It is also learning a different way of looking at the world. For example, one of your authors taught a student who had immigrated to the United States when she was a child. Although she was fluent in English, she said she always prayed in Polish; if she used English, the prayer didn't seem real to her.

PEOPLE DETERMINE MEANINGS

For the listener to understand what you intend, you should have something definite in mind. If an idea or impression is vague, the resulting message will be confused and ambiguous. Understanding is the core of meaning, and understanding is a two-way process; that is, you are responsible for presenting the idea clearly, and the listener is responsible for trying to understand it accurately. Meanings are ultimately determined by people, not by words.

When speaking of some subjects, you have to use a very specialized vocabulary. As Mary Boone, in her book *Managing Interactively* says, "The accountants have their language, the marketing people have their language, the businesspeople have their language, the IT people have their language. . . . That's what they've gotten their degrees in."[8] Here is how Keith Moffatt and Ytaka Shimomura, mathematicians, explain the forces at work on a spinning egg: "We may note that a raw egg does not rise when spun, simply because the angular velocity imparted to the shell must diffuse into the fluid interior; this process dissipates most of the initial kinetic energy imparted to the egg, the remaining energy being insufficient for . . . the state of gyroscopic balance to be established."[9]

You have undoubtedly had the experience of going home from college and talking with friends or family members who did not go to college. Often, the difference can be detected in vocabulary alone. Sometimes your friends or family members who did not go to college will be put off by your use of words that you have recently picked up from your psychology or sociology courses, from your political discussions with your college friends, or from lectures, speeches, and your extensive reading of college textbooks and related information. Your use of newly acquired words is healthy because it is only through use that new vocabulary is obtained and exact meanings for those words is applied. Your new vocabulary also will help you access an even greater amount of information, for it makes both reading and listening more comfortable and enjoyable.

New meanings are continually created by all of us as we change our ideas, our feelings, and our activities. As we think, read, travel, make friends, and experience life, the associations and connections that words have for us are changed.

THE LANGUAGE ENVIRONMENT

All language takes place within a particular environment. A minister speaks in the environment of a church; two friends have a conversation in the student center; an instructor gives a lecture in a classroom. Language that is appropriate to one environment might appear meaningless or foolish in another. The language you use in a dormitory, for example, might be completely inappropriate in a classroom or at home.

People, Purposes, and Rules

According to Neil Postman, who writes about language and education, the **language environment** is made up of four elements: people, their purpose, the rules of communication by which they achieve their purpose, and the actual talk used in the situation.[10] To illustrate these elements, let's take the simple example of John and Mary, who greet each other:

Mary:	Hi. How are you?
John:	Fine. How are you?
Mary:	Good.

The rules for this sort of conversation are known to you, since you often participate in it yourself. If John had failed to follow the rules, however, and had stopped to talk for five minutes about how miserable he felt, Mary might have been annoyed. John would have gone beyond the limits of that sort of conversation.

The kind of conversation Mary and John had illustrates language as a ritual. **Ritual language** takes place in environments where a conventionalized response is expected of you.[11] Greetings are a ritual; you briefly respond to someone—usually only half listening to what the other person has said—and then go about your business.

The rituals you use are determined by the language environment. If you are at a baptism or *bris,* you are expected to say how good-looking the child is or how well he or she behaved during the service. At a wedding you wish the couple happiness and tell the bride she looks beautiful.

Every society's language rituals are determined by the cultural values of that society. In rural East Africa, it would be rude to pass a man you know well with a brief "Hello." You are expected to stop and inquire about the person, his home, his livestock, and his health. In some cultures it is appropriate to tell a couple at their wedding that you hope they will have many sons; in American society, such a comment would be considered inappropriate.

You learn ritualized language when you are very young, from your parents or other adults around you. Researchers have found that young children do not automatically make the conventional responses of "Hi," "Good-bye," or "Thanks"—even though they hear adults doing so. If children are going to use these conventional terms, they must be taught.[12]

As children grow older, they begin to learn and use ritual language. Anyone who has handed out candy on Halloween can tell you that although the younger children may have to be prompted, this is no longer necessary with the older children; they offer their thanks spontaneously.

Appropriate Language

For any society to function it must have some sort of understanding about which words are inappropriate. As children grow up, they try out the new words they hear and, from the reactions of the adults around them, learn the words they shouldn't use. Generally, Americans (and probably most cultures) would agree that the following are inappropriate: First are racial or ethnic epithets against members of groups to which you do not belong. For example a white person should never use the word *nigger* to describe an African American. African Americans, however, can use this word within their own culture because in that context it has a different emotional meaning. Second are words that insult others' appearance or behavior. These words may range from *stupid* or *ugly* to *clumsy* or *incompetent*. Third are words that are blasphemous (religious words) or obscene (body-function words). Fourth are aggressive words intended to control others, such as *shut up* or *drop dead*. Words in any of these categories are highly loaded, emotional words that can do serious damage to human relationships.

Sometimes you have to refer to something for which it would be impolite to use the direct word. To do this you use a **euphemism**—an inoffensive word or phrase that is substituted for other words that might be perceived as unpleasant. For example, you ask "Where's your bathroom?" even when you don't intend to take a bath. If somebody has died, you might use the phrase "passed away." In one instance, when a restaurant in Taiwan wanted to serve dog meat, the owners knew that it would offend some people, and so rather than admit what it was, they called it "fragrant meat." Closer to home, you call your own meat "beef," "veal," and "pork" to veil that it is really dead cow, calf, and pig.

Whereas euphemisms are substitutions for unpleasant words, **doublespeak** refers to words deliberately constructed for political purposes—words specifically intended to impose a desirable mental attitude on those using them. Doublespeak and euphemisms are identical except for two things: (1) Doublespeak does not always have to do with unpleasant words, and (2) doublespeak always relates to a political agenda. For example, the military used *aerial ordinance* for bombs and missiles. George W. Bush used *axis of evil* to refer to countries to be attacked (Iran, North Korea, and Syria). The words *collateral damage* have been used to refer to bystander casualties, ecological destruction, and environmental contamination that result from war. *Freedom fighters* are terrorists with whom our government agrees; *rogue nations* are enemies, usually ones that are not aligned with a group of other nations in agreements that regard the conduct of warfare.[13]

You learn appropriate language as you become more sophisticated and mature. By the time you reach late adolescence, you probably know what language to use for a particular language environment. Whether you want to use the prescribed words is largely irrelevant. The language environment dictates the language that is expected of you. If you violate these expectations, you run the risk of having people respond to you negatively.

Specialization

Most language environments have words that are specialized and are used only in those environments. If your plumber tells you that your toilet needs a new sleeve gasket, you probably won't know what that means. You would understand if the plumber told you that the toilet needs a new seal at the bottom to keep the water from leaking out onto

Here, now, is an opportunity for your group to make a significant contribution to the whole world. Based on the combined backgrounds and experiences of the members of your group, you are to combine all of your knowledge and expertise to establish a set of rules for members of *your* generation. We will call these rules "Handy Reminders for Comfortable Communication." These are rules that could be distributed to every member of your generation that would absolutely ensure the use of appropriate language.

Come up with as many rules as you can given the amount of time you have. Then, as you have established the fundamental rules, arrange them in the order of most importance, with the most important rules at the top of your list. Brainstorm, first, for rules on which every member of the group can agree. Arrange them only after a set of 5 to 10 rules has been agreed upon.

the floor. Most professions and occupations have a language that only its practitioners understand. Professional cooks make a *roux*, teachers write up their *behavioral objectives*, and contractors install *I-beams*. Members of an occupational group must learn their specialized language to master their field.

Some language environments can be specialized even if the communicators are trying to reach a mass audience. For example, if you watch a jewelry show on a home shopping network on television, you soon discover that there are many words for describing jewelry. For example, the clasp used to keep the jewelry on your body may be a *lobster claw clasp*, a *box closure*, or a *snap bar* closure. Do you want a *faceted stone*, an *emerald cut*, or a *diamond cut?* You can't make choices until you learn this language. The language of the Internet is an excellent example of specialization.

Other groups develop a language that is never intended to be understood by outsiders. Car salespersons, for example, have many words for describing customers who are out of earshot. A *tire-kicker* is a person who pretends expertise but has none. A *roach*, *flake*, or *stoker* is a person with a bad credit rating, while a *be-back* is a customer who promises to return but probably won't.[14] Sometimes people create a special language when they feel they don't have as much power as the people around them. Quite often it is a language that those in power do not understand, and it is deliberately used to keep information from them. Students, especially those in high school and college, are one example of special-language groups. They use slang or a special meaning to exclude outsiders or members of the adult establishment. When away from adults, they may also use some of the language the culture considers inappropriate.

When a group has created a special language, you usually cannot step into that group and use its language unless you have some legitimate claim to membership. Students, for example, might secretly make fun of a teacher who tries to talk as they do. How you are expected to speak in a language environment depends on the role you are playing.

Whenever you shift roles, you shift your language environment and your speech as well. Let's say that in a single day you talk to your roommate, you go to class, and you speak to your mother on the telephone. Your role has shifted three times: from peer relating to peer, to student relating to instructor, to child relating to parent. Each circumstance has entailed a different language environment, and you have probably changed your speech accordingly—perhaps without even realizing it.

The important thing to remember about a language environment is that you must choose language that is appropriate to it. The language used in one environment usually does not work in another. When you think about the environment, you need to ask yourself who it is you are going to be talking with and in what context your language is going to be used. If you don't adapt to the environment, your language will not work, and you will lose the chance for effective communication.

STYLE, ROLES, AND GROUP MEMBERSHIPS

The words you use are determined by all your past experiences, by everything in your individual history. Stephen King, in his book *On Writing,* says it this way: "You undoubtedly have your own thoughts, interests, and concerns, and they have arisen, as mine have, from your experiences and adventures as a human being."[15] You learn words to express thoughts, and thought and language develop together, as discussed in the section on cognitive development at the beginning of this chapter. The way you think and the way you talk are unique; they form a distinctive pattern. In a sense, you are what you say because language is the chief means of conveying your thoughts. Neither language nor thought can be viewed in isolation because they are so interrelated. Together, they determine your verbal style.

Sheryl Perlmutter Bowen, a teacher of communication and women's studies at Villanova University, describes her own language and verbal style in this way: "My own speech . . . is often marked by a preference for personal topics, abrupt topic shifts, storytelling (in which the preferred point is the teller's emotional experience), a fast rate of speech, avoidance of inter-turn pauses, quick turn-taking, expressive phonology, pitch and amplitude shifts, marked voice quality, and strategic within-turn pauses. Given these characteristics," she adds, "my complaining and teasing should both be seen as normal interaction strategies."[16]

Style is the result of the way you select and arrange words and sentences. People choose different words to express their thoughts, and every individual has a unique verbal style. Not only do styles vary among people, but each person uses different styles to suit different situations. In the pulpit, a minister usually has a scholarly and formal style. At a church dinner, however, his or her style is likely to be informal and casual. When a football player signs autographs for fans, he speaks to them in the role of athlete—even though he might drop this role when he is with friends and family.

Sometimes style can negate a communicator's other good qualities. You probably know someone who is extremely shy and speaks in a faltering manner. You might also know some people who can never seem to get to the point. If you are critical of these people, it is probably because of their style.

Style, because of its power and influence, is just as important to the acceptance of ideas as all the other aspects of communication. Even if you have the proper information, the right occasion, and a listener interested in your message, what you have to say may be lost if your style is inappropriate.

Impressions of personality are often related to verbal style. When you characterize a person as formal and aloof, your impression is due in part to the way that person talks. Since your style partially determines whether others accept or reject you, it also influences how others receive your messages. Style is so important that it can influence people's opinion of you, win their friendship, lose their respect, or sway them to your ideas.

Like language environment, verbal style is often connected with the roles you play. Professionals, for example, are expected to speak grammatically correct English—both in private and in professional life. A college student is also expected to use correct grammar. Yet if he takes a factory job during summer vacation, using correct grammar might get him into trouble with his fellow workers, for his verbal style could identify him as a "college kid."

Gender and Language

Sociolinguist Deborah Tannen has found that men and women have almost completely different styles of speaking.[17] In fact, she maintains that their languages are so different that they might as well come from different worlds. According to Tannen, when women have conversations, they use the language of **rapport-talk.** This language is designed to lead to intimacy with others, to match experiences, and to establish relationships. Men, however, speak **report-talk.** In this type of speech the speaker's goal is to maintain status, to demonstrate knowledge and skills, and to keep the center-stage position.[18] Because of their different ways of speaking, men and women often have problems when they try to talk to each other, Tannen says. For example, a stock cartoon shows a man and woman at the breakfast table, with the man reading the newspaper and the woman trying to get his attention. The man is using the newspaper as a source of information he needs for future report-talks. The woman, however, is looking for interaction, or rapport-talk.

Tannen also says that men are more likely than women to look at problems in terms of "fixing them." A woman, for example, might tell her husband that someone insulted her. Her husband's reaction is to take revenge as a way of fixing the problem. For the woman, this probably is not a satisfactory solution; she would prefer a statement of understanding or an expression of empathy from him.[19]

Other researchers have also looked at differences between the way men and women interact. They have found that when men and women talk together, men are more likely to interrupt ("Let's go on to the next topic") and give directives ("Why don't you write this down?"). Women use more personal pronouns and more intensive adverbs ("I really like her"). The researchers also found that women use more questions and more justifiers ("The reason I say this . . . ").[20]

Tannen believes that gender differences in language are important considerations in the college classroom. In a typical classroom, she says, male students are likely to say what they know before the whole class and to welcome arguments and challenges from their classmates. They are also likely to reject anecdotal information as unimportant. Female students, on the other hand, do not find much pleasure in verbal conflict and are much more comfortable when they work in small groups and offer personal anecdotes. Since most classrooms are organized on the male model, Tannen believes that many women find the classroom to be a hostile space.[21]

An interesting example of gender differences in language occurred when a teacher asked her students to make up words that described experiences unique to their sex but that did not already exist in English. She found that women's and men's words were in entirely different categories. Women created words that tended to put women into passive roles, such as *perchaphonic* ("waiting for someone to phone you") and *herdastuda-phobia* ("fear when passing a group of strange men"). Men, however, created words that focused on competency and the power to change things, such as *gearheaditis* ("making your car the best on the road") and *beer muscles* ("believing you are tough after you have had something to drink").[22]

Where does gender-specific language come from? Tannen believes that it begins in childhood and that children learn it from their peers. She reports that one researcher who observed preschool children found that when the children wanted to do something, the girls would start with, "Let's . . . " while the boys would give direct commands, "Sit down."[23] In looking at videotapes of second-graders, Tannen says that in language and behavior, second-grade girls were more similar to adult women than they were to second-grade boys.[24] When the same second-graders were put in pairs and were asked to talk about "something serious," the girls did so. The boys, however, resisted or mocked authority.[25] Since language behavior starts so young, it's not surprising that it soon becomes automatic.

While some scholars have criticized the emphasis put on differences between male and female language because they feel that those who do the studies often interpret the results in a way that reinforces stereotypes society already holds about men and women, others attempt to explain the female advantage in language aptitude. In her

Some Criticisms of Tannen's Work

Seems to be based on anecdotes.

Seems to overgeneralize.

Seems to consider only white middle-class women and men.

Seems to focus on heterosexual women and men.

Sees problems in relationships between men and women as based in difference and not dominance.

Seems to ignore political and economic differences between men and women.

Relies on individuals' intentions ("He didn't intend to dominate") rather than on facts and also others' interpretations.

Tries to separate dominance and gendered culture. Doesn't explain why men and women have these different styles.

Questions

1. To what extent does criticism of an author automatically convey truth? How difficult would it be to verify the criticisms of Tannen's work?

2. Does criticism of a work nullify the value of or findings in that work? To what extent do sales of a work or the effect of a work mitigate (cause to become less harsh or harmful) criticism of that work?

3. If you were the author of a criticized work, how would you go about addressing that criticism?

Source: "Language and Gender" (1998) University of Colorado. Retrieved July 27, 2002, from **http://www.colorado.edu/ linguistics/sp98/2400/tannen.hyp**

book *The War Against Boys*, Christina Hoff Sommers—the W. H. Brady Fellow at the American Enterprise Institute in Washington, DC, who has a PhD in philosophy from Brandeis University and was formerly professor of philosophy at Clark University—offers research to support her contention that physiological sex differences correlate with differences in preferences and aptitudes. She cites the research of Bennett and Sally Shaywitz, neuroscientists at Yale University.[27] Using brain-imaging technologies—specifically functional magnetic resonance imaging (MRI)—to look for sex differences in the brain, they gave 19 men and 19 women volunteer subjects a simple language task. "In both men and women," writes Sommers, "the front of the cortex in the left hemisphere lit up brightly, indicating that to be the area where this task is carried out. But in 11 of the 19 women—and none of the men—an area in the right hemisphere also lit up. If two parts of the female brain focus on language, this might explain the female advantage in this area".[28]

Michael Gurian, in his book *What Could He Be Thinking?*, gives further evidence of the role that gender plays in language. The cerebral cortex is the area of the brain known for transforming emotion into thought. Females use more cortical areas for verbal experience (talking, writing, and reading), and they turn their experiences into emotive verbal responses. "Because the female brain does language in about seven brain centers, whereas the male brain does it in only one or two," Gurian notes, "there is a greater tendency in the female brain to process all of its experience, including emotive experiences, by using words."[29]

Powerful Talk

Powerful talk is talk that comes directly to the point—talk that does not use hesitation or qualifications. People who engage in powerful talk are found to be more credible, more attractive, and more persuasive than those who do not.[30] In the college classroom, teachers who used powerful language are considered by their students to be more believable and to have more status.[31]

Powerful talk is characterized by the *nonexistence* of certain communication behaviors. First, hedges and qualifiers—expressions such as "I guess" and "kind of"—weaken the power of speech. Hesitation forms such as "uh" and "you know" make speakers sound too uncertain. Third, tag questions—comments that start out as statements but end as questions ("It would be nice to go on a picnic, wouldn't it?") make speakers seem less assertive. Finally, disclaimers—words and expressions that excuse or ask listeners to bear with the speaker—weaken communications. Examples are "I know you probably don't agree with me, but . . . " or "I'm really not prepared to speak today."[32]

The number of women in powerful positions is increasing steadily, but it has been a struggle for them. Why has there been a struggle? Supreme Court Justice Sandra Day O'Connor says that "In the past there was a widespread belief—declining today, but certainly still there—that women are unfit for power positions." Whether it has to do with powerful talk or assertiveness, O'Connor says "The image of the aggressive leader does not lie easily with traditional notions of femininity."[33]

Many of us dilute our conversations and speeches with powerless words and expressions. However, the use of these expressions is mainly a matter of habit. Once you recognize your bad habits, you can start to break them.

Besides using powerful language, you can use several other techniques to make your language more lively. A sense of urgency is communicated mainly by verbs—the action words of language. "Judy slapped him" and "The children jumped up and down" are both sentences that sound energetic. Language is also livelier when you put sentences in the active rather than the passive voice. "The boy hit the ball" is more energetic than "The ball was hit by the boy."

Culture and Language

The number of U.S. residents age five and older speaking a language other than English at home jumped from 32 million in 1990 to 47 million in 2000. That means that nearly one in five Americans speak a language other than English at home and the top five languages, excluding English, are Spanish, Chinese, French, German, and Tagalog (Philippines). The difference between those speaking Spanish (28.1 million) and those speaking Chinese (2 million) is enormous. School districts are scrambling to find bilingual instructors, governments are looking for ways to help those who don't speak English well, and more and more companies are diversifying their advertising and marketing campaigns to reach people who speak other languages.[34] Why wouldn't companies want to diversify? African Americans and Latinos/Latinas account for one-quarter of department store sales, according to strategic marketing communications agency Meridian.[35]

Although English is unlikely to become the world's dominant language, it will remain one of its most important languages. For routine language, people will probably switch between two or more languages, but, according to British language expert David Graddol, "English-only speakers may find it difficult to participate in a multilingual society."[36] "In 1995, English trailed Chinese as the most common native language. Native English speakers were 9% of the world. That is expected to fall to 5% by 2050," Graddol said, "as Arabic and Hindi-Urdu overtake English."[37]

Why is an understanding of the impact of culture on language important? The following are stories cited by Marilyn Carlson Nelson, chair and CEO of the Carlson Companies, in her speech "On the Path." She says that Chevrolet tried to launch its Nova car in Latin America where *Nova* in Spanish actually means "no go." The successful "Got Milk?" campaign was almost trashed when the translation for "Got Milk?" was discovered to mean "Are You Lactating?" When the phrase "Pepsi, the choice of a new generation" was translated into Chinese, it came out as "Pepsi, the drink that will awaken your ancestors from the dead." Buick planned to launch its new Lacrosse in Quebec, until it learned that the name was Quebec slang for sexual self-gratification. These examples simply underscore the importance of understanding how culture affects language and language choices.[38]

Dialect

Toward the end of the summer in central Pennsylvania, many cooks begin to fry or preserve "mangoes." Outsiders are always surprised that Pennsylvania cooks are so interested in this tropical fruit. What they don't know is that in that part of the country a mango isn't a fruit at all; it's what everyone else calls a green pepper or a bell pepper. The central Pennsylvanians' use of the word *mango* is an example of dialect.

A **dialect** is the habitual language of a community. It is distinguished by unique grammatical structures, words, and figures of speech. The community members who use the dialect may be identified by region or by such diverse factors as education, social class, or cultural background. Many people will hold on to their dialects because they are a tie to their own community. See Figure 5-4 for some examples of dialects.

When radio and television became widespread, linguists predicted that their popularity might herald the end of dialect because people would imitate the standard American speech they heard on these media. However, it didn't work that way. Linguists have found that dialect is growing stronger, especially in many urban areas.[39]

It is important to understand what a dialect is and is not. Clearly it is *not* Mexican-Americans living in a Mexican-American neighborhood in Dallas, Texas, using a dialect when they speak Spanish to each other. But, what if an American from the south, who learned Spanish in high school, went into this Mexican-American neighborhood in Dallas, Texas, and talked with the Mexican-Americans living there? This American would likely speak his or her high-school learned Spanish using his or her Southern dialect of American English. True to his or her background, this American would *not* have the variations of idiom, vocabulary (or phonemes [units of sound] and morphemes [meaningful units]) peculiar to the Mexican-Americans from the neighborhood. He or she could not. His or her language would quickly reveal itself to the Mexican-Americans from the neighborhood as "off their standard"—an imperfect use of the standard language used by those Mexican-Americans from the neighborhood for whom Spanish is their native language.

Any language (French, German, Spanish, etc.) learned solely in the classroom will retain recognizable elements of the parent language, but it will have distinctive vocabulary, pronunciation, forms, and idiom that will quickly distinguish it as a linguistic branch of—and not the same as—the parent language. It is exactly the same as when the person, above, speaking Spanish using his or her Southern dialect of American English, traveled north in the U.S. and found him- or herself anywhere in the north using the Southern dialect of American English. The Southern dialect would have similar distinctions to his or her Spanish, from people in the north who speak American English.

Although there are no clear-cut rules for where and when it is appropriate to use a dialect, it is possible to make some generalizations. A dialect is appropriate in a group with a strong ethnic identity, but it may be inappropriate in situations where standard English is used. Linguistic scholars agree that some dialects have more prestige than others and that prestige is determined by both the people who speak the dialect and those who hear it. Thus, if you want to be accepted by and identified with people who use a dialect or who use a standard English different from your own, you might have to adapt to their way of speaking. Many people in America have discovered that it is not difficult to speak two "languages," a dialect and standard English. By so doing, they find it possible to keep their ethnic identity as well as function in a world where expectations are different.

Speaking and Writing

We use language in both speaking and writing, but the transactional nature of speaking makes it very different from writing.

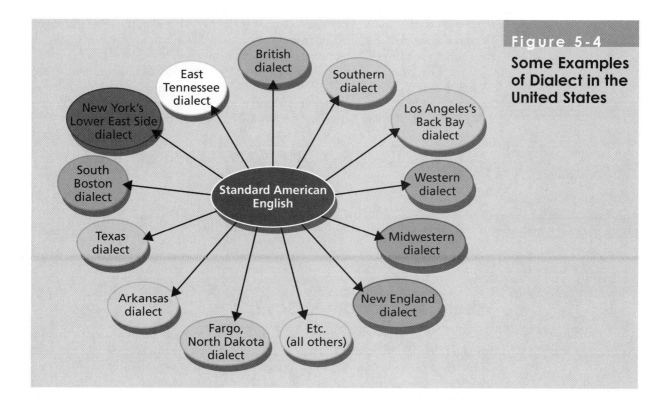

Figure 5-4

Some Examples of Dialect in the United States

When two people are engaged in conversation, they interact continuously and simultaneously. Both get and give information, form impressions, and respond to each other. On the basis of each other's responses, both can change their comments to explain, backtrack, hurry up, slow down, or do whatever is necessary to be understood.

Sometimes conversation reflects the participants' past knowledge of each other. They can use a kind of shorthand because of the experiences they've had together. If you are in a close relationship or desire one, you know that the words you speak may affect your present and future relationship. If the relationship is more impersonal, the choice of words might not be so important.

You also are able to change your language to reflect the circumstances. When you get negative feedback, you can change language to appease your listeners. You can use simpler words or concepts if listeners don't seem to understand. Spoken language is also accompanied by **paralanguage**—vocal cues, or the way you say your words. For example, your meaning can be influenced by your pitch and rate (high and fast if you are excited), your volume, and how often you pause. This kind of adaptation occurs in every conversation. Whether you are talking to your father, a professor, or a friend, your language will reflect your impression of this person, the kinds of experiences you have had together, and the role you are playing.

In contrast, it's not so easy to change your written language. In fact, writers have an entirely different set of problems than speakers do. When you are speaking, people are reacting to you as the message occurs. For writers, reaction from their audience is unusual, and they have no way of knowing if they have pleased or offended someone, or if they have even communicated their ideas. This means that their words must be chosen very carefully. Also, they have time to go over their words, polish their phrases, and check their grammar. Their readers have more time too. They can always reread the words if they're not clear the first time. Writers are more likely to use a larger vocabulary than speakers do, and readers can look up the words if they don't understand them. Writers do not have the paralanguage of speakers to add to their meaning. If the words they choose don't work, their attempt at communication fails.

Writers have no way of taking the future effects of their words into account. When an Indian author, Salman Rushdie, wrote *The Satanic Verses,* he could not predict that his words would be seen as blasphemous and would be condemned by an Iranian religious leader, who "gave permission" for any Moslem to kill the author.

WORKING ON YOUR COMMUNICATION

When you set out to communicate verbally, you are more likely to be successful if you use words and ideas that have the same meaning to the person with whom you are communicating as they do to you. Sometimes, although you think you are being clear, the other person might not perceive what you think you have communicated.

Communication can go awry at various stages. Let's look at some of the places where this might happen.

What Do You Want to Say?

In 1938, Orson Welles broadcast *The War of the Worlds,* a radio play about martians invading the United States. You can assume that in writing this play, Welles intended to entertain his audience. Although Welles's intent was clear to him, at least one million people misunderstood it and believed that the play was real. They believed that martians really had landed and that their lives were in peril. By the time the network announced that the broadcast was only a play, many people had already reacted to it by fleeing their homes to find a place of safety.

Although this is an extreme example of intent going astray, most of us have had times when people's responses were different from those we intended. You intend to tell your roommate to meet you at 7:00, but she thinks you said 7:30. You intend to make a joke, but you end up insulting someone. When you are involved in one-to-one communication, you often have a chance to clear up misunderstandings. If you see that the other person looks confused or annoyed or if the response you get indicates that you have not communicated something as precisely as you had intended, you can attempt to clarify what you said.

When you are talking to an audience, however, it is not so easy to clear up misunderstandings. In a public-speaking or mass-communication setting, you may not have a chance to respond to feedback or you may not be able to respond until the communication is over. Therefore, when you are going to communicate to a large audience, you must prepare your words much more carefully than you do in an interpersonal setting.

The first thing you must consider is, What exactly do you want to say? Students who are new to public speaking often do not think through this step clearly enough. Speakers who do not know precisely what they want to say frequently end up confusing their audience. The same may happen if they have not clearly thought out their words.

How Do You Want to Say It?

Although you are often told that you should make careful language choices, you might not know how to go about doing so. Command of language requires years of practice and study. Since it is impossible to lay down strict rules that govern the choice of language for all occasions and for all circumstances, the discussion here is limited to three important aspects of language choice: clarity, vividness, and ethics.

What are your perceptions of people who use English that is different from your own? Let's say the person has difficulty speaking the language correctly—as you have come to understand it. In her book *The Opposite of Fate*, Amy Tan talks about the perceptions others have of her mother who uses "broken" or "fractured" English:

I know this for a fact, because when I was growing up, my mother's "limited" English limited my perception of her. I was ashamed of her English. I believed that her English reflected the quality of what she had to say. That is, because she expressed them imperfectly, her thoughts were imperfect. And I had plenty of empirical evidence to support me: the fact that people in department stores, at banks, and in restaurants did not take her seriously, did not give her good service, pretended not to understand her, or even acted as if they did not hear her.

Source: *The Opposite of Fate: A Book of Musings* (p. 274), by Amy Tan, 2003, New York: Putnam's Sons.

Questions

1. When you speak imperfectly—using improper or broken English—do you think it influences others in negative ways?

2. Do you think there might be a relationship, as indicated in Tan's quote, between ideas expressed imperfectly and imperfect thoughts?

3. What means do people who use imperfect English have to discover that they are using imperfect English? When it is discovered, how can they improve their use of English? Do you think such improvement is advantageous, or do you think people should not worry about it?

Clarity

A pilot died in the crash of a private jet because the instructions on how to open the emergency door were so unclear that she could not get it open. Although a lack of clarity is usually not a matter of life or death, it can lead to frustration and misunderstanding. In most situations, you have to speak as clearly as possible if you want to be understood. **Clarity** is that aspect or characteristic of style by means of which a thought is so presented that it is immediately understood, depending on the precision and simplicity of the language. Clarity is especially important when there is little opportunity for feedback. For example, if you are saying something of special importance, making a formal speech, or being interviewed by the media, clarity is essential since you will probably not get another chance.

Jargon is a language that can be so specialized that it is inappropriate to use it outside the field where it originated. Emanuel Rosen, in his book *The Anatomy of Buzz*, writes this about the use of jargon: "From ancient fortified cities to current gated communities, people have always put walls and other barriers around themselves to keep intruders away to differentiate themselves from others. Networks have their own walls and fences, but instead of wire or bricks, people use dialect, jargon, and acronyms to keep strangers out."[40] Physicians often use a highly specialized language to describe illnesses and injuries. Although doctors can communicate with each other, sometimes they have problems communicating with patients because of the walls and fences. Many newspapers carry a column in which a physician answers questions from readers who do not understand what their own doctors told them—a way to break down the walls and add gates to the fences.

Other language that might not be clear to everyone is slang. Slang has its place when you are talking informally with your friends. However, many slang words have such broad and vague meanings that they could apply to almost anything. If you use the word *cool* to compliment someone's shirt and use it again to describe beautiful scenery, you reduce everything to a common element.

Sometimes people feel that if they have taken the trouble to learn long and complicated words, they should use them whenever they can. On a bottle of fluoride solution, the consumer is advised to "hold the solution in the mouth for one minute and then expectorate." In case the consumer doesn't understand the word *expectorate*, the phrase *spit it out* follows in parentheses. Since the purpose of this message is to communicate with the consumer, the simpler words, *spit it out,* should have been used in the first place.

Use more complicated words only when they help make your meaning clearer. For example, if you want your car painted red, you'll be happier with the final results if you use a more precise description than *red.* What shade do you prefer? Burgundy? Crimson? Vermilion? Garnet?

When you increase your vocabulary, you increase your chances of getting your intended meaning across to your listener. The more words you have at your command, the more precise you will be. This does not mean that you should search for big words; on the contrary, familiar words are often the best.

One of the delights of language is that it offers you many subtleties and shades of meaning. Choosing the same words to express all your ideas is like eating a Big Mac for dinner every night. Language is a marvelous banquet providing you with a vast array of choices for anything and everything you want to say.

Vividness

Remember those ghost stories you heard when you were a child? The best ones were those that filled you with terror—the ones laced with bloodcurdling shrieks, mournful moans, mysterious howling. They were usually set in dark places, with only an occasional eerie light or a streak of lightning. If any smells were mentioned, they were sure to be dank and musty.

The teller of a ghost story usually speaks in the first person. Any narrative told from the point of view of "I was there" or "It happened to me" is particularly vivid. By recreating an experience for your listeners, you can often make them feel what you felt. **Vividness** is the aspect or characteristic of style by which a thought is so presented that it evokes lifelike imagery or suggestion.

Vividness also comes from unique forms of speech. Some people would say that a person who talks too much "chatters like a magpie," a phrase that has become a cliché. To one Southern speaker, however, this person "makes a lot of chin music." When we say that language is vivid, we often mean that someone has found a new way of saying old things. Children often charm us with the uniqueness of their language because they are too young to know all the clichés and overused expressions. Another place to look for vivid language is in poetry and song. Although more words have been written about love than any other subject, many songwriters have given us new expressions and therefore new ways of looking at the experience. Their unique perspectives make an old idea sound original and exciting.

To Whom Are You Talking?

STRATEGIC FLEXIBILITY
Your success in being strategically flexible rests on this aspect: *Know* to whom you are talking. Your sensitivity to other people—along with your awareness of language choice and use—will largely determine your communication effectiveness.

As you talk to people, become conscious of them as particular individuals for whom you need to adapt your message. Note the language environment in which your conversation is taking place, and make the adjustments that are necessary. Also, when you are talking about a particular subject, see if you can find words that are unique to the subject—even if you have to define them. Often, learning about a subject is also learning the vocabulary of the subject. Be conscious of what you are saying. This added consciousness will increase your sensitivity to other people as well as your awareness of language choice and use.

Sometimes people confuse personal authenticity with inflexible language usage, and they equate undisciplined speech with spontaneity. "Telling it like it is" becomes an excuse for allowing the first words that come into your head to spill out in a torrent. Such language choices reflect a kind of self-centered indulgence that says to your listener, "Never mind who you are—listen to me." Adapting your language to the individual with whom you are talking can result in a more satisfying exchange.

What Metamessages Are You Sending?

You probably choose your words carefully when you are making a public presentation. It might not occur to you, however, to be so careful when you are talking to a friend or conversing with a small group of people. Yet you might occasionally have had a conversation that made you feel uneasy—the words all sounded right, but there was something else going on.

In such cases, you need to think about the **metamessage** (sometimes called *subtext*)— the meaning apart from what actual words express. For example, when one spouse tells the other, "We need to talk," he or she really might be saying, "I want to complain."

Metamessages take many forms. At a graduation ceremony, the president of the university introduced everyone on the stage except one of the deans. The dean realized that this was more than a simple oversight, that he might be in serious trouble. He was right: he was fired the next term.

Many metamessages don't involve words at all. Deborah Tannen believes that American men refuse to ask directions because it puts them in an inferior position and the person they ask in a superior position.[41]

Sometimes metamessages are recognizable to people within a specific culture but not to outsiders. A Polish professor complained that when she was in the United States, one of her American colleagues kept saying, "Let's have lunch sometime." When she tried to pin him down, he looked annoyed. What she didn't realize until much later was that this is an expression that some Americans use to terminate a conversation.

Language is filled with metamessages, and you have to listen for this kind of talk and understand its meaning if you are going to have accurate communication. You also should be aware of the metamessages you yourself send. For example, it is not unusual for a student speaker to begin a speech by implying that the speech will not be very good: "I just finished this speech this morning," "I couldn't find any research on this topic," or "You'll have to excuse me because I am feeling sick." If you say anything of this sort, you may be engaging in a metamessage; what you may really be saying is, "I am feeling extremely nervous and anxious about giving this speech."

Ethics

Ray Penn, a communications professor, points out that "a choice of words is a choice of worlds."[42] He reminds us that we can cause considerable damage to others by choosing the wrong words. For example, if you are asked to remember your most painful moment, the response will most likely be something someone said.

Penn asks us to consider whether "our analogies create a self-fulfilling prophecy that will ultimately keep us from relating to others unless we get our way." For example, how often in life do you talk of "winners" and "losers," condemning the losers to permanent failure? On the international scene, does calling Osama bin Laden "another Hitler" create a self-fulfilling prophecy? When political figures in the Middle East refer to the United States as "Satan" or "the devil," does such labeling influence the way we, as a country, react to them?

Penn also reminds us that language choices can influence people's perceptions of themselves. Insulting words, he points out, can reduce an individual to a mere trait ("dyke," "queer"); they can reduce someone to less-than-human status ("pig," "chicken"); or they can tell the person "I know all about you and you have no mystery" by means of labels ("hillbilly," "redneck," "geek").[43]

Penn reminds us that we make moral choices when we choose the language we are going to use. Many of the choices you make not only determine how you present yourself to others but also decide the nature of your relationships in the years to come. For this reason, it is important that you choose your words wisely and well.

THE INTERNET AND VERBAL COMMUNICATION

Besides the globalization and subsequent multilingualization (one-quarter of the world's languages—about 1,500—have some sort of cyberexistence[44]) of the Internet, there are four other clear and distinct influences where the Internet has affected language and language use. The first is the effect of e-mail messages on language. This effect has nothing to do with the obvious Internet characteristics of typing inaccuracies, misspellings, and lack of capitalization and punctuation which are all nonstandard, playful, and highly deviant. It has to do with **framing**—the way in which messages are divided, arranged, shaped, composed, constructed, and put together as a new whole. For example, let's say you receive a message that contains three different points. Instead of responding to the entire message, you can respond to just a single point, and send back the message. Then, you can respond to the second point, and send back the message, and, likewise, with the third. Your respondent can then respond to each point individually, or he or she can choose to dissect the message even further.

The point is, when you get the message back, an issue—with its development and history—is framed on the screen. Issues can go on and on, reply after reply, all unified and with their history intact. Never before in human written communication, says David Crystal, in his book *Language and the Internet,* has this been possible.[45]

The second influence of the Internet on verbal communication occurs on the World Wide Web. One thing that can be said about traditional writing is that it is *permanent.* When you open a book to page 10, close the book, then open it to page 10 again, the same thing appears on the page. *Impermanence* is what occurs on the Web. Pages can change in front of your eyes. Page content can be updated, rearranged, deleted, or presented in entirely new ways. Words not only appear and disappear, but they also arrive in varied sizes, textures, colors, and fonts, and images fade in and out. The Web offers an animated linguistic channel that is more dynamic than traditional writing and more permanent than traditional speech. "It is," says Crystal, "neither speech nor writing. It is a new medium."[46]

The third arena in which a language revolution has occurred is in chat rooms. Not only do you get screen messages from all over the world, but you get messages from a large number of people at the same time (the number is unlimited) on a theme. Often, conversations cluster into a half-dozen or more subconversations. Similar to being at a cocktail party with numerous conversations going on around you, there is no way to pay attention to all of them. Never before in human communication has it been possible to listen to that many people at the same time.

The fourth arena is the blurring of the division between speaking and writing. E-mails are written, as noted, in a much less formal way than is usual in writing. With voice recordings, it is possible to speak to those who are not in the same place or

Verbal Communication Self-Evaluation Form

How effective is your verbal communication? For each question circle the numerical score that best represents your verbal communication. Select an event, a situation, a context, and a time when you recently gave a speech or presentation, and analyze it using the following scale: 7 = Outstanding; 6 = Excellent; 5 = Very good; 4 = Average (good); 3 = Fair; 2 = Poor; 1 = Minimal ability; 0 = No ability demonstrated.

1. *Did you use extended conversation?* That is, did you use language that was not highly formal, that was easy for you to use (not a stretch), that seemed like normal conversation, and that revealed a natural, comfortable, relaxed vocabulary and approach?   7 6 5 4 3 2 1 0

2. *Did you reveal clarity in your word choices?* That is, were your words immediately meaningful? Did they arouse specific and definite meanings? Was there no ambiguity or confusion revealed?   7 6 5 4 3 2 1 0

3. *Did you reveal simplicity in your word choices?* That is, did you use simple words? Was your vocabulary instantly understandable? Did you avoid using vague and confusing words? Were you sensitive to audience knowledge and background?   7 6 5 4 3 2 1 0

4. *Did you reveal accuracy in your word choices?* That is, did your words seem to convey exactly what you meant? Did you give your listeners enough, but not too much, information? In your examples, did you give complete details such as names, places, dates, and other facts? When you used an uncommon or technical word, did you accurately define it for your listeners?   7 6 5 4 3 2 1 0

5. *Did your verbal communication reveal appropriateness?* That is, did the words you chose have a direct relationship to your listeners? Did all your facts, examples, illustrations, opinions, statistics, and personal experiences relate directly to your audience? Did you use personal pronouns such as *you, us, we,* and *our?* Did you ask your listeners questions or use rhetorical questions that did not require an answer but which created the impression of direct audience contact?   7 6 5 4 3 2 1 0

6. *Did you reveal dynamism in your choice of words?* That is, was your language vivid? Was it impressive? Did your language appear planned and prepared—like you had given it some specific thought? Did your language reveal your own personal imprint?   7 6 5 4 3 2 1 0

TOTAL POINTS: _____

Go to the *Communicating Effectively* CD-ROM and the Online Learning Center at **www.mhhe. com/hybels8** to see your results and learn how to evaluate your attitudes and feelings.

mhhe.com/hybels8

time as you. You can speak or listen in such situations but not interact. Live television broadcasts can include a mixture of recordings, telephone calls, incoming faxes, as well as e-mails. "One effect of this new technology and the modern universality of writing," says Josef Essberger, "has been to raise the status of speaking. Politicians who cannot organize their thoughts and *speak* [Essberger's emphasis] well on television win very few votes."[47]

CHAPTER REVIEW

SUMMARY

Your ability to use words depends on your native architecture, cognitive development, and environmental influences. It is a key component in strategic flexibility because, as the Sapir-Whorf hypothesis emphasizes, it influences the way you view and think about the world around you.

A word is a symbol; it stands for the object or concept it names. For us to understand one another, we must agree on what the particular word symbol stands for—in both its denotative and its connotative meanings. S. I. Hayakawa's ladder of abstraction helps convey meaning accurately to listeners. It helps analyze communications, understandings, and misunderstandings. It helps immunize against political propaganda, advertising, and vacant rhetoric, and it also helps communicators make personal adjustments as they become aware of their own abstracting.

Language is directly linked to your perception of reality and to your thought processes, which begin in earliest childhood. You create meanings for words as ideas, feelings, and activities change. Because you determine meanings, it is important to present ideas as clearly as possible while your listener tries to understand.

For language to be successful, it must be appropriate to the language environment. The language you should use in a particular environment is determined by the role you are playing in that environment. Certain language rituals are predetermined for you by the values of your society (culture and co-cultures). You learn these and other forms of appropriate language during your childhood. When you become an adult and enter the work world, often you must learn a specialized language used by your occupational or professional group.

Style, the way you express yourself, is an important aspect of language. The style that is expected of you often is determined by the roles you play. If you do not modify your language to fit your role, you may speak in ways that are inappropriate for the occasion.

Your gender influences the language style you use. Men are more likely to use report-talk, a language that maintains their status, demonstrates their knowledge and skills, and keeps them at the center of attention. In contrast, women are more likely to use rapport-talk, a language that leads to intimacy with others, establishes relationships, and compares experiences. Powerful talk, too, will influence your effectiveness.

English is losing its place as a dominant world language. One in five Americans speak a language other than English at home. If you belong to an ethnic group, you may use a dialect—the habitual language of your community. The advantage of dialect is that it helps a person fit into an ethnic community; the disadvantage is that it might not have prestige in a community where standard American English is spoken.

There are many differences between writing and speaking. Writing is formal and structured; uses words alone; and is nonimmediate, with delayed feedback. Speaking is informal and less structured; uses words along with facial expressions, gestures, and tone of voice; and is immediate with, for the most part, instant feedback. Knowing these and the other differences will help you increase both the clarity and accuracy of your messages.

When you work on your communication, you have to decide what you want to say and how you want to say it. In choosing how you wish to communicate, you should aim for clarity, vividness, and ethical choices. Then you should ask to whom you are speaking and what metamessages—the meaning apart from the actual words—you are sending.

There are four influences of the Internet on verbal communication. The first is the framing that occurs in e-mail messages. The second is the impermanence and animation of Web pages. The third is the unlimited number of people with whom you can communicate in chat rooms; and the fourth is the blurring of the division between speaking and writing.

KEY TERMS AND CONCEPTS

Use the *Communicating Effectively* CD-ROM and the Online Learning Center at **www.mhhe.com/hybels8** to further your understanding of the following terms.

Clarity 123
Cognitive development 108
Connotative meaning 109
Denotative meaning 109
Dialect 120
Doublespeak 114
Euphemism 114

Framing 125
Ladder of abstraction 109
Language environment 113
Metamessage 125
Paralanguage 121
Powerful talk 118
Rapport-talk 116

Report-talk 117
Ritual language 113
Sapir-Whorf hypothesis 108
Style 116
Vividness 124

QUESTIONS TO REVIEW

1. How did you acquire your ability to use words?

2. What is the Sapir-Whorf hypothesis? How does it influence strategic flexibility?

3. What is meant when a word is referred to as a symbol?

4. What is the difference between denotative meaning and connotative meaning?

5. What is the ladder of abstraction, and why is it useful?

6. What are the four elements that make up a language environment?

7. Define *euphemism* and *doublespeak* and give an example of each.

8. What do you mean when you talk about verbal style? How is it developed?

9. What is the difference between report-talk and rapport-talk, and why is it important?

10. How is powerful talk characterized? When people use it, what impression do they make?

11. What cultural changes are having an effect on language?

12. What is dialect, and what does it have to do with one's cultural background?

13. How do speaking and writing differ? What is the benefit of knowing the differences?

14. What is the difference between clarity and vividness, and what would be an appropriate example of each that reflects the difference?

15. What is the difference between paralanguage and metamessage?

16. What are some of the moral choices you should make in choosing the words you use?

17. What influences does the Internet have on verbal communication?

Go to the self-quizzes on the *Communicating Effectively* CD-ROM and the Online Learning Center at **www.mhhe.com/hybels8** to test your knowledge of the chapter contents.

CHAPTER

6

Nonverbal Communication

After reading this chapter, you should be able to:

- Frame a clear definition of nonverbal communication and provide examples to reveal its use.

- Explain the role of nonverbal communication in communicating effectively and achieving strategic flexibility.

- Point out differences between verbal and nonverbal communication and the way the brain processes the information from each.

- Describe and provide an example of the various types of nonverbal communication.

- Point out some of the ways culture influences nonverbal communication.

- Explain some of the ways you can become more aware of and improve your use of nonverbal communication.

- Describe the relationships among the Internet, social presence, media richness, and nonverbal communication.

U NTIL THE AGE OF 27, BRIAN LEWIS WAS OVERWEIGHT, UNPOPULAR, SHY, and depressed. Two years ago he reached a point where he couldn't take it anymore. He started working out, changed his diet, and started talking to new people. After a year, he had reinvented himself as a 100-pound-lighter, in-shape, social, and confident individual.

Toward the end of Brian's transition, he met Angela. She was smart, pretty, athletic, and funny—someone he had never dreamed of even talking to when he was overweight. Angela accepted Brian for who he is and who he was. He wants to spend the rest of his life with her, and Angela feels the same. Angela gave Brian confidence and reinforced his commitment to continue dieting and exercising, but he credits his reinvention of himself to changes in his opportunities, beliefs about himself and others, personality, confidence, social poise, and views of his future.

Nonverbal communication is information communicated without using words. Much of it—like Brian's overweight, unpopular, shy, and depressed personality—is unintentional. People may not be aware they are sending some nonverbal messages. On the other hand, Brian knew that being overweight, unpopular, shy, and depressed conveyed negative stereotypes he did not like, and with a great deal of personal effort and commitment he set out to change them.

THE ROLE OF NONVERBAL COMMUNICATION IN COMMUNICATING EFFECTIVELY AND ACHIEVING STRATEGIC FLEXIBILITY

As much as 93 percent of communication is nonverbal,[1] with 55 percent sent through facial expressions, posture, and gestures and 38 percent through tone of voice.[2] It is essential to understand how nonverbal communication works and how you can communicate better when you use it.

Communicating Effectively

If you look closely at the communication model discussed in Chapter 1, you will *not* find nonverbal communication as one of the elements depicted there. It is however embedded in every element in the model. Think about it. The size or dress of the sender-receiver is information communicated without using words, just as the pace or loudness of the message or the frown on his or her face is feedback to your message. Information could include noise from others talking too loudly and too close to where you are, or it could be a desperate, clinging handshake—the use of touch as an additional channel—to reinforce the urgency of the meeting. It could be the setting, like a cafeteria, that tells you to moderate what you say so others cannot hear; or, finally, it could be the culture, which may dictate conversational decorum or language choices. Now, when you look at the model—see Figure 6-1—you can see information possibilities in every element.

There are four other things you can learn from Figure 6-1. First, nonverbal communication plays an important role in communicating effectively. Second, to be unaware of nonverbal communication is to miss a significant portion of what goes on in any communication situation. Third, as Figure 6-1 indicates, communication is complex; look at the number of factors you take into consideration—some more important or obvious than others—before, during, and after communicating. Fourth,

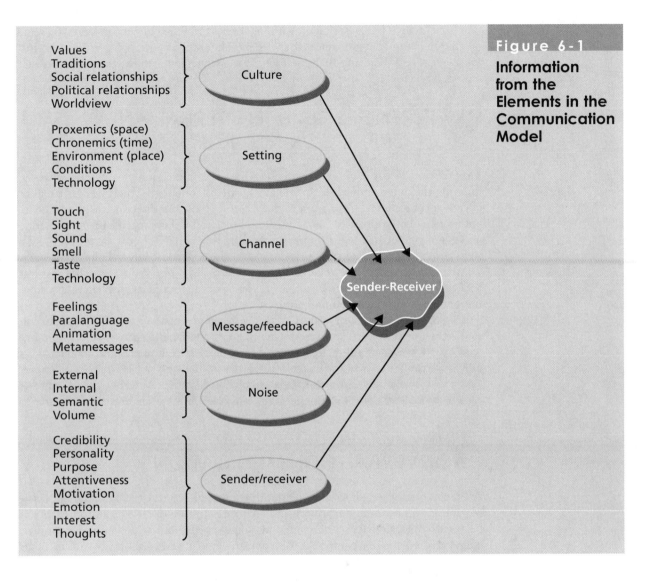

Figure 6-1

Information from the Elements in the Communication Model

no two communications can ever be the same. There are so many elements and so many different ways to interpret them.

Strategic Flexibility

You are aware of all the nonverbal elements that are likely to affect any communication you have with others. Now, think about all the processing procedures that your brain engages in (your unique perceptual filter depicted in Figure 2-3 of Chapter 2) as it takes in all or some of these elements. You make use of them as you anticipate, assess, evaluate, select, apply, then reassess and reevaluate each communication.

If you are attentive to verbal and nonverbal elements, responsive to current usage, and respectful of differential usage, you will probably be able to move into any social setting in your own society. You will be perceptually fluent, rising to all the demands of both verbal and nonverbal communication. It is both language fluency and nonverbal awareness that are most likely to result in strategic flexibility. When you examine the number of nonverbal factors alone (see Figure 6-1), you quickly understand why some people are better communicators than others. They are not just aware of the elements, but they process them and then use them in the strategic flexibility framework. It isn't a mystery; such ability can be learned.

DIFFERENCES BETWEEN VERBAL AND NONVERBAL COMMUNICATION

Most differences between verbal and nonverbal communication are obvious; however, knowing the differences can help you emphasize the one with which you can be most effective. For example, if you want to make certain that your directions are understood, put your emphasis on verbal communication because it follows specific rules of structure and grammar, because words represent specific things like schools, factories, or stop signs, and because verbal communication has culture- and context-bound meanings. On the other hand, if you want to express your feelings to a spouse who has just lost a close friend, words may be insufficient: your spontaneous nonverbal signs of sorrow, hurt, and loss may be far more significant.

One of the most important distinctions between verbal and nonverbal communication is the way the brain processes the information. Verbal information is conveyed linearly, one word after another. In nonverbal communication, however, the brain creates a composite of all the signals given off by a new experience. It is "a holistic phenomenon," says Carlin Flora, "in which clues (mellifluous voice, Rolex watch, soggy handshake, hunched shoulders) hit us all at once and form an impression larger than their sum."[3]

CHARACTERISTICS OF NONVERBAL COMMUNICATION

All forms of nonverbal communication have five characteristics in common. First, much nonverbal communication is unique to the culture or co-culture to which you belong. Second, verbal and nonverbal messages may be in conflict with one another. Third, much nonverbal communication operates at a subconscious level—you are often not aware of it. Fourth, your nonverbal communication shows your feelings and attitudes. Fifth, nonverbal communication varies by gender.

Nonverbal Communication Is Culturally Determined

Your culture affects almost all your communication behaviors. For example, it governs how close you stand while talking with another person, how you use or avoid eye contact, and how you express or suppress powerful emotions such as joy, disapproval, and anger. Your culture determines whether you feel free to express your love of another in public settings by holding hands, hugging, or kissing—what has come to be known as public displays of affection (PDA).

Much nonverbal behavior is learned in childhood, passed on to you by your parents and others with whom you associate. A good deal of it is learned simply through imitation. Growing up in a particular society, you adopt the traits and mannerisms of your cultural group. In Japan bowing shows rank. Slouching is rude in most northern European areas. Putting your hands in your pocket is disrespectful in Turkey.

Your culture governs your body movement. It determines what moves, when it moves, and where it moves, and it imposes restrictions on that movement. For example, your hips may move in sports and dancing, but not in the services of some churches. Children can move their bodies freely in gym class but not in math.

Nonverbal Messages May Conflict with Verbal Messages

Nonverbal communication is so deeply rooted, so unconscious, that you can express a verbal message and directly contradict it with a nonverbal message. For example, Terrence Sejinowski, of the Salk Institute for Biological Studies in La Jolla, California, has developed a computer program that can detect lies by analyzing fleeting facial expressions.[4] The computer is trained to analyze in real time the almost imperceptible expressions like eyelid flutters and strained smiles—the same expressions it used to take Paul Ekman, a psychologist at the University of California–San Francisco, and his team of researchers hours to catalog. With the new computer program, people can be screened for lying without their even knowing it.[5]

View "Nonverbal Messages," clip #4, on the CD.

Without computer assistance, most people can spot lies little better than half the time. In her study of lying, Maureen O'Sullivan, a University of San Francisco professor, found only 31 people of more than 13,000 who could do better. These so-called wizards read telltale signals such as fidgeting, pressing the lips together, raising the chin, moving the feet, and changing vocal pitch. Researchers warned, however, that such cues are not universal nor even always indicative of a lie.[6]

In **mixed messages** the verbal and the nonverbal contradict each other. The nonverbal communication is often more reliable than the verbal content. You can learn to manipulate words, but you might find it difficult to manipulate your nonverbal communication. You may not be aware of sending it; the message, however, comes through loud and clear.

Nonverbal Messages Are Largely Unconscious

You wake up feeling that you might be getting a cold. It's not yet bad enough to stay home, so you go to classes. The minute one of your classmates sees you, she says, "You look like you aren't feeling very well." She is making a nonverbal assessment: You don't have to say a word for her to know how you're feeling.

When you consider the amount and ordinariness of your nonverbal behavior, it is hardly surprising that you are unaware of much of it.

Nonverbal Communication Shows Your Feelings and Attitudes

The feelings and emotions others can detect in your face include happiness, sadness, surprise, fear, anger, interest, contempt, shame, shyness, and guilt.[7] But research shows that other people are as accurate, if not better, at detecting. emotions through vocal cues as through facial expression.[8] As a matter of fact, researchers Planalp and her associates have shown that vocal cues are the most recognizable signs of emotions.[9]

Your body is also quite capable of expressing emotions. In her report on communicating emotion in everyday life, Planalp reports that people easily interpret a person's emotional state from cues such as "being physically energetic, bouncy, jumping up and down, clenching hands or fists, making threatening movements, holding the body rigidly, shuffling, or having a slumped, droopy posture, dancing around, and using hand emblems."[10] If you wanted to demonstrate greater warmth and immediacy to another person, you might reveal a happy facial expression, enthusiastic gestures, closer interpersonal distances, and friendly touches.[11]

Nonverbal Communication Varies by Gender

Men and women use and interpret nonverbal communication differently. North American women not only initiate more eye contact during conversations than men, but they are more comfortable returning eye contact as well. Women maintain a gaze longer, but they are less likely than men to stare at someone—they break eye contact more frequently than men. This is not a contradiction; men are simply less likely to *make* the eye contact, but when they do, they often get "locked in" without realizing their eye contact is being returned.[12]

When surveyed, female students felt that they typically use more gestures than males.[13] Some authorities think women use fewer gestures with other women but more with men. Others think the difference is in the types of gestures used, not in their frequency of use. Although you will automatically return a smile if someone smiles at you first, experts agree that women smile more than men. It is also useful to point out that females are more attracted to others who smile.[14]

Although the experts agree that males use more personal space than females, when students were surveyed, 56 percent of the females felt they required more personal space than males.[15] In Edward T. Hall's book *The Hidden Dimension*, spatial zones are drawn closer for women than for men.[16] Hall notes that women tend to approach others more closely and seem to prefer side-by-side conversations. Men, on the other hand, prefer face-to-face conversations.

Men are more likely to initiate touch with others than are women. Women give and receive more touches than men except when initiating courtship and are more likely to associate touch with personal warmth and expressiveness. When students were surveyed, 57.8 percent of the females agreed that they touch others more than males do.[17] Touch is considered a feminine-appropriate behavior and a masculine-inappropriate one. Mothers touch female infants more than male infants, and female children tend to desire and offer more nonaggressive touch than male children.[18]

Which gender is likely to interpret nonverbal cues better? All experts agree on this one: females are better interpreters. When students were surveyed, 73.7 percent of the females agreed with the experts. There are two reasons for this. First, women tend to be more sensitive communicators. Second, women use a number of verbal and nonverbal channels to actively communicate to others the importance of relationships.

TYPES OF NONVERBAL COMMUNICATION

In this section, we will introduce paralanguage, body movement, eye messages, attractiveness, clothing, body adornment, space and distance, touch, smell, and time.

Paralanguage

Verbal communication consists of the words you use to communicate: nonverbal communication has a **paralanguage**—the way in which you say the words. Paralanguage, or paralinguistic cues, exists beside language and interacts with it. For example, a parent tells a child in a mild voice to clean up his room. When the room is still in the same condition two hours later, the parent says, "I thought I told you to clean up your room." This time the parent's voice communicates "If you don't do it soon, you're in big trouble."

One of the pioneers in the study of of nonverbal communication. Ray Birdwhistell shows how important paralanguage can be in its ability to modify everything that is said and place it into context:

> These cross-referencing signals [paralanguage] amplify, emphasize, or modify the formal constructions, and/or make statements about the context of the message situation. In the latter instance, they help to define the context of the interaction by identifying the actor or his audience, and furthermore, they usually convey information about the larger context in which the interaction takes place.[19]

An important aspect of paralanguage—and one noted in the quotation above when Birdwhistell says "by identifying the actor"—paralinguistic cues can create distinct impressions of you, the communicator. For example, what characterizes an attractive, influential voice? Researchers suggest that it is resonant and calm, less monotonous, lower pitched (especially for males), less regionally accented, less nasal, less shrill, and more relaxed.[20]

Albert Mehrabian estimates that 39 percent of the meaning in communication is affected by vocal cues—not the words themselves but the way they are said.[21] In languages other than English, this percentage may be even higher.

Rate

The **rate** (speed) at which one speaks can have an effect on the way a message is received.[22] Faster speakers are seen as more competent, credible, and intelligent.[23] But, they are also seen as less honest and trustworthy than slower speakers.[24]

Another aspect of rate is how one person will accommodate or adapt to another's rate. It's called **convergence.** Fast talkers slow down when interacting with slow talkers; slow talkers speed up when talking with fast talkers.[25] People who converge to another's rate are seen as more attractive and persuasive.[26]

Pitch

Pitch is the highness or lowness of the voice. Some people believe that high-pitched voices are not as pleasant as low-pitched voices. However, the same researchers who studied rate of speaking also found that speakers were judged more competent if they used a higher and varied pitch.[27] Lower pitches are more difficult to hear, and people who have low-pitched voices may be perceived as insecure or shy. Pitch can be changed, but it requires working with someone who has had professional training in voice modification.

Volume

The meaning of a message can also be affected by its **volume**—how loudly a person speaks. A loud voice is fine if it's appropriate to the speaker's purpose and is not used all the time. The same is true of a soft voice. Expert teachers know at what points to increase or decrease their volume when they want a class to be quiet.

Quality

The overall **quality** of a voice is made up of all the other vocal characteristics: tempo, resonance, rhythm, and articulation. Voice quality is important because research-ers have found that people with attractive voices are seen as more youthful, more competent, and more honest. However, people with immature voices were seen as less competent and powerful but more honest and warm.[28]

Vocal Fillers

A related aspect of paralanguage but not part of it is **vocal fillers**—the sounds you use to fill out your sentences or to cover up or fill pauses. You use many vocal fillers to let others know you are still speaking even though you may not know specifically what to say. They may be nonwords such as *uh, um,* and *er,* or they may be words and phrases such as *you know, like,* or *whatever,* when used to fill a pause. Although fillers are sometimes words, they are used in these instances as if they have no meaning.

Body Movement

Body movement, also called *kinesics,* comes "from the Greek word for 'movement' and refers to all forms of body movement, excluding physical contact with another's body."[29] Researchers Ekman and Friesen, divide body movement into five categories: emblems, illustrators, regulators, displays of feelings, and adaptors.[30]

Emblems are body movements that directly translate into words. In western society the extended thumb of a hitchhiker is an emblem that means "I want a ride." A circle made with the thumb and index finger can be translated into "OK." Emblems often cannot be carried from one culture to another. Shaking your head back and forth in southern India, for example, means "yes."

Emblems are often used when words are inappropriate. It would be impractical for a hitchhiker to stand on the side of the road and shout, "Please give me a ride!" Sometimes emblems can replace talk. You might cover your face with your hands if you are embarrassed, and you hold up your fingers to show how many of something you want. Subgroups in a society often use emblems that members of the group understand but whose meanings are intentionally kept from outsiders—the secret handshake of a fraternity is an example.

Illustrators accent, emphasize, or reinforce words. If someone asks how big your suitcase is, you will probably describe it with words and illustrate the dimensions with your hands. Illustrators can go beyond gestures. When an instructor underlines something she has written on the board, she is telling you that this point is particularly important.

In her book *Executive Charisma,* Debra A. Benton clearly defines the role that posture plays as an illustrator. "Stand tall and straight summons up visions of someone ethical, courageous, awake, alert, and alive. Good posture," Benton says, "shows confidence, vitality, discipline, and youthfulness. Slumped posture," she adds, "implies fright, insecurity, lack of self-acceptance or self-control, lack of discipline, a loser, sheepishness, shame, and guilt. To stand tall and straight is to have a demeanor that says, 'I expect acceptance.' "[31]

Regulators control the back-and-forth flow of speaking and listening. "They are the 'traffic cops' of conversation."[32] They are made up of hand gestures, shifts in posture, and other body movements that signal the beginning and end of interactions. At a very simple level, a teacher uses a regulator when she points to the person she wants to speak next. On a more subtle level, someone might turn away slightly when you are talking, perhaps indicating "I don't want to continue this conversation."

Displays of feelings show, through facial expressions and body movements, how intensely a person is feeling. If you walk into a professor's office and the professor says, "I can see you are really feeling upset," he or she is responding to nonverbal cues you are giving about your feelings. You could also come in with a body posture indicating

"I'm really going to argue about this grade"—with your clenched hands or stiff body position showing that you are ready for a confrontation.

Displays of feelings vary in different cultures. For example, many Asian cultures suppress facial expression as much as possible. Mediterranean (Latino/Latina and Arabic) cultures freely express grief or sadness while most American men hide grief or sorrow. Some people see animated expressions as a lack of control. Too much smiling is sometimes viewed as a sign of shallowness.

Adaptors are nonverbal ways of adjusting to a communication situation. They are behaviors that satisfy your physical or psychological needs. What do you do when you feel anxious, relaxed, crowded, or defensive? In general, adaptors are habits and are usually not intended to communicate.[33] However, often they convey a great deal of information.

Because people use such a wide variety of adaptors, and because they are so specific to each person's own needs and the individual communication situation, they are difficult to classify or even to describe generally.

For example, some people use adaptors when they are nervous or uncomfortable in a situation. You might play with jewelry, drum on the table, or move around a lot in your seat. Each of these behaviors is an adaptor—a way of helping you cope with the situation. We all use adaptors, but we are generally not aware of them unless someone points them out.

Eye Messages

Eye messages include all information conveyed by the eyes alone. The most important aspect of eye messages is eye contact, and in American culture, meeting another's eyes is a sign of honesty and credibility as well as warmth and involvement. In many cultures, conversing without eye contact can indicate disinterest, inattention, rudeness, shyness, or deception.[34]

When you think about the functions that eye messages can perform, you quickly realize their importance. Eye messages provide turn-taking signals in conversations that regulate interactions. They indicate attentiveness, involvement, immediacy, and connection to others. Prolonged stares, especially with negative facial expressions, can be intimidating. But one of their most delightful and wondrous aspects is their role in flirtation.[35]

Although eye messages have received marginal attention by intercultural scholars,[36] an African proverb says. "The eye is an instrument of aggression."[37] Many Asians and Pacific Islanders would agree. In their countries young people never make eye contact with their elders. In most African countries and many other parts of the world, if a person has more status than you, you should not look him or her in the eye.

Attractiveness

What is attractive to you? **Attractiveness** is having the power or quality of drawing, pleasing, or winning.[38] The importance of physical beauty to males is universal; men in all cultures around the world prefer young, nubile (of suitable age to marry) women. More than that, however, men prefer having a physically attractive mate because it is a sign of status.[39] Females, on the other hand, select men with sufficient resources to care for them and have stronger preferences for intelligent, considerate, and outgoing mates. Like men of all cultures, women are attracted to wealth, power, and status.[40]

Psychologists Sara Gutierres and Douglas Kenrick of Arizona State University have demonstrated that context counts. If you first see a highly attractive person, then you see a person of average attractiveness of the same sex, the average person seems a lot less attractive than he or she actually is. The reverse of this is also true: People of average attractiveness will seem more attractive than they are if they enter a room full of unattractive people of the same sex.[41]

Physical characteristics you can control are called **elective characteristics** and include clothing, makeup, tattoos, and body piercing. **Nonelective characteristics,** things you cannot change, are height, body proportion, coloring, bone structure, and physical disabilities. Many of the nonelective traits influence how you see the world. A six-foot woman, for example, would see life quite differently from her five-foot sister.[42]

There are some obvious benefits of attractiveness. People perceived as beautiful or handsome generally make more money and get more promotions. On the other hand, overweight and obese people face obstacles to fair pay and promotions. A study co-authored by Dan Cable, an associate professor at the University of North Carolina–Chapel Hill's Kenan-Flagler Business School, and Timothy Judge of the University of Florida has demonstrated that the taller you are, the more money you earn. The researchers controlled for gender, weight, and age and found that height was closely related to incomes in all kinds of professions. They showed, too, that each inch of height is worth an astonishing $789 more a year—six inches of height will net you $4,734 in annual income. Tall people get more of everything: notice, positive evaluations, promotions, and attention from the opposite sex. More than anything, these findings reveal our society's biases with respect to weight and height and how appearances rule over brains.[43]

Clothing

Because clothing gives such a strong and immediate impression of its wearer, it is enormously important to nonverbal communication. Besides communicating, however, clothing may serve as protection; communicate sexual attraction, self-assertion, self-denial, concealment, or group identification; and provide indications of status and role.[44] In addition, think of how much information you can gain from a person's clothing: sex, age, nationality, relation to opposite sex, socioeconomic status, group

Clothing projects a message; by choosing particular clothing, wearers commit themselves to the statements clothing makes.

and occupational identification, mood, personality, attitudes, interests, and values.[45] In his book *You Are What You Wear*, William Thourlby suggests that people make 10 decisions about others based on clothing: (1) Economic level, (2) Educational level, (3) Trustworthiness, (4) Social position, (5) Level of sophistication, (6) Economic background, (7) Social background, (8) Educational background, (9) Level of success, and (10) Moral character.[46]

Even though people may appear to dress in similar ways, they don't always see themselves as similar. An Amish woman points out that although Amish women wear dark clothes that cover the body, they are still aware of style. She writes: "Every culture has its own fashion expectations and requirements, and my people are no exception. They are concerned about how they look. They do not all wear black. They have individual color and style preferences. They enjoy shopping. And they talk about styles and fashions among themselves. . . . To these women, high and proper fashion means busy sewing machines, solid-colored, store-bought fabrics, and patterns passed down from generation to generation.[47]

Clothing falls into four categories: uniforms, occupational dress, leisure clothing, and costumes. Each conveys a different nonverbal meaning.

Uniforms identify wearers with particular organizations. They are the most specialized form of clothing. There is little freedom of choice in a uniform. Its wearers are told when to wear it (daytime, summer) and what they can and cannot wear with it (jewelry, medals, hairstyles).

By showing rank, military uniforms tell what positions the wearers hold in the hierarchy and what their relationships are to others in the organization. The uniform also implies that its wearer will follow certain norms.[48]

Occupational dress is clothing that employees are expected to wear, but it is not as precise as a uniform. It is designed to present a specific image of the employees.[49] Unlike wearers of uniforms, employees who wear occupational dress have choices. Flight attendants are required to wear specific pieces of clothing, but they can mix items and accessories to their own preferences. What teachers wear affects student perceptions. In a study of teaching assistants, researchers found that those who dressed the most informally were viewed the most positively by students. In this case, informal dress was faded jeans, T-shirts, and flannel shirts.[50]

Leisure clothing is worn when work is over. Because this kind of clothing is chosen by the individual, some people assert their personal identities through it.[51] However, not everyone sees styles of leisure wear as a choice. Many teenagers will wear only a particular brand of jeans because when their group agrees on a brand, everyone wears it. The mass media have had such a great influence on leisure clothing that it's hard to separate media influence from individual preference.

Costumes are a form of highly individualized dress. By putting on a costume like cowboy boots, bandanna, and hat, the wearer announces, "This is who I want to be." Costumes not only require thought regarding the image they convey but also go against many norms. As one student shrewdly observed as he changed his shoes for a job interview at a supermarket in the Northeast, "I better not wear my cowboy boots. They look too aggressive."

Body Adornment

Body adornment includes any addition to the physical body designed to beautify or decorate. Throughout the world people have found ways of changing the body they were born with. Americans are no exception. Hairstyles, facial hair, and makeup undergo

In this excerpt the importance of a single piece of clothing, the *hijab*, is described by Maryam Qudrat Aseel—a first-generation Afghan American girl, born and raised in Los Angeles—in her book *Torn Between Two Cultures*. The *hijab* is a simple head scarf—a small piece of fabric—for the hair, and it is "one element of being a true Muslim, and specifically a true Muslim woman" (p. 78). When Aseel wore the Muslim woman's head scarf, people automatically assumed she was some sort of fundamentalist, a terrorist, or a zealot preaching religion (p. 83). It is hard to believe how important a single nonverbal element could be, but here Aseel describes it:

On the day of my high school graduation, after three years of being looked upon as an outcast and deviant by both American and Afghan societies, I finally took off my hijab, which had caused so much contempt. I simply couldn't handle the scrutiny of my personal life. Even more ridiculous than being treated as a lesser human being because of my physical traits [deep tan skin, bold green eyes, full lips, and strong bone struc-

ture] I was being treated that way because of my clothes. And people had somehow assigned me the position of representing the entire religion of Islam. If I were to do one thing wrong or make one human mistake, I would not pay for it alone—so would Islam. If I so much as wore some lip gloss, I would be met with the attitude of "See, and she is supposed to be so religious—they're all just a bunch of hypocrites."

Source: From *Torn Between Two Cultures: An Afghan-American Woman Speaks Out* (p. 82), by Maryam Qudrat Aseel, 2003, Sterling, VA: Capital Books.

Questions

1. Do you expect a person who wears the symbol or uniform of a particular group to represent every other member of that group? Why or why not?

2. Do you expect a leader like a teacher, principal, or guidance counselor to follow a special code of conduct? Why or why not? Can you think of others expected to follow specific codes of conduct?

3. Have you been stereotyped by others because of your appearance or clothes? Do you think these stereotypes are fair? Why or why not?

conservative changes that are widely accepted. In fact, it's hard to believe that only about 100 years ago people were shocked when women used makeup and cut their hair short, or, more recently, when men began to wear earrings.

Space and Distance

The study of **space and distance,** called **proxemics,** examines the way people use the space around them as well as the distance they maintain from others. The minute you enter a classroom, you have to decide where to sit. As you can see in Figure 6-2, your choice depends on how much interaction you want to have with the instructor: If you are in the "action zone," you may be indicating that you want to participate in the class.

Territory is the space that a person considers as belonging to him or her—either temporarily or permanently. For example, you would probably be upset if you came into the classroom and found someone sitting in "your" chair.

Sometimes people unwittingly send out a mixed message about their space. Four students who rented a church that had been converted to student housing with four sleeping lofts found that they had little control over their space. Other students dropped in night and day—probably because the building looked more like a public than a private space. The minute their lease ended, they moved into more traditional housing.

Every culture has rules—usually informal—about the use of space and distance. Edward T. Hall, author of two classic books on nonverbal communication, discovered that North Americans use four distance zones when they are communicating with others: intimate distance, personal distance, social distance, and public distance.[52]

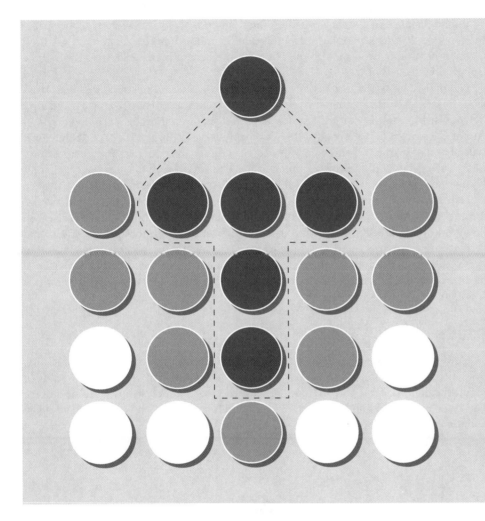

Figure 6-2

A Traditional Classroom Arrangement

In such an arrangement, those students occupying the blue seats will account for a large proportion of the total interaction that occurs between teachers and students. Those in the green seats will interact some; those in the white seats will interact very infrequently. The area enclosed in dotted lines has been called the "action zone."

Intimate distance, a range of less than 18 inches apart, places people in direct contact with each other. Look at a parent holding a baby. All our senses are alert when we are this close to someone. The parent can touch the baby, smell him, and hear every little gurgle he makes. People also maintain an intimate distance in love relationships and with close friends. Intimate distance exists whenever you feel free to touch the other person with your whole body.

When your intimate distance is violated by people who have no right to be so close, you feel apprehensive. If you are on a crowded bus, subway, or elevator and people are pressed against you, they are in your intimate distance. By not making eye contact you can protect your intimate distance psychologically, if not physically.

Personal distance, from 18 inches to 4 feet, is the distance you maintain from another person when you are engaged in casual and personal conversations. It is close enough to see the other person's reactions but far enough away not to encroach on intimate distance.

Social distance, from 4 to 12 feet, is the distance you are most likely to maintain when you do not know people very well. Impersonal business, social gatherings, and interviews are examples of situations where you use social distance and interaction becomes more formal.

Public distance, a distance of more than 12 feet, is typically used for public speaking. At this distance, people speak more loudly and use more exaggerated gestures. Communication is even more formal and permits few opportunities for people to be involved with each other.

Figure 6-3 shows the dimensions of the four distance zones. There are wide variations among cultures in the way people handle space and distance in relationships. When visiting another culture, you (as an American) would probably try to keep your "normal" distance between yourself and someone else—a large zone. Your behavior is typical of northern European communities, Scandinavian countries, and Great Britain but could appear "standoffish" in other cultures like Saudi Arabia, Latin America, Italy, France, and Spain, as well as other Middle Eastern countries. People there tend to keep a much closer distance—a small zone. You might view their maintaining nose-to-nose distance as "pushy" simply because their social space equates to our intimate space. You might find yourself backing away trying to regain your social space while an Arab would be pursuing you across the floor trying to maintain his. If you were visiting a friend in the Netherlands, on the other hand, your roles would be reversed. Their personal space equates to our social space; thus, to maintain your normal distance, you would continue trying to get closer to your friend.

Touch

The closer you stand to someone, the more you increase the likelihood of touching. **Touch** is to be in or come into physical contact with another person, and the study of touch is called **haptics.** You are familiar with the use of touch in intimate situations: You kiss babies, hold hands with loved ones, and hug family members. Touch "is a key component in growing, learning, communicating, and living."[53] The importance of

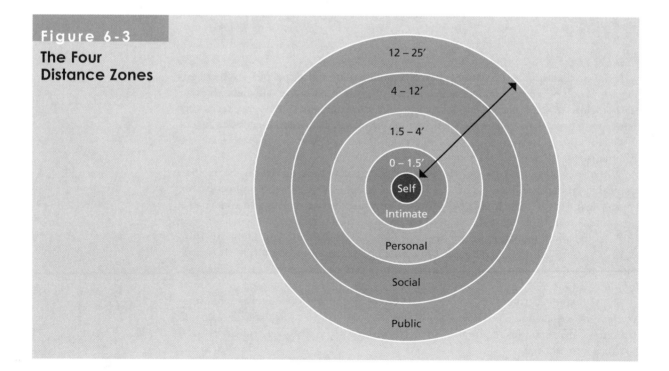

Figure 6-3

The Four Distance Zones

12 – 25′

4 – 12′

1.5 – 4′

0 – 1.5′

Self

Intimate

Personal

Social

Public

The distance people keep from other people is determined both by culture and occasion. The people in the left picture are Americans waiting in line at an airport. Those in the right picture are Chinese.

touch for babies was shown in a study of premature babies. For them to thrive, they had to be touched, releasing brain chemicals that promote growth. Premature infants who were massaged three times a day for 15 minutes gained weight 47 percent faster than those who were left alone in their incubators and later did much better on tests of mental ability and motor ability.[54]

When and where people touch one another is governed by a strict set of societal rules. Richard Heslin has described five different categories of touch behavior.[55] The first is *functional-professional touch,* in which you are touched for a specific reason, as in a physical examination by a doctor or nurse. This kind of touch is impersonal and businesslike. *Social-polite touch* is used to acknowledge someone else. The handshake is the most common form. Although two people move into an intimate distance to shake hands, they move away from each other when the handshake is over. In close relationships people use the *friendship-warmth touch.* This kind of touch involves hugs and casual kisses between friends. Touching is one way to communicate liking.[56] In more intense relationships the *love-intimacy touch* is common. Parents stroke their children; lovers and spouses kiss and fondle each other. The final touch Heslin describes is *sexual arousal touch*—touch used as an expression of physical attraction.[57]

Touch can quickly become a violation when it is unexpected or out of the message context. The improper touching of children is an obvious violation, and the most serious violation of touch, of course, is in assault and battery.[58] Inappropriate touch is discussed in the following "Consider This" box.

Smell

The study of smell is called **olfactics.** The sense of smell has long remained one of the most baffling of our senses. Richard Axel of the Howard Hughes Medical Institute at Columbia University and Linda Buck of the Fred Hutchinson Cancer Research Center in Seattle split the 2004 Nobel Prize in medicine for discovering how people discern individual odors.

There is much uncertainty about appropriate and inappropriate touch, but much of the uncertainty can be dealt with if some general guidelines are followed. Over time, courts will decide cases, and with respect to sexual harassment especially, a clear list of DOs and DON'Ts will emerge. Until then, however, guidelines—along with the common sense and decency of those involved—offer general parameters of acceptability.

- **Consider the context.** The totality of circumstances always must be considered. This includes the frequency and severity of the offending conduct as well as whether it is physically threatening or humiliating. In addition, whether it occurs in a public situation with other people around or in a private, isolated setting makes a significant difference.

- **Be mindful of the role that perception plays.** With respect to whether any behavior (touch included) is appropriate or offensive, it is always assessed only from the perspective of the recipient, not from the perspective of the alleged harasser. The intentions of the alleged harasser are irrelevant; no excuse is legitimate.

- **Know that unwelcome conduct is unacceptable.** For example, uninvited physical contact such as touching, hugging, patting, or pinching is inappropriate. In addition, repeated offensive sexual flirtations, advances, or propositions, displays of sexually suggestive objects or pictures, or sexually related jokes or remarks are improper. Verbal abuse or innuendo of a sexual nature, comments of a sexual nature about an individual's body, prolonged staring or leering, and obscene gestures or suggestive or insulting sounds are included.

- **Think before behaving.** Is the behavior I am about to engage in unwelcome? Is it of a sexual nature? Is it reciprocal or unilateral? Would a reasonable man or woman, under similar circumstances, react or be affected by such behavior? Are you being sensitive to the reactions of others? Are you honoring the other's request to avoid any behavior or discussion that is offensive or embarrassing? If you are a male, would you behave this way toward your mother or daughter?

Questions

1. What is the problem with any given set of rules or guidelines designed to govern, regulate, or control human conduct? What are the circumstances that cause rules to be broken, or guidelines to be ignored? What are some things that can be put into place that would furnish barriers, or hindrances, to rule breaking?

2. What should you do if you felt you had been subjected to inappropriate behavior? (One important point would be not to reciprocate in any way.)

3. Can you see that when it comes to appropriate or inappropriate behavior, that it can have very different meanings? Can you cite any examples?

Much of your sense of taste depends on your sense of smell. Thus, when you hold your nose or have a cold with stuffy nose, you lose much of the flavor of the food you eat. Odor preferences vary around the world, depending on cultural and genetic variations. If you are constantly or repeatedly exposed to an odor, your ability to perceive it will usually decline. This is called adaptation. About 85 percent of people have a childhood memory linked to a particular aroma, and the aroma most commonly mentioned is the fragrance of fresh baked goods.[59]

Time

The study of time is called **chronemics.** To say that time is very important in American culture is a huge understatement; we are obsessed with time. Our daily life is infused with a sense of urgency driven by the desire to beat the clock. Burgoon, Buller, and Woodall write, "Time is seen as a precious resource, a valuable and tangible commodity. We spend time, save it, make it, fill it, and waste it. It is seen almost as a container with defined boundaries. . . . The way we schedule events also reflects the urgent and precise way we deal with time. We expect classes to start on time (within a minute or so), and when they don't we wait only so long (20 minutes at the most) before leaving."[60]

You can use time for psychological effect. The student who is always late may be communicating considerable negative information. He is really not interested in this class or doesn't respect the instructor. You will probably not arrive too early for a date or party because this might make you appear too eager. If you dent the family car, you might wait for the right time to tell your parents about it. Your control of time, then, is an important form of nonverbal communication. The higher your status, the more control you have over your time. A parent can interrupt children's play to have them eat dinner or to make them go to bed far earlier than they want. Professionals in our society often make others wait for them.

Time differs greatly from one culture to another. Figure 6-4 shows what people in the United States regard as fashionably late, but suppose you were invited to a party in Venezuela, and the host said it would begin about 8 P.M. If you arrived at that time, you would be the only one there—the Venezuelans wouldn't arrive until 9 or 10 P.M. When interacting with people from different cultures, simply assume that their sense of time is different from yours.

FUNCTIONS OF NONVERBAL COMMUNICATION

Nonverbal communication has four functions. Nonverbal cues **complement** a verbal message by adding to its meaning. When you are talking to someone with a problem, for example, you might say, "I'm really sorry," and complement the message with a pat on the shoulder or a hug.

Nonverbal cues also **regulate** verbal communication. How would your boss or one of your teachers tell you that it's time for a meeting to end? He or she might do something obvious, like getting out of the chair, or something more subtle, like arranging papers on the desk, to communicate to you that the conversation is over.

Nonverbal messages can also **substitute** for verbal messages. Your instructor looks up, stares specifically at a couple of class members who are talking, then waits a couple

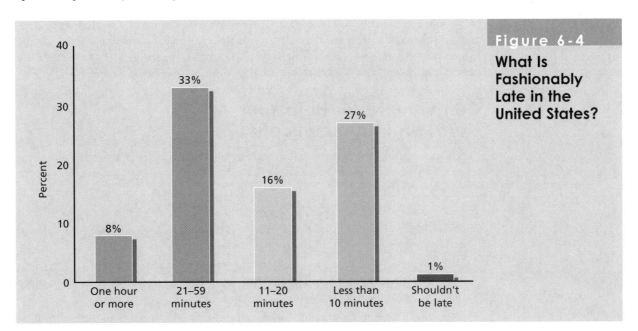

Figure 6-4

What Is Fashionably Late in the United States?

of seconds until everyone is quiet before she begins to speak. Her look says, "All right, everyone be quiet now. It's time to begin."

Often, nonverbal messages **accent** what you are saying. The instructor's voice is strong and firm when she tells the class she will accept no late papers; the teenager leans forward while she is trying to persuade her parents that she needs a new dress.

The key to controlling and thus improving your nonverbal communication is self-awareness. When you are fully aware of the signals you send, you have a greater opportunity not just for controlling them but for evaluating them as well. When you notice you are sending signals that aren't what you intend, you can either suppress them or change them. It is like using strategic flexibility on a personal—or intrapersonal—level or taking **control** of your life and your behavior.

One way to begin controlling your nonverbal communication is to control your emotions. Emotions often arise spontaneously and quickly—and produce subconscious (or unconscious) responses. But when you are aware of your emotions, you can begin to produce a counterresponse to mask, control, or subdue your actual reaction. For example, when someone asks you at the last minute how he or she looks, rather than express your surprise at what you consider to be an outrageous outfit, you mask your reaction.

Because you produce your emotions, you can control them. Once you are thinking rather than allowing your behavior to be at the mercy of your spontaneous feelings, you can better evaluate situations and consciously provide the responses you consider to be most appropriate.

STRATEGIC FLEXIBILITY

Thinking before acting (or emoting) is the basis for effective strategic flexibility because it requires thinking to anticipate, assess, evaluate, select, and properly apply your skills and behaviors. It is more likely that your strategies will be effective if you can control your initial emotional responses.

IMPROVING YOUR NONVERBAL COMMUNICATION

Below are some questions to ask about your nonverbal communication.

View "Nonverbal Messages," clip #4, on the CD.

How Do People React to You?

Do people ever react to you in a way that surprises you? You may be sending nonverbal messages that are being interpreted differently from the way you intended. For example, you may intend to tease someone but instead hurt his or her feelings. If you see that the person looks upset, you have a chance to explain what you really meant.

Can Videotapes Help Your Nonverbal Communication?

Videotape can tell you a great deal about behaviors you were not aware of and even some that you want to get rid of. Here are just a few items that you might look for when you see your tape.[61]

Eye contact. Since eye contact signals interest in others, increases credibility, and opens the flow of communication by conveying interest, concern, and warmth, make certain yours is comfortable and natural, but direct.

Facial expressions. Your face transmits happiness, friendliness, warmth, liking, and affiliation; thus, it pays to smile frequently. By smiling you will be perceived as more likable, friendly, warm, and approachable.

Gestures. Being lively and animated captures others' attention, makes your information more interesting, and provides conversational positive reinforcement.

Posture and body orientation. Posture and body orientation includes the way you walk, talk, stand, and sit. By standing erect, but not rigid, and by leaning slightly forward, you will communicate that you are approachable, receptive, and friendly.

Proximity. Cultural norms dictate the distances you need to stand for interacting with others. By increasing your proximity to others when in conversation, but not excessively, you not only make better eye contact, but you become more sensitive to the feedback of others.

Paralinguistics. You need to modulate your voice by changing such features as tone, pitch, rhythm, timbre, loudness, and inflection. Make sure you don't use a dull or boring voice.

Humor. When you reveal a willingness to laugh, you foster an inviting, warm, and friendly conversational environment. Laughter also releases stress and tension.

Is Your Nonverbal Communication Appropriate to the Role You Are Playing?

Like your language, your nonverbal communication should change as you play different roles. Observe other people in their roles. How much of their communication is nonverbal? What kind of nonverbal communication does a good teacher show? Who don't you want to be like? Is it their nonverbal behavior that turns you off? Do you do any of the same things? Can you stop doing them?

How Do You Use Your Space?

What messages are you sending out through the posters on your walls? Through the cuddly animals on your dresser? How tidy is your space? How much space do you occupy? Are you a sprawler; or do you keep your arms close to your body and your legs together? Are you conscious of certain space as "belonging" to you? Is it important that you have some spaces that you can call your own? What does the way you regard space tell others about you?

How Do You Use Time?

Are you on time or always late? Are you a procrastinator, leaving everything until the last minute?

If your use of time creates a bad impression, is it possible for you to change your ways?

When you look at all the things you communicate about yourself nonverbally, you will see that you should give nonverbal communication attention and care. Although nonverbal behavior is difficult to change, it can be done, especially if you are aware of how you use it.

THE INTERNET AND NONVERBAL COMMUNICATION

When you compare face-to-face communication with computer-mediated communication (CMC)—with its lack of visual and other nonverbal cues—CMC is extremely low in social presence. **Social presence** is the ability of CMC users to project themselves socially and affectively (with feeling) into a communication event. When you interact with someone else on the Internet, the degree of intimacy and immediacy you perceive with that person or the degree to which you perceive the person to be real determines your level of social presence.

Closely related to social presence is a concept called **media richness**—how much information is carried by a media source. Lean media carry the least amount of information while rich media carry the most. In an online article on media richness, Brian Newberry ranked seven different media types into a hierarchy from richest to leanest. The hierarchy also reveals the degree of social presence likely in each medium—with the most social presence represented at the top of the list and the least at the bottom:

1. Face-to-face
2. Video conferencing
3. Synchronous audio (as in instant messaging)
4. Text-based chat
5. E-mail and asynchronous audio
6. Threaded discussion (as in bulletin boards, usenet newsgroups, mailing lists, Web conferencing, and Web forums)[62]

Forms that are media rich and that represent high levels of social presence include a greater degree and a wider variety of nonverbal cues. Synchronous forms (where interaction is immediate) tend to include more nonverbal cues than asynchronous forms (where interaction is delayed). "Synchronous by its very nature," says Newberry, "requires that all communicating parties be available and attending to the communication activity at the same time."[63]

Such a ranking does not suggest that one form is better than another. Each form has its own advantages and disadvantages and any one is likely to be more appropriate in certain situations than another. Faced with the question of which to choose, you need to consider both efficiency and the best opportunity for the intended message to be conveyed accurately. As Newberry notes, the choice depends on "technology availability, time constraints, familiarity with the technology, task appropriateness of the technology and desired outcomes of the . . . activity."[64]

The choice of form can directly affect the parties' perception, appreciation, participation, or level of satisfaction. Think about the difference between terminating a relationship with another person via e-mail instead of face-to-face, or learning something about your success on an assignment via an instructor's Web site instead of hearing it face-to-face from the instructor. "Environments where participants do not feel they are recognized as individuals, or in which their input does not seem to be valued, may result in a reduced motivation to participate," says Newberry.[65]

Are You Aware of Nonverbal Communication?

How nonverbally aware are you? For each statement circle the numerical score that best represents your nonverbal awareness using the following scale: 7 = Outstanding; 6 = Excellent; 5 = Very good; 4 = Average (good); 3 = Fair; 2 = Poor; 1 = Minimal ability; 0 = No ability demonstrated.

1. I look others directly in the eye when communicating with them.	7 6 5 4 3 2 1 0	
2. I gesture with my hands and arms when communicating.	7 6 5 4 3 2 1 0	
3. I turn my body fully toward the person with whom I am speaking.	7 6 5 4 3 2 1 0	
4. I use a pleasant, appropriate tone of voice when speaking to others.	7 6 5 4 3 2 1 0	
5. I use a vocal volume that is appropriate when speaking to others.	7 6 5 4 3 2 1 0	
6. When listening to others, I notice and respond to their nonverbal responses to me—their vocal tone, eye contact, facial expressions, posture, gestures, and body movement.	7 6 5 4 3 2 1 0	
7. When listening to others, I am quiet when they are talking and allow them to express their ideas without interruption.	7 6 5 4 3 2 1 0	
8. When listening to another person, I smile when the person uses humor, and I nod at appropriate times.	7 6 5 4 3 2 1 0	
9. When listening to another person, I reveal my full support and attention through my nonverbal cues.	7 6 5 4 3 2 1 0	
10. I feel the nonverbal cues I use when speaking, and those I use in responding to others when they are speaking, reveal my comfort, poise, and confidence as an effective communicator.	7 6 5 4 3 2 1 0	

TOTAL POINTS: _____

Go to the *Communicating Effectively* CD-ROM and the Online Learning Center at **www.mhhe.com/hybels8** to see your results and learn how to evaluate your attitudes and feelings.

mhhe.com/hybels8

One area where nonverbal cues are important in day-to-day communication is determining credibility. Although we can never be certain about the truth or validity of any communication, with the lack of nonverbal cues in CMC, the truth of claims made on the Internet cannot easily be determined and credibility is instead established in small increments. In their book *Rules of the Net*, Thomas Mandel and Gerard Van der Leun state, "If you show over time that you are someone whose opinions, demeanor, and attitude are worth taking seriously, more people will endow you with their attention."[66]

SUMMARY

Nonverbal communication is information that is communicated without using words. There are nonverbal elements embedded in every element in the communication model. Your degree of fluency in your native language and your level of awareness of nonverbal components are likely to result in greater strategic flexibility.

You send more messages through nonverbal communication than you do through verbal communication, and although they often reinforce each other, there are numerous differences between them. One clear difference is in the way the brain processes the information. In the nonverbal realm, it is a holistic phenomenon in which clues hit you all at once, and you form an impression larger than their sum.

There are five characteristics of nonverbal communication: It is unique to the culture or co-culture to which you belong; verbal and nonverbal communication may be in conflict with one another; much nonverbal communication operates at a subconscious level; your nonverbal communication shows your feelings and attitudes; and nonverbal communication varies by gender.

There are many different types of nonverbal communication. They include paralanguage, body movement, eye messages, attractiveness (which includes body image as well as elective and nonelective character-

istics), clothing, body adornment, space and distance, touch, time, and smell. In each case, there are cultural and co-cultural variations in what is acceptable and unacceptable practice.

Nonverbal communication serves important functions. It can complement, regulate, substitute for, or accent a verbal message. The key to controlling your nonverbal communication is self-awareness. One way to begin controlling it is to control your emotions. What you need to do is think before you express your feelings.

One way of evaluating your nonverbal communication is to ask some questions about how you use it: How do people react to you? Can you use videotapes to improve your nonverbal communication? How do you use your space? How do you use time? The answers to these questions will indicate areas in which you can improve.

Communication using most forms of the Internet tend to be low in social presence and lean with respect to media richness. High social presence and media richness are best represented in face-to-face communication. Video conferencing is next, followed by synchronous audio (as in instant messaging), then text-based chat, e-mail, and asynchronous audio, and finally threaded discussion such as bulletin boards, usenet groups, mailing lists, and Web forums.

KEY TERMS AND CONCEPTS

Use the *Communicating Effectively* CD-ROM and the Online Learning Center at **www.mhhe.com/hybels8** to further your understanding of the following terms.

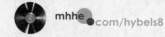

mhhe.com/hybels8

CHAPTER REVIEW

QUESTIONS TO REVIEW

1. What are some of the nonverbal components in each of the elements of the model of communication?

2. In what ways does nonverbal communication contribute to your ability to be strategically flexible?

3. In what ways do verbal and nonverbal communication differ, and of what value is knowing these differences?

4. What are the basic principles that govern nonverbal communication?

5. What is it called when verbal and nonverbal messages conflict? Give an example of this.

6. What are the different types of nonverbal communication, and what is an example of each type that clearly distinguishes it as the type it is designed to reveal?

7. What is paralanguage? What are the vocal qualities that contribute to paralanguage?

8. Can you give an example of nonverbal communication in each of the following body movements: Emblems? Illustrators? Regulators? Displays of feeling? Adaptors?

9. What does clothing communicate about you? How do the following kinds of clothing differ: Uniforms? Occupational dress? Leisure clothing? Costumes?

10. What is the study of space and distance called? What are the four distance zones, and how do they differ?

11. What are the five different categories of touch behavior? Give an example of each.

12. How does the process of smelling occur?

13. Can you give an example of how one's use of time communicates status? How does the use of time differ from culture to culture?

14. What are the functions of nonverbal communication, and how does each one relate to verbal communication?

15. In what ways does one's culture influence his or her nonverbal communication?

16. What ways do you have to control your nonverbal communication?

17. How would you go about improving your nonverbal communication?

18. In using the Internet, what ways do you have to increase your social presence, and what means would you use if you chose an approach designed to increase media richness?

mhhe.com/hybels8

Go to the self-quizzes on the *Communicating Effectively* CD-ROM and the Online Learning Center at **www.mhhe.com/hybels8** to test your knowledge of the chapter contents.

Interpersonal Relationships

After reading this chapter, you should be able to:

- Define *interpersonal communication*.
- Explain emotional intelligence and its importance to strategic flexibility.
- Define and explain *interpersonal needs*.
- Discuss how roles influence interpersonal communication.
- Explain how bids contribute to relationship development and some ways to encourage them.
- Define *self-disclosure*, and tell why it is important.
- Describe the four panes of the Johari Window.
- Describe the effect of the Internet on interpersonal relationships.

L ESLIE STEVENS' ONLINE DATING SERVICE HAD HER RATE HERSELF AND HER potential mate in categories ranging from sex drive to "socialistic-but-terflyosity." An algorithm then calculated her compatibility with a list of matches. Leslie wanted a vegetarian boyfriend who played piano and liked folk music, and she discovered the exact match in Cody Moore—he lived in a dorm on her campus as well. Leslie began sending Cody online messages, and the next thing they knew they were having lunch together and hanging out in real life. Stevens said, "The chances of meeting Moore without the help of an online community were pretty-much nil."

Online dating services have changed the way the college crowd interacts. Instead of getting to know classmates over coffee or through mutual friends, students can now access a goldmine of information about their peers—and potential mates—online.

Interaction with others is called **interpersonal communication**, and it occurs whenever one person interacts with another—usually in an informal setting. You cannot survive in society without interpersonal communication skills. They enable you to function socially and to maintain relationships important to you.

According to Clyde Lindley, Director of the Center for Psychological Services, Silver Springs, Maryland, "Much research shows the importance of interpersonal relationships to well-being, happiness, and satisfaction with life."[1] One study showed that lack of contact with others doubles the chance of getting sick or dying.[2] In a study of college roommates, the researchers discovered that the more roommates disliked each other, the more likely they were to go to the doctor and to come down with colds and the flu. Isolation has more impact on men than on women. Men without close social ties are two to three times more likely to die earlier than men who have them.[3]

This chapter begins by examining the big picture—how you understand and get along with others, who are you attracted to and why—and then discusses the specifics in the next two sections: talking to each other and self-disclosure. The final sections examine the essential elements of good relationships and the Internet's effect on interpersonal relationships.

EMOTIONAL INTELLIGENCE

Anyone who has taught long enough to see students mature can tell you of some who were smart in the classroom but never went anywhere and others who did not do particularly well in school but went on to have successful careers and relationships. Their success is due to what Daniel Goleman calls "emotional intelligence."[4] At its simplest level **emotional intelligence** is the ability to understand and get along with others. Goleman and other researchers see this kind of intelligence as made up of five characteristics: being self-aware, managing emotions, motivating yourself, recognizing emotions in others, and handling relationships. Let's look at each.[5]

Being Self-Aware

Before you can deal with the emotions of others, you need to recognize your own by paying attention to how you feel. Self-awareness requires the ability to get a little distance from the emotion so that you can look at it without being overwhelmed by it or reacting to it too quickly. For example, if you are having an argument with someone and act on your anger, you might tell the other person that you never want to see him or her again. On the other hand, if you can recognize how angry you are feeling, you might be able to say, "Let me think about this some more and talk to you about it later."

Distancing yourself from an emotion does not mean denying it ("I shouldn't feel this way"). Rather, it's a way to articulate to yourself what you are feeling so that you can act on it appropriately.

Managing Emotions

Managing your emotions means expressing them in a manner that is appropriate to the circumstances.[6] You may not be able to do this easily because emotions often come from below the surface of your consciousness. For example, there may have been a time that unexpected tears came to your eyes, or other times when you felt a terrible rage well up inside you.

Another emotion that gets out of control is anxiety.[7] When anxiety is out of control, you feel so worried or so upset that it interferes with the way you function. In a university setting, for instance, most teachers have had students who have been so worried about the right way to do an assignment that they didn't do it at all or did it poorly because they were afraid to take any chances.

Managing your emotions does not mean that you should never feel angry, worried, or anxious. These emotions are all part of being human, and if you don't find a way to express them, they can result in depression or antisocial acts. It's important that you control these emotions rather than letting them control you.

One interesting finding about emotions is that women are better than men at detecting them. In a study where men and women were shown video clips in which someone was having an emotional reaction, 80 percent of the time women were better than men at discerning the emotion.[8]

Motivating Yourself

Motivating yourself is setting a goal and then disciplining yourself to do what you have to do to reach it. Whether you are an athlete or a writer, talent is not enough to make you win the race or get your story published. Both writers and athletes will tell you that they worked hard on many boring activities before they mastered their discipline.

Self-motivation requires resisting impulses. If you are studying for a test, for example, it might be tempting to go to the computer and chat with a friend. If you give in to this impulse, you might become so engrossed in the computer that you completely forget the test.

Some of the most fascinating research on impulse control was done on a group of four-year-old preschoolers.[9] When a child was put into a room with a researcher, he or she was offered a marshmallow. However, the children were told that the researcher had an errand to run and that if they didn't eat the marshmallow, they would get two when the researcher returned. The researcher was gone 15 to 20 minutes—an eternity for a child. The minute he was gone, one-third of the children ate their marshmallows; the remainder found ways to distract themselves: They tried to go to sleep, they talked to themselves, or they engaged in play.

Later these same children were studied when they were teenagers. Those who waited when they were children were much better in social skills, more assertive, and better able to handle themselves in a crisis. Academically, they were far superior as students, and they scored an average of 210 points higher on SAT scores.[10]

Other influences on motivation, according to Goleman, were positive thinking and optimism. Those who had a strong sense of self could bounce back after they had a negative experience. Rather than dwelling on the failure, they looked at ways in which they could improve.[11]

Recognizing Emotions in Others

Empathy, the ability to recognize and share someone else's feelings, is essential to human relationships. It comes from hearing what people are really saying—both by listening to their words and by reading body language such as gestures and facial expressions, and recognizing what they mean by a particular tone of voice. When someone has the same feelings or experiences you have had, it's not difficult to feel empathy. You are really put to the test when you haven't had the other person's feelings or experiences. For example, how can you feel empathy with an African student who hasn't been home for three years and stays in the dorm over Christmas? You can feel sorry for him, and you could tell him that you would feel terrible if you couldn't go home for the holidays. However, these emotions are pity (feeling sorry for him) and sympathy (saying that you'd feel bad too), but they are not empathy because you have not shared his experience. You may go in the direction of empathy if you talk to him for a while, look at the pictures of his brothers and sisters, hear about all the delicious things his mother cooks for Christmas, and so on. Empathy is the extent to which you can sit in his place, see what he sees, and taste what he tastes.

Empathy has a strong moral dimension. Being able to recognize and share someone's distress means that you will not want to hurt him or her. Child molesters and sociopaths, for example, are people lacking in empathy.[12] Sharing empathy with others also means that you are able to reach out and help them because when you can feel as they feel, they are no longer alone.

Handling Relationships

What are some of the characteristics of popular people you know? Chances are that they are people who are largely positive and energetic and that being with them makes you feel positive too. Most likely, they are also the people who organize others (such as the child who suggests a game), negotiate solutions when there is a problem to be solved, and generally connect with others emotionally.[13]

Being popular, however, is not their only goal. People also need a sense of balance; they need to recognize their own needs and know how to fulfill them. For example, you might be popular if you are always willing to stop studying to go to a party. This, however, would not meet your own need to pass your courses.

THE IMPORTANCE OF EMOTIONAL INTELLIGENCE TO STRATEGIC FLEXIBILITY

Self-concept is the way you think about and value yourself. The way you look at others and the world around you, and how well you understand and get along with others, have direct influence on your self-concept, just as the way you think about and value yourself influences both perception and emotional intelligence.

Perception, emotional intelligence, and self-concept have a direct bearing on strategic flexibility simply because they either enhance or impair your ability to anticipate, assess, evaluate, select, and apply your skills and behaviors. The better your perceptive skills, the more likely that your emotional intelligence is high and your self-concept is positive.

Remember the first characteristic of emotional intelligence: self-awareness. Part of maturity is recognizing that just because you have emotions doesn't necessarily mean you must act on them. Not only do you recognize your own emotions, but you understand, too, the triggers that cause them to come to the surface. As you begin to recognize your emotions and their triggers, you will learn how to manage them and to reveal the appropriate ones in given circumstances.

As you become accustomed to using the strategic flexibility framework, you develop self-control through self-discipline. It is as if you are setting mini-goals for yourself. You anticipate situations with the goal of applying the appropriate and relevant skills and behaviors. You achieve success when you maximize your communication, enhance your credibility, and not only support but achieve your intentions.

Listening to others becomes easier when you are secure in your self. Your perceptions become more accurate, and your observations of the nonverbal behavior of others and attempts to really understand them improve. In the end there is a greater chance that you will be able to handle relationships more successfully. Handling relationships is not easy, nor is it automatic. It is learned behavior, and emotional intelligence can help you establish and sustain long-term, meaningful relationships. The problem is simply that emotional intelligence often develops slowly—along with emotional maturity. If you take each of the areas of emotional intelligence, and you make them an issue (see Figure 7-1) before thinking about any serious relationship, you are more likely to take the necessary time.

ATTRACTION TO OTHERS

Sometimes our attraction to others can be measured by individual features, but we are more than the sum of our individual parts. What makes you more is not only what others can see, but what goes on inside you as well—your confidence, your belief in yourself, your unwillingness to put yourself down (or up). Even if you are the world's best looking and brightest, you could still ruin another person's feeling of being special in your presence, by either attacking yourself or bragging.[14]

Every day you encounter scores of people, but most of them recede into a kind of human landscape. Occasionally, however, you think, "Hey, I would really like to get to know this

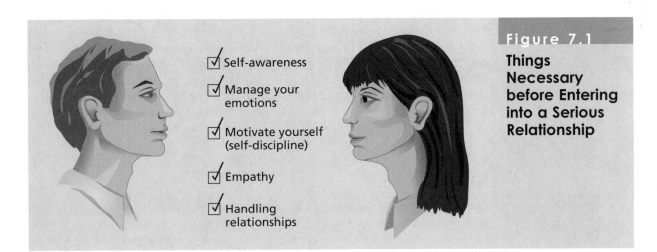

Figure 7.1

Things Necessary before Entering into a Serious Relationship

☑ Self-awareness

☑ Manage your emotions

☑ Motivate yourself (self-discipline)

☑ Empathy

☑ Handling relationships

There are many factors that make up attraction to others. Physical attraction, perceived gain, similarities, differences, and proximity are some of them. What are the likely factors at play here?

person better." Of the scores of people you meet, how do you pick one whom you want to know better? What are the ingredients that make up your attraction to others?

Physical Attraction

We are often attracted to others because of the way they look; we like their style and want to get to know them better. Physical attraction may be sexual attraction. In most cases, however, it goes beyond that. For adults who have had experience in the world, physical attraction usually recedes into the background as they get to know a person. Physical attraction can be a reason for getting to know someone, but it is usually not the basis for a long-term relationship.

Perceived Gain

Often we are attracted to people because we think we have something to gain from associating with them. For example, you join the ski club to get discounted lift tickets. Someone else joins a business management club because it will help her network when she enters the working world.

Although Americans believe they live in a classless society, this is not true. Even colleges and universities have a social hierarchy: Private schools (especially those in the Ivy League) have the most status, while junior and community colleges have the least. Colleges that are supported by a church are in a category of their own. What does this have to do with attraction? People will usually seek out others in their own class. Sometimes, however, they are motivated to move up and they try to blend into a higher class because the perceived awards will be greater.

Similarities

You may be attracted to someone who shares your attitudes and beliefs or seems knowledgeable about topics you find interesting and significant. Your **beliefs** are your convictions; your **attitudes** are the deeply felt beliefs that govern how you behave. When it comes to a strongly felt belief, you probably look for people who believe as you do. For example, in today's world it would be difficult for an Albanian and a Serb to be close friends—their politics have put them in opposing camps.

As adults grow older and meet more and more people, they become aware of the kinds of people they like and dislike, and they recognize the importance of compatibility. **Compatability** means having similar attitudes and personality, and a liking for the same activities.[15] For example, one couple decides to live in the city and focus on their careers rather than have a family. They like drama and excitement in their life—something the city provides. They often attend hockey and basketball games, and they spend their money on trendy clothes and eating out. Because they like the same things, their relationship is likely to last.

Differences

Although two people who have very different beliefs are unlikely to form a strong and lasting relationship, people with different personality characteristics might be attracted to each other. For example, a person who doesn't like making decisions might be attracted to a strong decision maker. Because these characteristics complement each other, they might help strengthen the relationship.

Specific interests may be so similar that they outweigh any differences. An American who runs in the Boston Marathon might have more in common with a runner from Kenya than with someone who spends every Sunday morning reading the newspaper and eating doughnuts. Association with a group might bring people together. Although a Rotary member from Indiana would have a different cultural background than a Rotary member from India, the fact that they both belong to Rotary will create a common ground for some of their interactions.

Proximity

Proximity is the close contact that occurs when people share an experience such as work, play, or school. Even when people might not otherwise have been attracted to each other, they may begin to know and like each other because they are together so much. For example, being in the same study group for a semester, sharing an office, or standing side-by-side on an assembly line are activities that place people in close proximity. Once they begin to share their lives on a day-to-day basis, they may find themselves becoming friends or even forming a romantic relationship.

Sometimes people who are attracted to each other form a strong friendship but lose touch when they no longer have proximity. Typically, friends who move to different cities vow to stay in touch, but it is not unusual for contact to drop to a yearly holiday card. Proximity, then, is important not just for starting relationships but also for keeping them going.

Cyberattraction

When you filter out those aspects of central importance in face-to-face communication—eye contact, self-contact gestures, posture, voice pitch, intensity, stress, rhythm, and volume—the process changes.[16] In cyberattraction, we depend on cues such as language, style, timing, speed of writing, and use of punctuation and emoticons. These form the substance of computer-mediated communication (CMC), discussed in Chapter 1.

CMC gives people an opportunity to interact without the weight of the physical-attractiveness stereotype and gives the smaller number of cues available a greater value. Partners build their stereotypical impressions of each other based on the language content of CMC messages. One researcher has found evidence that CMC groups gradually increase their impression development to a level approaching that of face-to-face groups,[17] but the process takes longer because the cues are fewer.

What are the specific cues of attractiveness in the cyberworld? First, you need to engage in an attentive and sensitive process of negotiation.[18] The negotiation needs to be both intriguing and enticing. Second, you need to simulate proximity by the shared use of a particular tool such as a chat room or newsgroup, and frequent contact is essential. Third, because people are attracted to someone they believe has attitudes similar to their own, because it is difficult and time consuming to learn how people think about multiple issues online, and because there is no way to compare someone's attitudes with their self-presentation (what people can see for themselves), there must be, according to one researcher, a strategic management of the similarity of perceptions.[19]

The fourth cue of attractiveness in the cyberworld is that you need to attract attention and show interest, usually with flatteries and verbal or multimedia compliments, such as virtual flowers. The fifth cue is humor. Humor is easily expressed in typed text, and those who excel at it increase their score on the interpersonal attraction scale.[20]

One of the most important cues to online attractiveness, the sixth, is a certain level of intimacy, or self-disclosure. Because you have no nonverbal cues on which to rely, and because online partners may be relative strangers, the degree of self-disclosure depends on inferring how the other person feels and how to pursue the relationship further. Anonymity often allows, even encourages, less inhibited behavior and opening oneself to another with little, or no fear of losing face.

MOTIVES FOR INTERPERSONAL COMMUNICATION

Everyone has needs that will vary with personality and moods. When you seek out others, you are trying to meet one or more of the following interpersonal needs: pleasure, affection, inclusion, escape, relaxation, control, health, and cybermotivation.[21]

Pleasure

We engage in a lot of interpersonal communication because it's fun. You chat online or gossip on the telephone with your best friend; you sit around and argue about sports teams with your buddies; you stop at the student center to have coffee, but also in the hope of meeting someone you know.

Affection

Whether it is expressed nonverbally (hugging, touching) or verbally ("I'm really glad you called me today"), affection is important to human happiness.

Unlike inclusion, affection is a one-to-one emotion.

Inclusion

Inclusion—involvement with others—is one of the most powerful human needs. Although nearly everyone has had the experience of being excluded, most people have had more experiences of being included. You may eat with a certain group at the cafeteria, go to parties at friends' houses, or join a club at the university. Belonging in this way is important to everyone's sense of well-being.

Escape

At one time or another, we all engage in interpersonal communication to try to avoid the jobs we are supposed to do. For example, before you begin writing your term paper, you decide to wander down the hall of your dorm to talk to a friend. A new form of escape is escape by computer. Chat rooms, e-mail, and surfing the Internet are particularly popular and enable you to escape without even going anywhere.

Relaxation

You often talk to your friends or families to relax and unwind from the activities of the day. You might sit with co-workers during a break, spend a few minutes with your spouse after work, or go out with a group of friends on the weekend.

Control

In a broad sense control means being able to make choices.

In the best relationships, the persons try to share control, which may change due to circumstances. For example, a couple we know moved to a new place where the wife had to commute two hours a day. This meant that she was not home to cook the evening meal, so her husband had to do it. He took control by reorganizing the kitchen to his liking—a legitimate action since he was now the main cook.

Researchers have found that people who have control over their own lives are healthier both mentally and physically.[22] Students learn better when teachers give them some independence, and workers feel better about their jobs when they can make some decisions about how their work should be done.[23] People who have the sense that they are in control of their lives are meeting one of their deepest needs.

Health

Research shows that people with strong social ties live longer than those who are isolated.[24] If you have a romantic partner, frequent contact with friends and family, or involvement with volunteer or religious organizations, the social support systems you form assist you in keeping heart rate, hypertension, and stress hormones under control. Lonely people often view the world as threatening, and although they want to be connected, they both expect negative responses and engage in self-protective behaviors that are self-defeating. Experts advise lonely people to join a local club or organization just because of the health-protective effects.

Cybermotivation

In computer-mediated communication, there is often considerably less anxiety than in real-life interactions. There is usually increased motivation because engaging in CMC is entertaining and exciting. In addition, CMC can bolster self-esteem, and you can self-disclose with little possibility of losing face. There is anonymity if you want it, and an opportunity to be who you want to be as well. The high levels of affiliation and trust often result in higher levels of self-disclosure, associated with our having a heightened sense of who we are when communicating via CMC.

TALKING TO EACH OTHER

Roles, Relationships, and Communication

All relationships are governed by the roles that the participants expect each other to play. Sometimes these roles are tightly defined; other times the participants have the flexibility to define them.

Often the roles you know best are those that are the most traditionally defined such as teachers and parents. Even though the people who work in these roles might want more flexibility than is allowed by traditional definitions, they often feel social pressure to conform to traditional roles and thus to traditional behavior.

Usually at the beginning of a relationship with someone your own age, you can choose the roles you want to play. Friends, for example, often decide on the role they will play within a friendship. Once the relationship is established, role expectations become fixed and friends expect each other to react in certain ways.

A critical question in a marriage is whether you want to play the role your father or mother played. If you don't, how will you set out to define your own role? Sherod Miller, a psychologist, says that once the partners give up old roles—the ones that were based on gender—they have to work out new ones: a process that leads to negotiating every aspect of their lives, especially when the first baby arrives.[25]

Other psychologists who have studied marriage found that the most successful marriages are ones where the male partners listen to their female partners rather than reacting defensively to complaints and criticism. A husband's willingness to listen shows that he understands and respects his wife's needs, and when this occurs, there is a much better chance of marital stability.[26]

As well as roles for your intimate relationships, there are roles for all aspects of your life and communication that work best in each of them. Your job is to find out which communication works best for all the roles you play. You will see, then, that much of your success in playing a role will depend on how well you communicate in that role.

Beginning Conversations: The Art of Small Talk

Have you ever felt nervous about entering a classroom where you didn't know any of the students? In many new social situations you might feel uneasy. You may wonder whether you will be able to begin a conversation and whether you will find people you like and, just as important, people who like you. The uncertainty you are feeling will probably be shared by other people in the room. How do you go about reducing it?

When most people begin conversations, they engage in **small talk**—social conversation about unimportant topics that allows a person to maintain contact without making a deep commitment. There are all sorts of conventions in small talk. Scholars who have studied conversation have found that it follows a routine that varies only slightly. Figure 7-2 shows this conversation pattern.

As you can see in this figure, many of the conversational responses are based on questions, some to find out information, others to establish common ground. Other questions are asked just to fill time or to be sociable. Since most people like answering questions about themselves, they are flattered when someone shows interest in them.

Dianna Booher, a business communications consultant, offers the following tips for beginning conversations:

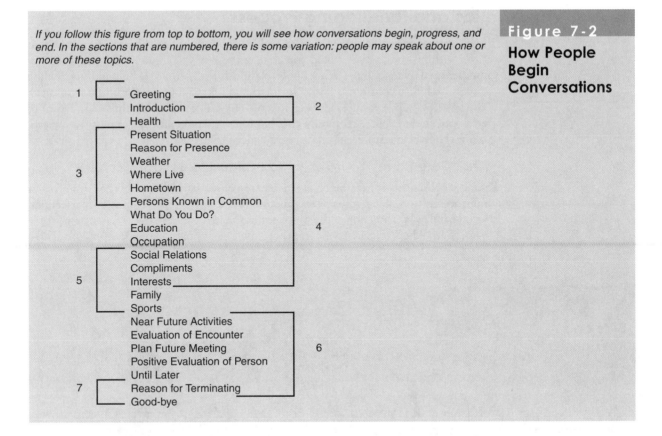

If you follow this figure from top to bottom, you will see how conversations begin, progress, and end. In the sections that are numbered, there is some variation: people may speak about one or more of these topics.

Figure 7-2

How People Begin Conversations

1
   Greeting
   Introduction   2
   Health
   Present Situation
   Reason for Presence
   Weather
3 Where Live
   Hometown
   Persons Known in Common
   What Do You Do?
   Education   4
   Occupation
   Social Relations
   Compliments
5 Interests
   Family
   Sports
   Near Future Activities
   Evaluation of Encounter
   Plan Future Meeting   6
   Positive Evaluation of Person
   Until Later
7 Reason for Terminating
   Good-bye

- *Introduce yourself in a way that gives the other person a way to respond to you.* This approach will uncover what the two of you have in common, and it will probably lead to subjects for conversation. Here, for example, is how a person who was much younger than most of the guests at the university president's party introduced himself: "Hi, I'm Jim Dolan, and I'm the student member of the Board of Trustees at the university."

- *Give people a way to remember your name.* The author of this text whose last name is Hybels told people that it rhymes with *bibles.* Not only did people learn how to pronounce her name, but often they remembered it when they met her again.

- *Personalize your greeting.* If you know something about the person, try to work it into your greeting. For example, "I liked the presentation you made in class last week."[27]

Booher also suggests that when you end the conversation, you do it as gracefully as possible. "Excuse me, I've enjoyed talking to you" is a short and graceful ending.

Because small-talk topics and questions are socially sanctioned, they create a safe meeting ground. They provide you with a chance to establish who you are with others. They also permit you to find out more about yourself through the eyes of others. Although you don't give away a lot of personal information in small talk, the image you give to others and the image you receive of them will let you know whether you want to see them again.

Bids and the Bidding Process

If you knew specifically what it was that holds relationships together, and you knew that it was within your control, would you change the way you conducted yourself in your interpersonal relationships? What holds relationships together are bids and the bidding process. A **bid**, according to John Gottman and his team of relationship researchers, "can be a question, a gesture, a look, a touch—any single expression that says, 'I want to feel connected to you.' A **response to a bid** is just that—a positive or negative answer to somebody's request for emotional connection." See Figure 7-3.[28]

What Determines Your Ability to Bid and to Respond to Bids?

Some people are likely to be better at bids and responses than others. There are three major influences at work. First, it may be a function of the way people's brains process feelings. Second, it may be a function of the way emotions were handled in the homes where people grew up. And third, it may be a function of people's emotional communication skills. These

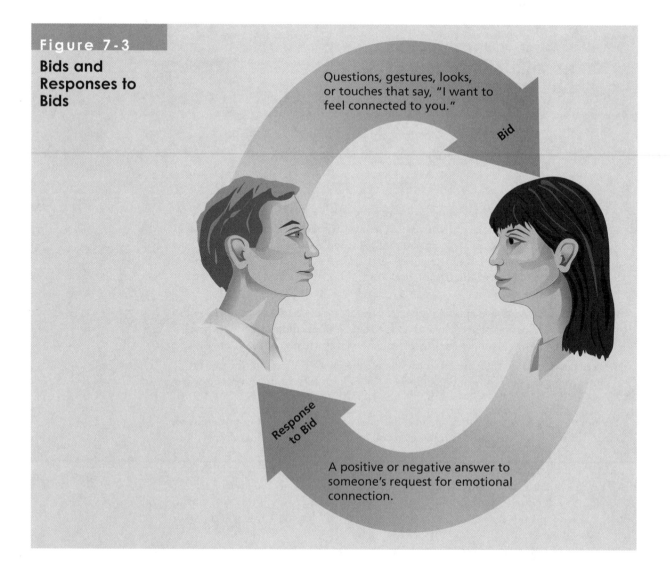

Figure 7-3

Bids and Responses to Bids

Questions, gestures, looks, or touches that say, "I want to feel connected to you."

Bid

Response to Bid

A positive or negative answer to someone's request for emotional connection.

three influences can be complex, interacting variables. Despite their influence, however, sometimes just knowing what ingredients can influence a relationship, or just knowing specifically what you can do to make a relationship you cherish a success, is enough. Placing bids and responding to bids is a skill that can be learned, practiced, and mastered.[29]

How Do Bids Contribute to Relationship Development?

In successful relationships, bids for emotional connection are responded to positively. Bids from either relationship partner are neither ignored nor dismissed, whether they are simple or mundane. It is the simple and mundane bids that weave the fabric that forms the backdrop for all future bids. Many come nonverbally and include vocalizing, affiliating gestures (like opening a door or offering a place to sit), playful touching, facial expressions, or affectionate touching.[30] Sure, some bids may be unseen, unheard, or overlooked just as some may be sent in a subtle, camouflaged, confused, or nonspecific manner. It is the overall pattern of behavior that is important, not necessarily any single, solitary bid. Remember, in most positive relationships thousands of bids take place daily.

Each encounter in a relationship is made up of many smaller exchanges—bids and responses to those bids. These exchanges of emotional information will either strengthen or weaken the connections between people, and these connections form the fabric we referred to earlier. Here, in the first example, the response to the bid is negative. In the next, the response is positive:

> *Hey, Chris. Did you get that class report finished?*
> *Would you stop nagging at me? You sound just like my mother!*

> *Would you get me a soda while you're up?*
> *No problem. Do you want anything else?*

The point is not the content, and the point has nothing to do with timing or circumstances. The point is that a positive response to a bid typically leads to continued interaction, and the chances for a successful relationship become better and better. And the reverse is just as clear. Negative responses to bids will shut down communication. Bids cease, and the relationship terminates.

How Can You Encourage Bids?

How can you make certain you respond positively to the bids of others if you choose to do so? Gottman and his researchers discuss six common sense ways to encourage and reinforce the bids of others. These are outlined in Figure 7-4.

Owned Messages

An **owned message** (also known as an I-message, as coined by Thomas Gordon[31]) is *"an acknowledgment of subjectivity by a message-sender through the use of first-person-singular terms* (I, me, my, mine). 'Responsible' communicators are those who 'own' their thoughts and feelings by employing these pronouns."[32]

Owned messages tend to provoke less interpersonal defensiveness than you-messages, and they are useful for conveying negative information. Some simple examples of owned and unowned messages will demonstrate the difference. To say "You make me mad" is an example of an unowned message (a you-message) and, as is obvious, has the potential for creating defensiveness in another person. To say "I'm feeling angry" is an example of owning a message and is less likely to create defensiveness.

Gordon said owned messages can be called "responsibility messages" because those who send them are taking responsibility for their own inner condition (listening to *themselves*) and

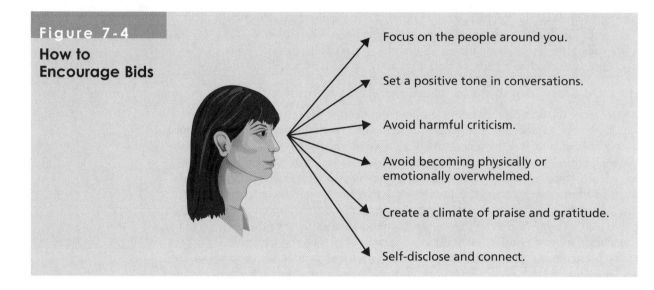

Figure 7-4

How to Encourage Bids

Focus on the people around you.

Set a positive tone in conversations.

Avoid harmful criticism.

Avoid becoming physically or emotionally overwhelmed.

Create a climate of praise and gratitude.

Self-disclose and connect.

assuming responsibility for being open enough to share their assessment of themselves with others. In addition, they leave the responsibility for the other person's behavior with them.[33]

What does an I-message look like? Gordon suggests a behavior/feelings/effects formula for constructing I-messages.

1. A description by the one concerned of the other's unacceptable (disruptive) behavior.

2. The feelings of the one concerned in reaction to the other's unacceptable behavior.

3. An explanation of how the other's behavior interferes with the one concerned's ability to answer his or her own needs.

Example: **"Jennifer, when you leave things everywhere (1) I get frustrated (2) because I cannot do what I have to do (3)."**

Remember as you use owned messages, any given behavior can be an asset or a liability, depending on the goal or situation. Interpersonal skills are competent when communicators employ them sensitively and sensibly according to the requirements of a particular social setting. Using owned messages is a skill that is generally perceived to be competent across contexts. It can increase your sense of control and responsibility, and control and responsibility are issues that are basic and paramount to interpersonal competence.[34]

SELF-DISCLOSURE: IMPORTANT TALK

To communicate who you are to other people, you have to engage in **self-disclosure**—a process in which one person tells another person something he or she would not reveal to just anyone.

The Importance of Self-Disclosure

Social penetration is the process of increasing both disclosure and intimacy in a relationship, and it is one of the most widely studied processes in relational development.[35] The theory is that relationships become more intimate over time as partners disclose more

Working Together

n a group, discuss bids and responses to bids by answering the following questions one at a time around the group:

1. In what way have you made bids for connection with important people in your life today?

2. How did you feel about the way people responded to your bids?

3. Did you notice anyone responding positively to your bids? In what ways?

4. Did you notice anyone turning away from your bids? In what ways?

5. Did you notice anyone turning against your bids? What did your behavior look like?

6. How have you responded today to other people's bids for connection?

7. Did you respond positively? How?

8. Did you turn away? How?

9. Did you turn against any bids for connection? How and why?

10. Do you think bids and responding to bids is an accurate way to assess the quality of interpersonal relationships?

Source: *The Relationship Cure: A Five-Step Guide for Building Better Connections with Family, Friends, and Lovers* (p. 15), by J. M. Gottman and J. DeClaire, 2001, New York: Crown Publishers.

and more information about themselves. When partners in a relationship are motivated, and when they exert the extra effort necessary not just to continue their relationship but to permit its growth, the relationship necessarily undergoes certain qualitative changes. Partners experience an additional sense of connectedness. At the same time, writes one researcher, "communicative transactions become increasingly interpersonal."[36]

Whether you want to encourage a relationship, hold it at the same level, or back off often depends on the information you get during the process of self-disclosure. Gerald Miller and his communication-research colleagues state that there are three kinds of information.[37] The first kind is **cultural information** which tells us about a person's most generally shared cultural attributes such as language, shared values, beliefs, and ideologies. Information at this level is as shallow and impersonal as is a greeting or good-bye. Knowing it allows you to perform acceptably in most social situations, but it is not very helpful when it comes to relationships.

The second kind of information is **sociological** and tells you something about others' social groups and roles. This level of communication allows you to be successful communicating with your doctor, dentist, lawyer, or hair stylist. You know something about their roles and affiliations, but you know relatively little about the person separate from his or her role.

The third kind of information is **psychological**, which is the most specific and intimate because it allows you to know individual traits, feelings, attitudes, and important personal data. This is the type of information on which most of your predictions about relationships will be based.

It is through self-disclosure, then, that you meet someone who believes the way you do—that you discover a common interest, for example, which you can pursue in greater depth because both of you have some background and information to share. Such a partner is likely to react to situations and events the way you would, and you trust him or her enough to reveal even more about yourself. The Assess Yourself box at the end of this chapter is on trusting others, because trust is an important part of the self-disclosure process.

Self-disclosure is important to relationships in other ways as well. You use it in the process of reciprocity: When someone discloses with you, your tendency is to self-disclose in return. You use self-disclosure for self-clarification—to clarify beliefs, opinions, thoughts, attitudes, and problems: "I thought you understood I was only kidding." You

Telling a secret might be one form of self-disclosure.

use it for identity management in attempts to make yourself more attractive: "I'm using a new fragrance; did you notice?" You use it for social control when revealing information may increase your control over the situation or a person: "I was given the authority to lead this group, and I think we should all stick to our agenda."

The Process of Self-Disclosure

One way to look at how the self-disclosure process operates was developed by Joseph Luft and Harry Ingham. Combining their first names, they labeled their model the **Johari Window** (see Figure 7-5).[38]

The "Free to self and others" area—the *open pane*—includes information about yourself that you are willing to communicate, as well as information you are unable to hide (such as a blush when you are embarrassed). When students meet for the first time in a class, they follow the instructor's suggestion and introduce themselves. Most of them stick to bare essentials: their names, where they come from, and their majors. When people do not know one another very well, the open pane is smaller than when they have become better acquainted.

The area labeled "Blind to self, seen by others"—the *blind pane*—is a kind of accidental disclosure area: There are certain things you do not know about yourself that others know about you. For example, a husband complains that every time his wife comes home from work, she looks mad—something she didn't realize until he pointed it out.

The *hidden pane*—self-knowledge hidden from others—is a deliberate nondisclosure area; there are certain things you know about yourself that you do not want known, so you deliberately conceal them from others. Most people hide things that might evoke disapproval from those they love and admire: "I was a teenage shoplifter"; "I don't know how to read very well." Others keep certain areas hidden from one person but open to another: A young woman tells her best friend, but not her mother, that her grades are low because she seldom studies.

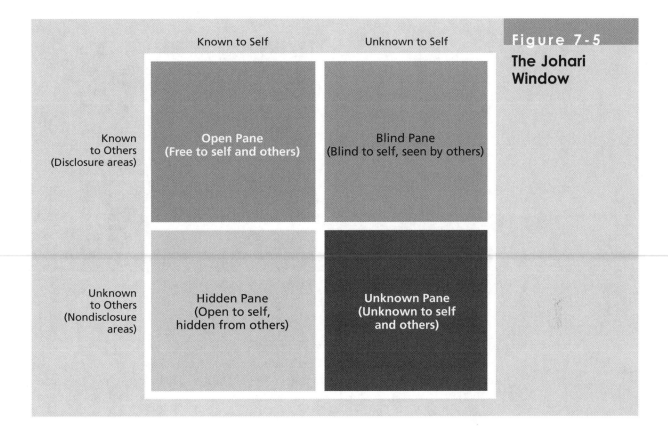

Figure 7-5

The Johari Window

The ***unknown pane*** is a nondisclosure area; it provides no possibility of disclosure because it is unknown to the self or to others. This pane represents all the parts of you that are not yet revealed. You might think that you are very brave, but you really don't know how you will react when you are faced with personal danger.

The disclosure and nondisclosure areas vary from one relationship to another, and they change all the time in the same relationship. Figure 7-6 shows how the Johari Window might look in a close relationship. The open pane becomes much larger because a person is likely to disclose more. When disclosure increases, people not only reveal more information about themselves but also are likely to discover things about themselves that they had not known before. If you apply the Johari Window to each of your relationships, you will find that the panes are different sizes in each one. In other words, you are likely to be more self-disclosing in some relationships than you are in others.

Self-Disclosure and Intimacy: Rewards and Fears

Self-disclosure is the most rewarding when it leads to greater intimacy. Only intimate relationships give you a chance to really be yourself, to share who you are with another person. This kind of intimacy can be found in romantic relationships and among family members and close friends. One study has found that both men and women are willing to self-disclose to about the same degree.[39]

Although in this chapter we take the position that self-disclosure is very important if you are going to have deep and satisfying relationships, we also acknowledge that many people fear the consequences of revealing themselves to another.

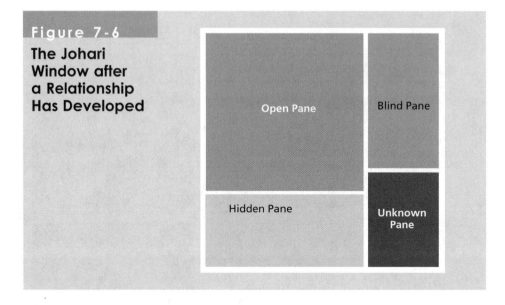

Figure 7-6

The Johari Window after a Relationship Has Developed

Open Pane

Blind Pane

Hidden Pane

Unknown Pane

Fear of Having Your Faults Exposed

Self-disclosure in a relationship may lead to communicating that you are not perfect and exposing things from your past that you would rather keep hidden. Once your fears, anxieties, or weaknesses are known to another person, that person could tell them to others or use them against you.

Fear That Your Partner Will Become Your Critic

By telling someone you are vulnerable, you open yourself to attack. A wife, for example, tells her husband how bad she felt when she wasn't invited to the senior prom. One day when they are having a fight, he says, "Don't tell me how much people like you. You didn't even get invited to the prom!"

Fear of Losing Your Individuality

Some people feel that if they reveal too much, they lose their sense of self, that there are private things that only they should know. This might be especially true during the years when teenagers are trying to gain autonomy from their families. Part of being autonomous is making decisions on your own and not telling everything to your parents.

Fear of Being Abandoned

Sometimes one partner is afraid that if the other knows something about him or her, he or she will be abandoned. For example, someone might not want to tell another about his struggle with alcoholism for fear that the other person will no longer love, accept, or want him.

When Should Self-Disclosure Occur?

Disclosure should occur only in relationships that are important to you. People who do not know you very well are likely to feel uncomfortable if you tell them too much about yourself too soon. Wait until you have some signs that a relationship has the possibility of developing further. For example, if someone seeks you out to invite you to go out

Discussion Prompt
Conduct a full-class discussion to answer the question: What are some of the fears you face in relationships that hold you back from full self-disclosure?

with him or her, after three or four times this is a sign that the person wants the relationship to develop.

For disclosure to work, both parties must be involved in it. If one person does all the disclosing and the other party just sits back and listens, disclosure is not likely to continue. Remember that disclosure means taking a risk. You will never know how another person will respond to your openness until you give it a try. To avoid getting hurt, try testing the water before you plunge in. One way of doing this is to talk about a subject in general terms and see how the other person reacts before you talk about your own experience with it.

Finally, examine your own motives for self-disclosure. Why do you want the other person to know this information? Will it really enhance the relationship, or can it do harm? All of us have some secrets that we should probably keep to ourselves. Sharing them may cause injury or make the other person lose trust in us. Although some secrets are a burden to keep, it may serve the interest of the relationship to do so. Those in relationships who believe in full and complete disclosure with partners risk the possibility of damage and even loss.

STRATEGIC FLEXIBILITY
Because of the risks, knowing when to self-disclose requires that you think about potential situations (anticipate); take stock of the factors, elements, and conditions of the situation (assess); determine the value and worth of the factors, elements, and conditions (evaluate); and carefully select the skills and behaviors that are likely to be appropriate (select) before engaging in self-disclosure.

ESSENTIAL ELEMENTS OF GOOD RELATIONSHIPS

Once you have begun using bids, owned messages, and self-disclosure, a relationship has truly begun and you need to "grow" it. Here, we will look at elements that draw people together: verbal skills, emotional expressiveness, conversational focus, non-verbal analysis, conversational encouragement, care and appreciation, commitment, and adaptation.

Verbal Skills

Partners in good relationships must have ongoing conversations, or dialogues, about the relationship itself. They must be able to search together for ways of reducing conflict, to discuss expectations they have of each other, and to explore anything else that might affect the relationship. In her article "Finding Real Love," Cary Barbor ends by saying, "Learning how best to communicate with each other and treat one another will help us enjoy loving, lasting relationships."[40]

Not only do females begin talking earlier than males, on most national assessment tests they score well ahead of males in reading and writing, and many more major in English, comparative literature, and foreign languages than men.[41] To make certain the playing field remains level, males may need to apply themselves more when it comes to verbal skills, because for partners to continue in a relationship, they must find mutually beneficial ways of communicating. Also, males need to alter their perception of relationships as stable, static commodities that never need discussion or reexamination.

Emotional Expressiveness

Gottman noted that your ability to bid and to respond to bids depends on the way your brain processes feelings, the way emotions were handled in your home, and your emotional communication skills.[42] Christina Hoff Sommers claims that females' verbal skills "may be responsible for their superior emotional expressiveness."[43] Her claim is supported by Daniel Goleman in *Emotional Intelligence* who says, "Because girls develop language more quickly than do boys, this leads them to be more experienced at articulating their feelings and more skilled than boys at using words to explore and substitute for emotional reactions such as physical fights."[44] Not only are females more expressive and responsive to others, they "invite others into conversations."[45] Once again, to level the playing field, males need to improve their ability at emotional expressiveness.

Achieving emotional expressiveness may require discussing points of conflict. This is particularly important if relationships are to be successful. Some people are conditioned to stay away from conflict. Childhood messages such as "Hold your tongue" and "I don't ever want to hear you talk that way again" lead us to believe that it's wrong to say words that other people do not want to hear. As adults, however, we have to recondition ourselves to discuss areas of conflict: Withdrawing from or avoiding conflict is too harmful to relationships.

Conversational Focus

A third factor likely to affect your ability to handle relationships is what you choose to talk about. Sommers claims that "Males, whether young or old, are less interested than females in talking about feelings and personal relationships."[46] Researchers at Northwestern University analyzed the conversational focus of college students gathered around a cafeteria table.[47] They discovered that 56 percent of the women's targets were intimates, close friends, boyfriends, and family members, but only 25 percent of the conversational focus of men was friends and relatives.[48] When researchers simultaneously presented male and female college students with two images on a stereoscope, one of an object, the other of a person, male subjects more often saw the object while female subjects more often saw the person.[49] Males need to increase their focus on feelings and relationships—to not only make their feelings known, but to make other people, especially their relationship partner, know how they feel about them and about their relationship.

What are some of the obvious elements of good relationships being revealed in this group?

Nonverbal Analysis

A fourth factor that will affect your ability to handle relationships is your ability to read between the lines, to analyze the nonverbal cues of the other person. Dozens of experiments confirm "that women are much better than men at judging emotions based on the expression on a stranger's face."[50] Not only are women better at observing the nonverbal cues of others, they also "tend to give obvious visual and vocal clues to signal they are following what others say and are interested in it."[51] Clues might include nodding their heads, smiling, establishing eye contact, and offering responsive gestures.[52] Males need to increase their sensitivity to nonverbal cues. Because they are not conditioned to be as observant in this area, they need to be especially vigilant and aware.

Conversational Encouragement

Often, men listen to others without showing their feelings; they keep their responses and feelings to themselves, as noted in the section on emotional expressiveness. This can be interpreted as an unwillingness to listen or lack of interest.[53] Women, on the other hand, encourage others to continue talking using listening noises such as "um, hmmm," "yes," "that's interesting," "so," "and," and so forth. They are encouragers, and these vocalizations not only reveal they are listening and interested, but they also prompt others to continue talking and to elaborate on their ideas.[54]

Roger Axtell, in his book *Do's and Taboos Around the World for Women in Business*, quotes Kathi Seifert, group president of North American personal care products for the Kimberly-Clark Corporation, who says "Women are naturally more caring, nurturing, and better listeners. They like to help and to respond to people's needs."[55] Shmuley Boteach, dean of the L'Chaim Society, which hosts world figures and diplomats and concentrates on values-based leadership, says women "when speaking to their husbands, . . . stop talking in midsentence because they know they are not being listened to. They feel like a piece of furniture, and this experience of being ignored is a denial of their value. Their spirit is crushed."[56] Fein and Schneider, in *The Rules for Marriage*, write "Learn how to listen without interrupting or offering advice, so that you can understand your spouse's perspective on things."[57] Men need to open up more, show their feelings, listen better, and reveal their responses. It may help, too, if men view conversations as Mary Boone describes them: "The purpose of a conversation is not to *agree* with each other, it's to learn from each other on both an intellectual and emotional level."[58]

Care and Appreciation

Scholars have found that people consistently use ways to communicate whether they want to have a relationship with a person or whether they want to avoid him or her.[59] The approach people use most often to foster a relationship is expressing *caring and appreciation* for the other person. Typical remarks might be, "We had such a good time last night, I would like to see you again," or "I am so glad that we are friends"—bids expressing "I want to feel connected to you." The second most used technique is giving *compliments*: "That was such a funny joke you told last night," or "You look great today"—more bids seeking connection. The third technique they use is engaging in *self-disclosure*—(also a bid) telling someone something about themselves that they wouldn't tell most people: "I felt so bad when I failed the test," or "I really like her: I wish she would pay some attention to me."

Commitment

All relationships need **commitment**—a strong desire by both parties for the relationship to continue and a willingness on both parties to take responsibility for the problems that occur in the relationship. Trying to force a partner to make a commitment, however, is a waste of time, claims Adrienne Burgess, in an article "I Vow to Thee" in the *Guardian*. She says, "Not only does it (commitment) provide no guarantees, but it also causes resentment and hostility, which undermines any loving feelings. In relationships with a real future, therefore, commitment usually develops at much the same rate on both sides. But promises of commitment are meaningless in the long-term, too—commitment isn't an act of will (while we can promise to stay with someone physically, we can't promise the same emotionally), and isn't something we do in any active sense. Commitment is a spin-off from other things: how satisfied we are with our relationship; whether we see a viable alternative to it; and whether moving on would cause us to lose important investments (time, money, shared property, and children)."[60]

All relationships have some kind of commitment as their foundation, but sometimes the partners to the commitment have different expectations. *Unconditional* commitments are those in which you commit yourself to another regardless of what may happen. Marriage vows are often cited as examples of unconditional commitments; however, with divorce rates hovering around 50 percent, it is clear that nearly one out of every two couples who accept the unconditional commitment do not fulfill it. *Conditional* commitments set forth the conditions of the commitment and carry with them the implication of "only if." "I will commit to you only if I do not find something better in the meantime," or "I will commit to you only if something extraordinary doesn't happen."

Although commitments are important and reassuring, it is perhaps better to accept them for what they are worth, based on the trust and faith in the person making the commitment and with hope for a positive future. However, it is best to prepare for the fact that most commitments are conditional, and it is unlikely that all conditions will be, or even could be, revealed or even known. Of course marriage should be an unconditional commitment, but we live in a transient society where planned obsolescence, endless technological advances, and instant millionaires guarantee a rapid and regular turnover of products, information, and fortunes; why should we expect relationships, including marriages, to be anything other than of short duration? Dreams, faith, optimism, visualizations, and confidence are all fine, but they really don't prepare you for a realistic conditional future. Only you can do that.

STRATEGIC FLEXIBILITY

Adapting and adjusting your behaviors and skills to changing circumstances is the foundation of strategic flexibility. Having all the tools in your toolbox is important, but even more important in strategic flexibility is carefully selecting exactly those tools likely to have the greatest impact and applying them with care and concern.

Adaptation

The time and effort dedicated to supporting, encouraging, and nurturing relationships—even well-established ones—must be spent in both introspection (the act of contemplating one's mental processes and emotional state in the relationship) and communication. Introspection and communication within relationships are foreign to conventional masculinity.[61]

Verbal skills, emotional expressiveness, conversational focus, nonverbal analysis, conversational encouragement, care and appreciation, and commitment are tools that help hold relationships together. You need to speak, listen, negotiate, stay on course, and hold your relationship in warm regard.[62] But if you can't adapt and adjust your skills and behaviors to the changes that occur, as introspection and communication will help you to do, these tools are useless. "After years of research," says one writer, "it turns out that what makes for highly adaptive people is their capacity to adapt."[63]

THE INTERNET AND INTERPERSONAL RELATIONSHIPS

People in virtual communities use the words they type on screens to:

exchange pleasantries and argue, engage in intellectual discourse, conduct commerce, exchange knowledge, share emotional support, make plans, brainstorm, gossip, feud, fall in love, find friends and lose them, play games, flirt, create a little high art and a lot of idle talk.[64]

Leslie Stevens and Cody Moore (from our opening example) are a small testament to both the success and nature of the Internet. What has now become dramatically and emphatically clear is that the Internet is more a social creation than a technical one.

There have been numerous studies on the Internet's effect on users, and just as there have been dire predictions about the erosion of language, there were similar predictions about the Internet's effect on interpersonal relationships—that the Internet promotes social disengagement (less voting, going to church, and discussing government with neighbors; fewer voluntary organizations and dinner parties; and less getting together for civic and social purposes). *Time* magazine reported that the amount of time the average U.S. Internet user spends online is 3 hours each day, and that each hour of Internet use reduces face-to-face contact with family members by 23.5 minutes.[65]

Internet addiction also is a problem. John Douglas and Stephen Singular, in their book *Anyone You Want Me to Be*, write that "Surfing the Net for love can easily become a minor hobby that evolves into a major pastime that turns into an addiction that can be almost as demanding and consuming as a full-time job."[66] Dr. Kimberly S. Young, assistant professor of psychology at the University of Pittsburgh–at Bradford, has stated that those most vulnerable to Internet addiction are those who are lonely, bored, depressed, or introverted or who lack self-esteem or have a history of addictions.

In his speech "Avoiding Trends That Deprive Us of Humanity," D. Stanley Eitzen, professor emeritus in the Department of Sociology at Colorado State University, states:

We are becoming a society that finds it easier, and even preferable to hide behind our computer screens and chat with a faceless, nameless stream of words from across the country or across the globe rather than deal with people face to face and all the complexities, good and bad, of the human relationship.[67]

For those raised in an Internet world, it is just another form of relating, a form that is different from other forms, to be sure, but one that provides valuable, important, and worthwhile benefits. For many Americans, e-mail and instant messaging have become essential features of social life. Overall, because of its ease of use, efficiency, and ubiquity, the Internet has made a dramatic increase in the number of interpersonal relationships we are likely to have.

The benefits of Internet communication are too numerous to mention; however, here are a few:

- It promotes healthy communication and interaction.
- It offers a strong support system for interpersonal relationships.
- It allows otherwise marginalized people to be integrated into society (it removes all barriers that shy people never get past in person).

- It reduces the costs of communicating with geographically distant acquaintances and strangers.

- It increases social contacts beyond family and close friends.

- It offers opportunities for communicating on an international level, for meeting those who identify with us, and who aid us in gaining perspective from them and from their backgrounds.

- It loosens the social restrictions that have traditionally protected morality and manners.

Online dating alone is a fixture of single life for adults of all ages, backgrounds, and interests. The extent of its use is staggering. Rachel Greenwald, in her book *Find a Husband After 35*, lists the benefits: (1) You can reach far more interested parties than by any other means; (2) it is fast; (3) it is inexpensive; (4) it is convenient; (5) it gives you the opportunity to tap into new groups of people outside your regular social circle; (6) you can really get to know each other first; thus, physical appearance is not a barrier to learning what really counts about one another; and (7) it is anonymous—you decide whether you want to reply, what you want to reveal, whether you want to meet, and when and where.[68] We discuss pitfalls of online dating in the next chapter.

The Internet has proven its value in interpersonal relationships. Look at the benefit that cell phones and computers with e-mail and instant messaging capabilities provide in keeping families and friends in touch, even though spread over wide geographical areas. The Internet also can affirm, reinforce, and assist in maintaining good relationships.

Trusting Others Scale

Indicate the degree to which you agree or disagree with each statement using the following scale: 1 = Strongly agree; 2 = Mildly agree; 3 = Agree and disagree equally; 4 = Mildly disagree; 5 = Strongly disagree. Circle your response following each statement.

1. Most people in my life are reliable and dependable. 5 4 3 2 1 0
2. In general, when there is a task to be done, I prefer doing it myself rather than asking someone else to do it. 5 4 3 2 1 0
3. Other people, in general, possess what I consider to be core (essential) skills and abilities. 5 4 3 2 1 0
4. In general, people share relevant information with me. 5 4 3 2 1 0
5. I get overly anxious when an important job that directly affects me and that I could do is carried out by someone else. 5 4 3 2 1 0
6. In general, the actions others take live up to the values they claim to live by. 5 4 3 2 1 0
7. Sometimes I feel I am being taken advantage of when someone else is taking actions that directly affect me, and yet I have no control over those actions. 5 4 3 2 1 0
8. In general, other people have a benevolent attitude toward me. 5 4 3 2 1 0
9. When in a group, I prefer working independently rather than as part of the group. 5 4 3 2 1 0
10. People tell white lies. 5 4 3 2 1 0
11. I have confidence in the integrity, ability, character, and truth of most other people. 5 4 3 2 1 0
12. In general, when others promise they will do something, I believe it will be done. 5 4 3 2 1 0
13. When others perform actions that directly affect me, I expect positive outcomes to occur. 5 4 3 2 1 0
14. In general, other people are open and honest with me, sharing all of their information, not just selected facts or opinions. 5 4 3 2 1 0
15. Other people voluntarily share their information with me. 5 4 3 2 1 0
16. I prefer to let those around me work independently, even if their work directly affects me. 5 4 3 2 1 0
17. Other people listen to me and to my ideas. 5 4 3 2 1 0
18. In general, others do not do what they say they will do. 5 4 3 2 1 0
19. I prefer situations where people with whom I am working have full opportunities for mutual influence—me influencing them and they influencing me. 5 4 3 2 1 0
20. In general, people are considerate of the ideas and feelings of others. 5 4 3 2 1 0
21. I prefer to monitor the behavior of others when I know their actions will affect me in some way. 5 4 3 2 1 0
22. I am willing to allow others to take actions that are important to and directly affect me, even though I have no control over how those actions will be done. 5 4 3 2 1 0
23. In general, other people are not as important as I am. 5 4 3 2 1 0
24. In general, I prefer to work with others to obtain a mutually acceptable outcome rather than to work alone. 5 4 3 2 1 0
25. In general most people meet my expectations. 5 4 3 2 1 0

TOTAL POINTS: _____

Before totaling your score, go to the *Communicating Effectively* CD-ROM or the Online Learning Center at **www.mhhe.com/hybels8** and follow the directions there.

mhhe.com/hybels8

Source: See "Tools for Personal Growth: Building Trust. **Coping.org** Tools for Coping with Life's Stressors" (provided as a public service), by J. J. Messina and C. M. Messina, 2002. Retrieved October 20, 2005, from **http://www.coping.org/growth/trust.htm**. I have quoted from their Web page, and I have refrained from using quotation marks simply because quotation marks form a minor barrier to the case of reading the information.

CHAPTER REVIEW

SUMMARY

Interpersonal communication, or one-to-one communication, is necessary for you to function in society. It helps you connect with others and develop empathy, and it contributes to your mental and physical health. Emotional intelligence is made up of being aware of your feelings, managing your emotions, motivating yourself, recognizing emotions in others, and handling relationships. All these have a direct bearing on strategic flexibility.

Strategic flexibility benefits from the contributions of perception, self-concept, and emotional intelligence because together these factors promote self-control, assist in managing emotions, and foster effective listening. They help you maximize your communication, enhance your credibility, and accomplish your intentions—all factors that make your use of the strategic flexibility format both more likely and more effective.

The ingredients that make up your attraction to others include physical attraction, perceived gain, similarities, differences, and proximity. In cyberattraction, those communicating depend on cues such as language, style, timing, speed of writing, and use of punctuation and emoticons.

The motives for seeking out interpersonal relationships are pleasure, affection (warm emotional attachments with others), inclusion (involvement with others), escape, relaxation, control (getting others to do as you want them to or being able to make choices in your life), health, and cybermotivation. Cybermotivation involves less anxiety, entertainment, excitement, unwinding, forgetting about daily problems such as school and work, privacy, complete availability, relieving boredom, bolstering self-esteem, anonymity if you want it, and high levels of self-disclosure.

Relationships with others are governed by the roles you are expected to play. Small talk is an instrument of communication that renders people attractive. To engage in small talk plan ahead, ask open-ended questions, share feelings and information, and reconnect via your past.

Bids and the bidding process are the glue that holds relationships together. Bids can be questions, gestures, looks, or touches, and responses to bids are positive or negative answers to somebody's request for emotional connection. Owned messages are acknowledgments of subjectivity by message senders through the use of first-person singular terms. Their value is that they provoke less interpersonal defensiveness than you-messages.

Self-disclosure is the process of communicating oneself to another person, telling another who you are and what you are feeling. It can be understood through the Johari Window, which has four panes: open, blind, hidden, and unknown. As relationships develop and disclosure increases, the open pane gets larger.

The essential elements of good relationships include verbal skills, emotional expressiveness, conversational focus, nonverbal analysis, conversational encouragement, care and appreciation, commitment, and adaptation.

For many, the Internet serves as a valuable, important, and worthwhile form of communication because it promotes healthy communication and interaction; allows a strong support system; facilitates the social integration of otherwise marginalized people; reduces the costs of communication; increases the numbers of social contacts; offers opportunities for communication on an international level; and loosens social restrictions. The Internet affirms, reinforces, and assists in maintaining effective interpersonal relationships.

KEY TERMS AND CONCEPTS

Use the *Communicating Effectively* CD-ROM and the Online Learning Center at **www.mhhe.com/hybels8** to further your understanding of the following terms.

mhhe .com/hybels8

Attitudes 160
Beliefs 160
Bid 166
Blind pane 170
Commitment 176
Compatibility 161
Cultural information 169
Emotional intelligence 156

Empathy 158
Hidden pane 170
Interpersonal communication 156
Johari Window 170
Open pane 170
Owned message 167
Proximity 161
Psychological information 169

Response to a bid 166
Self-disclosure 168
Small talk 164
Social penetration 168
Sociological information 169
Unknown pane 170

CHAPTER REVIEW

QUESTIONS TO REVIEW

1. How is *interpersonal communication* defined, and when do you use it?

2. What role does emotional intelligence play in strategic flexibility?

3. How and why are you attracted to other people?

4. In what ways do your roles and relationships influence your communication? Provide specific examples to support your explanation.

5. What specific health benefits are likely to occur because of interpersonal relationships?

6. Why is small talk important, and what kind of environment supports small talk?

7. What is a bid, what is the bidding process, and how do bids contribute to interpersonal relationships?

8. What are the parts of an owned message, and how do they support both the bidding process and conflict reduction?

9. What contribution does self-disclosure make to nurturing and developing relationships?

10. What is the Johari Window, what are its four panes, and which pane is likely to grow in size along with a developing relationship? Why?

11. What are the essential elements of good relationships that tend to draw people together?

12. What is the effect of the Internet on interpersonal relationships?

mhhe.com/hybels8

Go to the self-quizzes on the *Communicating Effectively* CD-ROM and the Online Learning Center at **www.mhhe.com/hybels8** to test your knowledge of the chapter contents.

Evaluating and Improving Relationships

OBJECTIVES

After reading this chapter, you should be able to:

- Summarize the stages of a relationship in coming together and coming apart.

- Explain extrinsic, intrinsic, and instrumental rewards and costs and show why they are important.

- Define *aggressive talk* and *indirect aggression* and explain how to deal with them.

- Define *regrettable words* and explain how people respond to them and how they affect relationships.

- Distinguish between good and bad criticism.

- Describe the precautions for delivering criticism.

- List and explain the steps in conflict resolution.

- Summarize the precautions necessary to ensure safety and security in online relationships and in those online relationships that transfer to the real world.

WHEN VICKI VANCE LEFT FOR SCHOOL, SHE THOUGHT SHE HAD found the love of her life. Kent was popular, good looking, athletic, and deeply in love with her. Everyone who knew them, knew they were meant to be together—a "match made in heaven" they would say.

Vicki wanted to pursue politics, and she needed a political science major with a communication minor to make it possible. She was looking forward to her undergraduate education because she thought the challenge would be both inspiring and exciting.

Kent did not want to go to college; he didn't do well in high school, and he found reading, studying, and learning dull and boring. His close friends were not planning to further their education, and he liked hanging out with his friends and working at the local department store.

Things between Vicki and Kent were great when Vicki first left for college, but staying in touch with Kent was tough because he didn't like using the Internet, never called just to say "hi," and didn't believe in writing letters. Kent was jealous of Vicki and all the male contacts she had made at school. He resented her continued education, and the tension was magnified when she discussed her classes, assignments, professors, and campus activities. Every time Vicki went home she noticed the distance between them had widened; consequently she went home less and less.

Vicki met Mark in her first political science class, when she had to borrow a pen from him to take notes. Mark would walk her from class, wait for her before class, and always select a seat next to hers in lecture. Soon they were hanging out together, and through their many discussions they discovered they had several similar interests and goals.

Vicki was feeling torn. She had known Kent for nearly four years. They were close, and she knew it would hurt him deeply if she even talked about Mark, much less told Kent they should try to cool their relationship. She felt she had to keep quiet, hope that things would change in some way, and wait for Kent either to find someone else or realize that their relationship was over. Vicki didn't like her decision. She had no guts, and she didn't like that. But she didn't want to hurt Kent.

It would be wonderful if, once relationships were formed, they remained healthy, happy, and rewarding for both partners. Unfortunately, this is not true. If you look at the divorce statistics alone you realize that many relationships don't last, but the fact that 50 percent of marriages end in divorce is *not* true either. By the 5th year of marriage, 10 percent end in divorce; by the 10th year, another 10 percent (or 20 percent cumulatively) end in divorce; another 10 percent end in divorce by the 18th-year (30 percent cumulatively), and by 50 years, another 10 percent (or 40 percent cumulatively). These statistics vary by state, by region within states, and by religious affiliation, race, culture, and co-culture, too. Most marriages that fail, however, do so before the partners reach their mid-40s.

Partners often cite a number of reasons for their failed marriages, and these relate to failed relationships of any kind: poor communication, financial problems, lack of commitment, a dramatic change in priorities, and infidelity. Other reasons include failed expectations or unmet needs; addictions and substance abuse; physical, sexual, or emotional abuse; and lack of conflict resolution skills.

Five factors destroy relationships between young people:

1. The partners fail to anticipate differences resulting from diverse cultural backgrounds, family experiences, and gender.
2. They buy into the notion of a "fifty-fifty" relationship, honestly expecting their partner to meet them halfway.
3. They have been taught that humankind is basically good; therefore they fail to anticipate the conflict that will occur when either of two self-centered partners demands his or her own way.
4. They fail to cope with life's trials. Instead of standing together through hard times, they blame each other or think something is wrong with their partner and the way he or she handles difficulties.
5. They have a fantasy view of love. They quickly feel stuck with an unloving partner and become deceived into believing the next one will be better.

The purpose of this chapter is to discuss some of the ways to evaluate and improve relationships. We will first look at the stages of a relationship—both coming together and coming apart—which will help you better understand where a relationship is, especially if it is in one of the declining stages. We discuss some of the questions that need to be asked in evaluating relationships: questions to ask about yourself, your partner, rewards and costs, and relationship roles. In the section titled "Improving Relationships," we look at aggressive talk, regrettable talk, criticism and complaints, avoidance, defensive communication, resolving conflicts, and the communication strategies you can use in each case. We end the chapter by assessing and evaluating relationships established on the Internet.

Not all relationships are positive and should be saved. Some are highly resistant to any kind of alteration; thus, sometimes any kind of change that either partner attempts will fail.

Just one clarifying comment on the notion of a fifty-fifty relationship mentioned earlier: Often, couples honestly expect their relationship partner to meet them halfway. This is a fantasy. If you have no intention of committing yourself 100 percent to a relationship—on both an initial and an ongoing level—it is unlikely you will be successful. Fifty-fifty is unrealistic simply because when either partner cannot or fails to hold up his or her end of the bargain—which often happens when *any* other commitments come into play (like work or children)—the relationship fails.

THE STAGES OF A RELATIONSHIP

All relationships go through predictable stages as they grow and develop whether they are between romantic couples, friends, business partners, or roommates. Identifying the stages of a relationship and the attributes, stumbling blocks, and joys of each stage can help you negotiate it and the future with more success. The information is useful both to evaluation—do you like where you are, and is it bringing the rewards you want?—and to improvement—what can I do differently to achieve the goals I want?

Most relationships begin with superficial communication; then, if the people like each other, they take steps to see each other again. Mark L. Knapp, a writer and researcher who focuses on relationships, has found that relationships develop along rather predictable lines. He describes five stages in which relationships come together and another five in which they fall apart. Each stage is characterized by certain kinds of communication.[1] Let's begin with a relationship that is coming together, using the example of Vicki and Kent.

Coming Together

Stage 1: Initiating

There are numerous stumbling blocks when people want to initiate a relationship. The *initiating* stage is characterized by nervousness, caution, and a degree of hesitation,[2] but these are healthy stumbling blocks since engaging in the initiating stage bears some risks, the primary one being rejection. The specific suggestions in the last chapter regarding small talk, conversation starters, and bids and responses to bids should be of some help at this early stage.

The joys of entering the initiating stage are enormous. It is like beginning any new adventure where the outcome is unknown, but the trip can make it all worthwhile. Joys, of course, include happiness or just finding a friend (companion, soulmate, intimate, confidante, playmate, kindred spirit, buddy, pal, chum, homeboy, homegirl, or colleague). Sometimes just the boost to your self-esteem is sufficient.

Michael Leviric and Hara Estroff Marano, in an article titled "Why I Hate Beauty," explain the importance of beauty in the initiating stage. They claim that "In the world of abstract logic, marriage is looked on as a basic matching problem with statistical underpinnings in game theory." They state, "Logic says that everybody wants to do as well as they possibly can in selecting a life partner. And when people apply varied criteria for choosing a mate, everybody ends up with a partner with whom they are more or less satisfied. Not everybody gets his or her No. 1 choice, but everybody winds up reasonably content."[3]

Vicki and Kent were introduced by friends on both sides who not only knew they were perfect for each other but told them so. The buildup was so great, both knew the reality couldn't match the hype. Although Vicki didn't like Kent at first (she thought he was a showoff), he was a great dancer, and having a male friend who loved to dance was something Vicki found attractive. Often, first impressions tell you whether the other person is interesting enough for you to pursue a relationship. For Vicki and Kent, it was all the small talk and the bids and responses to bids that started to draw them together—even though the first impression may not have predicted movement to the next stage.

Stage 2: Experimenting

In the *experimenting stage,* people make a conscious effort to seek out common interests and experiences. They experiment by expressing their ideas, attitudes, and values and seeing how the other person reacts. For example, someone with strong feelings about the equality of all races might express an opinion to see whether the other person agrees or disagrees.

The stumbling blocks in stage 2 are fewer. Perhaps the biggest one is the length of time experimenting can take. Talking with someone superficially at school, work, church, or in a chat room can last for years. This is healthy because so many people do not take the time to get to really know another person, and decisions about moving to the next stage often occur without sufficient knowledge and understanding. Thus, it is good to draw out this stage. Most relationships never go beyond this stage and, it seems, many that did perhaps should not have—especially when no foundation for proceeding had been established.

The joy of stage 2 is that everything is generally pleasant, relaxed, and uncritical, although still a bit uncertain.[4] Stage 2 is rewarding, too, if you like getting to know someone else: seeking common ground, testing the waters with self-disclosure, and providing personal histories. Vicki went through this stage with Kent, and it went on and on simply because dancing and talking together served their purposes early in the relationship, and, particularly, because Vicki was not especially impressed with him early on. Kent would tell Vicki about his family, upbringing, interests, and hobbies, but Vicki was reluctant to open up as much for some time.

Between Vicki and Mark, things were quite different. When Mark waited after class to walk her across campus, the two of them covered more territory getting to know each other in that first meeting than Vicki and Kent did in weeks. They not only found they had common interests and values, but they both decided they wanted to talk even more. Vicki and Mark engaged in an equal amount of self-disclosure. The connectedness and comfort they experienced with each other led them to going for coffee after class, meeting outside class to eat together, and going to campus events together. It was as if stage 1, initiating, was defined and completed when Vicki asked Mark for a pen, and Mark gave her his extra one.

Many relationships stay at this particular stage—the participants enjoy the level of the relationship but show no desire to pursue it further.

Stage 3: Intensifying

There are many joys associated with the *intensifying stage*. Vicki and Mark have discovered that they like each other quite a lot. They spend more time with each other because they are happy, loving, and warm. They swap DVDs and CDs and spend free time together. Not only do they enjoy each other's company, but closeness is both wanted and needed, so they hold hands, kiss, and hug. They start to open up to each other—telling each other private things about their families and friends. They talk about their moral values. They also begin to share their frustrations, imperfections, and prejudices.

Other things happen in the relationship. Vicki and Mark call each other by nicknames; they develop a "shorthand" way of speaking; they have jokes that no one else understands. Their conversations begin to reveal shared assumptions and expectations. Trust becomes important. They believe that if either one tells the other a secret, it will stay between them. They start to make expressions of commitment such as making plans together: "Let's go to Ocean City to work next summer." Expressions of commitment include buying gifts for each other or doing favors without being asked.[5] They also start engaging in some gentle challenges of each other: "Do you really believe that, or are you just saying it?" Openness has its risks in the intensifying stage. Self-disclosure makes the relationship strong, but it also makes the participants more vulnerable to each other.

This is likely to be the only stumbling block—vulnerability. The key here is trust, and it underscores the value of the "getting-to-know-you" stages of initiating and experimenting. Trust often takes time to develop. When trust is secure, there is less chance of being wounded, injured, or attacked because of a breach of trust. Lack of fidelity, lying, or the sharing of personal information with others outside the relationship are breaches of trust and can cause deep wounds that are difficult to overcome.

Stage 4: Integrating

Vicki and Mark have reached the *integrating stage*—the point at which their individual personalities are beginning to merge. People expect to see them together, and they are unhappy when apart.[6] If people see just one of them, they ask about the other. The friendship has taken on a specialness. They do most things together and reflect about their common experiences—the things they do together. They go to the same parties and have a lot of the same friends; their friends assume that if they invite one, they should invite the other. Each of them is able to predict and explain the behavior of the other. They feel like one person.

This is where the problem occurred between Vicki and Kent. Their relationship had already reached stage 4, integrating, before she left for college and before she met Mark. She and Kent had developed a deep and important relationship and suddenly, without warning, Mark entered the picture. Vicki and Mark have not reached this stage; however, given what has already occurred in their relationship, it seems like it won't be very long. Those who reach this stage are usually best friends, couples, or parents and children. It is at this stage—if it hasn't happened before—that partners meet one another's family and friends.

Stage 5: Bonding

The last coming-together stage of a relationship is *bonding*. At this point, the participants make some sort of commitment that announces their relationship to those around them. An announcement of an engagement or marriage would be an example of bonding. In other cases, such as those between friends, the bonding agreement might be less formal—for example, agreeing to room together. Whatever form it takes, bonding makes it more difficult for either party to break away from the relationship. Therefore, it is a step taken when the participants have some sort of long-term commitment to their relationship.

Bonding occurs in nonromantic relationships as well. For example, good friends become best friends often because of some especially meaningful (good or bad) "bonding" experience. Dorm roommates are often randomly assigned, but nonromantic apartment mates, who must depend on each other for bill paying, housekeeping, amenities, and the like, are more likely to be successful if they've reached a bonded relationship before moving in together. Partners in business, in the police, or in the military—where success, reputation, and even survival depend on close bonding with and trusting of each other—each know exactly what to expect from the other in critical situations. This same kind of bonding can occur between dancers and ice skaters as well. Although there are times when you may want to believe it isn't so, sex on its own, or a "one-night stand" with a virtual stranger, is not bonding.

At the bonding stage, participants make a formal commitment that announces their relationship to those around them.

Advancing from Stage 1 to Stage 5

The five coming-together stages build on one another (see Figure 8-1). For a relationship to advance to the next stage, both parties must want the change to occur. Because most of us have only limited time and energy for intense relationships, we are willing to let most of our relationships remain at the second or third stage. The first three stages permit us to become involved in friendships and to carry out normal social activities. The fourth and fifth stages, integrating and bonding, demand much more energy and commitment—they are reserved for very special relationships.

Notice that, for the most part, in the coming-together stages, the joys both partners experience outweigh the stumbling blocks that occur. In all stages you have five

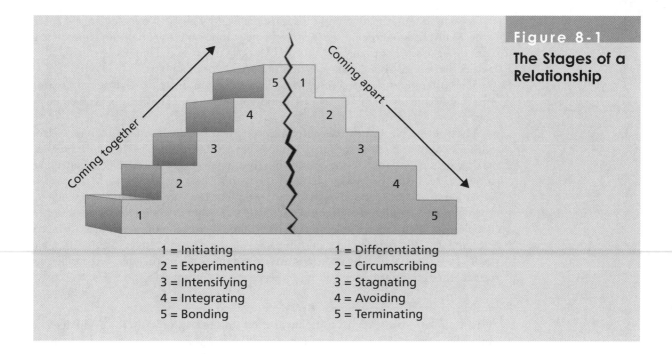

Figure 8-1

The Stages of a Relationship

1 = Initiating	1 = Differentiating
2 = Experimenting	2 = Circumscribing
3 = Intensifying	3 = Stagnating
4 = Integrating	4 = Avoiding
5 = Bonding	5 = Terminating

choices: to continue moving forward, to stagnate, to slow down, to go backward, or to exit.[7] Since stage 3 is the first in which there is self-disclosure, moving from stage 2 to stage 3 is particularly sensitive. If one person opens up too quickly, the other might feel so uncomfortable that he or she will be unwilling to go on to a new stage in the relationship.

Coming Apart

For a relationship to continue, the participants must grow and change together. If they cannot do this in ways that are satisfying to both of them, the relationship will come apart. Although it is more satisfying to look at relationships coming together, we all know that relationships also fail. Relationships that are failing can also be described in five stages—stages that reverse the process of coming together. Notice as you read about each stage that stumbling blocks have eliminated any joy that was there.

Stage 1: Differentiating

Time has passed, and Vicki and Mark have been married for over a year. The first months were a little rocky, but now serious problems are beginning to emerge. Vicki likes to go out several nights each week; Mark wants to stay home. Mark likes to cook new and exotic food; Vicki wants to eat meat and potatoes. Even their love for movies is causing conflict: Vicki wants to see them as soon as they open; Mark wants to wait until they are released as DVDs so that they can watch them at home.

Vicki and Mark have entered the *differentiating stage*. The interdependence of their courting stage is no longer so attractive. Now they are beginning to focus on how different they are, and much of their conversation is about their differences rather than their similarities. There is noticeable arguing, with talk about being incompatible.[8]

STRATEGIC FLEXIBILITY
If you are going to use strategic flexibility effectively—especially with respect to the coming-together stages—it requires great sensitivity. One measure that can be used to help you know what to do is your comfort level. When you evaluate factors, elements, and conditions, how comfortable are you with your assessment?

To some extent, the differentiating stage is a healthy phase that most couples experience. Many work out their differences by being autonomous sometimes and interdependent other times. For example, Vicki and Mark go together to family gatherings and to parties. However, when Mark goes hunting, Vicki goes shopping.

The differences the two recognized and tolerated during the stages of coming together become focal points for discussion and argument. They can be worked out if they are not too great.

The most visible sign of differentiating is conflict. But differentiating can take place without conflict. Even if nothing specific is bothering the couple, they may discover, as they mature and find new interests, that they have less and less to talk about. Vicki, for example, reads the newspaper every day and follows world events. Mark, on the other hand, gets his news from the Internet and finds it too depressing to talk about. Each experiences slight loneliness because the two of them are no longer as close as a couple, and regarding the relationship itself, there is some confusion and inadequacy creeping in.[9] Where is the relationship going? How long can it go on like this? Am I at fault? These are a few of the questions that one or the other partner may be considering; usually they are internalized and never expressed at this stage.

Stage 2: Circumscribing

When a relationship begins to fall apart, less and less information is exchanged. It seems better to stay away from points of conflict in the relationship in order to avoid a full-scale fight. Thus this is called the *circumscribing stage*.

Now conversation is superficial; everyday matters are discussed: "Your mail is on the desk." "Did I get any telephone calls?" "Do you want some popcorn?" The number of interactions is decreased, the depth of discussions is reduced, and the duration of each conversation is shortened. Because communication is constricted, the relationship is constricted.

Most people who find themselves in this stage try to resolve their problems by discussing the relationship itself. In response, the negative turn in the relationship might change. For example, Mark could go out to a movie with Vicki, and Vicki could agree to try some different food. In other cases, discussion about the relationship might reveal greater differences between the participants. In such cases, discussion about the relationship leads to even more conflict, so the participants limit discussion to "safe" topics. Vicki and Mark, for instance, stay away from the topic of having children because they know they will fight about it.

Often, people at this stage pursue different activities. Sometimes, too, they act aloof from each other. These experiences reveal coldness and distance. With respect to each other, partners are uncaring, and one or the other may become depressed or frustrated, feeling unloved and misunderstood.[10]

Persons who are in this stage often cover up their relationship problems. Although they might reveal problems to very close friends, in social situations they give the appearance of being committed to each other. They create a social or public face—in essence, a mask.

Stage 3: Stagnating

The *stagnating stage* is a time of inactivity. The relationship has no chance to grow, and when the partners communicate, they talk like strangers. The subject of the relationship itself is now off limits. Rather than try to resolve the conflict, the partners are more likely to think, "Why bother to talk? We'll just fight, and things will get even worse"; thus, for self-protection, they give short answers to questions.

How long this stage lasts depends on many things. If Vicki and Mark lead busy lives and just come home to sleep, they might go on in this stage for months or even years. However, if Mark stays home and broods about the relationship, he may look for some kind of resolution to their conflict. Most couples whose relationship reaches this stage feel a lot of pain. The partners may find it hard to separate and may hold on to the hope that they can still work things out. Either partner at this stage may feel unwanted, scared, bored, and sentimental.[11]

Stage 4: Avoiding

The *avoiding stage* involves physical separation. The parties avoid face-to-face interaction. They are not interested in spending time together, in building any kind of relationship, or in establishing any communication channels.

This stage is usually characterized by unfriendliness, hostility, and antagonism. Sometimes the cues are subtle: "I only have a minute. I have an appointment." They can also be direct and forceful: "Don't call me anymore" or "I'm sorry, I just don't want to see you." Often, responses are "I don't care" and "I don't know." If communication occurs, it covers general matters only; there is no talk about the relationship.

In relationships where physical separation is impossible, the participants may act as if the other person does not exist. Partners eat in silence, stay busy, and, if possible, spend a lot of time away.[12] Each one carries on his or her activities in a separate room and avoids any kind of interaction. In the case of Vicki and Mark, Vicki might sleep in the bedroom and Mark on the living room couch. Often, partners feel some sense of nervousness, as well as helplessness and annoyance.[13]

Stage 5: Terminating

In the *terminating stage*, the participants find a way to bring the relationship to an end. Differences are emphasized, and communication is difficult and awkward. Each party is preparing for life without the other. They may talk about staying in touch and discuss what went wrong. A goal at this stage may be to divide up their belongings. There are feelings of unhappiness, but these are accompanied by a sense of relief. Often one partner is lonely or scared because of having to face life alone again.[14]

Some relationships cannot be entirely terminated. Partners who have children might terminate their relationship with each other as marriage partners but decide to continue in some kind of relationship as parents to the children. The more amicably this can be done, the better it is for the children involved. Partners might set down a list of rules that will govern the new relationship.[15] When the termination is a divorce, the court is the one that establishes the rules.

Sociologist Diane Vaughan has studied the patterns that occur when a relationship is about to end. She says that one member of the couple, realizing he or she is unhappy, begins the process of ending the relationship. This person typically begins by finding alternatives—often in the form of a transitional person. Although the transitional person might be a romantic interest, the person could also be a minister, a therapist, or a good friend. When one partner begins to find satisfaction elsewhere, the couple's relationship becomes less endurable. At this point the dissatisfied person lets the other know of his or her discontent through body language and words.[16]

Finally the time comes when the dissatisfied person lets the partner know that he or she wants to end the relationship. The partner typically feels betrayed, hurt, and shocked—and is often unprepared. Vaughan says that during the breakup, both partners suffer emotional pain and go through the same stages of disengagement: the process just happens at different times for each of them.[17]

EVALUATING RELATIONSHIPS: ASKING THE RIGHT QUESTIONS

One reason many relationships fail is simply that people seldom take the time to ask the essential questions—especially the questions that should be asked *before* embarking on a serious relationship. It is true, of course, that some of us begin a relationship with no intention of its becoming serious and then discover it has evolved to that level without a decision ever being made. Perhaps some of the questions in this section will help you if this happens.

Our purpose is not to destroy spontaneity, surprise, and discovery, but to deal with some of the broad issues that often lead relationships to fail. When these are resolved to your satisfaction, and you have taken all the necessary precautions that would predict a satisfactory future partner, there will be plenty of room for spontaneity, surprise, and discovery.

Ask Yourself Questions

There are three questions to ask yourself.[18] The first has to do with fear of commitment. Are you concerned about the idea of forever? Do you fear you could make a mistake in the person you choose? Do you fear a loss of your freedom or autonomy? Are you afraid of a bad marriage—like your parents, for instance? Do you fear you would be a bad mate?

Antoinette Coleman, in her online newsletter *The Art of Intimacy*, states that "If you answered yes to any of these, it would be a good idea to begin working to understand where these feelings come from. Once you understand them better, you can choose to address them."[19] It may simply be that you are not ready to make any long-term commitment, and you know at this point in your life that you just need more time, or more emotional growth.

The second question is about fear of forming a relationship with another person. How many dating experiences have you had? Do you tend to rush into relationships, or do you move them along with thought and careful decision making? Can you live without a partner? Can you envision yourself in the immediate future with a partner? Do you really know and like yourself? Do you believe you could have a successful relationship?

The third question asks about making a commitment to *this* particular relationship and to *this* particular person. Is there a genuine connection? Do you have a vague feeling that something is missing? What is the quality of your intimate relating—*not* how often or how good the sex is, but how open, sharing, and real your interactions are with each other. Does it seem like the two of you are just killing time? Does your partner want what you want? Do you seem to be inconsistent in your level of contact and affection? Is your partner still not over a past relationship? Do you (and does your partner) really know what you want?

Ask Questions about Your Partner

Let's say that through frequent contact and increased levels of self-disclosure you have discovered a potential relationship partner, but you don't know whether this partner is even ready for a relationship. What questions should you ask yourself to determine a partner's readiness? Six are absolutely essential:

1. Is this person able to communicate with you openly and honestly?

2. Does this person appear to have a strong self-concept?

3. Is this person aware of the time and effort required to have a long-term, loving relationship?

4. Is this person willing to put forth the necessary time and effort along with you to make a long-term, loving relationship possible?

5. Does this person see the commitment necessary for a long-term, loving relationship as *more than simply fifty-fifty?*

6. Is this person prepared—as you are—to make a relationship partner his or her *first* priority, after himself or herself, in life?[20]

If the answer to any of these questions is "no," then this partner is probably not for you.

Here is a key point: Entering into a relationship hoping that the other person will change, or thinking that you will change the other person, "is not a solid foundation for a loving, committed relationship. In most cases, with rare exceptions, you are wasting your time."[21] Instead, get into the habit of looking for what you can love and appreciate about your partner, rather than how he or she needs to change or be fixed, and it will change the whole dynamic of your relationship.

Ask Questions about Rewards and Costs

In Chapter 7 we introduced a small portion of Altman and Taylor's social penetration theory. Their theory is based on social exchange—the idea that relationships are sustained when they are relatively rewarding and discontinued when they are relatively costly.[22] **Rewards** are the pleasures that result from being in a relationship. **Costs** are the problems. The essential question is, "Do the rewards outweigh the costs?" or, phrased a bit differently, "Are you willing to live with the costs considering the strength of the rewards?" When you know your relationship partner well—see the Consider This box—it is easier to weigh rewards and costs.

Altman and Taylor listed three types of rewards and costs: extrinsic, intrinsic, and instrumental. **Extrinsic** means outside the relationship. **Intrinsic** means within the relationship. **Instrumental** refers to the basic exchange of goods and services. To make sense of these, let's put them into the context of a relationship you have that has not yet progressed to the level of sexual intimacy. Whether or not you want to take it to that level depends on weighing the rewards and costs.

Extrinsic rewards: You like the people your partner has introduced you to and the friends he or she hangs out with.

Intrinsic rewards: You appreciate the attention, warmth, and affection you gain from being in the relationship.

Instrumental rewards: You know that if you decide to raise the current level of intimacy, one of the rewards when you move in with your partner (which you have already discussed) is you will share both the rent and the furniture.

Extrinsic costs: You are not going to have as much time for your friends, and you are going to have to share them with your partner.

Intrinsic costs: Not only will you feel obligated to return the attention, warmth, and affection you are receiving—probably at an increased level if the level of intimacy increased—but you will also spend time listening, communicating, and self-disclosing.

Instrumental costs: You will have to share your belongings.

Now it is up to you. Often, it is good to actually list the rewards and costs honestly not just so you can compare them but so that you can think about them specifically and over time.

Mira Kirshenbaum, a therapist who works with families and couples, holds that since the dynamics of a relationship are constantly shifting, it is better to ask questions about the relationship that go right to the heart of it. For example, she maintains that

Consider This

Know Your Relationship Partner

Test the strength of your relationship by taking this quiz prepared especially for *Newsweek* by John Gottman. Happy couples have a deep understanding of their partner's psyche.

	True	False
1. I can name my partner's best friends.	___	___
2. I can tell you what stresses my partner is currently facing.	___	___
3. I know the names of some of the people who have been irritating my partner lately.	___	___
4. I can tell you some of my partner's life dreams.	___	___
5. I can tell you about my partner's basic philosophy of life.	___	___
6. I can list the relatives my partner likes the least.	___	___
7. I feel that my partner knows me pretty well.	___	___
8. When we are apart, I often think fondly of my partner.	___	___
9. I often touch or kiss my partner affectionately.	___	___
10. My partner really respects me.	___	___
11. There is fire and passion in this relationship.	___	___
12. Romance is definitely still a part of our relationship.	___	___
13. My partner appreciates the things I do in this relationship.	___	___
14. My partner generally likes my personality.	___	___
15. Our sex life is mostly satisfying.	___	___
16. At the end of the day my partner is glad to see me.	___	___
17. My partner is one of my best friends.	___	___
18. We just love talking to each other.	___	___
19. There is lots of give and take (both people have influence) in our discussions.	___	___
20. My partner listens respectfully, even when we disagree.	___	___
21. My partner is usually a great help as a problem solver.	___	___
22. We generally mesh well on basic values and goals in life.	___	___

Score your results: Give yourself one point for each "True" answer. Above 12: You have a lot of strength in your relationship. Congratulations. Below 12: Your relationship can stand some improvement and will probably benefit from some work on the basics, such as improving communication.

Source: *Newsweek*, by B. Kantrowitz and P. Wingert, "The Science of a Good Marriage," April 19, 1999, pp. 52–57. Although the survey was intended for married partners since that is the focus of the entire article, it seems to work as well for most established relationships.

the answer to a question like the following will tell a lot about a relationship: "Does it seem to you that your partner generally and consistently blocks your attempts to bring up topics or raise questions, particularly about things you care about?"[23]

Ask Questions about Roles

Roles are important simply because to be happy and content in a relationship, both parties must be satisfied with the roles and expectations. Roles may evolve naturally and spontaneously for males, but for females, they must be discussed and negotiated.

One of the questions we asked students in interpersonal-communication classes had to do with relationship expectations: "What role do you expect to play in any future intimate relationship you have?" Sometimes students referred to the roles their parents played, sometimes they offered a politically correct response such as, "That would have to be worked out with my future partner," and sometimes a few would take the traditional stance that males were the breadwinners and females the homemaker raising the kids. Most female students wanted to play a role equal to that of their partner and have an equal say in how roles would be determined.

In successful relationships, the participants have usually worked out their roles and expectations. But circumstances change through the course of a relationship, and if the communication channels are not available and open, unexpected problems can occur down the road.

Consider an example. Doug and Rita had never directly discussed roles; things were essentially equal. Then unexpectedly Rita found herself pregnant, but Doug and Rita never stopped to talk about how their roles would change once the baby was born. Who was going to take care of the baby during the day? Were there going to be any changes in school commitments or workloads, and who was going to make changes if necessary? Who was going to get up at night when the baby cried? Who would adjust his or her schedule if the baby became sick?

There is no way to ask all the questions that will prepare you for changes likely to occur in relationships. There are, however, some questions you could ask while dating that might give you important information about how your partner views relationship roles. For example, "What do you want in a wife (or husband)?"[24] Many women think males want a maid—a wife who stays home, cooks, cleans, and isn't too smart; however, many males *say* they want, more than anything else, a capable, assertive, happy partner, not just a housekeeper. On the other hand, some men think women want a partner who is a big, burly, hairy, handsome "he-man" with money. Most women, however, want a loving, gentle, warm, caring, intelligent, capable, self-confident man who is willing to stand up for his beliefs.

Some other key questions might be, "Who do you think should be responsible for financially supporting the family?" or, a related question, "Who do you think should be responsible for caring for the house and family?" "If you were the husband of a working woman, would you be willing to do an equal share of the housework and child care?" "What determines who will be the boss in a marriage?" "Do you think it's necessary for a couple to be roughly equal in ability in love, in neediness, and in education to have an egalitarian [equal] relationship?"[25]

Both men and women are likely to know how their partner would want them to respond. In the period of infatuation and, often in the early stages of a loving relationship, partners want to please each other. That is sufficient grounds for observing the behaviors of possible future partners to see whether what they say is supported by activities with which you agree—that is, that there are no mixed messages.

Can you ask "too many questions"? Never. Just don't act like it's an interview. Spread them out over a sufficient amount of time, and work them in among other thoughts and feelings, and remember a key point: Often men do not want to open up, share feelings, or even communicate. Accept this as a signal. Do you want to have a long-term relationship in which there is little or no communication?

IMPROVING RELATIONSHIPS: USING COMMUNICATION STRATEGIES

Negative influences are a natural and expected part of relationships. It is *not* the frequency of their occurrence; it is how carefully, delicately, and respectfully they are resolved to *both* partners' satisfaction that is important. All the motivation and willingness to communicate, assertiveness training, owned messages, and listening and communication skills in the world cannot prevent relationships from becoming fertile ground for silence and stonewalling, for anger and frustration, or for just plain hard times. No speech, article, book, or expert can protect you from the range of painful emotions that make you human.[26] The greater the number of skills and behaviors you have in your toolbox, however, the greater the likelihood that you will be able to face and resolve all the negative influences that come your way. This is where your ability in and use of strategic flexibility has its real payoffs—not just in holding your relationships together (the big picture), but in satisfactorily resolving all those daily, nuisance-type issues that seem to provoke and keep you in a negative frame of mind.

In this section we will look at six of the big issues: aggressive talk and aggression, regrettable talk, criticism and complaints, avoidance, and defensive communication. In the final sections of this chapter we will focus on resolving conflicts and the role of the Internet.

Aggressive Talk and Aggression

Aggressive talk is talk that attacks a person's self-concept with the intent of inflicting psychological pain.[27] This kind of talk includes disparaging words such as *nigger, faggot,* and *slut,* and phrases such as "You are so stupid," or "You are an inconsiderate idiot." Aggressive talk makes recipients feel inadequate, embarrassed, or angry, and because of the impact it has on receivers, it is seldom justified. Not only does aggression breed aggression, but it can escalate, and verbal aggression can quickly lead to physical aggression. People who can control verbal aggression are those who can recognize their anger and control it when it occurs—usually by giving themselves a cooling-off period.

When aggressive talk leads to aggression—an unprovoked attack—in relationships, often the relationship is doomed. People tempted to use verbal aggression should be aware that such actions can destroy relationships.

A more subtle act, and one we are often not aware of committing, is **indirect aggression** (sometimes called *passive aggression*)—when aggression is a mental act (usually characterized by manipulation, scheming, cunning, deviousness, or conniving). People who use this form of communication often feel powerless, and they respond in the only way they can, by doing something to thwart the person in power. For example, if your mother asked you to clean the kitchen, and you did a poor job so that she would never ask you again, you are using passive aggression. Or, if you were forced to go to college, and you flunked all your courses just to show your parents their decision was wrong.

It is difficult to deal with those who are aggressive, and if the acts of aggression are excessive, uncontrolled, or frequent, it may be necessary to seek professional assistance—for you, your partner, or the two of you together.

If your goal is to deal with the aggressive talk of a partner, your first step is to make every effort to see the situation *from his or her point of view:* with empathy. When the time is appropriate—usually *not* immediately after the aggressive talk has occurred because emotions have been triggered and normal conversation may not take place—you might begin a conversation by asking your partner to explain his or her point of view. Encourage him or her to talk about underlying assumptions, beliefs, or background factors that may have led to the behavior you are upset about. Summarize the person's words and *emotions* from his or her point of view (so that he or she agrees you understand it). Understanding the other's situation, point of view, and reasons for beliefs and behavior is usually the major task to accomplish.

If it is impossible to have this kind of conversation, it might be helpful for you to imagine a scenario that will allow you to defuse your anger. Or you may interpret your partner's aggressive talk as a legitimate need to take care of himself or herself. If you can focus on evidence from the present or past that proves he or she loves you and is not trying to hurt you, it is easier to forgive the behavior, forget about it, and move on.

Regrettable Talk

Regrettable talk is talk you regretted after saying it. You invited someone to help you move into a new place, and he tells you he has just been diagnosed with cancer and will be in the hospital. Of course you couldn't have known that, but you are now embarrassed for having asked him. Regrettable talk might have hurt someone, or it may have shared a secret you were not supposed to tell.

Mark Knapp, Laura Stafford, and John Daly, all communication researchers, studied regrettable words. They discovered that 75 percent of regrettable words fell into five categories. The most common was the blunder—forgetting someone's name or getting it wrong, or asking "How's your mother?" and hearing the reply "She died." The next category was direct attack—a generalized criticism of the other person or of his or her family or friends. The third was negative group references, which often contained racial or ethnic slurs. The fourth involved direct and specific criticism, such as "You never clean house," or "Don't go out with that guy; he's a sleazeball!" The fifth category—revealing or explaining too much—included telling secrets or reporting hurtful things said by others.

When people were asked why they had made the remark in the first place, the most common response was, "I was stupid. I just wasn't thinking." Some said their remarks were selfish—intended to meet their own needs rather than the other person's. Others admitted to having bad intentions. They deliberately set out to harm the other person. On a less negative level, people said that they were trying to be nice but the words just slipped out. Some people said that they were trying to be funny or to tease the other person, and the words were taken in the wrong way.

How did the people who were the objects of the regrettable words respond? Most often they felt hurt. Many got angry or made a sarcastic reply. Some hung up the phone, walked away, or changed the subject. Others were able to dismiss the statement or to laugh about it. When the speaker acknowledged the error, the listener often helped to "cover" the incident by offering an explanation or justification.

One of the most interesting aspects of this study addressed whether regrettable words had a negative impact on the relationship. Of the respondents, 30 percent said there was a long-term negative change, 39 percent said there was no change in the relationship at all, and 16 percent said that the change was positive—for example, "In the long run. I think our relationship is stronger since it happened."

Criticism and Complaints

Most people experience anger from time to time in close relationships. Anger does not have to destroy a relationship: University of Michigan researchers found that the average couple has one serious fight a month and several small ones.[28] John Gottman, psychologist at the University of Washington, found that anger is not the most destructive emotion in a marriage, since both happy and miserable couples fight. He calls the real demons "the Four Horsemen of the Apocalypse"—criticism, contempt, defensiveness, and stonewalling.[29]

Experts agree that it's *how* partners fight that makes the difference. The most effective kind of anger is that which expresses one's own feelings while conveying concern for one's partner.[30] Since most anger begins with a complaint or criticism, let's look at the most effective way to express it.

Criticism is a negative evaluation of a person for something he or she has done or the way he or she is. In more distant relationships, criticism usually originates from a higher status person and is directed toward one with lower status.[31] If the participants are equals, such as friends or a couple, criticism could come from either partner.

Most people experience anger from time to time in close relationships. Anger doesn't have to destroy relationships. It is *how* people fight that makes the difference.

Researchers have discovered that criticism has five targets: appearance (body, clothing, smell, posture, and accessories); performance (carrying out a motor, intellectual, or creative skill); personhood (personality, goodness, or general ability); relationship style (dealing with others); and decisions and attitudes (opinions, plans, or lifestyle). They found that the target of most criticism is performance, followed by relationship style, appearance, and general personhood.[32]

The researchers also looked at what the recipients perceived as "good" and "bad" criticism. Most of the study's respondents believed that those who did not know them very well didn't have the right to criticize them. They were much more likely to identify criticism as bad if it was given in front of others rather than privately.

Criticism was labeled "bad" if it contained negative language (profanity or judgmental labels such as "stupid jerk") or if it was stated harshly by screaming or yelling. It was better received if it was specific and gave details on how to improve ("If you are going to be home after midnight, please call and let me know where you are"). Criticism was considered good if the person who made it also offered to assist in making the change or if its receiver could see how it would be in his or her best interest to change ("If you called me when you are going to be late, I wouldn't be so upset once you got home"). Finally, good criticism places negative remarks into a broad positive context ("If you called, it would reduce a lot of tension and anxiety in our relationship").

A **complaint** is an expression of dissatisfaction with some behavior, attitude, belief, or characteristic of a partner or of someone else. A complaint differs from criticism in that it is not necessarily directed at any specific person.

In studies of complaints between partners, researchers found that, as with criticism, some responses to complaints were more useful than others.[33] First, when complaints are trivial, they can probably be ignored. "This spaghetti is overcooked," or "Why do I have to be the only one to shovel the snow?" are trivial complaints. Second, a complaint should not be directed at anyone specifically. When you say, "Why doesn't anyone ever close doors?" you are not pointing to any one person, so the guilty party can change his or her behavior without losing face. Third, a complaint should be softened or toned down so that

In her book *The Dance of Connection*, Harriet Lerner writes about some of the advantages of anger:

> My point is not that you should deny your anger or ignore its sources. On the contrary, anger is an important signal that something is wrong. It always deserves our attention and respect. Anger can sharpen our passion and clarity and inspire us to speak honestly and truly. It can motivate us to say no to the demands and expectations of others, and yes to the dictates of our inner self. Our anger can help us clarify where we stand, what we believe, and what we will and won't do. Our anger tells us when the other person has crossed a line that shouldn't be crossed. In all these ways, our anger preserves the very dignity and integrity of our voice. If we didn't have our anger to motivate us, our fear might lock us into passivity, silence, and accommodation.

Questions

1. Do you have any personal examples of the positive expression of your own anger?

2. Do you think anger when expressed tends to be more positive than negative? Do you think when anger is expressed, it is more frequently negative than positive?

3. Taking the opposite point of view, what are some negative things that occur because of anger?

4. How can the negative outcomes of anger be changed to positive by our own efforts? In a relationship, what can you do specifically to help encourage anger to become positive and not negative?

Source: From *The Dance of Connection: How to Talk to Someone When You're Mad, Hurt, Scared, Frustrated, Insulted, Betrayed, or Desperate*, by H. Lerner, 2001, New York: HarperCollins.

---

the complainer can express his or her frustration or dissatisfaction without provoking a big argument. Fourth, if the complaint is serious, the partners should discuss it and try to arrive at a solution or a compromise before the complaint turns into a serious conflict.

The most useful communication strategy for dealing with criticism is to use owned messages, as discussed in Chapter 7. Rebecca Cline and Bonnie Johnson's research emphasized the importance of making the careful language choices that owned messages require.[34] People react negatively and defensively when conversation is filled with you-messages such as "You always blame others for your problems," or "You need to have the last word, don't you?"

Avoidance

Many people who are in unsatisfying relationships try to dodge any discussion of their problems. Some people use silence; others change the subject if their partners try to begin a discussion. Often people who refrain from discussing relationships are trying to avoid any kind of conflict. The downside of **avoidance**—refusing to deal with conflict or painful issues—is that unless the problem is discussed, it probably will not go away.

The best communication strategy to use with respect to avoidance is a combination of owned messages—"I need to deal with the conflict we're having. I cannot continue avoiding talking about it, because it eats away at me and makes me angry"—and assertiveness. **Assertiveness** is taking the responsibility of expressing needs, thoughts, and feelings in a direct, clear manner. "I know you think that if we don't talk about it, it will just go away, but I know it's going to come up again. I want to talk about it right now [assertiveness]."

Defensive Communication

Defensive communication occurs when one partner tries to defend himself or herself against the remarks or behavior of the other. The problem with defensive communication is that we are so busy defending ourselves that we cannot listen to what the other

STRATEGIC FLEXIBILITY
Plan what you want to say before you say it! This is exactly what strategic flexibility demands: To anticipate, assess, evaluate, and select *requires advanced thought*, so that when you assert yourself you do it with care, concern, and attention.

For an example of defensive communication, view clip #1, "Defensive Communication."

person is saying. Also, defending ourselves is dealing with past behavior; it gives us no chance to think about resolving the problem.

How can we avoid defensive communication? A researcher, in a classic article, came up with six categories of defensive communication and supportive strategies to counter each of them[35] (see Table 8.1). Consider the supportive response in each instance, as communication strategies.

Evaluation versus Description

Evaluative statements involve a judgment. If the judgment is negative, the person you are speaking to is likely to react defensively. If you tell your roommate, "It is inconsiderate of you to slam the door when I am trying to sleep," he might respond, "It's inconsiderate of you to snore every night when I am trying to sleep." On the other hand, if you tell your roommate, "I had trouble sleeping last night because I woke up when I heard the door slam," he is much more likely to do something about the problem. Since you have merely described the problem, the message is not as threatening.

Control versus Problem Solving

People who consistently attempt to exert control believe that they are always right and that no other opinion (or even fact) is worth listening to.

Others tend to respond negatively if they think someone is trying to control them. For example, if you are working on a class project with a classmate and you begin by taking charge and telling him or her what to do, you will probably be resented. A better approach is for you and your classmate to engage in problem solving together. The same applies to close relationships. If conflict arises and you decide what should be done ("I'll take the car and you take the bicycle"), your partner is not likely to respond positively. It is better to discuss the options together.

Strategy versus Spontaneity

Often strategy is little more than manipulation. Rather than openly asking people to do something, you try to manipulate them into doing what you want by using strategies such as making them feel guilty or ashamed. A statement that begins "If you love me, you will . . . " is always manipulative. A better approach is to express your honest feelings spontaneously: "I am feeling overwhelmed with all the planning I have to do for the party. Will you help me out today?"

Neutrality versus Empathy

If you receive a low grade on a paper and are feeling bad about it, you don't want your friend to say, "Maybe the teacher was right. Let's look at both sides." When feelings are high, no one wants a neutral, objective response. What is needed is for the other person to show **empathy**— the ability to recognize and identify with/our feelings. An empathic response to a poor grade in a course might be, "You must feel bad. You studied hard for that class."

Superiority versus Equality

People who always take charge of situations seem to imply that they are the only ones qualified to do so. Even if we have a position that is superior to someone else's, people will react less defensively if we do not communicate this

Table 8-1	**Categories of Defensive and Supportive Behavior**

Defensive Climate	Supportive Climate
1. Evaluation	1. Description
2. Control	2. Problem solving
3. Strategy	3. Spontaneity
4. Neutrality	4. Empathy
5. Superiority	5. Equality
6. Certainty	6. Provisionalism

magine that you have caught your relationship partner in a bald-faced lie, and it is clear that he or she cannot deny it, explain it away, or otherwise retreat from the situation. Go around your group, and have each member supply first a defensive statement and then a supportive statement of the same level—or a supportive statement designed to offset, dispel, or otherwise ameliorate the defensive one. For example, the first person in the group supplies an evalua-

tive statement: "You really annoy me when you lie to me like that. We agreed that is unacceptable behavior." The next person will supply a descriptive statement. The next student will offer a controlling statement, and the next a problem-solving one. The next student will offer a manipulative statement, the next a spontaneous one. The next student will offer a neutral statement followed by the next student with an empathic one. A superior statement is offered and then an equal one. And, finally, the next-to-the-last student offers a statement of certainty, and the final one a provisional comment.

superiority. An attitude of equality—"Let's tackle this problem together"—produces much less defensive behavior.

Certainty versus Provisionalism

Don't confuse people who are confident and secure with people who think they are always right. Confident and secure people may hold strong opinions; they are likely, however, to make many provisional statements that permit another point of view to be expressed. For example, someone might say, "I feel strongly on this subject, but I would be interested in hearing what you have to say."

Avoiding Defensive Communication: A Practical Example

Although we have discussed each of the six defensive categories separately, in most communication situations several of them appear simultaneously. You can see how this works in the following situations:

A Defensive Dialogue

Boss:	You're an hour late. If you're going to work here, you have to be on time. (superiority, control)
Employee:	My car wouldn't start.
Boss:	That's no reason to be late. (certainty, evaluation) You should have called. (evaluation)
Employee:	I tried, but . . .
Boss:	When work starts at 8 A.M., you must be here at 8 A.M. (superiority, control) If you can't make it, you should look for another job. (superiority, control, certainty) If you're late again, don't bother coming to work. (superiority, control, strategy)

This dialogue leaves the employee feeling defensive, angry, and unable to say anything. Let's take a look at how it might have gone if the boss had been more willing to listen:

A Supportive Dialogue

Boss:	You're an hour late. What happened? (description, equality)
Employee:	My car wouldn't start.
Boss:	Weren't you near a phone? (still no evaluation)

201

Employee:	Every time I tried to call, the line was busy. I finally decided that it would be faster to walk here than to keep trying to call.
Boss:	When people don't get here on time, I always worry that we're going to fall behind schedule. (spontaneity) Wasn't there any way of letting me know what happened? (problem solving)
Employee:	Yeah. I guess I panicked. I should have asked my sister to keep trying to call to let you know what happened. If it ever happens again, that's what I'll do.
Boss:	Good. Now let's get to work. There's a lot of catching up to do.

RESOLVING CONFLICT

When two people are in conflict and have decided that nothing will be served by avoidance or aggression, the option left open to them is **conflict resolution**—negotiation to find a solution to the conflict. Conflict arises because two individuals do not have compatible goals. Through the negotiation process, the two try to find out how they can both reach their goals. For the negotiation to be considered successful, both sides must be satisfied and feel that they have come out ahead. This is often referred to as *win-win negotiating.*

Deborah Wieder-Hatfield, a researcher in this area, has suggested a useful model for resolving conflict. In this model, each individual looks at the conflict intrapersonally. Then the partners get together to work out the problem.[36]

In the first stage, *intrapersonal evaluation,* each person analyzes the problem alone. This analysis is accomplished through a series of questions: How do I feel about this problem? How can I describe the other person's behavior? What are the facts?

In the second stage, the parties in the conflict get together to work out an *interpersonal definition* of the problem. It is important that both parties believe there is a problem and can define what it is. In this stage, it is important that each person listen carefully and check the accuracy of what he or she has heard by paraphrasing what was said. The same is true for feelings. At the end of this stage, both partners should agree on the facts of the problem.

In the third stage, the partners should discuss *shared goals.* Still focusing on the problem, the individuals should ask, "What are my needs and desires?" and "What are your needs and desires?" Then they should work to see whether their needs and goals overlap.

At the fourth stage, the partners must come up with *possible solutions* to the problem. Here it is useful to create as long a list as possible. Then each individual can eliminate solutions he or she considers unacceptable.

In the fifth stage, the partners move on to *weighing goals against solutions.* Some compromises are inevitable at this stage. The solutions may not be entirely satisfactory to either party, but they are a compromise that both hope they can live with. Negotiators would label this a win-win solution.

Since all resolutions are easier to make than to keep, the last stage of the process is to *evaluate the solution* after some time has passed. Did the solution work? Does it need to be changed? Should it be discussed again at a later date? As we mentioned earlier, it is not easy to change human behavior. When partners work to resolve conflict, even when they come up with good solutions there is likely to be some backsliding. It therefore makes good sense to give partners a chance to live up to their resolutions. Letting time pass before both negotiators are held accountable helps achieve this goal.

Gottman, from all of his research on couples, says that happy couples have a different way of relating to each other during disputes. Partners make frequent "repair attempts," reaching out to each other in an effort to prevent negativity from getting out of control in the midst of conflict. Humor, too, is often part of a successful repair attempt. If partners can work together and appreciate the best in each other, they learn to cope with the problems that are part of every relationship. Partners must learn to love each other not just for what they have in common but for things that make them complementary as well.[37]

The Bottom Line

The Institute for American Values conducted a study whose results bear directly on the discussions in this chapter.[38] Their research countered what they labeled the "divorce assumption"—that most people assume that a person stuck in a bad marriage has two choices: stay married and miserable or get a divorce and become happier. The study found no evidence that unhappily married adults who divorced were typically any happier than unhappily married people who stayed married.[39]

Two-thirds of unhappily married spouses who stayed married reported that their marriages were happy five years later. Those in the most unhappy marriages reported the most dramatic turnarounds. These unhappy partners had endured serious problems, including alcoholism, infidelity, verbal abuse, emotional neglect, depression, illness, and work and money troubles. The study found three principal techniques for their recovery; those in unhappy unions of any kind can learn something about what it takes to improve relationships.

The first technique is *endurance*. Many couples, the study found, did not so much solve their problems as transcend them—they simply and stubbornly outlasted their problems. By taking one day at a time and pushing through their difficulties, the unhappy spouses said in their focus groups, many sources of conflict and distress eased—whether it was financial problems, job reversals, depression, child problems, even infidelity.

The second technique is *work ethic*. Unhappy spouses actively worked to solve problems, change behavior, and improve communication. They tackled their problems by arranging for more private time with one another, seeking counseling, receiving help from in-laws or other relatives, consulting clergy or secular counselors, and even by threatening divorce and consulting divorce attorneys.

The third technique was *personal happiness*. In these cases, the unhappy partners found other ways to improve their overall contentment, even if they could not markedly improve their marital happiness. That is, they improved their own happiness and built, for themselves, a good and happy life, despite a mediocre marriage.

The bottom line to improving relationship happiness proved to be *commitment*—having a positive attitude toward the relationship. Unhappy partners minimized the importance of difficulties they couldn't resolve, and they actively worked to belittle and downplay the attractiveness of alternatives to their current relationship.

THE INTERNET AND EVALUATING AND IMPROVING RELATIONSHIPS

When you are using the Internet, and when your goal is to evaluate an online relationship, the key is to move slowly. The potential for lies, deceit, half-truths, hidden agendas, and misunderstandings is real, and they are more likely to reveal themselves over time simply because people have difficulty being on their best behavior for a long period. What are the red flags to look for?

Does the other person avoid direct answers to questions about issues that are important to you?

Does the other person make demeaning or disrespectful comments about you or other people?

Is there any inconsistency in basic information? For example, do the answers about marital status, children, employment, and location appear consistent? How about the information on age, appearance, education, and career?

Is the other person pushing too quickly for an in-person meeting or avoiding phone contact?

Is he or she engaging in overly sexy conversation right from the start?

Is the other person asking for money?

Ask direct questions when you find an inconsistency. Do the answers make sense? If you don't get direct answers, how are the questions declined? If you attempt to dig deeper, which is your right, mature people may respectfully ask you to back off, tell you that you are frightening them, or let you know that your questions are premature. These responses let you know the other person knows, first, how to be respectful and, second, how to take care of himself or herself.

There are seven tips for making the transition from virtual to real world smooth and safe:

1. *Don't give out personal information.* If someone asks for a phone number, get theirs, and call back from a pay phone. Don't tell where you live or work, or what you do.

   Gather as much information about the other person as possible, but stop communicating with anyone who pressures you for personal information or who in any way attempts to trick you into revealing it.

2. *Move slowly.* This not only helps you assess the other person by looking for odd behavior or inconsistencies, but it also allows you to find out whether the other person is indeed who he or she says. One of the problems with online communication is the ease of self-disclosure. You share too much of yourself too quickly, thinking it will make you close, but intimacy is cultivated over time.

3. *Use caution.* Careful, thoughtful decisions yield better relationship results. Trust builds gradually. Pay attention, and look for the red flags.

4. *Be honest.* If you are realistic about your own claims, you will have little anxiety about trying to control and manage your information. Exaggeration is often difficult to explain if you decide to meet later. Be yourself.

5. *Request a photo.* Request photos, not just a single photo. Not only does this give you an idea of a person's appearance, but when you have several images in several settings—like casual, formal, indoor, and outdoors—you have contexts in which to place verbal comments. When you hear excuses about why you can't see photos, consider that the person may have something to hide.

6. *Chat on the phone.* After using the Internet—or along with it—the telephone is the next step. It is another way to find out about a person's communication and social skills, and with the addition of all the vocal cues—volume, pitch, rate, tone, and quality—and the elements of enthusiasm, force, and variety, you begin to form a better, bigger picture of the other person.

7. *Meet only when you are ready.* When you are ready, you can choose whether to pursue the relationship in the offline world. No matter what level of online intimacy was attained, you can still decide not to meet offline. Even if you decide to arrange a meeting, you have the right to change your mind.

If you should decide to meet in person, meet in daylight in a safe, public place where other people will be present. Always tell a friend where you are going and when you will return, and provide your own transportation. If you feel unsafe or uncomfortable, leave.

Assess Yourself

Relationship Survey

The statements below refer to people in a close relationship (e.g., a relationship between two partners in an intimate relationship). For each statement decide to what extent it is characteristic of your feelings and behaviors using the following scale: A = Not at all characteristic of me; B = Slightly characteristic of me; C = Somewhat characteristic of me; D = Moderately characteristic of me; E = Very characteristic of me. Write the letter for the answer in each blank.

_____ 1. I am a good partner for an intimate relationship.

_____ 2. I am depressed about the relationship aspects of my life.

_____ 3. I am better at intimate relationships than most other people.

_____ 4. I feel good about myself as an intimate partner.

_____ 5. I sometimes have doubts about my relationship competence.

_____ 6. I am disappointed about the quality of my close relationship.

_____ 7. I am not very sure of myself in close relationships.

_____ 8. I cannot seem to be happy in intimate relationships.

_____ 9. I tend to be preoccupied with close relationships.

_____ 10. I think of myself as an excellent intimate partner.

_____ 11. I am less than happy with my ability to sustain an intimate relationship.

_____ 12. I would rate myself as a "poor" partner for a close relationship.

_____ 13. I feel down about myself as an intimate partner.

_____ 14. I am confident about myself as a relationship partner.

_____ 15. I feel unhappy about my interpersonal relationships.

_____ 16. I am not very confident about my potential as an intimate partner.

_____ 17. I feel pleased with my love relationships.

_____ 18. I sometimes doubt my ability to maintain a close relationship.

_____ 19. I feel sad when I think about my intimate experiences.

_____ 20. I have few doubts about my capacity to relate to an intimate partner.

_____ 21. I am not discouraged about myself as a loving partner.

Go to the *Communicating Effectively* CD-ROM and the Online Learning Center at **www.mhhe. com/hybels8** to see your results and learn how to evaluate your attitudes and feelings.

mhhe.com/hybels8

Source: Adapted from *The Relational Assessment Questionnaire (RAQ)*, by W. E. Snell, Jr., Department of Psychology, Southeast Missouri State University, September 11, 1999. Retrieved January 10, 2005, from **http://www4.semo.edu/snell/scales/RAQ.htm**

CHAPTER REVIEW

SUMMARY

The most important relationships in our lives go through five stages as they are coming together: initiating, experimenting, intensifying, integrating, and bonding. Relationships that remain superficial go through only the first or second stage. When relationships come apart, they also go through five stages: differentiating, circumscribing, stagnating, avoiding, and terminating.

In evaluating relationships, ask yourself questions about commitment, forming a relationship with another person, and making a commitment to a specific relationship and particular person. Next, you need to ask yourself questions about your partner. Following that, ask yourself questions about rewards and costs and, finally, ask yourself questions about roles.

To improve relationships you are likely to have to deal with aggressive talk and aggression, regrettable talk, criticism and complaints, avoidance, defensive communication, and conflict. There are no universal, all-encompassing, always successful ways for dealing with each of these areas; however, it should be clear that the better you are at applying the strategic flexibility framework, the better you will be at revealing empathy, using owned messages, and displaying assertiveness when necessary.

The bottom line was revealed in a study by the Institute for American Values and the techniques the survey uncovered that unhappy couples use to recover. The first is endurance; simply outlast the problems. The second is work ethic; put forth effort to solve problems, change behavior, and improve communication. The third is personal happiness; find other ways to improve your overall contentment. All of these techniques require commitment—a positive attitude toward relationships.

There are several ways to evaluate online relationships. We looked at red flags, tips for making the transition from online to real life smooth and safe, and suggestions for meeting in person.

KEY TERMS AND CONCEPTS

Use the *Communicating Effectively* CD-ROM and the Online Learning Center at **www.mhhe.com/hybels8** to further your understanding of the following terms.

mhhe
.com/hybels8

Aggressive talk 196
Assertiveness 199
Avoidance 199
Complaint 198
Conflict resolution 202
Costs 193
Criticism 197

Defensive communication 199
Empathy 200
Evaluative statements 200
Extrinsic costs 193
Extrinsic rewards 193
Indirect aggression 196
Intrinsic costs 193

Intrinsic rewards 193
Instrumental costs 193
Instrumental rewards 193
Regrettable talk 197
Rewards 193

CHAPTER REVIEW

QUESTIONS TO REVIEW

1. When a relationship comes together, it goes through five stages: initiating, experimenting, intensifying, integrating, and bonding. What happens in each stage?

2. When a relationship is in the process of breaking down, it goes through the following stages: differentiating, circumscribing, stagnating, avoiding, and terminating. What happens in each of these stages?

3. When engaged in the process of evaluating relationships, what are the categories of questions you need to ask? Provide a sample question for each category.

4. What are the differences among extrinsic, intrinsic, and instrumental rewards and costs? Give an example of each.

5. What methods are suggested for diffusing aggressive talk and aggression?

6. What is regrettable talk and what can you do about it?

7. What are the guidelines for delivering criticism?

8. What are the six types of defensive communication, and how can each one be changed to supportive communication?

9. What are the six stages of conflict resolution?

10. When it comes to relationships, what are the three techniques unhappy partners can use to recover from an unhappy union?

11. What are red flags when it comes to online communication? What are some examples of red flag comments?

12. What are some of the essential tips that will help online communicators transition to the real world?

mhhe.com/hybels8

Go to the self-quizzes on the *Communicating Effectively* CD-ROM and the Online Learning Center at **www.mhhe.com/hybels8** to test your knowledge of the chapter contents.

CHAPTER

9

Communicating at Work: Professional Communication

OBJECTIVES

After reading this chapter, you should be able to:

- Define *professional communication*.
- Describe the ways information interviews are used.
- Explain the steps in preparing for the information interview.
- Outline the process of preparing for employment interviews.
- Identify cultural and gender differences in the workplace and show how to cope with them.
- Describe the important ingredients of communicating within a professional atmosphere.
- Demonstrate the process of dealing with conflict at work.
- Explain the strengths and weaknesses of the Internet in professional communication.

K YLIE BEGAN COLLEGE BY ENROLLING IN THE SCHOOL OF BUSINESS WITH an emphasis in sales and sales management and a minor in communication. She knew that a high grade point average (GPA) and a degree would not guarantee her career success; therefore, she wanted to do everything she could to develop and support her skills. Her undergraduate courses in the principles of selling, sales management, and advanced professional selling convinced her that selling was her specialty. She filled her résumé with evidence that she had the skills employers value: work ethic, communication, information-gathering, and people skills. She took courses that reinforced her analytical and problem-solving skills—skills she knew would be important to future employers as well.

To help support herself, Kylie took on part-time jobs, and she kept a journal that included the dates she worked at each, employers she met, names of potential employers and other contacts, and her impressions of them. She joined business and communication clubs, attended community meetings, volunteered whenever opportunities arose, and visited places of business to find out about potential jobs and to make new contacts. Kylie developed poise and self-confidence and learned to speak and think positively about herself and her abilities.

Kylie had great personal assets she knew would support her interest in sales. In addition, she was a happy person with lots of energy, and in her communication, she was open, honest, and direct.

This chapter focuses on **professional communication**—communication that relates to, engages in, is appropriate for, or conforms to business professions or occupations. We begin the chapter looking at principles of professional conduct as both an umbrella and a touchstone for all the other subjects discussed in the chapter. Second, we look at interviewing because, without a successful interview, it is unlikely that you will enter into the professional realm of business. We next discuss cultural and gender differences in the workplace. Then we examine communicating within a professional atmosphere and dealing with conflict at work, particularly with supervisors or managers and customers. The final section looks at the role of the Internet in professional communication. The Assess Yourself survey for this chapter allows you to measure your professionalism.

PRINCIPLES OF PROFESSIONAL CONDUCT

Every business expects you to conduct yourself professionally and to follow a line of conduct that suggests you are competent. Adhering to professional norms will win you active and supportive cooperation from others, professional success, and promotions, career advancement, and other opportunities. Unprofessional behavior generally results in lost collegiality, contracts, advancement, and jobs.

Following is a list of universal principles of conduct. Each area of business will likely adhere to additional principles or specific codes of acceptable behavior. Often, new employees must sign a code of ethical conduct along with their employment contract.

- **Integrity** is uprightness of character and honesty. Synonyms for integrity leave no question about its meaning: *honor, good character, righteousness, morality, virtue, decency, fairness, truthfulness,* and *trustworthiness.* These qualities are essential in providing a basis for trust, and they go to the core of what is expected from business professionals.

- **Respect** conveys regard and appreciation of the worth, honor, dignity, and esteem of all people. Relationships must be based on mutual respect and civility. Respect means that you will not engage in harassment or discriminate in any way on the basis of race, color, religion, gender, age, national or ethnic origin, political beliefs, marital status, disability, or social or family background.

- **Openness** means the free exchange of ideas within the bounds of reasonable behavior. When all members are receptive to exchanging ideas in an open and free manner, they will likely be amenable to reason, thoughtful consideration, and ideas that are supported by facts, evidence, and other forms of proof.

- **Responsibility** refers to your ability to meet your obligations or to act without superior authority or guidance, to discharge your duty, while perceiving the distinctions necessary between right and wrong, and with proper ethical discrimination. It relies on common sense, maturity, and dependability.

- **Teamwork** is unity of action by a group of workers to further the success of the business or organization while giving and receiving constructive criticism.

- **Self-improvement** means seeking all means available to maintain and enhance your professional competence by improving your knowledge and proficiency. There is a direct, positive correlation between success in your personal life and success on the job.

- **Ethics** is a set of standards that guides behavior in accordance with principles defined by your culture, your community, or your profession. You will not engage in fraud or make any false, misleading, disparaging, or defamatory comments, and your behavior will be in compliance with the rules and guidelines set forth by the business as well as with federal, state, and local laws.

There are a number of other issues involved in professional conduct. For example, it is expected that you will promote the aims of the business and conduct yourself to reflect positively on the business and your profession. You will use all proper means to maintain the standards of the business and your profession to extend its usefulness and sphere of influence, respect any confidence gained in your professional capacity, avoid unwarranted statements that reflect upon the character or integrity of other members of the business or profession, recognize your responsibility for the professional guidance of subordinates under your immediate control, and recognize your responsibility toward the environment and toward other employees.

STRATEGIC FLEXIBILITY
When the principles of professional conduct are a natural and automatic part of your entire skills and behaviors repertoire, then making ethical decisions as you anticipate, assess, evaluate, select, and apply your skills and behaviors becomes spontaneous and habitual.

INTERVIEWS

An **interview** is a series of questions and answers, usually exchanged between two people, that has the purpose of getting and understanding information about a particular subject or topic. Thus, when you ask a professor about a low grade you received on a paper, you are engaged in interviewing. You go in with a purpose—to find out why you received a low grade—and your conversation with the professor is a series of questions and answers.

What makes an interview different from interpersonal communication is that it is task oriented—it has the goal of finding out specific information. You interview someone for information you need to put together a speech, or you go into a job interview with the goal of presenting yourself so well that the interviewer will want to hire you.

Key Steps for Successful Interviewing

Step One: Be prepared. Adequate preparation and practice are essential to demonstrate that you are a knowledgeable and credible person.

1. Know the purpose and objectives of the interview.
2. Make certain the setting and time are satisfactory.
3. Remove any barriers that might interfere with a successful interview.
4. Make certain you have communicated effectively with the other interview participant or participants.
5. Dress appropriately.
6. Practice. Immediate impressions will be formed from your verbal and nonverbal communication; thus, make certain your self-confidence, personality, and speech habits convey a positive impression.

Step Two: Have an interview plan, but be adaptable and flexible. Even though the interview may not unfold exactly as you anticipate, a plan shows that you are thoughtful, knowledgeable, and organized. If there is dead space during the interview, your plan will help provide a way to move forward. If the interview drifts far afield from where it should be, having a plan will help you refocus and redirect the interview. Help make certain that the interview efficiently and effectively fulfills its primary purpose and objectives.

Step Three: Follow up. Any commitment to an interview requires both time and effort, and all who participate require a minimum of a thank-you. If they have provided you important information, taken time away from their regular job, or given you an employment interview, a formal thank you in the form of a short, timely letter of appreciation is important and further reinforces and underscores your credibility and thoughtfulness.

The interviews we are most likely to participate in are information interviews and job interviews. Of course, interviewers may discard the regular interview and opt for a phone or e-mail interview or even lunch.

One thing all interviewers will look for, despite the type or format of the interview, is communication skills. "Improved communication is a key to retaining employees."[1] Sherry Morreale, associate director of the National Communication Association, cites a study, "Three Out of Four Say Better Communication Equals Greater Employee Retention," that reports the results of a survey of 4,000 human resource professionals conducted by KnowledgePoint. Seventy-one percent of the respondents cited solid communication skills as the major reason to retain employees. To foster a culture of communication, interviewers will seek people who reveal effective communication skills.

The Information Interview

An **information interview** is an interview in which the goal is to gather facts and opinions from someone with expertise and experience in a specific field. Types of information interviews include the **appraisal interview,** where a supervisor makes a valuation by estimating and judging the quality or worth of an employee's performance and then interviews the employee in connection with the appraisal. A **disciplinary interview** concerns a sensitive area. The manager hears the employee's side of the story and, depending on the outcome, may institute disciplinary action. An **exit interview** occurs at the termination of an employee's employment and is designed to resolve any outstanding concerns of employers and employees. Some exit interviews occur by questionnaire only. A final kind of informative interview is a **stress interview,** which is sometimes part of the job search. A stress interview is

The goal of the information interview is to gather facts and opinions from someone with expertise and experience in a specific field.

designed to see how you act under pressure—to give interviewers a realistic sense of your response to difficult situations.

Interviews are a flexible means of information gathering. We can credit technology for expanding the media through which they are conducted; thus, often they are carried on in electronic chat rooms, in teleconferences, or via e-mail. The information interview is a useful tool when you are collecting information for a speech, a group discussion, or a paper. Also, it can serve as a way to get answers to questions you may have about a certain occupation, a career field, education, training, or work conditions.

Information interviews help us to get the most up-to-date information. Reporters, for example, make extensive use of information interviews. They interview the mayor of the town about her plans for increasing taxes. They talk to the governor of the state about his plans for reelection. On campus, an interview is the most effective way of getting information from members of the college community. A student interviews the vice president of administration about whether tuition will increase next year; another interviews a department head about the new requirements for a major.

One of the greatest advantages of the information interview is that it allows an opportunity for feedback and follow-up. If you don't understand something, you will have a chance to ask questions. An interview also permits you to explore interesting points of information as they arise—points you may not have been aware of beforehand. For example, if you are interviewing a member of the college administration about a tuition increase, she might mention that electricity costs have gone up this year. You can explore this area: Have they gone up because the utility company has raised its rates or because of greater electricity use on campus?

Preparing for the Interview

Preparation is one of the essential keys to success in most interviewing situations. It has three important benefits. First, it means you are less likely to waste the time of the interviewee because you will be able to focus on just the information you need. Second, with focused questions and pertinent follow-up questions, you are likely to gain a depth of understanding not available otherwise. (These benefits depend, of course, on your choosing the right person to interview.)

Finally, by preparing for the interview you will increase your credibility. If the people you are interviewing see that you have taken time to prepare, they are much more likely to be willing to spend their time with you. If you start out with such questions as "How do you spell your name?" or "I don't know much about this topic; do you have any ideas for questions?" you will not inspire confidence in your skills. On the other hand, if you show that you know something about the interviewee and about the topic, you will likely find much more willingness to discuss the topic seriously, and you will get better and more specific information.

Gathering Background Information. Typical information you should have before the interview includes the proper spelling of the subject's name and his or her title. If the person is well known, you might be able to discover some biographical information before the interview. *Who's Who in America* contains biographical information about prominent Americans. Don't forget to check out the specialized editions, such as *Who's Who in the South, Who's Who in American Women,* and so on. If you are going to talk to someone who works for the college or university, the public relations office is likely to have some biographical information about the person.

You should also have background information on the topic of your interview. The purpose of an interview is not to give you a crash course on a particular topic; it is to give you information that is not commonly known or new insight into an old topic. For example, if you're going to interview someone about using the Internet, you should have some experience in actually using it so that you can speak with some authority.

Deciding on the Format. **Open-format** interviews are relatively unstructured. As interviewer, you take note of or record the participant's statements but do not exert a great deal of control. In open-format interviews, you may ask interviewees to respond to a general topic or concern, and they determine the direction of the interview as they react to the points raised.

Closed-format interviews are highly structured. They are as formal, buttoned-down, and structured as the open format is freewheeling. As interviewer, you know exactly what you want to ask, and you work to keep your interviewee on track by asking one of your standardized questions and recording the respondent's answers to each one before moving on to the next question. Although this is an efficient technique for getting information because it is highly scripted, it doesn't allow much spontaneous information to emerge.

Semiopen format interviews occur when you have a core set of standardized questions that you ask in a standard manner and carefully record. However, this format allows you to deviate from the script with spontaneous follow-up questions if they are germane to the interview.

The best way to interview is to ask a variety of different kinds of questions, many of which emerge as the interview progresses. Thus, for most information interviews, our position is that the semiopen format works best because it most successfully accommodates this approach—requiring effective listening on the part of the interviewer and flexibility in adapting to what happens.

Preparing Questions. In this section we will look at primary, follow-up, open-ended, closed, neutral, and leading questions.

Primary Questions. **Primary questions** are designed to cover the subject comprehensively, and should be based on your background research. They often come first. Let's say you are interviewing a member of your counseling staff about depression. Some of the primary questions you might ask are:

- What is the clinical definition of depression?
- How does depression differ from being in a bad mood?
- What are the signs of a serious depression?
- Where can a student go to get help?
- How is depression treated?

Follow-Up Questions.   As the interview proceeds, you will think of other questions based on the answers given by your interviewee. These **follow-up questions** are useful when you want to go into a subject in greater depth. They also enable you to pursue an area that might be new to you or to clarify something you don't understand. Often the answers lead into such interesting areas that interviewers get information they hadn't planned on.

Open-Ended Questions.   **Open-ended questions** permit the person being interviewed to expand on his or her answers. They lead to explanations, elaboration, and reflection. Most in-depth questions are open-ended.

Closed Questions.   Questions worded in ways that restrict their answers are **closed questions.** "Do you plan to stay in this job?" "Are you going to graduate from school?" Other closed questions require only a short answer; for example: "Do you work better at home or in your office?" "What city would you most like to live in?" Closed questions have some advantages. They are designed to get a lot of information quickly, and they are good for eliciting facts.

When you prepare your interview's primary questions, they should be a mixture of closed and open-ended questions.

Neutral Questions versus Leading Questions.   Questions that do not show how the interviewer feels about the subject are **neutral questions.** For example, a reporter interviewing the mayor about a tax increase might ask this neutral question: "Many people think this tax increase will create a hardship for people who live in the city. What do you think?"

Leading questions point the interviewee in a particular direction. If you were to ask the dean, "When is the college going to stop exploiting women?" you would be implying that the college is currently exploiting women. A more neutral way of phrasing this question would be, "Do you think men and women have equal opportunities at this college?" or, if you want to get more specific, "Men's intramural sports are allotted twice as much money as women's. Why is that?"

Leading questions often show the bias of the interviewer, and if there is a negative bias, it might arouse hostility in the person being interviewed. Sometimes, however, leading questions can be used effectively. If you are interviewing a member of Alcoholics Anonymous, it might be appropriate to ask, "How did AA improve your relationships in your family?" Sometimes interviewers use a leading question to get a strong emotional reaction from the person being interviewed. Reporters and talk-show hosts often ask persons they are interviewing provocative questions like "How do you deal with the kind of negative comments being made about you?" or "What is it like to be known for your bad temper and rudeness?"

It's important to know when to ask leading questions. Since some questions can lead to hostility, especially when feelings run high, the inexperienced interviewer should leave them for the end of the interview and concentrate on neutral questions at the beginning. You should also remember that some leading questions can result in explosive replies, and so you should not ask them if you are not prepared for the answers they might evoke.

Working Together

Working with others as a group, come up with follow-up questions to these answers from an interview:

1. The people I hate most are drunken drivers. Ever since our family suffered such a tragic loss, I have been determined to devote my efforts to getting them off the roads.

2. The United States government is taking care of Native Americans through the reservation system.

3. People who live in earthquake-prone areas should take some basic safety precautions.

4. Once the United States has invaded a country, it has an obligation to stay and help the country become stable and functioning again.

5. The harmful chemicals and wastes that are discharged into the air and water of our nation not only make us sick but cause death as well.

6. Burnout, which is stress caused by the inability to cope and adjust to the demands of certain situations, causes irritability, fatigue, and low motivation.

Now the group should create several more statements that will lead to follow-up questions. Pass them along to another group so that they can come up with follow-up questions.

Using Tape or Notes? Before you conduct an interview, decide whether you want to record it on audio or videotape. The main advantage of taping is that it allows you to record the interview without taking notes. You can concentrate on listening and pay more attention to nonverbal cues. Taping also permits you to get precise quotations. This is particularly useful if the topic is controversial. If you are looking only for background information, however, exact quotations might not be your goal. Note taking has advantages of its own. You don't have to worry about equipment, and it is easier to review notes to find what you want than it is to go through a recording cassette. One advantage of conducting an online interview is that you can print out an exact copy of what occurred.

If you are taping, remember that your credibility is as affected by your professional handling of the equipment as it is by your conduct of the interview itself. Get your subject's permission beforehand to record the interview. Make certain you have a long-enough videotape to cover the entire interview and more, and check the lighting and sound conditions.

Sometimes tape recorders or video cameras make people feel self-conscious, and some of the spontaneous nature of an interview can be lost. A very controversial interviewee might not want to be pinned down to his or her exact words. Another disadvantage of taping is that if you have a very long interview, you will find it time consuming to watch or listen to the tape and pick out the main points.

If you decide to take notes instead of making an audio or video recording, it is useful to devise your own form of shorthand. After the interview is over, you should immediately write out your notes in greater detail while the comments are still fresh in your mind.

Conducting the Interview

Whenever you conduct an interview, the most important thing you can do is know what you are talking about. Most people will be pleased if you let them know you have been researching the topic of the interview and have taken the time to find out something about it.

People who are not accustomed to being interviewed might feel nervous, so it is important to help them feel at ease. You can best do this by thanking them for agreeing to the interview and expressing your interest in the topic you will be talking about. If you are taping the interview, try to put the recorder in an unobtrusive place so that it will not make the interviewee feel self-conscious.

Once you begin asking questions and listening to answers, don't be afraid to ask for clarification. Sometimes interviewers do not do this because they are afraid of appearing ignorant. If the person you are interviewing, for example, mentions a Supreme Court case you have never heard of, you should immediately ask for background information on the case.

It is important that you, as interviewer, keep control of the situation. As you ask your questions, you should set the tone for the interview and establish your authority, the course the interview will take, and your relationship to the interviewee.[2] When you are talking to people in their own area of expertise, quite often they will digress or tell you more than you want to know. If you have scheduled a half-hour interview and after the first 10 minutes you are still on your first question, you are losing control of the interview and won't have time to pose all the questions you want to ask. If this happens, the only thing you can do is interrupt. This can be done with such statements as "This is really very interesting and I would like to talk more about it, but I want to ask you a few more questions."

Watch for nonverbal cues. If the issue is sensitive, is the interviewee giving you cues that he or she is dodging the questions? Is he or she avoiding eye contact? Tapping a pen nervously on the desk? Nonverbal cues can often tell you whether to follow up on a point or to steer away from it.

If you are interviewing someone who is on a tight schedule, don't run beyond the time you have scheduled. If you need more time, ask for it at the interviewee's convenience or call back to tie up the loose ends over the telephone. Occasionally, when you listen to your tape or read your notes, you will discover something you missed or something that needs clarifying. The telephone is a good way to get this information after the interview is over.

Once the interview is complete, thank the interviewee. If it was a good interview, don't be afraid to say so. Even people who are interviewed frequently are pleased to hear they have been helpful. Also, let the person know how you plan to use the interview.

STRATEGIC **FLEXIBILITY**
A key part of strategic flexibility is the word *flexibility*. When you are truly anticipating, assessing, evaluating, and selecting, you will be sensitive to the changes in direction that interviews take, and you will be able to adapt and apply appropriately the skills and behaviors best suited to the situation.

Analyzing the Interview

When the interview is over, spend some time thinking about how you did. Your success can be measured by how the interviewee responded to you and whether you got the information you needed.

You can tell whether your questions were well worded by the way the person answered them. If he or she never quite dealt with the points you raised, the problem may have been with the questions. If he or she asked for clarification, that is another indication your questions weren't well structured.

Looking at your notes will tell you whether you covered the subject thoroughly and listened carefully. Are your notes confusing? Are there gaps in them? Finally, did you conduct the interview in a professional manner? Did you arrange the questions in a logical order beforehand? Had you researched the topic of your interview? Did you know how to run the equipment? The main measure of your professionalism is whether your interviewee took you and your questions seriously.

Information Interviews as Precursors to Job Interviews

Information interviews can help clarify and define career goals, introduce potential employers, and establish a network of contacts that could lead to future employment. Unlike job interviews, information interviews do not require that you sell yourself to employers. They are arranged with individuals who are most likely to provide information directly or who can refer you to persons with information. The best feature of information interviews as precursors to job interviews is that they are a way of exploring your possibilities—choosing academic majors, making career choices, changing careers, or beginning a job hunt.

To use information interviews as precursors to job interviews, analyze your skills, scrutinize your interests, and clarify your career goals. Next, you need to research the world of work. Select occupational fields that fit your career interests and needs, and research them. Then write a résumé.

Now, locate appropriate people to interview. The first and most immediate source of information consists of friends, family, neighbors, colleagues, former employers, and anyone else you know who might either supply an information interview or offer you a referral. Think, too, about contacting faculty, career center personnel, staff at other university offices, alumni, and any employer contacts the career center can provide. Other sources are community service agencies and trade and professional organizations such as the chamber of commerce, women's organizations, or the Information Management Association. You might also scan the *Yellow Pages* and articles in newspapers, magazines, and journals. Consider, as well, attending local, state, regional, or national meetings for professional associations in your career-interest field.

Once you locate someone to interview, prepare a variety of questions in different categories. Tailor your list of questions specifically to the individual and his or her organization. Background questions might include "Tell me about how you got started in this field," and "What educational background or related experience might be helpful in entering this field?" Work-environment questions might include "What do you do during a typical workday or workweek?" "What skills are most essential for effectiveness in this job?" and "What are the most difficult or challenging elements to the job?" Questions on career preparation might include "What kinds of prior experiences are absolutely essential?" and "What kind of lifestyle does your job permit?" You can also ask about current and future job availability and potential job advancement, any personal advice, and referrals to others to whom you could talk.

Setting up appointments requires that you be resourceful and sincere and, above all, show interest in what your target person does. Most people enjoy the opportunity to discuss their work. If they are too busy to meet you during their office hours, explore the possibility of meeting over lunch or after work. If a person cannot meet with you, ask whether you can ask her or him a few quick questions over the telephone.

Here are some final reminders for conducting information interviews as precursors to job interviews:

1. Remember that this is not a job interview. Your purpose is to acquire information. Nevertheless, dress as if it were an actual job interview. First impressions are always important.

2. Get to your appointment a few minutes early, and be courteous to everyone you meet.

3. Take the initiative in conducting the interview. The ball is in your court; you ask the questions.

4. Indicate your strengths and interests at appropriate times.

5. Do not exceed your requested time, but be prepared to stay longer in case the contact indicates a willingness to talk longer.

6. Before you leave, ask your contact if he or she could refer you to others in the same career. By doing this, you can establish a referral list and build a job-search network.

7. Write a thank-you note. Thank the person for his or her time and interest and cite any conclusions or decisions resulting from the interview.

8. Keep a record of each organization you visit. Record the information you obtained, too: names, comments, and new referrals for future reference.

The Employment Interview

The **employment interview** is an interview used by an employer to determine whether someone is suitable for a job. In an employment interview you have two goals: to distinguish yourself in some way from the other applicants, and to make a good impression in a very short time. The key to reaching both these goals is careful preparation.

A **résumé** is a summary of your professional life written for potential employers. It should give an idea of your career direction, present your achievements, and cite examples of your skills. The career center on your campus can provide you with sample résumés. A faster way of obtaining free advice, samples, and different options is to consult the Internet. "How to write a résumé" entered into the Google search engine (October 24, 2005) produced 19,700,000 hits; electronic résumés produced 4,450,000; cover letters, 79,400,000, and "how to write cover letters" produced 23,000,000 hits. The phrase "how to write application letters" produced 18,900,000 Web sites. There is no shortage of information available at your fingertips.

The employment interview is a structured form of communication.

The Interview

The actual interview—when you are sitting face-to-face with a potential employer or his or her representative—is the great equalizer. No matter what your GPA is, no matter how much background and experience you have, and no matter how much you know, if you cannot interview successfully, you will not get the job.

The key to reducing anxiety and trepidation about the interview is being well prepared. Career experts have made it clear that you should spend three, four, or even more hours preparing for the job interview. The best way to start researching a company is simply to type its name into any major search engine. Search for the answers to these types of questions:

- How old is the company?
- What are its products or services?
- Who are its customers?
- Who are its major competitors?
- What is its reputation or industry standing?
- What are its new products or services?
- How large is the company?
- What are its short- and long-term goals?
- How has the company resolved its problems?
- Have there been recent employee layoffs?
- Where is the company located?
- What are the backgrounds of its managers?
- What training programs are offered?
- What is the company philosophy?

Next decide exactly how your skills will benefit the company. Be able to answer simple interview questions like "Why do you want to work for us?" "What do you know about our company?" and "How can you benefit our company?"

Interview Questions.   Most employment interviews follow a predictable line of questioning. Spend time practicing your answers in the following areas.

Job Expectations.   The interviewer will want to find out whether what you are looking for in a job is compatible with the job the company has to offer. You will be asked what you want in a job, what kind of job you are looking for, and whether you would be content in this particular job. The best way to prepare for such questions is to study the job description carefully and see whether your qualifications and expectations match the job description.

Academic Background.   The interviewer will want to know whether you have had enough education to do the job. To find this out, he or she will ask you questions about the schools you attended, the degrees you have, and your grades. This is a good time to mention extracurricular activities that might be pertinent to the job.

Knowledge of the Organization.   All interviewers assume that if you are interested enough in the job, you will have taken the trouble to find out something about the employer. Sometimes you will be asked a direct question: "Why do you want to work for this company?" An answer might be, "I know several people who work here, and they like the company very much," or "I am impressed by your management training program."

You should be prepared to ask some questions yourself about the company or organization. For example, "Is it a new position?" "To what extent does the company promote from within versus hiring from the outside?"

Work Experience. The interviewer will want to know about other jobs you have had and whether anything in your work experience might relate to the job you are applying for. Even though your work experience might not be directly related to the job at hand, don't assume it is necessarily irrelevant. Let's say you are applying for a job as manager of a local store and your only job experience has been taking junior high students on canoe trips every summer. Although this summer job might not be directly relevant, it would certainly show that you are a responsible person—a characteristic an employer will be looking for in a manager.

Career Goals. *Short-term goals* concern what you want to do in the next year or so. *Long-term goals* are directed to a lifetime plan. Interviewers want to discover whether you are thinking about your future, to gauge your ambition, and to see whether you will fit into the company's long-term goals. If you are interviewing for a management trainee position in a bank, for example, the interviewer will try to find out whether you can foresee a long-term career with the bank and whether the bank is justified in putting you in its training program.

Strengths and Weaknesses. Most interviewers will want to find out whether hiring you will enhance their organization. To this end you might be asked directly "What do you see as your greatest strength?" or "What is your greatest weakness?" Think about both these points in relation to the job being offered before you go to an interview. Even if you are not asked directly about your strengths, you should be prepared to sell yourself on your good points during the interview. If on your last job you reorganized a department and improved its efficiency by 50 percent, now is the time to mention it. Be honest if you are asked about your weaknesses. If you are doing something about them, mention what it is. For example, "I am not always as well organized as I could be, but I am working on setting priorities and that seems to help" lets the interviewer know you are working on the problem.

Being Interviewed

Proper Behavior. There are some very clear and well-established norms for the face-to-face interview.

- Plan to arrive 10–15 minutes early. Lateness, whatever the reason, is never excusable.

- Treat all people you encounter with professionalism and kindness—including the receptionist, secretary, and maintenance people.

- Maintain a professional image no matter what happens, even if your interviewer takes a casual approach.

- Wait until you are offered a chair before sitting. Sit upright, look alert, and show interest at all times. Be both an effective listener and an effective communicator.

- Always look your prospective employer in the eye while speaking.

- Follow your interviewer's leads and don't interrupt, but try to get him or her to describe the position and duties early in the interview, so you can apply your background, skills, and accomplishments to the position.
- Always conduct yourself as if you are determined to get the job. Never close the door on opportunity.
- Show enthusiasm.

Improper Behavior. Do not smoke, smell like smoke, chew gum, or lie. Do not over-answer questions, and if the interview moves into politics or controversial issues, listen more than speak. Do not answer questions with a simple "yes" or "no"; explain whenever possible. Don't criticize your present or former employers, and never inquire about salary, vacations, bonuses, or retirement in the initial interview unless you are certain the employer is interested in hiring you. If asked about the salary you want, indicate what you've earned, but make it clear that you're more interested in opportunity than a specific salary.

Appropriate Dress. Dress makes up a great deal of the first impression you make. Your attire should be both professional and comfortable. If you are a woman, wear a straight-forward business suit, sensible pumps, and simple jewelry. Your hair and fingernails should be well groomed, and your makeup and perfume moderate.

If you are a man, wear a clean, ironed shirt with a conservative tie, a simple jacket and pants or business suit, and polished shoes. Your face should be clean-shaven, facial hair neatly trimmed, and hair and fingernails well groomed, and you should use cologne or aftershave sparingly.

After Your Interview. Make notes immediately so you don't forget any critical details. Send a short thank-you letter to the interviewer without delay. If several people interviewed you, send each a thank-you note. Restate your interest in the position and the confidence you have in your qualification. Do not call the employer back immediately, but if he or she said a decision would be made in a week, you may call back in a week. Again, thank him or her for the interview and, once again, reiterate your interest.

If you receive word that another candidate was chosen for the position you interviewed for, send a follow-up letter to the employer. Thank him or her for the opportunity to interview for the position. Let him or her know, too, that should another similar position open up in the future, you would love to have the opportunity to interview again.

CULTURAL DIFFERENCES IN THE WORKPLACE

Cultural differences, in the broadest sense, include not just obvious differences among people from other countries, but also "differences based upon income, regional origins, dress code and grooming standards, music preferences, and political affiliation."[3] An understanding of cultural differences may not only facilitate communication, but it can also avoid potentially embarrassing or even insulting situations.

Employers take diversity seriously and are willing to invest to establish and maintain it. Remember the principles of professional conduct, and make certain all your actions take place within that framework. First, treat others with respect and fairness as individuals, as if their opinion matters to you. Give others a chance to explain themselves and to "get things off their chests." Second, approach all others with an open mind. Third, put yourself in their place, and try to understand how others think and why they say and do what they do. Fourth, prepare yourself. If you need more information about others such as cultural attributes, religions, or ethnic differences and expectations, use the library or Internet. If co-workers are from another culture, learn about their culture's beliefs and values. Be conscious of things such as the amount of physical space between people who are talking with each other, the amount of eye contact that is appropriate, the significance of voice inflections when asking questions, or the purpose, if any, of head movements and other body language during conversations. Fifth, remember that you can be easily deceived by generalities and stereotypes. Just as there are significant differences among people from your neighborhood, home town, city, or state, there are equally significant differences among people from different countries or religions.[4]

GENDER DIFFERENCES IN THE WORKPLACE

A series of surveys of men and women at five U.S. companies discovered that men in the business world are driven by personal concerns such as career development and professional or financial rewards. Women are driven by the desire to increase communication, expand relationships in the workplace, or improve the quality and focus of customer service.[5] Basic characteristics like these not only drive but underscore many of the gender differences explained in this section.

The gender differences you notice in everyday life are apparent in the workplace. For example, as discussed in Chapter 5, men tend to use a **report style** of language (called report-talk) designed to preserve their independence and negotiate and maintain status. Women use a **rapport style** (rapport-talk) designed to establish connections and negotiate relationships. When both are asked to make a decision, in traditional circumstances men will make it without consultation. Men often believe that seeking input is unnecessary, and when put in charge of making the decision, they do it. Women, on the other hand, may discuss the decision with others and seek their input and feedback. They think it is important that everyone feels they have contributed to the decision in order to support it.[6]

Another report–rapport difference is in goal setting. Men are task oriented and focus on the end result and will move at once, often independently, to achieve it. Women are more concerned about the process and will connect with and involve others as they move toward their goals. Also, when achieving goals involves competition, men generally thrive because they enjoy it. Women, instead, thrive in arenas that involve collaboration.

Yet another result of the report–rapport difference is in giving feedback to others. Because women are more relationship oriented, they tend to use tact and sensitivity and reveal genuine concern about the other's feelings. Men, on the other hand, will be more direct, blunt, and to the point—a straightforward report style. In giving orders, too, men are direct. Women, disposed to maintain harmony, will give an order but follow it up with "If you don't mind," or "If it's okay with you."

Obviously, this is not a complete list of gender differences, nor do these differences apply universally to all men and all women. How these differences play out in actual business circumstances will vary greatly, but this discussion should give you a basic understanding of some of the differences that occur in the business environment and a premise for beginning to resolve differences and misunderstandings.

COMMUNICATING WITHIN A PROFESSIONAL ATMOSPHERE

Much of your success within any business environment will be based on your ability to communicate. Ineffective communication often results in poor cooperation and coordination, lower productivity, undercurrents of tension, gossip and rumors, and increased turnover and absenteeism. What can you do to ensure accurate, clear, and effective communication? Begin by showing concern about both the quality and quantity of your communication.

1. Give more attention to face-to-face communication with co-workers as well as superiors. Do not rely mainly on bulletin boards, memos, e-mail, or other written forms of communication. Trust is built better and faster when conversation is face-to-face.

2. Remember that the key to good communication is effective listening. Show respect for others when they speak. Don't interrupt; give them time to communicate; summarize and repeat what they just said; don't plan your response while the other person is talking; avoid checking your e-mail or shuffling paperwork while you're listening; and make an effort to look the other person in the eye.

3. Speak clearly and use good diction. People may miss your point if you are hard to understand. Be especially clear about deadlines and expectations.

    Rephrase thoughts and repeat what is being said to you back to those who are speaking. This ensures not only that you understood what they said but more importantly what they meant.

4. Maintain a positive attitude. People will be more interested in what you say.

5. Give and receive feedback. Everyone needs to know when they are doing a good job and when they need to make improvements. Give feedback in person, and always keep the criticism focused on the work and not on the individual.

6. If you get angry or upset, calm down before responding. Take a break, count to 10, go for a walk. Do whatever you need to do to cool off. Then sit down and think through how you want to approach the situation before taking any action.

7. Build your credibility. Demonstrate by both your messages and your actions that you subscribe to the principles of professional conduct discussed in the opening section of this chapter. They create a climate of trust and openness with others.

STRATEGIC FLEXIBILITY
The work environment reinforces the importance of strategic flexibility—especially when you are angry or upset. After you have taken a break and cooled down, you need to sit down and anticipate the coming situation, assess all elements, carefully evaluate everything, and select with sensitivity and care before you apply.

DEALING WITH CONFLICT AT WORK

Effective communication is the key to dealing with conflict at work. You can support effective communication with a well-thought-out, reasoned approach. This suggests that your emotions will not be engaged. How can you keep control in a potentially volatile situation? It isn't easy, of course, but the key is "emotional disengaging," according to Florence M. Stone of the American Management Association (AMA).[7] Stone says "it entails turning off your emotions to a situation and examining it as a scenario in a play or plot in a book—that is, objectively."

Some people, when facing conflict on the job, will put on gloves and come out swinging. Some will put on blinders and ignore the problem. But others will seek productive solutions, and the following steps will guide you through that process.[8]

First, *plan, prepare, and rehearse*. You must have a clear idea of your message, and to obtain this clear idea, you must do your homework and review the facts. It may even help to write out the problem. The better command you have of all the facts, the stronger your foundation throughout the process.

Second, *set an appropriate climate*. Anticipate your meeting with the other person by scheduling an uninterrupted time to work through the issues. Make your meeting private so nobody else will witness or overhear your conversation. Set the tone for the entire process by treating the other person as respectfully as you yourself would want to be treated.

Third, *adopt a constructive attitude*. Examine your motives and feelings carefully before delivering difficult or critical feedback. Emotions that reflect anger, frustration, and lack of respect will be quickly detected, as will awkwardness and discomfort. People will more likely be open to critical feedback if they are confident in, feel respected by, and trust the messenger.

Fourth, *assertively state the message*. Assertiveness is neither pushy, obnoxious, aggressive, nor confrontational. It means being open and straightforward about a situation, speaking calmly about what happened and keeping your emotions under control. This is where owned messages come into play. Instead of saying "You did this . . . " say "I was surprised when I heard . . . "

Fifth, *allow your message to sink in*. Stay quiet while your receiver processes your remarks. You do not need to elaborate, justify, or expand on your message at this point. You will have a better discussion if your receiver is allowed time to think and compose himself or herself.

Sixth, *listen carefully to the response*. Do *not* interrupt. Give your receiver an opportunity to express his or her reaction and response, even if this means some emotion is shown. Reveal your understanding and empathy by paraphrasing the remarks, if appropriate, and acknowledge his or her feelings.

Seventh, *restate, clarify, and recycle*. Work with your receiver until he or she has a clear understanding of your position. Encourage discussion to explore the issues, but stay on track. This is not an opportunity to debate and argue the issues. You may elaborate now in response to questions for clarification, but actively acknowledge both the reactions and viewpoints of your receiver as you do. Your active listening skills, accurate paraphrasing skills, and obvious respect for your receiver will help build the trust that forms the foundation for constructive problem solving.

Eighth, *focus on solutions*, not personalities. This is when you both need to offer solutions. It may require a compromise—not a complete adoption of one solution or another—to ensure there is closure to the conflict. It is not about one person winning and another losing; but rather, about both parties finding a way to resolve the conflict.

Ninth, *plan to evaluate solutions*. Schedule a time to meet after a solution has been put into practice, when both parties should be free to discuss it. Did it work? Can we make changes so it will work better?

Some people will never be able to get along with one another no matter what efforts are made. Rather than looking for issues to be upset about, you are more likely to work

STRATEGIC FLEXIBILITY
Dealing with conflict requires a thoughtful, rational approach to problem solving. If you apply the strategic flexibility framework at each stage of the problem–solution process, you are more likely to select just the right set of skills and behaviors that, when applied, will help move the problem toward a solution.

with such co-workers if you resolve to take the high road. You will be able to work in a more positive manner and environment if you think about the purpose of the work, the long-range goals of the company, and your individual contribution rather than co-worker problems and personality clashes.

THE INTERNET AND PROFESSIONAL COMMUNICATION

The Internet is the job market of the twenty-first century. Why go online? There are five reasons. (1) You can access current information at all hours of the day or night. (2) You can reach deeper into your local area as well as take your search far beyond your regular boundaries. (3) Using the Internet in your search demonstrates leading-edge skills. (4) The Internet lets you meet new people and initiate new relationships with others in your profession or region. (5) The Internet can help you explore career alternatives and options that you maybe haven't considered.[9]

Searching the Internet specifically for jobs, employment, and careers will bring up numerous results pertinent to you. A high-quality career Web site will include frequently updated job postings. Good sites update their listings several times a week at the minimum, adding new jobs and deleting old or already filled ones as soon as new information is available. The two technologies you should be sure to utilize during your online job search are searchable job databases and résumé databases.

High-quality career Web sites will include free, confidential résumé posting. Most sites offer free résumé posting with registration, but there is no shortage of less reputable sites that may try to trick you. A good one will offer a "private posting" option. This allows you to limit who has access to personal information such as your address, detailed work history, and salary information.

Résumé databases give job seekers additional exposure to recruiters who may search such databases to find candidates for their openings. To make your résumé fit numerous queries, supplement your résumé with industry buzz terms in line with your experiences and qualifications. Customize your résumé for each job. After sending a résumé electronically, mail a hard copy and call the hiring manager to follow up.

Finally, you need to be able to make contacts with people who can help you find information or secure you an interview. Most Web sites, career oriented or otherwise, feature message boards where users can post questions, comments, or the like. Message boards can be another great resource for industry information, as well as for making contacts with people in your area of expertise. Although the Internet is changing almost everything about finding a job, who you know still matters.

Measure Your Professionalism

How professional are you? Read the following statements. Then use the following scale to rate your level of agreement:

1	2	3	4	5	6	7
Not at all true			Moderately true			Absolutely true

_____ **1.** I am considered a person of good character.

_____ **2.** I convey regard and appreciation for the worth, honor, dignity, and esteem of all people.

_____ **3.** I fully support and demonstrate the free exchange of ideas within the bounds of reasonable behavior.

_____ **4.** I am amenable to changing my position based on the reasoned and thoughtful exchange of ideas when they are supported by facts, evidence, and other forms of proof.

_____ **5.** I always meet my obligations and act independently without superior authority or guidance.

_____ **6.** I am considered a good team player who knows the value of teams in developing creative solutions to challenges.

_____ **7.** I accept constructive criticism well and recognize its value in improving myself.

_____ **8.** I seek all available means to improving my professionalism and expertise.

_____ **9.** I always act in accordance with right principles of conduct.

_____ **10.** I never maliciously or intentionally make false, misleading, disparaging, or defamatory comments about others.

TOTAL POINTS: _____

Go to the *Communicating Effectively* CD-ROM and the Online Learning Center at **www.mhhe.com/hybels8** to see your results and learn how to evaluate your attitudes and feelings.

mhhe.com/hybels8

CHAPTER REVIEW

SUMMARY

Professional communication is that which in some way relates to business professions or occupations. Every business expects you to conduct yourself professionally and to follow a line of conduct that suggests you are competent. Universal principles of professional conduct include integrity, respect, openness, responsibility, teamwork, self-improvement, and ethics. When your skills and behaviors are anchored by these principles, then making the right, moral, honest, lawful, and ethical decisions becomes spontaneous, routine, and habitual.

An interview is a series of questions and answers, usually between two people, for the purpose of getting and understanding information about a particular subject. Interviews can be used for a wide variety of purposes including speeches, group projects, and research papers. Careful preparation is essential.

Information interviews will help you get the most up-to-date information and feedback; they are the most personal way of getting information. Preparation should include deciding on the angle you want to take, the format you plan to use, the kind of questions that will be most appropriate, and whether to use tape or notes.

Before you go to an employment interview, research the organization offering the job. Be prepared to talk about your job expectations, your academic and work backgrounds, your knowledge of the organization, your career goals, and your strengths and weaknesses as a potential employee. Your manner of dress, the kind of questions you ask, and your awareness of potential negative factors will affect the outcome. After the interview, write a follow-up letter or call the interviewer indicating that you are still interested in working for the organization.

There are cultural differences in the workplace, and an understanding of cultural differences may not only facilitate communication but also avoid potentially embarrassing or even insulting situations. To deal with cultural differences, follow the principles of professional conduct, approach others with an open mind, use empathy, prepare yourself, and avoid generalities and stereotypes about others.

Gender differences in the workplace often stem from the differences between men's report style and women's rapport style. This difference affects whom people choose to work with, goal setting, giving feedback, expressing feelings, handling problems, and asking questions.

Communicating within a professional atmosphere should place an emphasis on ensuring accurate, clear, and effective communication. You can do this by giving more attention to face-to-face communication, revealing effective listening, speaking clearly, sharing your ideas, giving and receiving feedback, calming down before responding, building your credibility, and being ethical.

The best way for dealing with conflict is to plan, prepare, and rehearse. You will need to set an appropriate climate; adopt a constructive attitude; assertively state your message; allow your message to sink in; listen carefully to the response; restate, clarify, and recycle; focus on solutions; and, finally, plan to evaluate the solutions adopted.

The Internet has become the job market of the twenty-first century. Two important technologies include searchable job databases and résumé databases. Make certain you use the private posting option when you post your résumé and remember the importance of personal contacts.

KEY TERMS AND CONCEPTS

Use the *Communicating Effectively* CD-ROM and the Online Learning Center at **www.mhhe.com/hybels8** to further your understanding of the following terms.

Appraisal interview 212	Integrity 210	Report style 223
Closed-format (interview) 214	Interview 211	Respect 211
Closed questions 215	Leading questions 215	Responsibility 211
Cultural differences 222	Neutral questions 215	Résumé 219
Disciplinary interview 212	Open-ended questions 215	Self-improvement 211
Employment interview 219	Open-format (interview) 214	Semiopen format (interview) 214
Ethics 211	Openness 211	Stress interview 212
Exit interview 212	Primary questions 214	Teamwork 211
Follow-up questions 215	Professional communication 210	
Information interview 212	Rapport style 223	

QUESTIONS TO REVIEW

1. What are the principles of professional conduct?

2. What is an information interview, and when do you use it?

3. What kind of information should you know before you go to an interview?

4. What are the differences among open-format, closed-format, and semiopen format interviews?

5. What are the differences among primary, follow-up, open-ended, closed, neutral, and leading questions? Give an example of each.

6. What preliminary planning must take place before you conduct information interviews that are precursors to job interviews?

7. What are some of the typical questions asked in job interviews?

8. When being interviewed, what are examples of proper and improper behavior?

9. What are some of the questions you should be prepared to ask in job interviews?

10. What are specific things you can do to reveal your sensitivity to cultural differences in the workplace?

11. What gender differences are likely to show up in the workplace?

12. What are some of the key guidelines for communicating within a professional atmosphere?

13. What are the basic strategies for dealing with conflict at work?

14. What contribution does the Internet make to professional communication?

 Go to the self-quizzes on the *Communicating Effectively* CD-ROM and the Online Learning Center at **www.mhhe.com/hybels8** to test your knowledge of the chapter contents.

References

Chapter 1

1. Boyer, P. (2003). *College rankings exposed: The art of getting a quality education in the 21st century*. Lawrenceville, NJ: Thomson/Peterson, p. 119.

2. Boyer, *College rankings exposed*, pp. 100 & 119; Haslam, J. (2003). Learning the lessons—Speaking up for communication as an academic discipline too important to be sidelined. *Journal of Communication Management, 7*(1), 14–20; Tucker, M. L., & A. M. McCarthy, (2003). Presentation self-efficacy: Increasing communication skills through service-learning. *Journal of Managerial Issues, 13*(2), 227–245; Winsor, J. L., D. B. Curtis, & R. D. Stephens. (1997). National preferences in business and communication education. *Journal of the Association of Communication Administration, 3*, 170–179; [No author]. (1992). What work requires of schools: A SCANS report for America. U.S. Department of Labor. *Economic Development Review, 10*, 16–19; Rooff-Steffen, K. (1991). The push is on for people skills. *Journal of Career Planning and Employment, 52*, 61–63; [No author]. (1998, December 29). Report of the national association of colleges and employers. *The Wall Street Journal, Work Week*, p. 1A; Maes, J. D., T. G. Weldy, & M. L. Icenogle. (1997). A managerial perspective: Oral communication competency is most important for business students in the workplace. *Journal of Business Communication, 34*, 67–80; Lankard, B. A. (1960). *Employability—The fifth basic skill*. ERIC Clearinghouse on Adult, Career, and Vocational Education, Columbus, OH (ERIC Document Reproduction Service No. ED 325659).

3. Ford, W. S. Z., & D. Wolvin (1993). The differential impact of a basic communication course on communication competencies in class, work, and social contexts. *Communication Education, 42*, 215–223.

4. Diamond, R. (1997, August 1). Curriculum reform needed if students are to master core skills. *The Chronicle of Higher Education*, p. B7.

5. Combs, P. (2003). *Major in success: Make college easier, fire up your dreams, and get a very cool job*. Berkeley, CA: Ten Speed Press.

6. Berlo, D. K. (1960). *The process of communication: An introduction to theory and practice*. New York: Holt, Rinehart and Winston.

7. Washington, D. (2000). *The language of gifts: The essential guide to meaningful gift giving*. Berkeley, CA: Conari Press.

8. Mehrabian, A. (1981). *Silent messages: Implicit communication of emotions and attitudes* (2nd ed.). Belmont, CA: Wadsworth.

9. Wilder, C. (1979, Winter). The Palo Alto Group: Difficulties and directions of the transactional view for human communication research. *Human Communication Review, 5*, 171–186.

10. Barnes, S. B. (2003). *Computer-mediated communication: Human-to-human communication across the Internet*. Boston: Allyn & Bacon, p. 4.

11. Gilster, P. (1997). *Digital literacy*. New York: John Wiley, p. 15.

12. Nieto, S. (1999, Fall). Affirming diversity: The sociopolitical context of multicultural education. In F. Yeo, The barriers of diversity: Multicultural education & rural schools. *Multicultural education, 2*–7; also in F. Schultz (ed.). (2001). *Multicultural education* (8th ed.), Guilford, CT: McGraw-Hill/Dushkin.

13. Griswold, W. (1994). *Cultures and societies in a changing world*. Thousand Oaks, CA: Pine Forge Press.

14. [No author]. (1999). *Ethical comm: NCA credo for ethical communication*. National Communication Association (NCA). Retrieved November 9, 2004, from **http://www.natcom.org/policies/External/EthicalComm.htm**

15. Ibid.

16. Ibid.

17. Ibid.

Chapter 2

1. Muriel, J., & D. Joneward (1971). *Born to win: Transactional analysis with gestalt experiments*. Reading, MA: Addison-Wesley, pp. 68–100.

2. Keillor, G. (1985). *Lake Wobegon days*. New York: Penguin/Viking Press, pp. 304–305.

3. Boone, M. E. (2001). *Managing inter@ctively: Executing business strategy, improving communication, and creating a knowledge-sharing culture*. New York: McGraw-Hill.

4. Manz, C. C., & H. P. Sims, Jr. (2001). *The new superleadership: Leading others to lead themselves*. San Francisco: Berrett-Koehler, p. 110.

5. Schwalbe, M. L., & C. Staples (1991). Gender difference in self-esteem. *Social Psychology Quarterly, 54*(2), 158–168.

6. Joseph, R. A., H. R. Markus, & R. W. Tafarodi. (1992, September). Gender and self-esteem. *Journal of Personality and Social Psychology, 63*(3), 391–402.

7. Maslow, A. H. (1970). *Motivation and personality* (2nd ed.). New York: Harper & Row.

8. Paul, A. M. (2001, March/April). Self-help: Shattering the myths. *Psychology Today*, 66.

9. Ibid., p. 66.

10. Ibid., p. 66.

11. Johnson, K. (1998, May 5). Self-image is suffering from lack of esteem. *The New York Times*, p. C7.

12. Ratey, J. R. (2001). *A user's guide to the brain: Perception, attention, and the four theaters of the brain*. New York: Pantheon Books, p. 56.

13. Ma, Miranda Lai-yee. (2003). *Unwillingness-to-communicate, perceptions of the Internet and self-disclosure in ICQ*. (A graduation project in partial fulfillment of the requirement for the degree of master of science in New Media, the Chinese University of Hong Kong, Hong Kong.) Retrieved March 20, 2004, from **http://216.239.41.104/search?q=cache:jqalB1tqnocJ:www.com.cuhk.edu.hk/courses/msc/Aca** p. 5 of 37.

14. Tidewell, L. C., & J. B. Walther, (2002). Computer-mediated communication effects on disclosure, impressions, and interpersonal evaluations—Getting to know one another a bit at a time. *Human Communication Research, 28*, 317–348.

15. Ma, Miranda Lai-yee, *Unwillingness-to-communicate*, pp. 20–21.

16. [No author]. (1999, December 28). *External reality and subjective experience*. Western Michigan University. Retrieved November 24, 2004, from **http://spider.hcob.wmich.edu/bis/faculty/bowman/erse.html**

17. Ibid.

18. Yeager, S. (2001, January 1). *Lecture notes: Self-concept*. DeSales University. Retrieved November 24, 2004, from **http://www4.allencol.edu/~sey0/selfla.html**

19. *External reality and subjective experience*.

Chapter 3

1. Morreale, S. (2003, November). Gender and diversity. *Spectra, 39*(11), 5. Morreale cites PEN Weekly NewsBlast, September 19, 2003. Survey by Futrell, Gomez, and Bedden, 2003.

2. Nieto, S. (1999, Fall). Affirming diversity: The sociopolitical context of multicultural education. In F. Yeo, The barriers of diversity: Multicultural education & rural schools. *Multicultural education, 2–7*; also in F. Schultz (ed.). (2001). *Multicultural education* (8th ed.). Guilford, CT: McGraw-Hill/Dushkin.

3. Harris, M. (1983). *Cultural anthropology*. New York: Harper & Row.

4. Gudykunst, W. B., & Y. Y. Kim. (2002). *Communicating with strangers: An approach to intercultural communication* (4th ed.). Boston: McGraw-Hill, p. 122.

5. Carnes, J. (1999). A conversation with Carlos Cortes: Searching for patterns. In Schultz, *Multicultural education*, pp. 50–53. From Cortes, C. (1999, Fall). *Teaching tolerance*, 10–15.

6. Beamer, L., & I. Varney. (2001). *Intercultural communication in the global workplace* (2nd ed). Boston: McGraw-Hill/Irwin, p. 3.

7. Rosaldo, R. (1989). *Culture and truth: The remaking of social analysis*. Boston: Beacon Press.

8. Samovar, L. A., & R. E. Porter. (2001). *Communication between cultures* (4th ed.). Belmont, CA: Wadsworth, pp. 2, 46.

9. Martin, J. N., & T. K. Nakayama. (2001). *Experiencing intercultural communication: An introduction*. Boston: McGraw-Hill.

10. Aseel, M. Q. (2003). *Torn between two cultures: An Afghan-American woman speaks out*. Sterling, VA: Capital Books, p. 67.

11. Schultz, F. (2001). Identity and personal development: A multicultural focus. In Schultz, *Multicultural education*.

12. Martin & Nakayama, *Experiencing intercultural communication*, p. 185.

13. Cruz-Janzen, From our readers; Howard, G. R. (1999). *We can't teach what we don't know: White teachers, multiracial schools*. New York: Teachers College Press.

14. Carnes, A conversation with Carlos Cortes.

15. Schultz, Identity and personal development, p. 113.

16. Martin & Nakayama, *Experiencing intercultural communication*, p. 8.

17. Liu, Jun. (2001). *Asian students' classroom communication patterns in U.S. universities: An emic perspective*. Westport, CT: Ablex. As reviewed by Mary M. Meares, Book Reviews. (2004). *Communication Education, 53*(1), 123.

18. Martin & Nakayama, *Experiencing intercultural communication*.

19. Triandis, H. (1990). Theoretical concepts that are applicable to the analysis of ethnocentrism. In R. Brislin (ed.), *Applied cross-cultural psychology*. Newbury Park, CA: Sage.

20. [No author]. (2001). *Dimensions of culture*. Retrieved December 2, 2004, from **http://cwis.kub.nl/~fsw2iric/vms.htm**

21. Hall, E. T. (1976). *Beyond culture*. New York: Harper & Row, 1983; Hall, E. T. (1994). Context and meaning. In Samovar & Porter (eds.), *Intercultural communication*.

22. Ibid.

23. Chang, I. (2003). *The Chinese in America: A narrative history*. New York: Viking Press, p. xiii.

24. Hofstede, G. (2001). *Culture consequences: International differences in work-related values* (2nd ed.). Beverly Hills, CA: Sage.

25. Hall, *Beyond culture*; Hall, Context and meaning.

26. Martin & Nakayama. (2001). *Experiencing intercultural communication*, p. 44.

27. Ibid.

28. Orbe, M. P. (1998). *Constructing cocultural theory: An explication of culture, power, and communication*. Thousand Oaks, CA: Sage.

29. Adair, N., & C. Adair. (1978). *Word is out*. New York: Dell.

30. Raybon, P. (1996). *My first white friend*. New York: Viking Press.

31. Fadiman, A. (1997). *The spirit catches you and you fall down*. New York: Farrar, Straus & Giroux, p. 182.

32. Raybon, *My first white friend*, pp. 1–2.

33. DuPraw, M. E., & M. Axner. (1997). *Working on common cross-cultural communication challenges: Toward a more perfect union in an age of diversity*. Study Circles Resource Center—AMPU. Retrieved December 2, 2004, from **http://www.wwed.org/action/ampu/crosscult.html**

34. Carnes, A conversation with Carlos Cortes.

35. Pool, K. (2002, February). Valuing diversity. *Personal Excellence*, 13.

36. Cruz-Janzen, From our readers.

37. DuPraw & Axner, *Working on common cross-cultural communication challenges.*

38. Ibid.

39. Gudykunst, W. B., & Y. Y. Kim. (2002). *Communicating with strangers: An approach to intercultural communication* (4th ed.). Boston: McGraw-Hill.

40. Karim, A. U. (2001, April). *Intercultural competence: Moving beyond appreciation and celebration of difference.* Interculturally Speaking, Kansas State University Counseling Services' Human Relations Newsletter, I(1). Retrieved December 2, 2004, from **http://www.ksu.edu/counseling/ispeak/people to people.htm**

41. Taylor, R. (2001). *Are you culturally competent? (intercultural communication).* Springhouse Corporation. Retrieved December 2, 2004, from **http://www.findarticles.com/cf0/ m3231/431/74091624/print.jhtml**. This World Wide Web article was excerpted and adapted from Taylor, R. (2000). Check your cultural competence. *CriticalCareChoices.* Springhouse, PA: Springhouse Corporation.

42. Maruyama, M. (1970). *Toward a cultural futurology.* Paper presented at the annual meeting of the American Anthropological Association, published by the Training Center for Community Programs, University of Minnesota, Minneapolis, MN. In Martin & Nakayama, *Intercultural communication in context.*

43. Martin & Nakayama, *Experiencing intercultural communication,* p. 320.

44. Hwang, J., L. Chase, & C. Kelly. (1980). An intercultural examination of communication competence. *Communication,* 9, 70–79.

45. Gudykunst & Kim, *Communicating with strangers.*

46. Ibid.

47. [No author]. (2004, February 28). New online friendship community helps like-minded Muslims link up. Associated Press. *The* (Toledo) *Blade,* p. B5.

Chapter 4

1. Thompson, K., & D. Dathe. (2001). *Moving students toward competent listening: The Thompson-Dathe integrative listening model (ILM).* Convention Paper Resource Center, International Listening Association (ILA). Retrieved December 6, 2004, from **http://www.listen.org/pages/cprc_2001.html**. The process of remembering has been added to the ILM framework as discussed in this chapter.

2. Friedman, P. G. (1978). *Listening processes: Attention, understanding, evaluation.* Washington, DC: National Education Association, p. 274.

3. Rubin, R. B., & C. V. Roberts. (1987, April). A comparative examination and analysis of three listening tests. *Communication Education,* 36, 142–153.

4. Youaver, J. B. III, & M. D. Kirtley. (1995). Listening styles and empathy. *Southern Communication Journal,* 60(2), 131–140.

5. Kiewitz, C., J. B. Weaver, H. B. Brosius, & G. Weimann. (1997, Autumn). Cultural differences in listening style preferences: A comparison of young adults in Germany, Israel, and the United States. *International Journal of Public Opinion Research,* 9(3), 233–247. Online abstract retrieved December 9, 2004, from **http://www3.oup.co.uk/intpor/hdb/Volume_09/Issue_03/090233. sgm.abs.html**

6. Ibid.

7. O'Brien, P. (1993, February). Why men don't listen . . . and what it costs women at work. *Working Women,* 18(2), 56–60.

8. Tannen, D. (1999, May 6). Listening to men, then and now. *New York Times Magazine,* 56ff.

9. O'Brien. Why men don't listen, pp. 56–60.

10. Ibid.

11. Golen, S. (1990, Winter). A factor analysis of barriers to effective listening. *The Journal of Business Communication,* 27, 25–36.

12. Burton, J., & L. Burton. (1997). *Interpersonal skills for travel and tourism.* Essex: Addison-Wesley Longman.

13. Purdy, M. (2002). Listen up, move up: The listener wins. Monster Career Center. Retrieved December 9, 2004, from **http://content.monster.com/listen/overview/**. Copyright 2005—Monster Worldwide, Inc. All Rights Reserved. You may not copy, reproduce or distribute this article without the prior written permission of Monster Worldwide. This article first appeared on Monster, the leading online global network for careers. To see other career-related articles visit **http:// content.monster.com**.

14. Youst, R., & J. C. Pearson. (1994). Antecedent and consequent conditions of student questioning: An analysis of classroom discourse across the university. *Communication Education,* 43(4). CommSearch 95, CD-ROM, National Communication Association, first release (no date).

15. Pryor, B. K., P. Taylor, R. W. Buchanan, & D. U. Strawn. (1980). An affective-cognitive consistency explanation for comprehension of standard jury instructions. *Communication Monographs,* 47, 69

16. Nichols, M. P. (1995). *The lost art of listening.* New York: Guilford Press.

17. Greider, L. (2000, February). Talking back to your doctor works. *AARP Bulletin.*

18. Elias, M. (2003, September 23). The doctor is inattentive: Med students will be tested on empathy, listening skills. *USA Today,* p. 9D.

Chapter 5

1. Ratey, J. J. (2001). *A user's guide to the brain: Perception, attention, and the four theaters of the brain.* New York: Pantheon Books, p. 253.

2. [No author]. (no date). *Let's talk about it: Fostering the development of language skills and emergent literacy.* The Whole Child, For Early Care Providers, (PBS) Public Broadcasting Service. Retrieved December 18, 2004, from **http://www.pbs.org/wholechild/providers/ talk.html**

3. Sapir, E. (1958). The status of linguistics as a science. In E. Sapir, *Culture, language and personality* (ed. D. G. Mandelbaum). Berkeley: University of California Press.

4. Whorf, B. L. (1940). Science and linguistics. *Technology Review,* 42(6), 229–231, 247–248; Whorf, B. L. (1956). *Language, thought and reality* (ed. J. B. Carroll). Cambridge, MA: MIT Press.

5. Paratore, J., & R. McCormack (eds.). (1997). *Peer talk in the classroom: Learning from research.* Newark, DE: International

Reading Association. As reviewed by Hoffman, J. (2004, July). *Communication Education, 53*(3), 297.

6. Hayakawa, S. I. (1991). *Language in thought and action* (5th ed). New York: Harcourt.

7. Cotrell, H. W. (2001). *Spice up that family history.* Retrieved December 2, 2001, from e-mail.

8. Boone, M. E. (2001). *Managing inter@ctively: Executing business strategy, improving communication, and creating a knowledge-sharing culture.* New York: McGraw-Hill, pp. 109–110.

9. [No author]. (2002, April 2). Egg mystery boils down to physics: Mathematicians unravel gyroscope effect. *The* (Toledo) *Blade,* p. 3A.

10. Postman, N. (1992). *Technopoly: The surrender of culture to technology.* New York: Vintage Books.

11. Goffman, E. (1971). *Relations in public.* New York: Basic Books, p. 62.

12. Greif, E. B., & J. B. Gleason. (1980). Hi, thanks, and goodbye: More routine information. *Language in Society, 9,* 159–166.

13. Lutz, W. (1996). *The new doublespeak.* New York: HarperCollins.

14. Bennet, J. (1995, March 29). A charm school for selling cars. *The New York Times,* pp. D1, D8.

15. King, S. (2000). *On writing: A memoir of the craft.* New York: Scribner's, p. 208.

16. Tanno, D. V. (2000). Jewish and/or women: Identity and communicative style. In A. Gonzalez, M. Houston, & V. Chen (eds), *Our voices: Essays in culture, ethnicity, and communication.* Los Angeles: Roxbury., p. 33.

17. Tannen, D. (1990). *You just don't understand.* New York: Morrow, pp. 42–43.

18. Ibid., p. 76.

19. Ibid., pp. 51–52.

20. Mulac, A., J. M. Wiemenn, S. J. Widenmann, & T. W. Gibson. (1988). Male/female language differences and effects in same-sex and mixed-sex dyads: The gender-linked language effect. *Communication Monographs, 55,* 316–332.

21. Tannen, D. (1992, February). How men and women use language differently in their lives and in the classroom. *Education Digest, 57,* 3–6.

22. Turner, L. H. (1992). An analysis of words coined by women and men: Reflections on the muted group theory and Gilligan's model. *Women and Language, 15,* 21–27.

23. Tannen, *You just don't understand,* p. 153.

24. Ibid, p. 245.

25. Ibid., pp. 255–256.

26. Weatherall, A. (1998). Re-visioning gender and language research. *Women and Language, 21*(1), 1.

27. Shaywitz, B. A. (1995, February 16). Sex differences in the functional organization of the brain for language. *Nature, 37*(3), 607–608.

28. Ibid., pp. 89–90.

29. Gurian, M. (2003). *What could he be thinking? How a man's mind really works.* New York: St. Martin's Press.

30. Johnson, C. E. (1987, April). An introduction to powerful talk and powerless talk in the classroom. *Communication Education, 36,* 167–172.

31. Haleta, L. L. (1996, January). Student perceptions of teachers' use of language on impression formation and uncertainty. *Communication Education, 45,* 20–27.

32. Johnson, An introduction to powerful talk, p. 167.

33. O'Connor, S. D. (2003). *The majesty of the law: Reflections of a supreme court justice.* New York: Random House, p. 197.

34. [No author]. (2003, October 9). Foreign languages spoken in U.S. homes on rise. Census Bureau Study. *The* (Toledo) *Blade,* pp. 1, 7.

35. Nelson, M. C. (2004, March 15). On the path: Business's unfinished journey to diversity. *Vital Speeches of the Day, LXX*(11), 337.

36. [No author]. (2004, February 27). English declining as world language. *USA Today,* p. 7A.

37. Ibid.

38. Nelson, On the path, p. 339.

39. Hummel, S. (1999, January 25). Do you speak Bostonian? *U.S. News and World Report,* 56–57.

40. Rosen, E. (2000). *The anatomy of buzz: How to create word of mouth marketing.* New York: Doubleday, p. 215.

41. Tannen, *You just don't understand,* p. 62.

42. Penn, C. R. (1990, December 1). A choice of words is a choice of worlds. *Vital Speeches of the Day,* 117.

43. Ibid.

44. Crystal, D. (2000). *The Internet: A linguistic revolution.* Retrieved December 18, 2004, from **http://www.crystalreference.com**

45. Crystal, D. (2001). *Language and the Internet.* New York: Cambridge University Press.

46. Crystal, *The Internet: A linguistic revolution.*

47. Essberger, J. (2001). *Speaking versus writing.* For ESL learners. EnglishClub.com. Retrieved December 18, 2004, from **http://learners.englishclub.com/esl-articles/200108.htm**

Chapter 6

1. Mehrabian, A. (1981). *Silent messages: Implicit communication of emotions and attitudes* (2nd ed.). Belmont, CA: Wadsworth.

2. Brody, J. (1992, August 19). Personal health: Helping children overcome rejection. *The New York Times,* p. C12.

3. Flora, C. (2004, May/June). Snap judgments: The once-over. Can you trust first impressions? *Psychology Today,* 60.

4. Boyce, N. (2001, January 15). Truth and consequences: Scientists are scanning the brain for traces of guilty knowledge. *U.S. News & World Report,* 42.

5. Ibid.

6. [No author]. (2004, November 8). They can't tell a lie—some people just know. *The* (Toledo) *Blade,* p. 1D.

7. Ekman, P., & W. V. Friesen. (1969). The repertoire of nonverbal behavior: Categories, origins, usages, and coding. *Semiotica, 1,* 49–98.

8. Goodman, E. (2002, May 1). Some prefer to smile, furrow brows to Botox. *The* (Toledo) *Blade*, p. 11A.

9. Planalp, Communicating emotion in everyday life; Planalp, S., V. L. DeFrancisco, & D. Rutherford. (1996). Varieties of cues to emotion occurring in naturally occurring situations. *Cognition and emotion, 10*, 137–153.

10. Planalp, Communicating emotion in everyday life.

11. Andersen, P. A., & L. K. Guerrero. (1998). The bright side of relational communication: Interpersonal warmth as a social emotion. In Andersen & Guerrero, *Handbook of communication and emotion*, pp. 303–324.

12. Griffin, M. A., D. McGahee, & J. Slate. (1998). *Gender differences in nonverbal communication.* Valdosta State University, Valdosta, Georgia. Retrieved December 28, 2004, from **http://www.bvte.edc.edu/ACBMEC/p1999/Griffin.htm**. Throughout this section, Griffin, McGahee, and Slate site three sources: Burgoon, J. K., D. B. Buller, & W. G. Woodall (1996). *Nonverbal communication: The unspoken dialogue* (2nd ed.). New York: McGraw-Hill; Hanna, M. S., & G. L. Wilson (1998). *Communicating in business and professional settings* (4th ed.). New York: McGraw-Hill; Ivy, D. K., & P. Backlund (1994). *Exploring genderspeak.* New York: McGraw-Hill.

13. Griffin, McGahee, & Slate, *Gender differences in nonverbal communication.*

14. Ibid.

15. Ibid.

16. Hall, E. (1966). *The hidden dimension.* Garden City, NY: Doubleday.

17. Griffin, McGahee, & Slate, *Gender differences in nonverbal communication.*

18. Ibid.

19. Birdwhistell, R. L. (1970). *Kinesics and context.* Philadelphia: University of Pennsylvania Press, p. 117.

20. Addington, D. W. (1968). The relationship of selected vocal characteristics to personality. *Speech Monographs, 35*, 492–505; Pearce, W. B. (1971). The effect of vocal cues on credibility and attitude change. *Western Speech, 35*, 176–184; Zuckerman, M., & R. E. Driver. (1989). What sounds beautiful is good: The vocal attractiveness stereotype. *Journal of Nonverbal Behavior, 13*, 67–82; Zuckerman, M., H. Hodgins, & K. Miyake. (1990). The vocal attractiveness stereotype: Replication and elaboration. *Journal of Nonverbal Behavior, 14*, 97–112.

21. Mehrabian, A. (1968, September). Communication without words. *Psychology Today*, 53; Mehrabian, A. (1981). *Silent messages: Implicit communication of emotions and attitudes* (2nd ed.). Belmont, CA: Wadsworth, pp. 42–47.

22. MacLachlan, J. (1979, November). What people really think of fast talkers. *Psychology Today*, 113–117.

23. Ray, G. B. (1986). Vocally cued personality prototypes: An implicit personality theory approach. *Communication Monographs, 53*, 272; Buller, D. B., & R. K. Aune. (1988). The effects of vocalics and nonverbal sensitivity on compliance: A speech accommodation theory explanation. *Human Communication Research, 14*, 301–332; Street, R. L., & R. M. Brady. (1982). Speech rate acceptance ranges as a function of evaluative domain, listener speech rate and communication context. *Communication Monographs, 49*, 290–308.

24. Burgoon, J. K. (1978). Attributes of a newscaster's voice as predictors of his credibility. *Journalism Quarterly, 55*, 276–281.

25. Street, & Brady, Speech rate acceptance ranges as a function of evaluative domain, pp. 290–308.

26. Buller, & Aune, The effects of vocalics and nonverbal sensitivity on compliance, pp. 301–332.

27. Ray, Vocally cued personality prototypes, p. 273.

28. Berry, D. S. (1992, Spring). Vocal types and stereotypes of vocal attractiveness and vocal maturity on person perception. *Journal of Nonverbal Behavior, 16*(1), 41–54.

29. Burgoon, Buller, & Woodall, *Nonverbal communication*, p. 33.

30. Ekman, P., & W. V. Friesen. (1969). The repertoire of nonverbal behavior: Categories, origins, usages, and coding. *Semiotica, 1*, 49–98.

31. Benton, D. A. (2003). *Executive charisma.* New York: McGraw-Hill, p. 90.

32. Burgoon, Buller, & Woodall, *Nonverbal communication*, p. 42.

33. Ibid.

34. Andersen, P. A. (1999). *Nonverbal communication: Forms and functions.* Mountain View, CA: Mayfield, p. 40.

35. Kendon, A. (1967). Some functions of gaze direction in social interaction. *Acta Psychologica, 26*, 22–63; Exline, R. V., S. L. Ellyson, & B. Long. (1975). Visual behavior as an aspect of power role relationships. In P. Pliner, L. Drames, & T. Alloway (eds.), *Nonverbal communication of aggression.* New York: Plenum, Vol. 2, pp. 21–52; Fehr, B. J., & R. V. Exline. (1987). Social visual interaction: A conceptual and literature review. In A. W. Siegman & S. Feldstein (eds.), *Nonverbal behavior and communication* (2nd ed.). Hillsdale, NJ: Erlbaum, pp. 225–236; Andersen, P. A. (1985). Nonverbal immediacy in interpersonal communication. In A. W. Siegman & S. Feldstein (eds.), *Multichannel integrations of nonverbal behavior.* Hillsdale, NJ: Erlbaum, pp. 1–36; Silver, C. A., & B. H. Spitzberg. (1992, July). *Flirtation as social intercourse: Developing a measure of flirtatious behavior.* Paper presented at the Sixth International Conference on Personal Relationships, Orono, ME.

36. Gudykunst, W. B., & Y. Y. Kim. (1997). *Communicating with strangers: An approach to intercultural communication* (3rd ed.). New York: McGraw-Hill; Jensen, J. V. (1985). Perspective on nonverbal intercultural communication. In L. A. Samovar, & R. E. Porter (eds.), *Intercultural communication: A reader.* Belmont, CA: Wadsworth, pp. 256–272; Samovar, L. A., R. E. Porter, & N. C. Jain. (1981). *Understanding intercultural communication.* Belmont, CA: Wadsworth.

37. Richmond, Y., & P. Gestrin. (1998). *Into Africa: Intercultural insights.* Yarmouth, ME: Intercultural Press, p. 95.

38. Feingold, A. (1990). Gender differences in effects of physical attraction on romantic attraction: A comparison across five research paradigms. *Journal of Personality and Social Psychology, 59*, 981–993.

39. Andersen, *Nonverbal communication*, p. 113.

40. Andersen, P. A. (1998). Researching sex differences within sex similarities: The evolutionary consequences of reproductive differences. In D. J. Canary & K. Dindia (eds.), *Sex differences and similarities in communication*. Mahwah, NJ: Erlbaum, pp. 83–100; Berscheid, E., K. K. Dion, E. H. Walster, & G. W. Walster. (1971). Physical attractiveness and dating choice: Tests of the matching hypothesis. *Journal of Experimental Social Psychology, 7,* 173–189; Berscheid, E., & E. H. Walster (1969, 1978). *Interpersonal attraction* (2nd ed.). Reading, MA: Addison-Wesley; [No author]. (1972, September). Beauty and the best. *Psychology Today, 5,* 42–46, 74; Berscheid, E., & E. H. Walster. (1974). Physical attractiveness. In L. Berkowitz (ed.), *Advances in experimental social psychology*, Vol. 7. New York: Academic Press, pp. 158–215; Brislin, R. W., & S. A. Lewis. (1968). Dating and physical attractiveness: Replication. *Psychological Reports, 22,* 976; Coombs, R. H., & W. F. Kenkel. (1966). Sex differences in dating aspirations and satisfaction with computer-selected partners. *Journal of Marriage and the Family, 28,* 62–66; Walster, E., V. Aronson, D. Abrahams, & L. Rottman. (1966). Importance of physical attractiveness in dating behavior. *Journal of Personality and Social Psychology, 4,* 508–516.

41. Levine, M., & H. E. Marano. (2001, July–August). Why I hate beauty. *Psychology Today,* 41.

42. Dimitrius, J. E., & M. Mazzarella. (1998). *Reading people: How to understand people and predict their behavior—Anytime, anyplace.* New York: Random House, p. 31.

43. [No author]. (2004, January 18). Pay scale follows its natural height. *The* (Toledo) *Blade,* p. 1B.

44. Schwartz, J. (1963). Men's clothing and the Negro. *Phylon, 24,* 224–231.

45. Kelly, J. (1969). *Dress as nonverbal communication.* Paper presented at the Annual Conference of the American Association for Public Opinion Research.

46. Thourlby, W. (1978). *You are what you wear.* New York: New American Library, pp. 143–151.

47. Stolzafus, L. (1998). *Traces of wisdom: Amish women and the pursuit of life's simple pleasures.* New York: Hyperion, pp. 134–135.

48. Joseph, N. (1986). *Uniforms and nonuniforms.* New York: Greenwood Press, pp. 2–3, 15.

49. Ibid., p. 143.

50. Morris, T. L., J. Gorham, S. H. Cohen, & D. Hoffman. (1996, April). Fashion in the classroom: Effects of attire on student perceptions of instructors in college classes. *Communication Education, 45,* 142–148.

51. Joseph, *Uniforms and nonuniforms*, pp. 168–169.

52. Hall, *The hidden dimension*, pp. 116–125.

53. Ratey, J. (2001). *A user's guide to the brain: Perception, attention, and the four theaters of the brain.* New York: Knopf, p. 76.

54. Goleman, D. (1988, February 2). The experience of touch: Research points to a critical role. *The New York Times,* p. C1.

55. Heslin, R. (1974). *Steps toward a taxonomy of touching.* Paper presented at the Western Psychological Association Convention, Chicago, IL, 1974; Winter, R. (1976, March). How people react to your touch. *Science Digest, 84,* 46–56; Thayer, S. (1988). Touch encounters. *Psychology Today, 22,* 31–36.

56. Anastasi, A. (1958). *Differential psychology.* New York: Macmillan; Mehrabian, A. (1970). Some determinants of affiliation and conformity. *Psychological Reports, 27,* 19–29; Mehrabian, A. (1971). *Silent messages: Implicit communication of emotions and attitudes* (2nd ed.). Belmont, CA: Wadsworth.

57. Heslin, *Steps toward a taxonomy of touching;* Winter, R, How people react to your touch.

58. Hickson, & Stacks, *NVC—Nonverbal communication.*

59. Ibid. Many of the facts cited here are quoted directly from the U of C wellness letter.

60. Burgoon, Buller, & Woodall, *Nonverbal communication*, pp. 127–128.

61. Ritts, V., & J. R. Stein. Six ways to improve your nonverbal communications. Faculty Development Committee, Hawaii Community College. Retrieved January 2, 2005, from **http://www.hcc.hawaii.edu/intrnet/committees/FacDevCom/guidebk/teachtip/commun-1.htm**

62. Newberry, B. (2002). *Media richness, social presence and technology supported communication activities in education.* Technology Enriched Learning, University of Kansas. Retrieved January 2, 2005, from **http://learngen.org/resources/module/lgend101_norm1/200/210/211_3.html**

63. Ibid.

64. Ibid.

65. Ibid.

66. Mandel, T., & G. Van der Leun. (1996). *Rules of the net: Online operating instructions for human beings.* New York: Hyperion.

Chapter 7

1. Lindley, C. (1996). *Clyde's corner.* International Personnel Management Association Assessment Council. Retrieved January 5, 2005, from **http://www.ipmaac.org/acn/dec96/clyde.html**

2. Goleman, D. (1995). *Emotional intelligence.* New York: Bantam, p. 179.

3. Ibid., p. 178.

4. Goleman, *Emotional intelligence.*

5. Ibid., pp. 43–44.

6. Ibid., pp. 81–82.

7. Ibid., p. 193.

8. Goleman, D. (1998). *Working with emotional intelligence.* New York: Bantam, pp. 322–223; Covey, S. (1998). *7 habits of highly effective families.* New York: Golden Books, pp. 22–23, 238.

9. Ibid.

10. Ibid., p. 193.

11. Ibid., pp. 86–90.

12. Ibid., pp. 106–110.

13. Ibid., pp. 111–126.

14. Weinberg, G. (2002). *Why men won't commit: Getting what you both want without playing games.* New York: Atria Books, p. 30.

15. Hatfield, E., & R. L. Rapson. (1992). Similarity and attraction in close relationships. *Communication Monographs, 59,* 209–212.

16. Sias, P. M., & D. J. Cahill. (1998). From co-workers to friends: The development of peer friendships in the workplace. *Western Journal of Communication, 62*(3), 173–299.

17. Mantovani, F. (2001). Cyber-attraction: The emergence of computer-mediated communication in the development of interpersonal relationships. In L. Anolli, R. Ciceri, & G. Riva (eds.), *Say not to say: New perspectives on miscommunication.* IOS Press. Retrieved January 2, 2005, from **http://www.vepsy.com/communication/book3/2CHAPT_10. PDF+Revealing+attractiveness+int.CMC&hl=en&start=4**

18. Walther, J. B. (1993). Impression development in computer-mediated interaction. *Western Journal of Communication, 57,* 381–398.

19. Chenault, B. G. (1998). Developing personal and emotional relationships via computer-mediated communication. *CMC Magazine, 5* (online): **http://www.december.com/cmc/mag/1998/ may/chenault.html**

20. Baym, N. K. (1995). The performance of humour in computer-mediated communication. *Journal of Computer-Mediated Communication, 1* (online): **http://jcmc.mscc.huji.ac.il/vol1/ issue2/baym.html**

21. Rubin, R. B., E. M. Perse, & C. A. Barbato. (1998). Conceptualization and measurement of interpersonal communication motives. *Human Communication Research, 14,* 602–628.

22. Goleman, D. (1988, October 7). Feeling of control viewed as central in mental health. *The New York Times,* pp. C1, C11.

23. Ibid.

24. Wolfer, S. (2004, January/February). Save the date: Relationships ward off disease and stress. *Psychology Today, 37*(1), 32.

25. Joinson, A. (2003, November 4). *Intimacy and deception on the Internet: The role of the user, media and context.* Institute of Educational Technology—The Open University (*Instytucie Psychologii Uniwersytetu Gdannskiego*). Retrieved January 3, 2005, from **http://64.233.167.104/search?q=cache:ljEQ9LVhkTUJ: iet.open.ac.uk/pp/a.n.joinson/anima.ppt+motivation+for+using +CMC+for+romance&hl=en&start=9**

26. Marano, H. E. (1997, May 28). Rescuing marriages before they begin. *The New York Times,* p. C8.

27. Ibid.

28. Booher, D. (1996, May). How to master the art of conversation. *Vitality,* 5.

29. Gottman, J. M., & J. DeClaire. (2001). *The relationship cure: A five-step guide for building better connections with family, friends, and lovers.* New York: Crown, p. 4.

30. Ibid., p. 25.

31. Ibid., p. 31.

32. Gordon, T. (1974). *T.E.T.—Teacher effectiveness training.* New York: Wyden.

33. Proctor, R. F. II. (1991). *An exploratory analysis of responses to owned messages in interpersonal communication.* Unpublished doctoral dissertation, Bowling Green State University, Bowling Green, OH, p. 11.

34. Weaver, R. L. II. (1996). *Understanding interpersonal communication* (7th ed.). New York: Harper/Collins, pp. 149–154.

35. Gordon, *T.E.T.,* p. 139.

36. Parks, M. R. (1985). Interpersonal communication and the quest for personal competence. In M. L. Knapp & G. R. Miller (eds.), *Handbook of interpersonal communication.* Thousand Oaks, CA: Sage, pp. 171–201.

37. Littlejohn, S. W. (1992). *Theories of human communication* (4th ed.). Belmont, CA: Wadsworth, p. 274.

38. Miller, G. R., & M. J. Sunnafrank. (1982). All is for one but one is not for all: A conceptual perspective of interpersonal communication. In F. E. X. Dance (ed.), *Human communication theory: Comparative essays.* New York: Harper & Row. All is for one but one is not for all, pp. 222–223.

39. Ibid.

40. Luft, J. (1970). *Group process: An introduction to group dynamics* (2nd ed.). Palo Alto, CA: Science and Behavior Books.

41. Dindia, K., M. A. Fitzpatrick, & D. A. Kenny. (1997, March). Self-disclosure in spouse and stranger interaction: A social relationships analysis. *Human Communication, 23*(3), 388.

42. Barbor, C. (2001, January/February). Finding real love. *Psychology Today,* 42–49.

43. Kimura, D. (1999, Summer). Sex differences in the brain. *Scientific American Presents, 10*(Special Issue, no. 2), 26; Hedges, L. V., & A. Nowell. (1995, July 7). Sex differences in mental test scores, variability, and numbers of high-scoring individuals. *Science, 269,* 41–45; Halpern, D. F. (1992). *Sex differences in cognitive ability* (2nd ed.). Hillsdale, NJ: Erlbaum; Blum, D. (1997). *Sex on the brain: The biological differences between men and women.* New York: Viking Press.

44. Gottman & DeClaire, *The relationship cure,* pp. 65–87.

45. Sommers, C. H. (2000). *The war against boys: How misguided feminism is harming our young men.* New York: Simon & Schuster, p. 87.

46. Goleman, *Emotional intelligence,* p. 131.

47. Wood, J. T. (1997). But I thought you meant. . . . Misunderstandings in human communication. Mountain View, CA: Mayfield, p. 69. In D. Vaughan, *Uncoupling: How relationships come apart.* New York: Random House.

48. Sommers, *The war against boys,* p. 151.

49. Levin, J., & A. Arluke. (1985). An exploratory analysis of sex differences in gossip. *Sex Roles, 12,* 281–285.

50. Ibid.

51. McGuinness, D., & J. Symonds. (1977). Sex differences in choice behaviour: The object-person dimension. *Perception, 6*(6), 691–694.

52. Sommers, *The war against boys;* Brody, L. R., & J. A. Hall. (1993). Gender and emotion. In M. Lewis & J. Haviland (eds.), *Handbook of emotions.* New York: Guilford Press, pp. 447–460.

53. Wood, But I thought you meant . . . , p. 69. In Vaughan, *Uncoupling.*

54. Ibid.

55. Ibid.

56. Ibid.

57. Axtell, R. (1997). *Do's and taboos around the world for women in business.* New York: John Wiley, pp. 161–162.

58. Boteach, S. (2000). *Dating secrets of the ten commandments.* New York: Doubleday, p. 165.

59. Fein, E., & S. Schneider. (2001). *The rules for marriage: Time-tested secrets for making your marriage work.* New York: Warner Books, pp. 187–188.

60. Boone, M. E. (2001). *Managing inter@ctively: Executing business strategy, improving communication, and creating a knowledge-sharing culture.* New York: McGraw-Hill, p. 223.

61. Mottet, T. P., & V. P. Richmond. (1998). An inductive analysis of verbal immediacy: Alternative conceptualization of relational verbal approach/avoidance strategies. *Communication Quarterly,* 46(1), 25–40.

62. Burgess, A. (2002, January 26). I vow to thee. *Guardian.* Retrieved March 24, 2003, from **http://www.guardian.co.uk/Archive/Article/0,4273,4342138,00.html**

63. Real, T. (2002). *How can I get through to you? Reconnecting men and women.* New York: Scribner's, p. 198.

64. Ibid., p. 202.

65. Ibid., p. 74.

66. Perrole, J. A. (1991). Conversations and trust in computer interfaces. In C. Dunlop & R. Kling (eds.), *Computerization and controversy.* Boston: Academic Press, pp. 350–363. As cited in Chenault, B. G. (1998, May). Developing personal and emotional relationships via computer-mediated communication. CMC magazine, p. 1. Retrieved January 10, 2004, from **http:www.december.com/cmc/mag/1998/chenault.html**

67. [No author]. (2005, January 10), "Numbers," *Time,* 19. From the Stanford Institute for the Quantitative Study of Society.

68. Douglas, J., & S. Singular. (2003). *Anyone you want me to be: A true story of sex and death on the Internet.* New York: Scribner's (a Lisa Drew Book), p. 91.

69. Eitzen, D. Stanley. (2003, December 15). Avoiding trends that deprive us of humanity: The atrophy of social life. *Vital Speeches of the Day, LXX*(5), 144.

70. Greenwald, Rachel. (2003). *Find a husband after 35: Using what I learned at Harvard Business School.* New York: Ballantine Books, pp. 114–135.

Chapter 8

1. Knapp, M., & A. Vangelisti. (1995). *Interpersonal communication and human relationships* (3rd ed.). Boston: Allyn & Bacon.

2. Avtgis, T. A., D. V. West, & R. L. Anderson. (1998, Summer). Relationship stages: An inductive analysis identifying cognitive, affective, and behavioral dimensions of Knapp's relational stages model. *Communication Research Reports,* 15(3), 281.

3. Levine, M., & H. E. Marano. (2001, July–August). Why I hate beauty. *Psychology Today,* 42.

4. Avtgis, West, & Anderson, Relationship stages, pp. 280-287.

5. Ibid., p. 283.

6. Ibid., p. 284.

7. Ibid.

8. Ibid.

9. Ibid.

10. Casto, M. L. (2004). *The 7 stages of a romantic relationship.* The All I Need. Retrieved January 11, 2005, from **http://www.theallineed.com/ad-self-help-2/self-help-010.htm**. This article is adapted from the book: Casto, M. L. (2000). *Get smart! About modern romantic relationships: Your personal guide to finding right and real love.* Cincinnati, OH: Get Smart! Publishing.

11. Avtgis, West, & Anderson, Relationship stages, p. 284.

12. Ibid.

13. Ibid., p. 285.

14. Ibid.

15. Ibid.

16. Ibid.

17. Ibid.

18. Knapp, M. L., R. P. Hart, G. W. Friedrich, & G. M. Shulman. (1973). The rhetoric of goodbye: Verbal and nonverbal correlates of human leave-taking. *Speech Monographs, 40,* 182–198.

19. Banks, S. P., D. M. Altendorf, J. O. Greene, & M. J. Cody. (1987). An examination of relationship disengagement perceptions: Breakout strategies and outcomes. *Western Journal of Speech Communication, 51,* 19–41.

20. Mauchline, P. (2000). *Evaluating whether a potential partner may be the one for you.* The Art of Loving. Retrieved January 8, 2005, from **http://aboutyourbreakup.com/potential.html**. Mauchline lists five questions only. Some of the information here is taken directly from his Web site.

21. Littlejohn, S. W. (1992). *Theories of human communication* (4th ed.). Belmont, CA: Wadsworth, p. 274.

22. Kirshenbaum, M. (1996). *Too good to leave, too bad to stay.* New York: Dutton, p. 94.

23. [No author]. (no date). *Competition and feeling superior to others.* Retrieved January 9, 2005, from **http://mentalhelp.net/psyhelp/chap9/chap9q.htm**. The questions and comments in this section have been taken from this source.

24. Ibid.

25. Lerner, H. (2001). *The dance of connection: How to talk to someone when you're mad, hurt, scared, frustrated, insulted, betrayed, or desperate.* New York: HarperCollins.

26. Infante, D. A. (1995, January). Teaching students to understand and control verbal aggression. *Communication Education,* 44(1), 51.

27. Guerrero, L. K. (1994, Winter). I'm so mad I could scream: The effects of anger expression on relational satisfaction and communication competence. *Southern Communication Journal,* 59(2), 125–141.

28. Kantrowitz, B., & P. Wingert. (1999, April 19). The science of a good marriage. *Newsweek,* 52–57.

29. [No author]. (1993, September–October). The rat in the spat. *Psychology Today,* 12.

30. Tracy, K., D. Van Duesen, & S. Robinson. (1987). "Good" and "bad" criticism: A descriptive analysis. *Journal of Communication,* 37, 46–59.

31. Ibid., p. 48.

32. Alberts, J. K., & G. Driscoll. (1992). Containment versus escalation: The trajectory of couples' conversational complaints. *Western Journal of Speech Communication, 56,* 394–412.

33. Cline, R. J., & B. M. Johnson. (1976). The verbal stare: Focus on attention in conversation. *Communication Monographs, 43,* 1–10.

34. Gibb, J. (1961). Defensive communication. *Journal of Communication, 11,* 141–148.

35. Wieder-Hatfield, D. (1981). A unit in conflict management education skills. *Communication Education, 30,* 265–273.

36. Kantrowitz, & Wingert, The science of a good marriage, 56.

37. Waite, L. J., D. Browning, W. J. Doherty, M. Gallaher, Y. Luo, & S. M. Stanley. (2002, July 11). *Does divorce make people happy? Findings from a study of unhappy marriages.* The Institute for American Values. Retrieved January 11, 2005, from **http:// www.americanvalues.org/html/r-unhappyii.html**

Chapter 9

1. [No author]. (2002). *Types of interviews and how to handle them.* CareerJournal.Jobpilot. Retrieved January 17, 2005, from **http:// www.jobpilot.co.th/content/channel/journal/typeinterview.html**

2. Morreale, S. (2001, May). Communication important to employers. *Spectra,* 8.

3. Misler, E. G. (1975). Studies in dialogue and discourse: II. Types of discourse initiated by and sustained through questioning. *Journal of Psycholinguistic Research, 4,* 99–121.

4. Campullo, J. L. (no date). *Cultural differences in the workplace: Stereotypes vs. sensitivity.* Fisher & Phillips LLP (Attorneys at Law). Retrieved January 16, 2005, from **http://www.laborlawyers.com/ CM/Seminar%20Materials/seminar%20materiala548.asp**, p. 1.

5. [No author]. (2004, March 3). *Workforce diversity issues: The role of cultural differences in workplace investigations.* Cultural Differences in Workplace Investigations. Texas Workforce. Retrieved January 16, 2005, from **http://www.twc.state.tx.us/ news/efte/cultural_differences.html**

6. [No author]. (2004, September 1). Studies find women, men motivated on job by differing concerns. *The* (Toledo) *Blade,* p. 8B (originally published in the *Boston Globe*).

7. Tymson, C. (no date). *Business communication: Bridging the gender gap.* Retrieved January 16, 2005, from **http://www.tymson. com.au/pdf/gendergap.pdf**

8. Lifland, S. (2002, February). *Interview with Florence M. Stone.* AMA–American Management Association. Retrieved January 15, 2005, from **http://www.amanet.org/arc_center/archive/ experts_feb2002.htm**

9. Wisinski, J. (1993). *Resolving conflicts on the job: A WorkSmart book.* New York: AMACOM, Chap. 1.

10. Dikel, Margaret F. (2003, September). *How to use the Internet in your job search.* The Riley Guide: Execute a Campaign. Retrieved May 7, 2004, from **http://www.rileyguide.com/ jobsrch.html**

Chapter 10

1. Sharpe, R. (1999, May 27). *Contributing to online discussions.* University of Plymouth. Retrieved January 20, 2005, from **http:// sh.plym.ac.uk/eds/LO/LOnet6.html**

2. Chadwick, T. B. (2001, September 21). *How to conduct research on the Internet.* Infoquest! Information Services. Retrieved January 20, 2005, from **http://www.tbchad.com/resrch.html**

3. Sharpe, *Contributing to online discussions.*

4. [No author]. (2005). *Internet usage statistics: The big picture.* Internet World Stats: Usage and Population Statistics. Retrieved January 20, 2005, from **http://www.internetworldstats.com/ stats.htm**

5. [No author]. (2001, January 1). *Help with Internet e-mail and mailing lists.* City of Grand Prarie, Alberta, Canada. Retrieved January 20, 2005, from **http://www.city.grandeprare.ab.ca/h_ email.htm#Frinding_And-Subscribing_toMls**

6. Beebe, S. A., & J. T. Masterson. (2002). *Communicating in small groups: Principles and practices* (7th ed.). Boston: Allyn & Bacon.

7. Whetten, D. A., & K. S. Cameron. (1984). *Developing management skills.* Glenview, IL: Scott, Foresman, p. 6.

8. Ibid.

9. Tubbs, S. L. (2003). *A systems approach to small group interaction* (8th ed.). New York: McGraw-Hill.

10. Svinicki, M. (no date). *Using small groups to promote learning: Section 5. Improving specific teaching techniques.* Center for Teaching Effectiveness, the University of Texas at Austin. Retrieved January 19, 2005, from **http://www.utexas.edu/academic/cte/ sourcebook/groups.pdf**, p. 1.

11. Wilson, G. L. (2004). *Groups in context: Leadership and participation in small groups* (7th ed.). New York: McGraw-Hill.

12. Beebe & Masterson, *Communicating in small groups.*

13. Ibid.

14. Goleman, D. (1990, December 25). The group and the self: New focus on a cultural rift. *The New York Times,* pp. 37, 41.

15. Ibid.

16. Thelen, H. A. (1997, March). Group dynamics in instruction: Principle of least group size. *School Review, 57,* 142.

17. Lawren, B. (1989, September). Seating for success. *Psychology Today,* 16–20.

18. Beebe & Masterson, *Communicating in small groups,* p. 113.

19. Janis, I. L. (1972). *Victims of groupthink.* Boston: Houghton Mifflin, p. 9.

20. Ibid., p. 3.

21. Greenhalgh, L. (2001). *Managing strategic relationships: The key to business success.* New York: Free Press.

22. Ibid., p. 237.

23. Janis, *Victims of groupthink,* pp. 174–175.

24. Larson, C. E., & F. M. J. LaFasto. (1989). *Teamwork.* Newbury Park, CA: Sage, p. 19.

25. Dyer, W. G. (1985). *Team building: Issues and alternatives* (2nd ed.). Reading, MA: Addison-Wesley, p. 24.

26. [No author]. (no date). *What makes a good team?* Center for Service and Leadership, George Mason University, Fairfax, Virginia. Retrieved January 19, 2005, from **http://www.gmu.edu/student/csl/goodteam.html**

27. Barnett, S. (no date). *Teams in the workplace.* LIS 405. Retrieved January 20, 2005, from **http://lrs.ed.uiuc.edu/students/sbarnett/lis405le/teams.htm**

28. Drucker, P. F. (no date). *There's more than one kind of team.* Retrieved January 20, 2005, from **http://web.cba.neu.edu/~ewertheim/teams/drucker.htm**

29. Hersey, P., & K. H. Blanchard. (1982). *Management of organizational behavior: Utilizing human resources* (4th ed.). Englewood Cliffs, NJ: Prentice Hall.

30. Benne, K. D., & P. Sheats. (1948). Functional roles of group members. *Journal of Social Issues, 4,* 41–49.

31. Ibid.

32. Gahran, Amy (1999, June 20). The content of online discussion groups, Part 1: Introduction. *Contentious.* Retrieved May 11, 2004, from **http://www.contentious.com/articles/V2/2-3/feature2-3a.html**, p. 1.

33. [No author]. (no date). *Types of group communication tools.* University of Illinois. Retrieved March 24, 2003, from **http://illinois.online,uillinois.edu/stovall/GroupTools/GT/index.html**

34. Gahran, The content of online discussion groups.

35. Maeroff, G. I. (2003). *A classroom of one.* New York: Palgrave Macmillan, p. 43.

Chapter 11

1. Arnold, H. J., & D. C. Feldman. (1986). *Organizational behavior.* New York: McGraw-Hill, pp. 120–121.

2. Abrams, R. (1999). *Wear clean underwear: Business wisdom from mom.* New York: Villard Books, p. 36.

3. Cramer, R. J., & T. R. Jantz. (2005). *An examination of personality traits among student leaders and nonleaders.* PSI CHI. The National Honor Society in Psychology, Loyola College. Retrieved January 24, 2005, from **http://www.psichi.org/pubs/articles/article_421.asp**

4. Bennis, W. (1998). *Managing People Is Like Herding Cats.* London: Kogan Page.

5. Burbules, N. C. (1993). *Dialogue in teaching.* New York: Teachers College Press.

6. Doyle, M. E., & M. K. Smith. (2001, September 18). *Shared leadership.* Infed Encyclopedia—The Encyclopedia of Informal Education. Retrieved January 25, 2005, from **http://www.infed.org/leadership/shared_leadership.htm**

7. Zigarmi, P., D. Zigarmi, & K. H. Blanchard. (1985). *Leadership and the one minute manager: Increasing effectiveness through situational leadership.* New York: William Morrow.

8. Hargrove, R. (2001). *E-leader: Reinventing leadership in a connected economy.* Cambridge, MA: Perseus, p. 7.

9. Chang, H. K. (2003, March 14). *Sustainable leadership requires listening skills.* Graduate School of Business, Stanford University. Retrieved January 25, 2005, from **http://www.gsb.stanford.edu/news/headlines/vftt_vanderveer.shtml**

10. Simonton, B. (2003). *Leadership skills—Listening, the most important leadership skill—Don't shoot the messenger.* Retrieved January 25, 2005, from **http://www.bensimonton.com/messenger-leadership-skills.htm**

11. McCutchen, B., & Heller, Ehrman, White, & McAuliffe, LLP. (2003, September). Preserving diversity in higher education. *A Manual on Admissions Policies and Procedures After the University of Michigan Decisions.* Retrieved January 25, 2005, from **lhttp://www.bingham.com/bingham/webadmin/documents/radb5f5a.pdf.**

12. Nelson, C. S. (2004). *What makes a great leader great?* ConcreteNetwork.com. Retrieved January 25, 2005, from **http://www.concretenetwork.com/csn_archive/greatleader.html**

13. Giuliani, R. W. (2002). *Leadership.* New York: Miramax Books, p. 184.

14. Sieler, A. (1999). *Leadership and change.* Observing Differently, Newfield, Australia. Retrieved January 20, 2005, from **http://www.newfieldaus.com.au/Articles/leadership&change.htm**

15. Goleman, D. (1990, December 25). The group and the self: New focus on a cultural rift. *The New York Times,* pp. 37, 41.

16. Deutsch, M. (1973). *The resolution of conflict: Constructive and destructive processes.* New Haven, CT: Yale University Press; Johnson, D. W. (1970). *Social psychology of education.* Edina, MN: Interaction Book Company; Johnson, D. W., & F. Johnson. (1994). *Joining together: Group theory and group skills* (5th ed). Boston, MA: Allyn & Bacon; Johnson, D. W., & R. T. Johnson. (1995). *Teaching students to be peacemakers* (3rd ed.). Edina, MN: Interaction Book Company.

17. Blake, R. R., & J. S. Mouton. (1964). *The managerial grid.* Houston, TX: Gulf Publishing, p. 11; Blake, R. R., & J. S. Mouton. (1978). *The new managerial grid.* Houston, TX: Gulf Publishing.

18. Gahran, A. (1999, June 20). The content of online discussion groups, Part 3: Improving content in the discussion groups you run. *Contentious.* Retrieved May 11, 2004, from **http://www.contentious.com/articles/V2/2-3/feature2-3a.html**

19. Munro, K. (2002, May). Conflict in cyberspace: How to resolve conflict online. *Psychology of Cyberspace.* Rider University. Retrieved May 12, 2004, from **http://www.rider.edu/~suler/psycyber/conflict.html**, p. 1.

Appendix

1. Markoff, J. (2004, December 30). Internet use said to cut into TV viewing and socializing. *The New York Times,* p. C5.

2. Ibid.

3. Chenault, B. G. (1998). Developing personal and emotional relationships via computer-mediated communication. *CMC Magazine.* University of Illinois at Urbana–Champaign. Retrieved November 10, 2004, from **http://www.december.com/cmc/mag/1998/may/chenault.html**

4. [No author]. (1999). *Resource guide: Media literacy.* Ontario, Canada: Ministry of Education; [No author]. (1999, May 30). A

few words about media literacy. Retrieved March 10, 2003, from **http://www.cmpl.ucr.edu'exhibitions/education/vidkids/medialit.html**; Hobbs, R. (1998). Media literacy in Massachusetts. In A. Hart (ed.), *Teaching the media: International perspectives.* Mahwah, NJ: Erlbaum, pp. 127–144.

5. Freed, K. (2002, May 11). Deep literacy: A proposal to produce public understanding of our interactivity. *Media & Education, Media Visions Journal.* Retrieved March 2, 2005, from **http://www.media-visions.com/ed-deeplit.html**

6. Flaherty, L. M., K. J. Pearce, & R. B. Rubin. (1998, Summer). Internet and face-to-face communication. Not functional alternatives. *Communication Quarterly, 46*(3), 250–268.

7. O'Sullivan, P. B. (2000). What you don't know won't hurt me: Impression management functions of communication channels in relationships. *Human Communication Research, 26*(3), 405–406.

8. Barnes, S. B. (2003). *Computer-mediated communication: Human-to-human communication across the Internet.* Boston: Allyn & Bacon, p. 15. Throughout this appendix, I depend heavily on the work of Susan B. Barnes.

9. Mazur, M. A., R. J. Burns, & T. M. Emmers-Sommer. (2000). Perceptions of relational interdependence in online relationships: The effects of communication apprehension and introversion. *Communication Research Reports, 17*(4), 397–406.

10. Barnes, *Computer-mediated communication*, p. 148.

11. Loughlin, T. W. (1993, January). Virtual relationships. The solitary world of cmc. *Interpersonal Computing and Technology: An Electronic Journal for the 21st Century, 1*(1). Retrieved March 20, 2002, from **http://jan.uce.edu/~ipct-j/** (7 pages).

12. Keen, P. G. W. (1988). *Competing in time.* New York: Ballinger.

13. Barnes, *Computer-mediated communication*, p. 116.

14. Ibid., p. 125.

15. Ibid., p. 213.

16. Ibid., p. 230.

17. Rheingold, H. (1993). *The virtual community.* Reading, MA: Addison-Wesley, p. 6.

18. Rheingold, H. (1998). Virtual communities. In F. Hesselbein, M. Goldsmith, R. Beckhard, & R. F. Schubert (eds.). *The community of the future.* San Francisco: Jossey-Bass, p. 116.

19. Barnes, *Computer-mediated communication*, p. 226.

20. Ibid., p. 227.

21. Ibid., p. 227.

22. [No author]. (2004, March 6). You're on. *The* (Toledo) *Blade*, p. 1D.

23. [No author]. (2004, September 27). Who's blogging now? *Newsweek*, 62.

24. Ibid.

25. Ibid.

26. Mintz, J. (2005, January 21). When bloggers make news: As their clout increases, web diarists are asking: Just what are the rules? (Marketplace) *The Wall Street Journal*, p. 1B.

Chapter 12

1. Tucker-Ladd, C. E. (1996–2000). *Chapter 5: Signs of stress.* Psychological self-help/mental health net. Retrieved February 2, 2005, from **http://www.mhnet.org/psyhelp/chap5/chap5c/htm**

2. Levasseur, D. G., K. W. Dean, & J. Pfaff, (2004, July). Speech pedagogy beyond the basics: A study of instructional methods in the advanced public speaking course. *Communication Education, 53*(3), p. 247.

3. Chadwick, T. B. (2001, September 21). *How to conduct research on the Internet.* Infoquest! Information Services. Retrieved February 2, 2005, from **http://www.tbchad.com/resrch.html**

4. Ormondroyd. J., M. Engle, & T. Cosgrave. (2001, September 18). *How to critically analyze information services.* Olin Kroch, Uris Libraries, Research Services Division, Cornell University Library. Retrieved February 2, 2005, from **http://www.library.cornell.edu/okuref/research/skill26.htm**

5. Cuomo, M. (1998). Graduation speech at Iona College. In A. Albanese & B. Trissler (eds.), *Graduation day: The best of America's commencement speeches.* New York: Morrow, pp. 72–73.

6. Selnow, G. (2000, November 1). The Internet: The soul of democracy. *Vital Speeches of the Day, 67*(2), 59.

7. [No author]. (2004). *Trends Journal.* The Trends Research Institute. Rhinebeck, New York. Retrieved November 3, 2005, from **http://www.trendsresearch.com/**

8. [No author]. (2002). *Trends in college binge drinking during a period of increased prevention efforts: Findings from 4 Harvard School of Public Health College alcohol study surveys: 1993–2001.* School of Public Health, Harvard University. Retrieved March 25, 2003, from **http://www.hsph.harvard.edu/cas/Documents/trends/**

9. Franklin, W. E. (1998, September 15). Careers in international business: Five ideas or principles. *Vital Speeches of the Day, 64.*

10. Ibid., p. 719.

11. Walters, F. M. (2000, December 15). We, the people: Prize and embrace what is America. *Vital Speeches of the Day, 67*(5), 144.

Chapter 13

1. Mann, W., & J. Lash. (2004). *Some facts psychologists know about: Test and performance anxiety.* Psychological Services Center and the Division of Student Affairs and Services, University of Cincinnati. Retrieved November 3, 2005, from **http://www.psc.uc.edu**, p. 3.

2. Probert, B. (2003). *Test anxiety.* University of Florida Counseling Center. Retrieved November 3, 2005, from **http://www.counsel.ufl.edu/selfHelp/testAnxiety.asp**

3. [No author]. (no date). *Health, exercise, diet, rest, self-image, motivation, and attitudes.* Learning Strategies Database, Center for Advancement of Learning, Muskingum College, Muskingum, MI. Retrieved November 3, 2005, from **http://muskingum.edu/~cal/database/Physiopsyc.html**

4. [No author]. (no date). *Dealing with test anxiety.* SUNY Potsdam Counseling Center. Retrieved November 3, 2005, from **www.potsdam.edu/COUN/brochures/test.html**

5. [No author]. (no date). *Study skills for college.* Pennsylvania State University. Retrieved November 3, 2005, from **http://www.bmb.psy.edu/courses/psu16/troyan/studyskills/examprep.htm**

6. *Dealing with test anxiety.*

7. Probert, *Test anxiety.*

8. Mann, & Lash, *Some facts psychologists know about,* p. 3.

9. [No author]. (2002). *Test-taking strategies.* Academic Services, Southwestern University. Retrieved November 3, 2005, from **http://www.southwestern.edu/academic/acser-skills-terstr.html**.

10. Mann & Lash, *Some facts psychologists know,* p. 3.

11. [No author]. (2002, January 17). *Test anxiety.* Counseling Center, University of Illinois at Urbana. Retrieved November 3, 2005, from **http://www.couns.uiuc.edu/brochures/testanx.htm**

12. [No author]. (2001, August 31). *Test anxiety: Overcoming test anxiety.* Counseling Center, University of Florida. Retrieved November 3, 2005, from **http://www.counsel.ufl.edu/selfHelp/testAnxiety.asp**

13. Lamm, R. D. (2003, September 1). Sustainability: The limited use of history in the new world of public policy. *Vital Speeches of the Day, 69*(22), 678.

14. Kreahling, L. (2005, February 1). The perils of needles to the body. (Health & Fitness). *The New York Times,* p. D5.

15. McKerrow, R. E., B. E. Gronbeck, D. Ehninger, & A. H. Monroe. (2003). *Principles and types of speech communication* (15th ed.). Boston: Allyn & Bacon.

16. Gruner, C. B. (1985, April). Advice to the beginning speaker on using humor—What the research tells us. *Communication Education, 34,* 142.

17. Keillor, G. (1998). Commencement address—Gettysburg College. In A. Albanese & B. Triller (eds.), *Graduation day: The best of America's commencement speeches.* New York: Morrow, p. 181.

18. Dilenschneider, R. L. (2001, July 15). Heroes or losers: The choice is yours. *Vital Speeches of the Day, 67*(19), 605.

Chapter 14

1. Knight, B. (2000). *Women who love books too much: Bibliophiles, bluestockings and prolific pens.* Berkeley, CA: Conari Press.

2. Sellnow, D. D., & K. P. Treinen. (2004, July). The role of gender in perceived speaker competence: An analysis of student peer critiques. *Communication Education, 53*(3), 293.

3. Argyle, M. (1991). Intercultural communication. In L. A. Samovar & R. E. Porter (eds.), *Intercultural communication: A reader* (6th ed.). Belmont, CA: Wadsworth, p. 43.

4. Hahner, J. C., M. A. Sokoloff, & S. Salisch. (2001). *Speaking clearly: Improving voice and diction* (6th ed.). New York: McGraw-Hill.

5. [No author]. (2005). *How many online?* ComputerScope, Ltd., Scope Communications Group, Prospect House, 3 Prospect Road, Dublin 9, Ireland. Retrieved February 8, 2005, from **http://www.nua.ie/surveys/how_many_online/**, p. 1.

6. Ibid.

7. Motley, M. T. (no date). *Overcoming your fear of public speaking.* Communication Resource Center for Students, Fundamentals of Communication, Faculty Services Center, Houghton Mifflin Company. Retrieved February 7, 2005, from **http://college.hmco.com/communication/resources/students/fundamentals/fear.html**

8. Ibid.

9. Ibid.

10. Schacter, D. L. (2001). *The seven sins of memory: How the mind forgets and remembers.* Boston: Houghton Mifflin.

11. Manz, C. C., & H. P. Sims, Jr. (2001). *The new superleadership: Leading others to lead themselves.* San Francisco: Berrett-Koehler.

12. Ibid.

Chapter 15

1. Petersen, J. A. (1999, August 12). *Better families.* Quoted on the Christianity New home page, Preaching Resources. Copyright 1996 by *Christianity Today, Inc/LEADERSHIP, 17*(3), 69.

2. Lamm, R. (1998, September 15). Unexamined assumptions: Destiny, political institutions, democracy, and population. *Vital Speeches of the Day, 64*(23), 712.

3. Ehrensberger, R. (1945). An experimental study of the relative effects of certain forms of emphasis in public speaking. *Speech Monographs, 12,* 94–111.

4. [No author]. (2005, February 25). *Visual communication of ideas.* Presentation Helper. Retrieved March 8, 2005, from **http://www.presentationhelper.co.uk/visual_communication.htm**

5. This study was cited in Arredondo, L. (1994). *The McGraw-Hill 36-hour course: Business presentations.* New York: McGraw-Hill, p. 177. Also see Weaver, R. L. II. (2001). *Essentials of public speaking* (2nd ed.). Boston: Allyn & Bacon, p. 186.

6. Knapp, M. L., & A. L. Vangelisti. (1996). *Interpersonal communication and human relationships* (3rd ed.). Boston: Allyn & Bacon.

7. Kluger, J. (2004, December 20). The buzz on caffeine. *Time,* 52.

8. Finerman, E. (1996, March 1). Humor and speeches: A standup history. *Vital Speeches of the Day, 62*(9), 313.

9. Price, Technical presentations, pp. 1–3.

10. Ibid., p. 6.

11. Templeton, M., & S. S. Fitzgerald. (1999). *Schaum's quick guide to great presentations.* New York: McGraw-Hill, pp. 46–48.

12. Ringle, W. J. (1998). *TechEdge: Using computers to present and persuade.* (Essence of Public Speaking Series). Boston: Allyn & Bacon, pp. 120–121.

13. Price, Technical presentations, p. 4.

14. [No author]. (1999, February 4). *Technical presentations.* Toastmasters International. Retrieved March 24, 2003, from **http://www.toastmasters.bc.ca/ed-program/man-technical.html**

15. Tham, M. (1997). *Poster presentation of research work.* Chemical and Process Engineering. University of Newcastle upon Tyne. Retrieved March 24, 2003, from **http://lorien.ncl.ac.uk/ming/dept/tips/present/posters.htm**

16. Birdsell, D. S. (1998). *The McGraw-Hill guide to presentation graphics.* Boston: McGraw-Hill, pp. 8–11.

17. Nordgren, L. (1996, September 23). *Designing presentation visuals*. Media Services. Robert A. L. Mortvedt Library. Pacific Lutheran University. Retrieved March 24, 2003, from **http://www.plu.edu/~libr/media/designing_visuals.html**

18. Dershern, H. L. (1998, June 24). *How to give technical presentations*. Retrieved March 24, 2003, from **http://www.cs.hope.edu/~dershern/reu/howtopresent/**

Chapter 16

1. Rokeach, M. (1968). *Beliefs, attitudes, and values: A theory of organization and change*. San Francisco: Jossey-Bass, p. 124.

2. Bell, P. (2001, July 1). The new entrepreneurship: From exuberance to reality. *Vital Speeches of the Day, 67*(18), 572–575.

3. Haines, M. P. (2001, July 23). Facts change student drinking. *USA Today*, p. 15A.

4. Lane, T. (2001, December 3). Colleges develop better awareness of drinking risks. *The* (Toledo) *Blade*, p. 1A.

5. Ibid., p. 6A.

6. Kluger, J. (2001, June 18). How to manage teen drinking (the smart way). *Time*, 42–44.

7. Lane, Colleges develop better awareness of drinking risks, p. 1A.

8. Waldron, R. (2000, October 30). Students are dying: Colleges can do more. *Newsweek*, 16.

9. Morse, J. (2002, April 1). Women on a binge. *Time*, 56–61.

10. Ibid., p. 56.

11. Haines, M. P. (2001, July 23). Facts change student drinking. *USA Today*, p. 15A.

12. Ibid.

13. Kluger, How to manage teen drinking, p. 43.

14. Haines, Facts change student drinking, p. 15A.

15 Ibid.

16. Lane, Colleges develop better awareness of drinking risks, p. 1A.

17. Haines, Facts change student drinking, p. 15A.

18. Dunn, C. P. (1976). *Logical fallacies in argument*. Department of Management, San Diego State University. Retrieved March 26, 2003, from **http://www.rohan.sdsu.edu/faculty/dunnweb/logicafall.html**. Adapted from Engel, S. M. (1976). *With good reason: An introduction to informal fallacies*. New York: St. Martin's Press, pp. 66–130. These logical fallacies in argument are quoted directly from C. P. Dunn's adaptation.

19. Bauer, J., & M. Levy. (2004). *How to persuade people who don't want to be persuaded*. New York: John Wiley, pp. 17–18. The study cited is Davenport, T., & J. Beck. (2000, September–October). Getting the attention you need. *Harvard Business Review*.

20. Ibid., pp. 17–18.

21. Maslow, A. H. (1970). *Motivation and personality* (2nd ed.). New York: Harper & Row.

22. Tracy, L. (2005, March 1). Taming hostile audiences: Persuading those who would rather jeer than cheer. *Vital Speeches of the Day, 71*(10), 312.

23. Odden, L. R. (1999, March 1). Talk to your children about the tough stuff: We are all in this together. *Vital Speeches of the Day, 65*(10), 301.

24. Thompson, W. N. (1978). *Responsible and effective communication*. Boston: Houghton Mifflin.

25. [No author]. (2004, February). Optimism and longevity: What's the connection? *University of California, Berkeley Wellness Letter, 20*(5), 1.

26. [No author]. (2002, August 28). College education includes lessons in credit cards. *The* (Toledo) *Blade*, p. 7B. *The Blade* cited the *Kansas City Star*.

27. Mooney K. with L. Berghheim. (2002). *The ten demandments: Rules to live by in the age of the demanding customer*. New York: McGraw-Hill, p. 174.

Glossary

A

abstract symbol A symbol that represents an idea. (ch 1) (10)

accent Nonverbal message designed specifically to place stress on the verbal message. (ch 6) (148)

access to roles A characteristic of the Internet that makes it unique from normal face-to-face communication because there are no limitations; whoever has the technical capacity to receive messages with a computer can also send them. (ch 1) (24)

accommodation An approach that works toward getting the dominant group to reinvent, or at least change, the rules so that they incorporate the life experiences of the nondominant group. Something that occurs in groups when people on one side of an issue give in to the other side. (ch 3) (69)

accommodation strategies When people are not part of a dominant culture, those processes people use to get the dominant group to reinvent or change the rules through the use of nonassertive, assertive, or aggressive accommodation. (ch 3) (69-70)

action listening style That kind of listening in which the listener wants precise, error-free presentations and is likely to be impatient with disorganization. (ch 4) (85)

active listening Making a mental outline of important points, thinking up questions or challenges to the points that have been made, and becoming mentally involved with the person talking. (ch 4) (92)

adaptors Nonverbal ways of adjusting to a communication situation. (ch 6) (139)

ad hominem A fallacy that occurs when an argument diverts attention away from the question being argued by focusing instead on those arguing it. (ch 16) (408)

agenda A list of all the items that will be discussed during a meeting. (ch 11) (235)

aggressive talk Talk that attacks a person's self-concept with the intent of inflicting psychological pain. (ch 8) (196)

analogy In reasoning, comparing two similar cases and concluding that if something is true for one, it must also be true for the other. (ch 16) (407)

anecdote A short, interesting story based on an experience. (ch 15) (381-382)

anticipate The first of six steps of the strategic flexibility format in which users think about potential situations and the needs and requirements likely to arise because of them. (ch 1) (6)

anxiety A disturbance that occurs in your mind regarding some uncertain event, misgiving, or worry. (ch 4, 14) (89, 361-363)

appeal to authority A fallacy that occurs whenever an idea is justified by citing some source of expertise as a reason for holding that idea. (ch 16) (408)

appeal to ignorance A fallacy that occurs when an argument is based on an opponent's inability to disprove a conclusion as proof of the conclusion's correctness. (ch 16) (408)

apply The fifth of six steps of the strategic flexibility format in which users, with care, concern, and attention to all the factors that are likely to be affected—including any ethical considerations that may be appropriate—apply the skills and behaviors they have selected. (ch 1) (7)

appraisal interview A type of information interview in which a supervisor makes a valuation by estimating and judging the quality or worth of an employee's performance and then interviews the employee in connection with the appraisal. (ch 9) (212)

articulation The ability to pronounce the letters in a word correctly. (ch 14) (352)

assertiveness Taking the responsibility of expressing needs, thoughts, and feelings in a direct, clear manner. (ch 8) (199)

assess The second of the six steps of the strategic flexibility format in which users take stock of the factors, elements, and conditions of the situations in which you find yourself. (ch 1, 4) (6, 95)

assimilation When nondominants use assimilation, they drop cultural differences and distinctive characteristics that would identify them with the nondominant group. (ch 3) (68)

assimilation strategies When people are not part of a dominant culture, those processes they use to drop cultural differences and distinctive characteristics that would identify them with the nondominant group include the use of nonassertive, assertive, and aggressive assimilation strategies. (ch 3) (68-69)

assumption A taking for granted or supposition that something is a fact. (ch 3) (72)

asynchronous communication Communication in which people are not directly connected with each other at the same time. (ch 1, 10, Appendix A) (23, 251, 277)

attentiveness Focusing on the moment. (ch 14) (346)

attitudes Deeply felt beliefs that govern how one behaves. Also, a group of beliefs that cause us to respond in some way to a particular object or situation. (ch 12, 16) (297, 401)

attractiveness Having the power or quality of drawing, pleasing, or winning. (ch 6) (139-140)

audience analysis Finding out what one's audience members know about a subject, what they might be interested in, and what their attitudes and beliefs are. (ch 12) (295-300)

authoritarian leader One who holds great control over a group. (ch 11) (261-262)

avoidance A refusal to deal with conflict or painful issues. (ch 8) (199)

B

begging the question A fallacy that occurs when an argument, instead of offering proof for its conclusion, simply reasserts the conclusion in another form. (ch 16) (408)

beliefs One's own convictions; what one thinks is right and wrong, true and false. Also, they are classified as statements of knowledge, opinion, and faith. (ch 7, 12, 16) (160, 297, 400-401)

bid A question, gesture, look, touch, or other single expression that says, "I want to feel connected to you." (ch 7) (166)

bifurcation A fallacy that occurs when one presumes that a distinction is exclusive and exhaustive, but other alternatives exist. (ch 16) (408)

blind pane That area in the Johari Window known as an accidental disclosure area. (ch 7) (170)

blog (or Web log) A spontaneous public online journal (or diary) in which Internet users share their lives. (Appendix A) (282-283)

body adornment Any addition to the physical body designed to beautify or decorate. (ch 6) (141-142)

body movement (kinesics) Describes a phenomenon responsible for much of our nonverbal communication. (ch 6) (138)

body (of speech) The main part of the speech. (ch 13) (318)

brainstorming A technique of free association; in groups, when all members spontaneously contribute ideas in a group without judgments being made. The goal of brainstorming is for the group to be as creative as possible. (ch 10) (242)

bulletin boards An online group discussion originally designed for swapping files and posting notices. (ch 10) (251)

C

causal reasoning A logical appeal that pertains to, constitutes, involves, or expresses a cause and therefore uses the word *because*, which is either implicitly or explicitly stated. (ch 16) (407)

cause-and-effect order Organization of a speech around why something is happening (*cause*) and what impact it is having (*effect*). (ch 13) (320)

central idea The essential thought that runs through the speech or communication. (ch 4, 12) (93, 294-295)

channel The route traveled by a message; the means it uses to reach the sender-receivers. (ch 1, Appendix A, ch 12) (10, 277, 300)

chronemics The study of time. (ch 6) (146-147)

clarity That property of style by means of which a thought it so presented that it is immediately understood, depending on the precision and simplicity of the language. (ch 5) (123)

closed-format Interviews that are highly structured. (ch 9) (214)

closed questions Interview questions that are worded in ways that restrict their answers (e.g., questions that can be answered with a yes or a no). (ch 9) (215)

co-culture People who are part of a larger culture but also belong to a smaller group that has some different values, attitudes, or beliefs. (ch 1, 3) (19, 59)

coercive power In an organization, the ability of a leader to punish followers (e.g., by criticizing them, refusing to pay attention to them, using power to demote them, refusing to raise their pay, or firing them). (ch 11) (259)

cognitive development The development of the thinking and organizing systems of your brain that involves language, mental imagery, reasoning, problem solving, and memory development. (ch 5) (108)

cognitive dissonance A psychological theory, applied to communication, that states that people seek information that will support their beliefs and ignore information that does not. (ch 4) (89)

cohesiveness The feeling of attraction that group members have toward one another. It is the group's ability to stick together, to work together as a group, and to help one another as group members. (ch 10) (239)

commitment A strong desire by both parties for the relationship to continue. In groups, it is the willingness of members to work together to complete the group's task. (ch 7, 10) (176, 239)

communication Any process in which people share information, ideas, and feelings. (ch 1) (8)

comparison Supporting material that points out the similarities between two or more things. (ch 12, 15) (304-305, 377)

compatibility Similar attitudes, personality, and a liking for the same activities. (ch 7) (161)

complaint Expression of dissatisfaction with the behavior, attitude, belief, or characteristic of a partner or of someone else. (ch 8) (198-199)

complement Nonverbal cues designed specifically to add to the meaning of a verbal message. (ch 6) (147)

composition The makeup of a thing. (ch 15) (379)

computer (or online) databases A collection of items of information organized for easy access via a computer. (ch 12) (301)

computer-generated graphics Refers to any images created or manipulated via computer—art, drawings, representations of objects, pictures, and the like. (ch 14) (357-359)

computer-mediated communication (CMC) A wide range of technologies that facilitate both human communication and the interactive sharing of information through computer networks, including e-mail, discussion group, newsgroups, chat rooms, instant messages, and Web pages. (ch 1) (18)

conclusion (of speech) In a speech, the closing remarks that tie a speech together and give listeners the feeling that the speech is complete. (ch 13) (327-328)

concrete symbol A symbol that represents an object. (ch 1) (10)

conflict Expressed struggle between at least two individuals who perceive incompatible goals or interference from others in achieving their goals. (ch 11) (269)

conflict resolution Negotiation to find a solution to the conflict. (ch 8) (202-203)

connotative meaning The feelings or associations that each individual has about a particular word. (ch 5) (109)

constructing meaning The complicated and unique process of making sense of the cues, signals, and impulses received. (ch 4) (81-82)

content listening style That kind of listening in which the listener prefers complex and challenging information. (ch 4) (85)

content openness A characteristic of the Internet that makes it unique from normal face-to-face communication because there are no limitations on content. (ch 1) (24)

context High context occurs when most of the meaning of the message is either implied by the physical setting or is presumed to be part of the individual's beliefs, values, and norms. It is considered low context when most of the information is in the code or message. (ch 3) (65)

contrast Supporting material that points out the differences between two or more things. (ch 12, 15) (305, 377)

controlling listeners People who prefer talking to listening and seek to control their listeners by looking for ways to talk about themselves and their experiences. (ch 4) (90)

convergence An aspect of rate (the speed at which one speaks) demonstrated by how one person will accommodate or adapt to another's rate. (ch 6) (137)

conversational quality When speakers talk to audiences in much the same way they talk when they are having a conversation with another person. (ch 14) (345)

costs The problems associated with relationships. (ch 8) (193)

costumes The type of clothing that is a form of highly individualized dress. (ch 6) (141)

creativity The capacity to synthesize vast amounts of information and wrestle with complex problems. (ch 1, 12) (7, 301)

credibility The believability of a speaker based on the speaker's expertise, dynamism, trustworthiness, and ethics. (Appendix A, 16) (281, 415-417)

critical listening Includes all the ingredients for active listening and, in addition, evaluating and challenging what is heard. (ch 4) (92)

critic-analyzers Group members who look at the good and bad points in the information the group has gathered. (ch 10) (245)

criticism A negative evaluation of a person for something he or she has done or the way he or she is. (ch 8) (197-198)

cultural differences Includes not just obvious differences between people from other countries, but also differences based upon income, regional origins, dress code and grooming standards, music preferences, political affiliation, how long an individual has been in this country, skin tone, language ability, religion, etc. (ch 9) (222-223)

cultural identity The degree to which you identify with your culture. (ch 3) (58)

cultural information Information used in making predictions based on a person's most generally shared cultural attributes such as language, shared values, beliefs, and ideologies. (ch 7) (169)

culture The ever-changing values, traditions, social and political relationships, and worldview created and shared by a group of people bound together by a combination of factors (which can include a common history, geographic location, language, social class, and/or religion). (ch 1, 3) (19, 57)

D

deductive reasoning Reasoning from the general to the specific. (ch 16) (404-405)

defensive communication When one partner tries to defend himself or herself against the remarks or behavior of the other. (ch 8) (199-200)

definition Supporting material that is a brief explanation of what a word or phrase means. (ch 12, 15) (305, 376))

delegating That style of situational leadership in which leaders hang back and let members plan and execute the job. (ch 11) (264)

deletions The blotting out, erasing, or canceling of information that makes people's perceptions less than perfect because their physical senses are limited. (ch 2) (46)

democratic leader One who lets all points of view be heard and lets group members participate in the decision-making process. (ch 11) (262)

demographic analysis Reveals data about the characteristics of a group of people, including such things as age, sex, education, occupation, race/nationality/ethnic origin, geographic location, and group affiliation. (ch 12) (297)

demonstration speech A speech that teaches people "how to" perform a process. (ch 15) (375)

denotative meaning The dictionary definition of a particular word. (ch 5) (109)

dialect The habitual language of a community. (ch 5) (120)

digital literacy The ability to understand and use information in multiple formats from a wide range of sources when it is presented via computers. (Appendix A) (277)

directness Being natural and straightforward. (ch 14) (347)

disciplinary interview A type of information interview that concerns a sensitive area, where the employee is notified, and the interview involves hearing the employee's side of the story and, depending on the outcome, instituting disciplinary action. (ch 9) (212)

discrimination The overt actions one takes to exclude, avoid, or distance oneself from other groups. (ch 3) (67)

displays of feelings Face and body movements that show how intensely we are feeling. (ch 6) (138)

distortions The twisting or bending of information out of shape that makes people's perceptions less than perfect because they observe only a small part of their external environment. (ch 2) (46)

dominant culture Includes white people from a European background. (ch 3) (68)

doublespeak A term that refers to euphemisms created by an institution, such as government, to cover up the truth. (ch 5) (114)

dynamism For speakers, a great deal of enthusiasm and energy for their subject. (ch 16) (416-417)

dysfunctional (individual) roles Any role played by a group member that can be characterized as aggressor, blocker, recognition-seeker, self-confessor, playboy or play-girl, dominator, help-seeker, or special-interest pleader. (ch 10) (250-251)

E

elective characteristics The nonverbal, physical characteristics over which you have control such as clothing, makeup, tattoos, and body piercing. (ch 6) (140)

e-mail lists Group discussions that are completely passive; the discussion contributions arrive through e-mail. (ch 10) (251)

emblems Body movements that have a direct translation into words. (ch 6) (138)

emotional appeal A persuasive strategy that focuses on listeners' needs, wants, desires, and wishes. (ch 16) (409)

emotional intelligence The ability to understand and get along with others. (ch 7) (156)

empathic listening Involves trying to understand what others are feeling from their point of view and reflecting those feelings back. (ch 4) (92)

empathy The process of mentally identifying with the character and experiences of another person. (ch 4) (95) The ability to recognize and identify with someone's feelings. (ch 7) (158)

employment interview An interview used by an employer to determine whether someone is suitable for a job. (ch 9) (219-222)

enunciation How one pronounces and articulates words. (ch 14) (352)

ethical communication Communication that is honest, fair, and considerate of others' rights. (ch 1) (20)

ethics Behavior that is in accordance with right principles as defined by a given system of ethics (such as your culture and co-culture), or professional conduct within a specific business environment. (ch 9, 16) (211, 417)

ethnocentrism The belief that one's own cultural group's behaviors, norms, ways of thinking, and ways of being are superior to all other cultural groups. (ch 3) (65)

etymology The study of the origin and development of words. (ch 15) (376-377)

euphemisms Inoffensive words or phrases that are substituted for words that might be perceived as unpleasant. (ch 5) (114)

evaluate The third of the six steps of the strategic flexibility format in which users determine the value and worth of the factors, elements, and conditions to all those involved and how they bear on one's own skills and abilities. (ch 1) (6)

evaluation Determining the value and worth of the factors, elements, and conditions. (ch 4) (82)

evaluative statements Expressions that involve a judgment. (ch 8) (200)

example Supporting material that is a short illustration that clarifies a point. (ch 12) (305)

exit interview A type of information interview that occurs at the termination of an employee's employment, and is designed to resolve any outstanding concerns of employers and employees. (ch 9) (212)

expertise Having the experience or knowledge of an expert. (ch 16) (416)

expert power The influence and power that an expert has because he or she knows more than anyone else. (ch 11) (259)

extemporaneous speaking Speaking from notes. (ch 14) (349)

external noise Interference with the message that comes from the environment and keeps the message from being heard or understood. (ch 1) (11)

extrinsic Means outside the relationship. (ch 8) (193)

extrinsic costs The sacrifices, losses, or suffering as a result of things that occur outside the relationship (could include not having as much time for your friends or sharing your friends with your partner). (ch 8) (193)

extrinsic rewards The gifts, prizes, and recompenses that occur outside a relationship (could include liking the people your partner has introduced you to or the friends he or she hangs out with). (ch 8) (193)

eye messages As an aspect of nonverbal communication, they include all information conveyed by the eyes alone. (ch 6) (139)

F

fable cause A fallacy that occurs when events are causally connected but in fact no such causal connection has been established (ch 16) (408)

fact Something that can be verified in a number of ways. (ch 4) (95)

fallacy An improper conclusion drawn from a premise. (ch 16) (407-409)

false analogy A fallacy that occurs when a comparison between an obscure or difficult set of facts and one that is already known and understood, and to which it bears a significant resemblance, is erroneous and distorts the facts of the case being argued. (ch 16) (408)

feedback The response of the receiver-senders to each other. (ch 1) (11)

femininity versus masculinity That way of contrasting a group of cultures to another group of cultures that involves the division of roles between women and men. (ch 3) (64)

flaming The exchange of rude or hostile messages between online participants. (Appendix A) (282)

flip chart A series of pictures, words, diagrams, and so forth. It is made up of several pages that speakers "flip" through. (ch 14) (354)

follow-up questions Interview questions that are based on the answers given by interviewees and useful when interviewers want interviewees to go into a subject in greater depth. (ch 9) (215)

FOXP2 gene The gene directly linked to developing the fine motor skills needed for the development of language and speech. (ch 5) (107)

framing The way in which messages are divided, arranged, shaped, composed, constructed, and put together as a new whole. (ch 5) (126)

full-sentence outline A complete map of what a speech will look like. (ch 13) (330)

functional leadership When leadership varies with the task of the group and moves from one individual to another as the group finds it suitable. (ch 11) (262)

G

general purpose The intention of the speaker to inform or persuade. (ch 12) (293)

generalizations The process of drawing principles or conclusions from particular evidence or facts that makes people's perceptions less than perfect because once people have observed something a few times, they conclude that what has proven true in the past will prove true in the future as well. (ch 2) (46)

globalization A characteristic of the Internet that makes it unique from normal face-to-face communication because there are no limitations due to borders. (ch 1) (24)

groupthink A group dysfunction in which the preservation of harmony becomes more important than the critical examination of ideas. (ch 10) (239-241)

H

haptics The study of touch. (ch 6) (144)

hasty generalization A fallacy that occurs when an isolated exceptional case is used as the basis for a general conclusion that is unwarranted. (ch 16) (408)

hidden agendas Unannounced goals, subjects, or issues of individual group members or subgroups that differ from the group's public or stated agenda. (ch 11) (267)

hidden pane That area of the Johari Window where self-knowledge is hidden from others—a deliberate non-disclosure area in which there are certain things you know about yourself that you do not want known and deliberately conceal them from others. (ch 7) (170)

hierarchy of needs The relative order of the physical and psychological needs of all human beings. (ch 16) (409-411)

high context versus low context That way of contrasting a group of cultures to another group of cultures that involves the degree to which most of the information is carried in the context (high) or most of the information is in the code or message (low). (ch 3) (65)

hyperpersonal computer-mediated communication (CMC) When the levels of affection and emotion developed through CMC equal or surpass face-to-face communication. (Appendix) (280-281)

hypothetical example An example that is made up to illustrate a point. (ch 12) (305)

I

illustrators Gestures or other nonverbal signals that accent, emphasize, or reinforce words. (ch 6) (138)

immediacy It occurs when the communicator is completely focused on the communication situation. (ch 14) (346-347)

impromptu speaking Speaking on the spur of the moment with little time to prepare. (ch 14) (347)

indirect aggression (also called *passive aggression*) People who use this form of communication often feel powerless and respond by doing something to thwart the person in power. (ch 8) (196)

individualism versus collectivism The way of contrasting a group of cultures to another group of cultures that involves the degree of integration and orientation of individuals within groups. (ch 3) (64)

inductive reasoning Reasoning from the specific to the general. (ch 16) (405-407)

inflection A change in pitch used to emphasize certain words and phrases. (ch 14) (352)

influence The power of a person or things to affect others—to produce effects without the presence of physical force. (ch 16) (399)

information interview An interview in which the goal is to gather facts and opinions from someone with expertise and experience in a specific field. (ch 9) (212)

information-sharing group A type of group that meets to be informed or to inform others, to express themselves and to listen to others, to get or give assistance, to clarify or hear clarification of goals, or to establish or maintain working relationships. (ch 10) (236-237)

informative speech A speech that concentrates on explaining, defining, clarifying, and instructing. (ch 15) (372-373)

initial partition A preview of the main points of a speech at the outset (often, in the introduction of the speech). (ch 13) (323)

instrumental Refers to the basic exchange of goods and services. (ch 8) (193)

instrumental costs The sacrifices, losses, or suffering as a result of exchanging goods and services (could include sharing your belongings). (ch 8) (193)

instrumental rewards The gifts, prizes, and recompenses that occur as a result of the basic exchange of goods and services (could include raising the current level of relational intimacy with one of the rewards being moving in with your partner and sharing in both the rent and the furniture). (ch 8) (193)

Integrative Listening Model (ILM) A framework for assessing listening both systematically and developmentally. (ch 4) (80)

integrity Uprightness of character and honesty. (ch 9) (210)

intercultural communication When a message is created by a member of one culture, and this message needs to be processed by a member of another culture. (ch 1, 3) (19, 60)

internal noise Interference with the message that occurs in the minds of the sender-receivers when their thoughts or feelings are focused on something other than the communication at hand. (ch 1) (11)

interpersonal communication One person interacting with another on a one-to-one basis, often in an informal, unstructured setting. (ch 1, 7) (15, 156)

interview A series of questions and answers, usually exchanged between two people, that has the purpose of getting and understanding information about a particular subject or topic. (ch 9) (211, 220)

intimate distance The distance zone, a range of less than 18 inches apart, that places people in direct contact with each other. (ch 6) (143)

intrapersonal communication Communication that occurs within you; it involves thoughts, feelings, and the way you look at yourself. (ch 1) (15)

intrinsic Means within the relationship. (ch 8) (193)

intrinsic costs The obligation to return the attention, warmth, and affection you receive, and the time you will spend listening, communicating, and self-disclosing. (ch 8) (193)

intrinsic rewards The gifts, prizes, and recompenses that occur within a relationship could include the attention, warmth, and affection you gain from being in a relationship. (ch 8) (193)

introduction (of speech) In a speech, the opening remarks that aim to get attention and build interest in the subject. (ch 13) (323-327)

J

Johari Window A model of the process of disclosure in interpersonal relationships, developed by Joseph Luft and Harry Ingham. (ch 7) (170-171)

K

keyword outline An outline containing only the important words or phrases of a speech that helps remind speakers of the ideas they are presenting. (ch 13) (300)

knowledge class A class of individuals supported solely by its participation in the new information industries with little, if any, reliance upon traditional manufacturing, production, or agriculture. (ch 3) (56)

L

ladder of abstraction A diagram of how we abstract, through language, classifications, types, categories, etc. (ch 5) (109-112)

laissez-faire leader One who does very little actual leading. This leader suggests no direction for and imposes no order on a group. (ch 11) (262)

language environment The environment in which language takes place (e.g., in a classroom). (ch 5) (113)

leader A person who influences the behavior of one or more people. (ch 11) (258)

leadership style The amount of control a leader exerts over a group. (ch 11) (261)

leading questions A question designed to point the interviewee in a particular direction. (ch 9) (215)

learning group The purpose is to increase the knowledge or skill of participants. (ch 10) (237)

legitimate power (also called *organizational power*) Leaders in formal organizations who derive their influence because they are "the boss" or because of the organizational hierarchy and its rules. (ch 11) (259)

leisure clothing The type of clothing that is up to the individual and that is worn when work is over. (ch 6) (141)

listening Includes the processes of listening preparation, receiving, constructing meaning, responding, and remembering. (ch 4) (80)

listening preparation Includes all the physical, mental, and behavioral aspects that create a readiness to listen. (ch 4) (80)

logical appeal An appeal that addresses listeners' reasoning ability. (ch 16) (404-409)

long-term orientation The way of contrasting a group of cultures to another group of cultures that involves the trade-off between long-term and short-term needs gratification. (ch 3) (65)

M

mailing lists Group discussions that are completely passive; the discussion contributions arrive through e-mail. (ch 10) (251)

main heads or main points The points that reinforce the central idea. All the broad, general ideas and information that support your central idea. (ch 4, 13) (93, 316)

maintenance roles Group members who play these roles focus on the emotional tone of the meeting. (ch 10) (249-250)

manuscript speaking Writing out an entire speech and reading it to the audience from the prepared script. (ch 14) (358)

map versus territory The map is the personal mental approximation and the territory is the actual land or external reality that people experience. Map versus territory simply contrasts the subjective internal experience with the objective external reality. (ch 2) (41-44)

media literacy The ability to access, analyze, evaluate, and communicate information in all its forms—both print and nonprint. (Appendix A) (277)

media richness How much information is carried by a media source. (ch 6) (150)

memory (speaking from) This type of delivery involves writing out the entire speech and then committing it to memory word for word. (ch 14) (348-349)

mental outline A preliminary sketch that shows the principal features of the speech or lecture. (ch 4) (93)

message The ideas and feelings that a sender-receiver wants to share. (ch 1) (9)

metamessage The meaning, apart from the words, in a message. (ch 5) (125)

minor points The specific ideas and information that support the main points. (ch 13) (316)

mixed message A message in which the verbal and nonverbal contradict each other. (ch 6) (135)

mnemonic device A memory trick used to remember factual information. (ch 4) (83-84)

mob appeal A fallacy that occurs when an appeal is made to emotions, particularly to powerful feelings that can sway people in large crowds. (ch 16) (408)

model A replica of an actual object that is used when the object itself is too large to be displayed (e.g., a building), too small to be seen (e.g., a cell), or inaccessible to the eye (e.g., the human heart). (ch 14) (354)

monotone Little variety of pitch in a speech. (ch 14) (352)

motivated sequence Organization of a speech that involves five steps: attention, need, satisfaction, visualization, and action and works because it follows the normal process of human reasoning. (ch 13, 16) (322, 414-415)

motivation The stimulation or inducement that causes people to act. (ch 16) (399)

multimedia Refers to various media (e.g., text, graphics, animation, and audio) used to deliver information. (ch 14) (359)

N

national communities Co-cultural groupings within a country. (ch 3) (62)

natural delivery The collection of speech and actions that best represents your true self—that is, free from artificiality, affectation, and constraint. (ch 15) (386)

naturalistic fallacy A fallacy that occurs when something is identified as being good or desirable because it appears to be a natural characteristic. (ch 16) (407)

netiquette (or net etiquette) It includes the common practices, customs, conventions, and expectations expected of individuals using the Internet. (ch 10) (232)

neutral questions Interview questions that do not show how the interviewer feels about the subject. (ch 9) (215)

neutrality Not taking sides (in a group discussion). (ch 11) (265)

noise Interference that keeps a message from being understood or accurately interpreted. (ch 1) (11)

nondominant culture Includes people of color, women, gays, lesbians, and bisexuals, and those whose socioeconomic background is lower than middle class. (ch 3) (68)

nonelective characteristics The nonverbal physical characteristics over which you have no control and cannot change such as height, body proportion, coloring, bone structure, and physical disabilities. (ch 6) (140)

nonverbal communication Information we communicate without using words. (ch 6) (132)

nonverbal symbol Anything communicated without words (e.g., facial expressions or hand gestures). (ch 1) (10)

norms Expectations that group members have of how other members will behave, think, and participate. (ch 10) (235)

O

objective reality The actual territory or external reality everyone experiences. (ch 2) (48)

objectivity Basing conclusions on facts and evidence rather than on emotion or opinions. (ch 11) (265)

occupational dress The type of clothing that employees are expected to wear, but not as precise as a uniform. (ch 6) (141)

olfactics The study of smell. (ch 6) (145-146)

open-ended questions Interview questions that permit the person being interviewed to expand on his or her answers. (ch 9) (215)

open-format Interviews that are relatively unstructured. (ch 9) (214)

openness The free exchange of ideas within the bounds of reasonable behavior. (ch 9) (211)

open pane The area of the Johari Window that involves information about yourself that you are willing to communicate, as well as information you are unable to hide. (ch 7) (170)

opinion A personal belief. (ch 4) (95)

organizational chart A chart that shows the relationships among the elements of an organization, such as the departments of a company, the branches of federal or state government, or the committees of student government. (ch 14) (354)

outline A way of organizing material so all the parts and how they relate to the whole can be seen. (ch 13) (329-330)

owned message (also known as an I-message) An acknowledgment of subjectivity by a message-sender through the use of first-person singular terms (*I, me, my, mine*). (ch 7) (167-168)

P

pace How quickly or slowly a person speaks. (ch 14) (352)

paralanguage The way we say something. (ch 5, 6) (121, 136-137)

paraphrasing Restating the other person's thoughts or feelings in your own words. (ch 4) (96)

participating That style of situational leadership in which leaders state the problem but immediately consult with group members. (ch 11) (264)

passiveness The suspension of the rational functions and the reduction of any physical functions to their lowest possible degree. (ch 4) (90)

people listening style That kind of listening in which the listener is concerned with the other person's feelings. (ch 4) (85)

perception How people look at themselves and the world around them. (ch 2) (30)

perceptual filters The limitations that result from the narrowed lens through which people view the world. (ch 2) (47)

personal distance The distance zone, a range from 18 inches to 4 feet, that people maintain from others when they are engaged in casual and personal conversations. (ch 6) (143)

personal inventory Appraising your own resources. (ch 12) (291)

persuasion The process of trying to get others to change their attitudes or behavior; also, the process that occurs when a communicator (*sender*) influences the values, beliefs, attitudes, or behaviors of another person (*receiver*). (ch 16) (398)

PETAL In using presentation graphics, (1) develop pertinent materials, (2) choose an engaging format, (3) present your materials in a timely manner, (4) satisfy yourself that they are appropriate to the audience, and (5) ensure that everything is legible. (ch 15) (387)

pitch Highness or lowness of the voice. (ch 6) (137)

place Refers to the physical stage for the speech and the interaction with the audience. (ch 12) (300)

polls Surveys taken of people's attitudes, feelings, or knowledge. (ch 12) (308)

power distance The way of contrasting a group of cultures to another group of cultures that involves social inequality. (ch 3) (63)

powerful talk Talk that comes directly to the point, that does not use hesitation or qualifications. (ch 5) (118)

PowerPoint One of the most widely used software programs designed for use in presentations. (ch 14) (359-360)

prejudice A negative attitude toward a cultural group based on little or no experience. (ch 3) (67)

premise The reasons given in support of a conclusion. (ch 16) (407)

presentation A descriptive or persuasive account that is created to communicate ideas in a compelling and graphic manner (e.g., explain concepts, communicate complex data, make recommendations, or persuade and motivate others). (ch 15) (385-387)

primary questions Interview questions that often come first in the interview or that come first with each new topic the interviewer introduces. (ch 9) (214-215)

problem–solution order Organization of a speech into two sections: one dealing with the problem and the other dealing with the solution. (ch 13) (320-321)

professional communication Communication that is connected with, preparing for, engaged in, appropriate for, or conforming to business professions or occupations. (ch 9) (210)

pronunciation The ability to pronounce a word correctly. (ch 14) (352)

propriety The character or quality of being proper, especially in accordance with recognized usage, custom, or principles. (ch 4) (100)

proxemics The study of how people use space. (ch 6) (142)

psychological information The kind of information that is the most specific and intimate because it allows you to know individual traits, feelings, attitudes, and important personal data. (ch 7) (169)

psychological risk Taking a chance on something new (e.g., on a new person or place). (ch 2) (37)

psychological safety Approval and support obtained from familiar people, ideas, and situations. (ch 2) (37)

psychological sets A type of psychological filter that includes your expectations or predispositions to respond. (ch 2) (45)

public communication The sender-receiver (*speaker*) sends a message (the *speech*) to an audience. (ch 1) (18)

public distance The distance zone, a distance of more than 12 feet, typically used for public speaking. (ch 6) (144)

public-speaking anxiety The disturbance of mind regarding the uncertainty surrounding a forthcoming public-speaking event for which you are the speaker. (ch 14) (361-363)

Q

quality (of voice) Comprised of all voice characteristics: tempo, resonance, rhythm, pitch, and articulation. (ch 6) (137-138)

question-begging epithets A fallacy that occurs when slanted language is used to reaffirm what we wish to prove but have not yet proved. (ch 16) (408)

questions of fact Questions that deal with what is true and what is false. (ch 10, 16) (245, 412)

questions of policy Questions that are about actions that might be taken in the future. (ch 10, 16) (245, 412-413)

questions of value Questions of whether something is good or bad, desirable or undesirable. (ch 10, 16) (245, 413)

R

rapport style A style of communication designed to establish connections and negotiate relationships. (ch 9) (223)

rapport-talk Type of language women use in conversation, designed to lead to intimacy with others, to match experiences, and to establish relationships. (ch 5) (116)

rate (of speech) Speed at which one speaks. (ch 6) (137)

RDAT In using slides in a presentation, read the visual, describe its meaning or significance, amplify it with an explanation or illustration, and, finally, transition to the next slide. (ch 15) (387)

reassess and reevaluate The sixth of six steps of the strategic flexibility format in which users closely examine the results of any steps taken or not taken by them. (ch 1) (7)

receiving The process of taking in, acquiring, or accepting information. (ch 4) (80)

reference list A list of all the material you have used—and only that which you have used—in preparing your speech. (ch 13) (330-331)

referent power When leaders enjoy influence because of their personality. (ch 11) (259)

reflected appraisals Messages we get about ourselves from others. (ch 2) (32)

regrettable talk Saying something embarrassing, hurtful, or private to another person. (ch 8) (197)

regulate Nonverbal cues designed specifically to direct, manage, or control behavior. (ch 6) (147)

regulators (1) Nonverbal signals that control the back-and-forth flow of speaking and listening, such as head nods, hand gestures, and other body movements. (2) Group members who play this role help regulate group discussion by gently reminding members of the agenda or of the point they were discussing when they digressed. (ch 6) (138)

remembering Information that is learned well and stored securely in your memory system. (ch 4) (82)

report style A style of communication designed to pre-serve independence and negotiate and maintain status. (ch 9) (223)

report-talk Type of language men use in conversation, designed to maintain status, to demonstrate knowledge and skills, and to keep center-stage position. (ch 5) (117)

respect Conveys regard and appreciation of the worth, honor, dignity, and esteem of people. (ch 9) (211)

responding Using spoken and/or nonverbal messages to exchange ideas or convey information. (ch 4) (82)

response to a bid A positive or negative answer to some-body's request for emotional connection. (ch 7) (166)

responsibility Your ability to meet your obligations or to act without superior authority or guidance. (ch 9) (211)

résumé A summary of a person's professional life written for potential employers. (ch 9) (219)

reward power A leader can have an influence if he or she can reward the followers (e.g., through promotions, pay raises, or praise). (ch 11) (259)

rewards The pleasures that come as a result of being in a relationship. (ch 8) (193)

rhetorical question A question that audience members answer mentally rather than aloud. (ch 15) (384)

ritual language Communication that takes place when we are in an environment in which a conventionalized response is expected of us. (ch 5) (113)

roles Parts we play, or ways we behave with others. (ch 1) (14)

rules Formal and structured directions for behavior. (ch 10) (236)

S

Sapir-Whorf hypothesis The language you use to some extent determines—at least influences—the way in which you view and think about the world around you. (ch 5) (108-109)

scripts Lines and directions given to people by parents, teachers, coaches, religious leaders, friends, and the media that tell them what to say, what they expect, how to look, how to behave, and how to say the lines. (ch 2) (32)

select The fourth of six steps of the strategic flexibility format in which users carefully select from their repertoire of available skills and behaviors those likely to have the greatest impact on the current (and future) situations. (ch 1) (7)

selective attention The ability to focus perception. (ch 4) (82)

self-concept How a person thinks about and values himself or herself. (ch 2) (30)

self-disclosure Process by which one person tells another something he or she would not tell just anyone. (ch 7) (168)

self-esteem See *self-concept*.

self-fulfilling prophecies Events or actions that occur because a person and those around her or him expected them. (ch 2) (33)

self-improvement Seeking all means available to improve your professionalism and expertise. (ch 9) (211)

self-perception The way in which one sees oneself. (ch 2) (35)

selling That style of situational leadership in which leaders state the problem and decide what to do, but they sell the other group members on the idea to gain majority support. (ch 11) (264)

semantic noise Interference with the message that is caused by people's emotional reactions to words. (ch 1) (12)

semiopen format Interviews that occur based on a core set of standardized questions that are asked in a standard man-ner and carefully recorded. (ch 9) (214)

sender-receivers In communication situations, those who simultaneously send and receive messages. (ch 1) (8)

sensory acuity Paying attention to all elements in the com-munication environment. (ch 1) (11)

separation When nondominants do not want to form a com-mon bond with the dominant culture, they separate into a group that includes only members like themselves. (ch 3) (70)

separation strategies When people are not part of a dominant culture, those processes that people use to get the dominant group to reinvent or change the rules through the use of nonassertive, assertive, or aggressive separation. (ch 3) (70-71)

servant leader Person who works for the well-being and growth of all employees and is committed to creating a sense of community and sharing power in decision making. (ch 11) (259)

setting Where the communication occurs. (ch 1) (12)

shared leadership It occurs when all group or team members assume both decision-making authority and responsibility for the group or team's results. (ch 11) (262)

situational leadership It occurs when leaders adopt different leadership styles depending on the situation. (ch 11) (263)

small-group communication It occurs when a small number of people meet to solve a problem. The group must be small enough so that each member has a chance to interact with all the other members. (ch 1) (17)

small groups Gatherings of 3 to 13 members who meet to do a job, solve a problem, or maintain relationships. (ch 10) (233)

small talk Social conversation about unimportant topics that allows a person to maintain contact with a lot of people without making a deep commitment. (ch 7) (164)

social comparisons When people compare themselves with others to see how they measure up. (ch 2) (33)

social distance The distance zone, a range from 4 to 12 feet, that people are most likely to maintain when they do not know people very well. (ch 6) (143)

social groups Groups designed to serve the social needs of their participants. (ch 10) (236)

social penetration The process of increasing both disclosure and intimacy in a relationship. (ch 7) (168)

social presence The ability of computer-mediated communication users to project themselves socially and affectively (with feeling) into a communication event. (ch 6) (149)

sociological information Information that tells you something about others' social groups and roles. (ch 7) (169)

space and distance Those distances people maintain between themselves and others that convey degrees of intimacy and status. (ch 6) (142-144)

spatial order Organization of a speech by something's location in space (e.g., left to right, top to bottom). (ch 13) (319-320)

specific purpose A statement for a speech that tells precisely what the speaker wants to accomplish. (ch 12) (294)

statistics Facts in numerical form. (ch 12) (306)

stereotypes Oversimplified or distorted views of another race, ethnic group, or culture. (ch 3) (65)

strategic flexibility Expanding your communication repertoire (your collection or stock of communication behaviors that can readily be brought into use) to enable you to use the best skill or behavior available for a particular situation. (ch 1) (6)

stress interview A type of information interview that is sometimes part of the job search and is designed to see how an interviewee acts under pressure. It is designed to give interviewers a realistic sense of their response to difficult situations. (ch 9) (212)

style The result of the way we select and arrange words and sentences. (ch 5) (116)

subjective view The personal, internal, mental map of the actual territory or external reality that people experience. (ch 2) (48)

substantive conflict Conflict that arises when people have different reactions to an idea. Substantive conflict is likely to occur when any important and controversial idea is being discussed. (ch 11) (269-270)

substitute Nonverbal message designed specifically to take the place of a verbal message. (ch 6) (147)

supporting material Information that backs up your main points and provides the main content of the speech. (ch 12) (304-308)

supporting points The material, ideas, and evidence that back up the main heads. (ch 4) (93)

sweeping generalization A fallacy that occurs when a general rule is applied to a specific case to which the rule is not applicable because of specific features of the case. (ch 16) (408)

symbol Something that stands for something else. (ch 1) (9)

supportive behavior A way of avoiding defensive communication by using supportive strategies such as description, problem solving, spontaneity, empathy, equality, or provisionalism. (ch 8) (200-201)

synchronous communication Online group discussion in which group members communicate at the same time. All participants are virtually present at the same time (e.g., in a telephone conversation, a face-to-face encounter, or a real-time, online group format). (ch 1, 10, Appendix A) (23, 251, 277)

T

target audience A subgroup of the whole audience that you must persuade to reach your goal. (ch 2, 16) (296, 404)

task-oriented group A type of group that serves to get something specific accomplished, often problem-solving or decision-making goals. (ch 10) (236)

task roles Roles that help get the job done. Persons who play these roles help groups come up with new ideas, aid in collecting and organizing information, and assist in analyzing the information that exists. (ch 10) (248-249)

team Two or more people with a specific goal to be attained who coordinate their activity among the members to attain their goal. (ch 10) (241)

teamwork The unity of action by a group of workers to further the success of the business or organization. (ch 9) (211)

telling That style of situational leadership in which the leader is focused more on the task and less on the group. (ch 11) (263)

temporality A characteristic of the Internet that makes it unique from normal face-to-face communication because there are no time limitations. (ch 1) (24)

territory Space we consider as belonging to us, either temporarily or permanently. (ch 6) (142)

testimony Another person's statements or actions used to give authority to what the speaker is saying. (ch 12) (307-308)

time The three facets of time that matter in analyzing the speech occasion are: time frame for the speech, time of day, and the length of time of your speech. (ch 12) (300)

time order Organization of a speech by chronology or historical occurrence. (ch 13) (318-319)

time-style listening That kind of listening in which the listener prefers brief and hurried interaction with others and often lets the communicator know how much time he or she has to make the point. (ch 4) (85)

topical order Organization of a speech used when the subject can be grouped logically into subtopics. (ch 13) (322-323)

touch To be in contact or come into contact with another person. (ch 6) (144-145)

transactional communication Communication that involves three principles:(1) people sending messages continuously and simultaneously; (2) communication events that have a past, present, and future; and (3) participants playing certain roles. (ch 1) (13)

transitions Comments that lead from one point to another to tell listeners where speakers have been, where they are now, and where they are going. (ch 13) (328-329)

transpection The process of empathizing across cultures. (ch 3) (73)

trustworthiness In the giving of a speech, the speaker is perceived as reliable and dependable. (ch 16) (417)

U

uncertainty avoidance The way of contrasting a group of cultures to another group of cultures that involves tolerance for the unknown. (ch 3) (65)

uniforms The most specialized form of clothing and that type that identifies wearers with particular organizations. (ch 6) (141)

unknown pane Area of the Johari Window that is known as a nondisclosure area and provides no possibility of disclosure because it is unknown to the self or to others. (ch 7) (171)

Usenet newsgroups Online group discussions that handle individual messages sorted by broad subject areas that can be subscribed to through Internet or corporate network host providers. (ch 10) (251)

V

values A type of belief about how we should behave or about some final goal that may or may not be worth attaining. (ch 16) (400)

verbal symbol A word that stands for a particular thing or idea. (ch 1) (10)

virtual community A group of people who may or may not meet one another face-to-face, and who exchange words and ideas through the mediation of computer bulletin boards and networks. (Appendix A) (282)

vision Foresight, insight, and imagination. (ch 11) (268)

visual support Visual material that helps illustrate key points in a speech or presentation. Visual support includes devices such as charts, graphs, slides, and computer-generated graphics. (ch 14) (353-360)

vividness That property of style by which a thought is so presented that it evokes lifelike imagery or suggestion. (ch 5) (124)

vocal fillers Words we use to fill out our sentences or to cover up when we are searching for words. (ch 6) (138)

volume (of vocal sound) How loudly we speak.(ch 6) (137)

W–Z

Web conferencing or Web forums Online group discussions that use text messages (and sometimes images) stored on a computer as the communication medium. Messages are typed into the computer for others to read. (ch 10) (252)

Web log (or blog) A spontaneous public online journal (or diary) in which Internet users share their lives. (Appendix A) (282-283)

worldview An all-encompassing set of moral, ethical, and philosophical principles and beliefs that governs the way people live their lives and interact with others. (ch 3) (58)

Credits

Photos

Chapter 1

3: John Giustina/Iconica/Getty Images; **10:** Stockbyte/Getty Images; **12** *(left):* Sven Martson/The Image Works; **12** *(right):* Rosebud Pictures/Stone/Getty Images; **19:** Digital Vision/Getty Images

Chapter 2

29: Spencer Grant/PhotoEdit Inc.; **34:** David Young-Wolff/PhotoEdit Inc.; **37:** David Young-Wolff/PhotoEdit Inc.; **45:** Ryan McVay/Photodisc Green/Getty Images

Chapter 3

55: Juan Silva/The Image Bank/Getty Images; **58:** Jose Luis Pelaez, Inc./Corbis; **64:** Robert Essel NYC/Corbis

Chapter 4

79: Tom Stewart/Corbis; **93:** Rubberball; **98:** George Shelley/Corbis

Chapter 5

105: Walter Hodges/Stone/Getty Images; **106:** Jim West/The Image Works

Chapter 6

131: Michael Jang/Stone/Getty Images; **140:** Alan Carey/The Image Works; **145** *(left):* Bob Daemmrich Photography, Inc./The Image Works; **145** *(right):* Michael S. Yamashita/Corbis

Chapter 7

155: Cassy Cohen/PhotoEdit Inc.; **160:** Steven Rubin/The Image Works; **170:** Rolf Bruderer/Corbis; **174:** Tim Mantoani/Masterfile

Chapter 8

183: Barry Yee/Taxi/Getty Images; **188:** Michael Newman/PhotoEdit Inc.; **198:** David Young-Wolff/PhotoEdit Inc.

Chapter 9

209: Digital Vision/Getty Images; **213:** Karen Preuss/The Image Works; **219:** Michael Newman/PhotoEdit Inc.

Chapter 10

231: Masterfile; **239:** Bob Mahoney/The Image Works; **249:** Loren Santow/Stone/Getty Images

Chapter 11

257: Charles Gupton/Stone/Getty Images; **261:** Michael Goldman/Masterfile; **270:** Mark Richards/PhotoEdit Inc.

Appendix A

280 *(left):* Comstock/Getty Images; **280** *(right):* VStock LLC/Index Stock Imagery, Inc.

Chapter 12

289: Pierre Tremblay/Masterfile Corporation; **293:** Ebsin-Anderson/The Image Works; **296** *(left):* David Butow/Corbis SABA; **296** *(right):* AP/Wide World Photos; **302:** Jon Riley/Stone/Getty Images; **306:** Jose Luis Pelaez, Inc./Corbis

Chapter 13

313: Michael Newman/PhotoEdit Inc.; **318:** A. Ramey/PhotoEdit Inc.; **324:** Chuck Savage/Corbis

Chapter 14

343: Cleve Bryant/PhotoEdit Inc.; **348:** Barbara Stitzer/PhotoEdit Inc.; **359:** Lon C. Diehl/PhotoEdit Inc.

Chapter 15

371: Michael Newman/PhotoEdit Inc.; **374:** Susan Van Etten/PhotoEdit Inc.; **377:** James Schnepf/Getty Images; **380:** Michael Newman/PhotoEdit Inc.; **385:** Fisher/Thatcher/Stone/Getty Images

Chapter 16

397: Bob Daemmrich/The Image Works; **400:** David Young-Wolff/PhotoEdit Inc.; **401:** A. Ramey/PhotoEdit Inc.; **410:** AP/Wide World Photos; **415** *(left):* Michael Newman/PhotoEdit Inc.; **415** *(right):* Bob Daemmrich/The Image Works

Text and Illustrations

Chapter 1

20: "Credo for Communication Ethics" reprinted by permission of National Communication Association, Washington, DC.

Chapter 2

32: Garrison Keillor, "Revival" from *Lake Wobegon Days.* Copyright © 1985 by Garrison Keillor. Used by permission of Viking Penguin, a division of Penguin Group USA Inc. **51:** In *Measures of Personality and Social Psychological Attitudes* by J.P. Robinson, P.R. Shaver, & L.S. Wrightsman, 1991, San Diego: Academic Press (p. 127-31). Adapted from *The Antecedents of Self-Esteem* by S. Coopersmith, 1967, San Francisco: W. H. Freeman and Company. Used by permission of W. H. Freeman.

Chapter 3

75: Adapted from www.literacynet.org/icans. Used by permission of Adult Basic Education Office, Professional Development Services, Washington State ABE Literacy Resource Center, formerly ABLE Network.

Chapter 4

90: Table 4-1 From "A Factor Analysis of Barriers to Effective Listening" by Steven Golen in *Journal of Business Communication:* 27, 25-36 (Winter 1990). Reprinted by permission of the author. **91:** From *Listen Up, Move Up: The Listener Wins* by Michael Purdy. Reprinted by permission of Michael Purdy. **98:** From "Talking Back to Your Doctor Works" by Linda Greider, *AARP Bulletin:* February 2000. Reprinted by permission of Linda Greider. **101:** Adapted from www.literacynet.org/icans. Used by permission of Adult Basic Education Office, Professional Development Services, Washington State ABE Literacy Resource Center, formerly ABLE Network.

Chapter 5

118: From "Sex Differences in the Functional Organization of the Brain for Language" by B.A. Shaywitz, 1995, Nature 37 (3) 89-90. Used by permission of the Nature Publishing Group.

Chapter 7

165: Quotation from Dianna Booher, 1996, *Vitality,* 5. Used by permission of the author. **171:** Table 7-5 Figure from *Group Processes: An Introduction to Group Dynamics* by Joseph Luft, 1984. Mayfield Publishing Company. Reprinted with permission of The McGraw-Hill Companies. **176:** From "An Inductive Analysis of Verbal Immediacy," by T. P. Mottet & V. P. Richmond, *Communication Quarterly.* Copyright 1998 from Communication Quarterly by T. P. Mottet & V. P. Richmond. Reproduced by permission of Taylor & Francis Inc., www.taylorandfrancis.com. **177:** From "Avoiding Trends that Deprive Us of Humanity," by D. Stanley Eitzen, 2003. Reprinted by permission of Vital Speeches of the Day. **179:** Reprinted by permission of Constance Messina.

Chapter 8

192: © 2003 Antoinette Coleman. www.Consum-mate.com, 703-847-1768, Toni@conum-mate.com. All rights reserved. **194:** From *Newsweek,* April 19, 1999. Copyright © 1999 Newsweek Inc. All rights reserved. Reprinted by permission. **205:** The Relational Assessment Questionnaire, adapted from W.E. Snell Jr., 1999. Used by permission of William Snell.

Chapter 9

226: From How to Use the Internet in Your Job Search, by M. F. Dikel, 2003. The Riley Guide: Execute a Campaign. Used by permission of Margaret F. Dikel, author of The Riley Guide (Rileyguide.com).

Chapter 10

243: Table 10-1 From "Brainstorming Guidelines" by J.M. Fritz. Used by permission of Jane Fritz, University of New Brunswick. **253:** Adapted from www.literacynet.org/icans. Used by permission of Adult Basic Education Office, Professional Development Services, Washington State ABE Literacy Resource Center, formerly ABLE Network.

Chapter 11

272: From Conflict in Cyberspace: How to Resolve Conflict Online by Kali Munro, 2002, www.kalimunro.com/article_conflict_online.html. Used by permission of the author. **273:** Adapted from www.literacynet.org/icans. Used by permission of Adult Basic Education Office, Professional Development Services, Washington State ABE Literacy Resource Center, formerly ABLE Network.

Appendix A

279, 282: From *Computer-mediated Communication: Human-to-human Communication Across the Internet* by Susan B. Barnes, 2003. Used by permission of Allyn and Bacon / Pearson Education, Boston, MA. **280:** From "Virtual relationships: The Solitary World of CMC" by T. W. Loughlin, *Interpersonal Computing and Technology: An Electronic Journal for the 21st Century,* 1993. Used by permission of Thomas Loughlin, SUNY Fredonia.

Chapter 12

292: Fig 12-2 From *Analyzing Your Topic.* Research Tutorial for Freshman and Transfer Seminars, Webster University. Used by permission of Webster University, St. Louis. MO. **305:** From "The Internet: The Soul of Democracy," by G. Slenow, 2000. Reprinted by permission of Vital Speeches of the Day. **307:** From "Trends in College Binge Drinking During a Period of Increased Prevention Efforts: Findings from 4 Harvard School of Public Health College Alcohol Study Surveys: 1993-2001." Retrieved 3/25/03 from www.hsph.harvard.edu/cas/Documents/trends/. Journal of American College Health, 2002; 50(5): 203-217. Reprinted by permission of the Helen Dwight Reid Educational Foundation and the author. Published by Heldref Publications, 1319 18th St. NW, Washington, DC 20036. Copyright © 2002. **307:** From William Franklin, President, Franklin International, 2001. Reprinted by permission of Vital Speeches of the Day. **309:** From *Insight vs.*

Chapter 13

317: From "Sustainability," by Richard Lamm, 2003. Reprinted by permission of Vital Speeches of the Day. **319:** From *Public Speaking: Make 'em Wonder*, C. M. McKinney. Advanced Public Speaking Institute. © Tom Antion. Reprinted with permission. **325:** From Commencement address by Robert L. Dilenschneider, 2001. Reprinted by permission of Vital Speeches of the Day. **332:** Fig. 13-2 "Tech Tips for Teachers - Citing Internet Sources" from the Classroom Connect website www.classroom.com/community/connection/howto/citeresources.jhtml, copyright 2004 by Classroom Connect, reprinted by permission of the publishers.

Chapter 14

356: Fig 14-3 From "Snakes Scarier than Public Speaking," USA TODAY. March 26, 2001. Reprinted with permission.

Chapter 15

374: From "Unexamined Assumptions: Destiny, Political Institutions, Democracy, and Population" by Richard Lamm, 1998. Reprinted by permission of Vital Speeches of the Day. **377:** From "The Buzz on Caffeine," © 2002 TIME Inc. Reprinted by permission. **378:** From "Humor and Speeches: A Stand-Up History" by Eugene Finerman, 1996. Reprinted by permission of Vital Speeches of the Day.

Chapter 16

405: From "The New Entrepreneurship" by Peter Bell, 2001. Reprinted by permission of Vital Speeches of the Day. **406:** From "Facts Change Student Drinking," USA TODAY. June 23, 2001. Reprinted with permission. **412:** From "Talk to Your Children About the Tough Stuff: We Are All in This Together" by Lance R. Odden, 1999. Reprinted by permission of Vital Speeches of the Day and the author.

Index